Shadow Archives

Shadow Archives

The Lifecycles of African American Literature

Jean-Christophe Cloutier

Columbia University Press / *New York*

Columbia University Press
Publishers Since 1893
New York   Chichester, West Sussex
cup.columbia.edu
Copyright © 2019 Columbia University Press

Library of Congress Cataloging-in-Publication Data
Names: Cloutier, Jean-Christophe, author.
Title: Shadow archives : the lifecycles of African American literature / Jean-Christophe
    Cloutier.
Description: New York : Columbia University Press, 2019. | Includes bibliographical
    references and index.
Identifiers: LCCN 2019006299 (print) | LCCN 2019011302 (ebook) |
    ISBN 9780231550246 (e-book) | ISBN 9780231193306 (cloth : alk. paper) |
    ISBN 9780231193313 (pbk. : alk. paper)
Subjects: LCSH: American literature—African American authors—History and
    critcism. | American literature—20th century—Information resources. |
    American literature—20th century—Research—Methodology. | African
    Americans—Intellectual life—20th century.
Classification: LCC PS153.N5 (ebook) | LCC PS153.N5 C53 2019 (print) |
    DDC 810.9/896073—dc23
LC record available at https://lccn.loc.gov/2019006299

Columbia University Press books are printed on permanent and durable acid-free paper.
Printed in the United States of America

Cover image: Background photograph courtesy of the Samuel Roth estate.
Cover design: Lisa Hamm

À Aimée, et au tout petit qui s'en vient

I have not hesitated to use words which are old, and in some circles considered poetically overworked and dead, when I thought I could make them glow alive by new manipulation.

—CLAUDE MCKAY, *HARLEM SHADOWS*

In approaching our subject with the sensibilities of statisticians and dissectionists, we distance ourselves increasingly from the marvelous and spell-binding planet of imagination whose gravity drew us to our studies in the first place. This is not to say that we should cease to establish facts and to verify our information, but merely to suggest that unless those facts can be imbued with the flash of poetic insight then they remain dull gems; semi-precious stones scarcely worth the collecting.

—DANIEL DREIBERG, "BLOOD FROM THE SHOULDER OF PALLAS"

CONTENTS

ILLUSTRATIONS

ACKNOWLEDGMENTS

As is typical of anything related to archives, this book has seen its lifecycle delayed, accelerated, flatline, and resurrected a number of times over the many years of its gestation. Without the assistance and support of a great many individuals and collectives, it would surely have remained in the depths of the backlog, left to mutely utter its own cry of terror alongside the counterfactual chimeras swarming in the bizarro world. Now that it has chosen its form and emerged at last, it is time to offer some well-deserved expressions of gratitude.

Departing from convention, let me begin and end by thanking my partner in crime and in life, Beth Blum, for all things must begin and end with her, my Alpha and Omega. Without her ceaseless support and love, this book would never have had a chance.

Somewhat like the secret agent in William Burroughs's novel *The Soft Machine*, this book seems to have originally been made of "UT," undifferentiated tissue—it grew yet stubbornly refused to assume its final form. Shades of what it eventually became were first manifested at Columbia University during my doctoral research. I took my first trip to the Library of Congress in 2008—in a broken-down Chinatown bus that had more than three inches of water caught between the windowpanes next to my seat—to consult the Ralph Ellison Papers, a dream I had nursed since my undergrad days at Concordia in Montréal. That's when I got the fever. And the only prescription was and remains more archives. I could not have asked for a better Virgil, as a guide and mentor through this perilous quest among the papers of the dead, than Brent Hayes Edwards, gentleman-scholar and academic superhero. Little did we know, back in the summer of 2009 when I stumbled upon Claude McKay's typescript of *Amiable with Big Teeth*, that we would end up working together for the better part of a decade trying to get the book to publication. Brent, I guess it's safe to say it now: I found the novel only as a con to force you to spend more time with me. Thank you for always pushing me to go beyond my limits, even when I thought it was hopeless. And thank you for the countless ways you have been a friend to me throughout this journey.

My time at Columbia was further sustained by the steady, inspirational presence of Bob O'Meally, who threw me fastballs when I needed them and curve balls when I least expected them. Our sessions in his office with Ellison's trusty *Webster's New International Dictionary*, second edition, opened between us are among my fondest memories. Rounding out my committee was Maura Spiegel, kindness personified, a holy presence who offered friendship and understanding at a time when the universe seemed on the brink of collapse. I am also grateful for the experience of serving on the board of advisers of the American Studies Center at Columbia thanks to the generosity and mentorship of Casey "Dr. Strange" Blake and Andrew Delbanco. My cohort and the fellow graduate travelers I met in passing were an indispensable source of debate and stolen moments of revelry: Emily Cersonsky Hayman, Nijah Cunningham, John Hay, Jang-Wook Huh, Irvin Hunt, Royden Kadyschuk, Vesna Kuiken, Emily Lordi, Ivan Lupic, Jarvis McInnis, Alastair Morrison, Imani Owens, Hiie Saumaa, Adam Spry, Kate Stanley, Jessica Teague, Courtney Thorsson, Lindsay Van Tine, Aaron Winslow, Autumn Womack, and many others. Columbia's secret comics society, Karen Green, Paul Levitz, and Jeremy Dauber, were also warm interlocutors who supported my work throughout my studies and long after I graduated.

Even though we met toward the end of my doctorate work, the inimitable and defiant Ann Douglas has since become one of my most cherished friends and mentors. I thank her for bringing back "telepathic shock and meaning excitement" into my work and for injecting me with life-sustaining doses of confidence during the rockiest moments of this book's evolution.

For the wonderfully cataclysmic impact it has had on my life and my scholarly trajectory, I must thank the archivists, librarians, and curators who dwell in Columbia's "pink palace," the Rare Book and Manuscript Library. My archival internship, spearheaded by then director Michael Ryan and supervised by the always upbeat and resourceful Alix Ross, ranks among the biggest thrills of my professional life. Even the days spent in solitude in darkened stacks, sifting through endless print matter or box after box of the exact same printed draft, were a joy. During my three years as an intern, I also benefitted from conversations with Gerald Cloud, Carrie Hintz, Karla Nielsen, Jane Siegel, and all of my fellow interns from myriad disciplines. It was also during my time working in Butler Library that I met the indefatigable Jay Gertzman, booklegger, smuthound, and Roth scholar extraordinaire. I cherish our ongoing friendship, enlivened through the sporadic lunches and dinners we manage to wrest from the jaws of time.

Ever since my arrival at the University of Pennsylvania in 2013, the Penn English Department has been an ideal and most welcoming home. Despite being one of the busiest humans I have ever met, Jim English has been unrelenting in his support of my work and a fount of professional, institutional, worldly advice in all aspects. I remain flabbergasted and humbled by the sheer amount of time and kindness he has devoted to me. Herman Beavers has similarly been a constant source of encouragement and wisdom. For their warmth, support, and helpful suggestions on a number of topics, this book is also indebted to Rita Barnard, Peter Decherney, Jed Esty, Al Filreis, Michael Gamer, Zack Lesser, Heather Love, Jo Park, and Paul Saint-Amour (who might possibly be the Kindest Man in the World on top of being, like Wolverine, the best at what he does). For their conversations and camaraderie, I am grateful to Charles Bernstein, Pearl Brilmyer, Tim Corrigan, Rich King, Brian Kirk, Rahul "Mr. Wolf" Mukherjee, Jennifer Ponce de León, Melissa Sanchez, Emily Steiner, Emily Steinlight, and David Wallace. Even though I have only just begun to know them as colleagues, I am everlastingly thankful for the newest members of our department: Margo Crawford, Dagmawi Woubshet, Simone White, and Whitney Trettien. I have already learned so much from them, and this book would not be the same without the conversations we have had late in the game. I have also benefitted from a triad of thoughtful, dedicated departmental chairs since my arrival at Penn—Nancy Bentley, Amy Kaplan, and Jed Esty—who have consistently made themselves available and looked out for all junior faculty. One initiative in particular has had a salutary effect on this book: the manuscript workshop. The judicious comments and suggestions offered by William Maxwell and Priscilla Wald on an earlier manuscript crystallized the final form this book would eventually adopt. I thank them for rescuing me from becoming too much like Stephen King's Jack Torrance. I would also like to take this time to thank our graduate students, especially those who shared their wonderful insights in my graduate seminar on archives or through our conversations over the years. Last but certainly not least, I cannot underscore enough how grateful I am for the mentorship and encouragement I received from Salamishah Tillet when I was lucky enough to have her as a colleague at Penn. From the moment I interviewed for the job and to this day across state lines, Salamishah has been a beacon of inspiration and wisdom without whose light I would surely have gone astray.

In the wider Penn community, I would be remiss not to thank the incredible cohort of rambunctious radicals who form the Workshop in the History of Material Text and all the wonderful staff of the Kislak Center. In particular, John Pollack, Lynne Farrington, Holly Mengel, David McKnight, and Mitch Fraas have been an invaluable resource for my graduate seminar on archival research methods and for my ongoing love affair with archives, special collections, and the history of the book.

Over the years, I have also had the good fortune of receiving assistance from an exceptional cadre of dedicated archivists and librarians at a great number of repositories: the New York Public Library on Forty-Second Street, the Schomburg Center for Research in Black Culture at the New York Public Library, the Beinecke Rare Book and Manuscript Library at Yale, the Library of Congress, the Howard Gotlieb Center at Boston University, the Amistad Research Center at Tulane, the Emory Library, the

Lilly Library at Indiana University, the Houghton Library at Harvard, the Syracuse University Library, the John Hay Library at Brown, and, of course, the Rare Book and Manuscript Library at Columbia, along with others I have likely forgotten in the fevered haze of nomadic research. Among those who were particularly helpful at crucial junctions of the project were Maricia Battle, Melissa Barton, Alice L. Birney, Michael Forstrom, Katherine Fortier, Steven Fullwood, Christopher Harter, Patrick Kerwin, and Sarah E. Pratt, just to name a few. Kalhil Muhammad and Diana Lachatenere of the Schomburg Center were instrumental in ensuring good progress on all things related to my work on Claude McKay. Diana has been an especially frequent interlocutor over the years, and I am so thankful for her generosity and spirit.

I am equally thankful for the support from the literary estates that have greatly facilitated—and sometimes quite directly made possible—my work. From my very first article on Ellison and comics, John Callahan and Donn Zaretsky of the Ralph and Fanny Ellison Charitable Trust have always propelled my research forward with "maximum enthusiasm." I thank Annie Kronenberg of John Hawkins & Associates for facilitating the permissions from the Estate of Richard Wright. Alexis Sattler and Jesseca Salky of the HSG Agency generously gave me a life-saving discount for materials related to Ann Petry; I am indebted to them and to Elisabeth Petry, Ann Petry's daughter, who took the time to answer my questions and blessed the project with immediate encouragement. Edward Burns, Van Vechten trustee and eternal fountain of literary lore, has further given me the unexpected gift of friendship; I wish we could have lunch at the Knickerbocker every week. A huge and heartfelt thanks goes to Peter Kunhardt Jr. and Amanda Smith of The Gordon Parks Foundation, with whom I have now had the good fortune of collaborating for some years, notably for the *Invisible Man: Gordon Parks and Ralph Ellison in Harlem* exhibition at the Art Institute of Chicago. As a literary scholar, I rarely have the chance to be part of something so far-reaching and historic and could not imagine a more meaningful outcome for my research work than what we were able to accomplish together with the curator Michal Raz-Russo in 2016. Needless to say, the project had a tremendous impact on this book. The generosity, encouragement,

ACKNOWLEDGMENTS

openness, and support The Gordon Parks Foundation has shown toward my work has made all the difference in the world and along the way has only widened admiration for Gordon Parks and his vibrant legacy.

I would also like to acknowledge those institutions and departments that provided financial support through scholarships, fellowships, and awards: the Social Sciences and Humanities Research Council of Canada; the Andrew W. Mellon Foundation; as well as Columbia University's Graduate School of Arts and Science, American Studies Center, and Rare Book and Manuscript Library. At Penn, I could not have completed the research necessary for this book without the generous contributions from the University Research Funds, the Research Opportunity Grants, and the Penn Undergraduate Research Mentoring Award. I am especially grateful to Skip Gates and the Hutchins Center for African and African American Research at Harvard University for allowing a French Canadian like me to live among the scholars there for an extended stay. The chance to share my work in progress in those hallowed halls and among such a vibrant community of scholars and artists is something I will always cherish. From that unforgettable first colloquium I attended when Cornel West electrified the room with his triumphant return to Harvard to all of the wonderful events, dinners, and tours we shared, it was a once-in-a-lifetime experience. The book as it stands would not be possible without the inspiration and feedback I received from my fellow fellows and the unflagging leadership of Henry Louis Gates Jr., Krishna Lewis, and Abby Wolf. I feel both proud and lucky to have journeyed alongside these magnificent humans at Harvard: Harry Allen, John Ataguba, Abidemi Babalola, Gaiutra Bahadur, Zelalem Kibret Beza, David Bindman, NoViolet Bulawayo, Kurt Campbell, Myisha Cherry, Christa Clarke, Cassi Pittman Claytor, Christian Ayne Crouch, Petrina Dacres, Genevieve Dempsey, Martha Diaz, Zebulon Dingley, Nikki A. Greene, Matheus Gato, Al-Yasha Ilhaam, John Jennings, Julie Kleinman, Márcia Lima, Treva Lindsey, Nomusa Makhubu, Ivor Miller, Myles Osborne, Shenaz Patel, Tef Poe, Jacqueline Rivers, Jenny Sharpe, LaFleur Stephens-Dougan, Candacy Taylor, and Belén Vega Pichaco.

Over the many years I have worked on this book, I have also been lucky to receive advice from a number of friends and colleagues at other

xviii

institutions: Ammiel Alcalay, Joan Allen, Alan Blum, Jeremy Braddock, Jason Camlot, Wayne Cooper, Mary Esteve, Laura Helton, Tsitsi Jaji, Damien Keane, John Edwin Mason, Adam McKible, Kirsten McLeod, Alessandro Porco, and many others who deserve my gratitude. A special note of thanks goes to Bart Auerbach, the energetic literary appraiser who assessed, among so many other collections, the Samuel Roth Papers and the Ralph Ellison Papers and who was kind enough to meet with me and share a wealth of unique information on the rarified world of literary auctions and institutional acquisitions.

I am deeply thankful to my editor at Columbia University Press, Philip Leventhal, who long championed and then steadfastly guided the book through the review process with an uncannily deft touch. Monique Briones and everyone at the press have been a joy to work with.

Last, I thank my family: even though much of what I "do" remains unclear to them—Why would a Québécois boy go off to work in the States and in an *English* department in the first place?!?—my parents, Estelle St-Pierre and Jean-François Cloutier; my sister, Marieke; my *beau-frère*, François; and my nephew and nieces, Félix, Floryane, and Évelyne, have been sources of rejuvenation and unfailing support throughout the years. *Merci de tout mon coeur pour votre amour et pour ce rappel quotidien qu'il faut toujours se souvenir de ses racines. Comme disait La Poune: met du sel, met du poivre . . . avec un peu de sauce!*

And now, a final word for the being who united our two solitudes: Beth Blum, *mon amour. C'est tout simplement impossible d'énumérer ou d'expliquer ou même d'exprimer comment ce livre doit son existence à cet être sublime qu'est ma femme et la mère de nos enfants, Aimée et celui que nous ne connaissons pas encore, celui qui s'en vient. Cette sage déesse terrestre est aussi la sage-femme de toutes mes créations, et de tout mon bonheur. Sans elle, le néant. Sans elle, ça vaut pas la peine.*

An earlier version of chapter 5 appeared as an article titled "The Comic Book World of Ralph Ellison's Invisible Man," *Novel: A Forum on Fiction* 43, no. 2 (2010): 294–319. Copyright © 2010, Novel Inc. All rights reserved. Republished by permission of the copyright holder and the publisher, Duke University Press. A version of chapter 2 was originally published as

ACKNOWLEDGMENTS

"Amiable with Big Teeth: The Case of Claude McKay's Last Novel," *Modernism/Modernity* 20, no. 3 (September 2013): 557–76. Copyright © 2013 The Johns Hopkins University Press. Reprinted by permission of Johns Hopkins University Press.

ABBREVIATIONS

BU	Boston University
FWP	Federal Writers' Project
HBCUs	historically black colleges and universities
HNM	*Harlem: Negro Metropolis*
JWJ Collection	James Weldon Johnson Collection
NAACP	National Association for the Advancement of Colored People
NARA	U.S. National Archives and Records Administration
NYPL	New York Public Library

Shadow Archives

INTRODUCTION

"NOT LIKE AN ARROW, BUT A BOOMERANG," OR

The Lifecycles of Twentieth-Century
African American Literary Papers

"I would hurl words into this darkness and wait for an echo," Richard Wright writes at the end of *Black Boy*, "and if an echo sounded, no matter how faintly, I would send other words to tell, to march, to fight, to create a sense of the hunger for life that gnaws in us all, to keep alive in our hearts a sense of the inexpressibly human."[1] What is all too easy to forget is that these rousing, now-famous words—words that have since reverberated loudly across the globe in multiple languages—lingered long in the shadows before sounding that first faint echo. For years they dried up likes raisins in the sun of Wright's archive until part 2 of *Black Boy*, known then as "American Hunger," at last appeared in print in 1977, seventeen years after the author's death and more than three decades after being hurled into this darkness. Perhaps as a reminder of its archival birth, the first edition closes with a reproduction of a page from the original typescript profuse with Wright's hand edits.[2] And finally in 1991, thanks to the Library of America's "restored text" edited by Arnold Rampersad, *Black Boy* appeared whole as the book we now know, teach, and love.[3] The hunger for life encoded in Wright's words was preserved in their creator's archive—that boxed site of enclosed darkness where words sit poised ready to tell, to march, and to fight for another day.

So fraught with absences, removals, and delayed restorations is the history of the black literary archive that it could perhaps best be described, after the poets Langston Hughes and Kevin Young, as a kind of "montage of a dream deferred" forming a vast, collective "shadow book."[4] In *The Grey Album*, Young proposes a triadic taxonomy of "shadow books": the unwritten, the removed, and the lost. He suggests that the legion books by African American authors that "fail to be written" symbolize "the life denied [them], the black literature denied existence."[5] We nevertheless journey to black authors' special collections to "search among the fragments of a life unlived," hoping to map out the counterfactuals that history refused to accommodate. Archives are where we attempt to mend the split lives of books whose original releases, like *Black Boy*, "involve textual removals."[6] For scholars, the preservation of the removed is precisely the condition upon which genetic criticism depends: the alternative versions and abandoned drafts retroactively cast their shadow back upon the maimed books that survived. By disrupting textual stability, special collections further encourage "a willingness to recognize the unfinished" as a condition of the literary—not only what has been removed but also what the removed may one day inspire.[7] The paradox here—namely, that future presence is born out of past absence, that anything saved serves only to remind us of all that was lost—forms the archivescape of African American literature. Perhaps unsurprisingly, given his latest role as the director of the Schomburg Center for Research in Black Culture at the New York Public Library (NYPL), Young's extended reflections on shadow books ultimately bring him to the archive; such lostness, he concludes, is the reason he became not only a poet but also a collector and curator, "to save what we didn't even know needed saving."[8]

This book argues that such an archival impulse is the invisible hallmark of twentieth-century African American literary practice. The word *archival* bespeaks an underlying notion that documents have an afterlife, that they can be put to new, unpredictable uses and form the basis for new interpretive and narrative acts. For this reason, I define the archival as a pastness to come—*un passé à venir*. Such a temporality is suggested by Ralph Ellison's famous definition of *hibernation* in *Invisible Man* (1952) as a "covert preparation for a more overt action," which may serve as an accurate definition of black archivism. As I discuss in more detail, this is a double hibernation: first, it occurs during the creator's lifetime of preserving and subsequently (re)deploying his or her records, and, second, it occurs in post-humous revelations. The archive is never an end in itself—otherwise we might as well call it a dumpster—but rather a speculative means to possible futures, including unknowable teleologies guided by unborn hands.

The case of Richard Wright, widely considered to be the first African American writer to enter mainstream American literature, is particularly telling because the bulk of his oeuvre comprises shadow books. Although Wright lived a relatively short life, dying in Paris in 1960 at the age of fifty-two, he left behind many more shadow books—along with some haikus—than books he was able to publish in his lifetime. And even those he was able to witness come into the world did so under difficult circumstances. His preeminence as an internationally recognized American writer imbued his unpublished works with an immediate aura of interest, despite what many of his contemporaries saw as his postexile "decline." Wright was thus one of the first African American writers whose archive was targeted for posthumous recuperation and reclamation. First came *Eight Men* in 1961—a collection of short stories Wright had begun preparing for publication—followed by what is now regarded as one of his best novels, the naturalist-modernist hybrid *Lawd Today!* (original title: *Cesspool*), completed in 1935, rejected everywhere, but finally published in 1963 by Walker and Company—although this first edition was filled with inconsistencies and unwarranted changes. In the decades that followed and up to *A Father's Law* in 2008, more Wright kept turning up, including *American Hunger* in 1977 and the young-adult novella *Rite of Passage* in 1994. Still waiting for an echo in the darkness of the Beinecke Rare Book and Manuscript Library at Yale University is the notorious "Island of Hallucination," an unfinished sequel to *The Long Dream* (1958), where the protagonist, Fishbelly, finds himself caught, much as his creator was, in a paranoid haze of CIA sur-veillance, betrayal, and international fascism.

Beyond the release of these previously unseen works, Wright's prolific posthumous publishing record points to another of the utilitarian hallmarks of literary archives—namely, the establishment of authoritative or corrected editions. When the Library of America brought the complete *Black Boy* out of the shadows in 1991, it was also able to restore Wright's underappreciated novel *The Outsider* (1953). The editor with whom Wright had worked at the time had failed to understand Wright's novelistic project—he wanted Wright to eliminate the discourse against fascism that lies at the heart of the novel—and tried to turn it into a murder mystery. As a result, the publisher, Harper & Brothers, deleted an entire section and removed a number of paragraphs throughout the manuscript, amounting to more than 16 percent of the original.[9] In language that reflects the way in which working in personal archives often leads us to feel as if we are dealing with the living proxy of the deceased, Arnold Rampersad, the editor in charge of the monumental Library of America volumes, explains that he "tried to give him [Wright] back his book" by following "Wright's last typescript that he submitted to the publisher" rather than relying on the first published edition.[10]

Yet that's not all; the case of Richard Wright further introduces another central concern of this book—namely, the unheralded labor of archivists. Rampersad's editorship also gave us at last, in 1991, the unexpurgated version of Wright's first and most famous novel, *Native Son* (1940), another shadow book made whole thanks to the fortuitous preservation of the novel's page proofs in Wright's papers at Yale Library. These proofs, however, which represent the final version of the book before the Book-of-the-Month Club's deletions, were "overlooked by scholars," the *New York Times* reported at the time, because they had been "catalogued in an unusual way."[11] This final detail, where the archivist's hand suddenly materializes, is an important reminder of the invisible labor that makes so much of archival literary scholarship possible. As the *Native Son* example shows, the manner in which an author's material is cataloged can make all the difference in the world. Thus, understanding—or, rather, failure to understand—how cataloging works can objectively mean the difference between finding something or leaving it in the shadows.

Indeed, this brief history of the Library of America Wright volumes exposes much of what is at stake in literary papers as a whole: the writer's perceived value on the rare book and manuscript marketplace (determining who acquires their papers and who can afford them); the myriad delays that define anything archival and the widespread revisionist consequences that come in the archive's sluggish wake (for reception history, canon formation, authorial biographies, and so much more); and the internal processing of the papers (the journey from acquisition to access that the records undertake within a repository). In other words, as Lisa Stead puts it, literary papers "offer us interrelated knowledge about the practices of editors and publishers and the power relations between writers and these figures and institutions."[12] Indeed, literary papers and the worlds they bring together—personal records and private estates, institutional libraries and the marketplace, archival science and copyright law—have increasingly determined the conditions of possibility for the future of literary study. For this reason, grasping the ways in which archivists have handled and conceived of literary papers since the midcentury boom is critical.

THE LIFECYCLES OF RECORDS

Upon its release in 1956, Theodore Schellenberg's manual *Modern Archives: Principles and Techniques* was immediately hailed as a new guiding light for the archival profession. *The American Archivist* called it "the most significant and useful statement yet produced on the administration of modern records and archives."[13] By consolidating methods and experiences developed "in the brief span of 20 years since the creation of the National Archives Establishment [*sic*]" in 1934—archives that were founded amid a growing panic that important federal records were then "kept in various basements, attics, abandoned buildings, and other storage places with little security or concern for storage conditions"[14]—Schellenberg's manual became proof of "the advanced stage reached by the rapidly maturing profession of archivist in the United States."[15] The incumbent authority in archival practice and thinking, Hilary Jenkinson, whose work had held strong influence in the field ever since the publication of *Manual for Archive Administration* in 1922, had been surpassed. So much for the "old fossil," as Schellenberg called Jenkinson.[16]

One of Schellenberg's most enduring contributions to modern records management is the "lifecycle" concept, which appears early in the manual.

After briefly explaining that effective records managers should optimize the ability of records to "serve the purposes for which they were created as cheaply and effectively as possible" and then should make "proper disposition of them after they have served those purposes," Schellenberg writes:

> Record management is thus concerned with the whole life span of most records. It strives to limit their creation, and for this reason one finds "birth control" advocates in the record management field as well as in the field of human genetics. It exercises a partial control over their current use. And it assists in determining which of them should be consigned to the "hell" of the incinerator or the "heaven" of an archival institution, or, if perchance, they should first be held for a time in the "purgatory" or "limbo" of a record center.[17]

This remarkable passage operates as a veritable petri dish of postwar anxieties over reproductive rights, population control, genocide, and eschatology. Even though archivists are here portrayed as a "prochoice" collective, Schellenberg's account nevertheless casts the archive in pseudotheological terms as "heaven," the site of an everlasting afterlife. Record managers stand as gatekeeping celestial Lutherans on the threshold of life and death, imposing limits on the number of births and decreeing salvation or damnation for those who have come to the end of their days. It would also be hard to miss the disturbing connotations of the invocation of "human genetics" and the "incinerator," coming a mere decade after revelations of concentration camps, mass killings, and the accompanying eugenics experiments in Nazi-occupied Europe. Despite its attempt at playfulness, Schellenberg's analogy retains the cold touch of the gloved clinician. Over the years, the curiously anthropomorphic concept of a record's "lifecycle," which has come to designate the different roles and phases through which documents pass before being "disposed of,"[18] has grown into an integral part of records administration.

The lifecycle concept has become common shorthand for the dynamics of records: their provenance, purpose, and telos. Elizabeth Shepherd and Geoffrey Yeo, the authors of an oft-used manual in library science,

Managing Records: A Handbook of Principles and Practice, explicate the life-cycle model as an indication "that records are not static, but have a life similar to that of biological organisms: they are born, live through youth and old age and then die. . . . Most models aim to show a progression of actions taken at different times in the life of a record: typically, its creation, capture, storage, use, and disposal."[19] Of all these terms, the most conspicuous is undoubtedly *capture*, which bears the taint of covert Cold War espionage and containment, a feeling reinforced by its definition as almost a form of informant hostage taking: the steps "taken to secure a record into an effective records management system, where the record can be maintained and made accessible for as long as it is needed."[20] What *capture* really means is that a record's information must be inscribed or seized in some kind of storage medium—in that sense, "a record is 'captured' on paper as soon as it is created," but this piece of paper then needs to be pulled into a records-management system—which still requires a physical infrastructure—in order to be used and controlled. The same goes for born-digital records, which are saved on various digital formats that require both hardware and software.[21]

To the linguistically alert, such language of capturing and securing—the language of records management—is redolent of the war-torn politics out of which the field emerged and expresses the instrumentalism of late capitalism. In particular, the paradoxically dehumanizing overtones of the lifecycle analogy are encapsulated by the graph in figure o.1, which, though innocently offered by Shepherd and Yeo as a visual illustration of the lifecycle model, adopts unsettling connotations when considered in light of its postwar institutional context.

It is difficult to entertain the anthropomorphic conceit of the lifecycle concept without considering the histories of actual lives reduced to disposable property—from concentration camp inmates to chattel slaves —created only to be captured, stored, maintained (fed, housed), used, and discarded once used up. Given these subtexts, it is not surprising that some of the most robust recent theorizing of the archive writ large has come from Jewish and Holocaust studies, African American studies, and postcolonial history. These fields, exemplified perhaps by the work of Giorgio Agamben,

'Progression of actions' lifecycle model

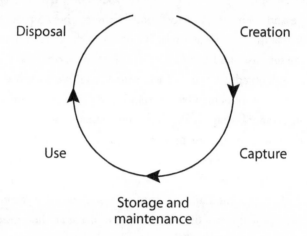

FIGURE 0.1. An ominous lifecycle.

Source: Elizabeth Shepherd and Geoffrey Yeo, *Managing Records: A Handbook of Principles and Practice* (London: Facet, 2003), 6.

Saidiya Hartman, and Ann Laura Stoler, forcefully remind us of the many literal lives behind the official record, whether they be subjects or administrators.[22]

Treating documents as alive can troublingly blur the line between property and the living, but this same metaphor can also underscore the ethical stakes of their use. As recent scholars of coloniality and the police state— Ann Laura Stoler, Michel Foucault, and William Maxwell, to name a few—have taken pains to remind us, the cold, administrative records found in colonial, prison, and intelligence-agency archives are the product of imperfect, fallible human hands, functionaries with "epistemic uncertainties," just as the fading traces of long ago prisoners, or "cargo"—as in Nour-beSe Philip's *Zong!*[23]—are remnants of lived lives, scars *en relief* of once vibrant beings. "[The archive] is proof that a life truly existed," Achille Mbembe writes, "that something actually happened."[24] In the face of such a clinical lifecycle system, humanist practices remind us that archived lives matter.[25]

African American studies holds an indelible archival relation where the living present is forever marked with what Salamishah Tillet calls "sites of slavery," a sentiment further echoed recently by Christina Sharpe in her book *In the Wake: On Blackness and Being*.[26] Emerging in the wake of the omnipresent vanishing point of slavery, African American criticism fuses archival theory and practice in thinking together afterlives, resilience, tradition, materiality, loss, translation, absence, recuperation, and civic engagement. The forensic imagination that informs much of contemporary African American scholarship (re)establishes the authority of a collective provenance, conjuring a kinship that, at its best, allows contemporary black life to imaginatively reclaim irretrievable losses. At the same time, as Hartman's "critical fabulation" makes clear, such retrieval, let alone epistemology or any notion of certainty, remains impossible. The black diasporic archive operates both within and beyond this paradigm; it grounds itself in the material as much as in the immaterial—accumulating paper and phantasms with relish and dread. Put another way, black archivism is another material means through which Amiri Baraka's elusive "changing same" comes into being.[27] In part because many African American authors lived with a constant threat of annihilation and in part because of a forced self-reliance, they deliberately developed an archival sensibility whose stakes were tied to both politics and aesthetics, to both group survival and individual legacy.

Motivated at once by private self-construction and public-minded group unity, the conscious building of black literary archives defines the midcentury period between the New Negro movement and the Black Arts Movement. Practiced under inimical conditions, this rising archivism may in fact be the clearest bridge between the two movements we so often keep apart, the tunnel that runs under the great American library. Thus, deep immersion in the idiosyncratic collecting practices of individual authors offers a unique counterpoint to the dominant forms of institutional thinking under whose shadow black writers lived. The archive becomes a site where an author's hidden identities, affiliations, and political ambivalences and fantasies can be hammered out, notably when these things were deemed too difficult, messy, shameful, or inchoate for public presentation. In this respect, an author's private archival practices foreground alternative forms of curation that remain simultaneously political and aesthetic.

As I trace in more detail in chapter 1, over the past hundred years an intergenerational consideration—a kinship across time reaching back to a common ancestry in Africa and hurled forward into a speculative future—distinguishes the archival practices of African American authors from purely mainstream desires for individual legacy or the lure of wealth and posthumous fame. That said, there is no question that a certain amount self-interest, indeed, self-love—an unshakable belief in one's own value and importance—is a necessary aspect of the self-archiving life, and thus the prominence of one's chief allegiance—to the group or the self—depends on the author in question. To take a literary example, when the troubled queer artist Paul commits suicide at the end of Wallace Thurman's novel *Infants of the Spring* (1932), he carpets "the floor with sheets of paper detached from the notebook in which he had been writing his novel," imagining that this dramatic flourish—pages found surrounding the bloody final bath of its author—would create enough "delightful publicity to precede the posthumous publication of his novel." Thurman's narrative criticizes Paul's failure to take "into consideration the impermanency of penciled transcriptions" as the pages are "rendered illegible when the overflow of water had inundated the floor, and soaked the sheets strewn over its surface."[28] Literary glory after death can come only to those who have taken the time and care to understand the brittle nature of the materials they work with and have pursued proper steps for long-term preservation.

By merging the dominant concept of "afterlives" in African American studies with the archival notion of records going through a series of "lifecycles," this book seeks to sustain an ethical grounding for the narration of history. Amid this literary study, I want to suggest that our methods of historicizing have in part been dependent on an archival lifecycle discourse in ways that have yet to be fully addressed. Indeed, from an archivist's perspective, much of Mbembe's oft-cited essay "The Power of the Archive and Its Limits" seems to emerge unwittingly out of the lifecycle discourse. For instance, Mbembe writes that "it is only at the end of this period of closure that the archived document is as if woken from sleep and returned to life. It can, from then on, be 'consulted.'" He concludes his essay with a paraphrase of the lifecycle model that archivists—and historians—have been using for decades: the use of an archive "results in the resuscitation of life, in bringing the dead back to life by reintegrating them in the cycle of time."[29]

Although the lifecycle model is a crucial and contentious context for the "archival turn" in literary studies, it remains useful in and of itself as a means of understanding the work that archives do. Despite being the target of some important critiques—notably the alternative "records-continuum" model—the lifecycle concept has largely been embraced by the archiving profession.[30] In fact, the current website of the U.S. National Archives and Records Administration (NARA), "America's record keeper," cites the life-cycle concept as key to its methods. When answering the age-old question "What's a record?" NARA follows its general mission statement with a detailed breakdown of the lifecycle model under the title "Records Have 'Lifecycles.'"[31] This breakdown is part of a series of educational capsules grouped under the simple rubric "ABCs About Archives." Roughly speaking, first, the "record is created, usually for a specific purpose, presumably for a legitimate reason and according to certain standards."[32] The record is then "active" and has what archivists call "maximum primary value." Once this initial activity is no longer necessary because its primary purpose is achieved, the record usually develops a related use (say, consultation) and is still kept on site but might not be used every day. After a time, the record creator must decide how to dispose of the record—a phase often called "appraisal": Should it be destroyed, or do we deem it to have "long-term, indefinite, archival value" and store it for posterity? Once stored—or "archived"—the record acquires what some archivists call "secondary value," a concept that was developed to distinguish between the types of purposes and context in which a record was first created and used and the new kinds of uses that same record can unpredictably acquire over time. NARA officials, the website states, "help documents through this process"—that is, through life. In other words, archivists are the life coaches of civilization's undead.

The NARA's lifecycle model primarily concerns bureaucratic documents, however, so when it comes to literary documents, the lifecycle concept becomes much more complex—indeed, literary archives have always presented peculiar challenges to the traditional ways archivists do business. Literary records may adopt a multiplicity of lives over an extended career—all the while remaining in the hands of a single creator. When we handle literary artifacts, we may never know how many lives they have already had.

Nor can we know how many they may have again. This book aims to bring into relief the unique powers and functions of writers' archives through meticulous excavation of previous lifecycles of key literary artifacts preserved in the papers of pioneering African American novelists who collectively helped to inaugurate an important midcentury shift in black literary collecting practices. In tracing the underappreciated archival sensibility of these novelists—namely, Claude McKay, Richard Wright, Ann Petry, and Ralph Ellison—this book demonstrates how these writers first preserved then reanimated their own living collections through novelistic practice. "In the beginning was not the shadow but the act," Ralph Ellison writes in his first book of essays to underscore how "all those acts, legal, emotional, economic and political, which we label Jim Crow" are the ontology upon which the shadow can be constituted. Indeed, if I may be allowed a counterintuitive *détournement* of Ellison's concept, without those acts of preservation, precarious performances laden with "legal, emotional, economic, and political" weight, there would be no resultant shadow archives out of which to reclaim and reaffirm. As Ellison puts it, the "digging up of corpses"—in this case literary ones—is a necessary part of the "process by which the role of Negroes in American life" can be newly demonstrated.[33] At the same time, this book is invested in how the novelistic valuation of wayward documents, now held in multiple repositories, has come to form the shadow archive of American literature.

In the remaining part of this introduction, I outline the book's key argumentative terms, stakes, and literary case studies, and then in chapter 1 I offer a historical survey of the rise of twentieth-century African American manuscript collections in the context of the wider growth of contemporary literary papers. Subsequent chapters serve as case studies, what Carlo Ginzburg calls "micro-histories,"[34] uncovering the multifaceted literary means by which authors redeploy their records, whether through revision, insertion, falsification, translation, redaction, remediation, or even simple fictionalization, sometimes across vast expanses of time. As investigative deep dives into the papers of specific writers, these chapters call for a radical reassessment of an author's overall oeuvre while at the same time serving as practical scenarios for negotiating literary archives in contemporary scholarly practice.[35] To this end, my chapter on Ann Petry departs from the tone and structure of the other chapters to expose the kind of prelabor that the longer, interpretive scholarship necessitates. Framed as a first-person account of an archival quest, punctuated by interruptions and a dearth of materials, this "interlude" chronicles the difficulties of locating and working with the papers of a fiercely private author who actively destroyed much of her archive. The chapter stands as a representative example of the many reasons why the papers of black female authors are so few in number and remain neglected even by the repositories that own them. At the same time, I narrate how the evidence gathered in the Ann Petry Collection at Boston University began to mysteriously point to another, undisclosed manuscript collection at Yale and the research efforts I undertook in my fevered attempt to find it.[36]

In the same spirit, this book concludes with a methodological reflection on the discovery and subsequent authentication of Claude McKay's novel *Amiable with Big Teeth*, the "lost" shadow book that launched this project many years ago. Chapter 4 and the coda thus mean to break the "fourth wall" of the scholarly monograph to address crucial questions of method and access that are too often concealed behind the glossy, finished academic product. The juxtaposition of three interpretive chapters alongside two methodological pieces aims to expose the ways in which these distinct forms of scholarship—what Jerome McGann calls "lower" and "higher" criticism, terms used to differentiate textual scholarship or philology from hermeneutics and "interpretive procedures"[37]—demand different kinds of intellectual and physical labor yet nevertheless mutually inform and reinforce each other. This book is thus an attempt to return to a more capacious way of engaging with literary artifacts by offering both an "analysis of the textual transcriptions" and the "sociohistory of the documents."[38] It is in part an answer to the call Lisa Stead makes in her introduction to the anthology *The Boundaries of the Literary Archive: Reclamation and Representation*, where she proposes that what literary scholars actually "do in the archive—physical or virtual" should "be positioned alongside (and in dialogue with) the conclusions, revelations and formulations we take out of the archive."[39]

PROLEPSIS: ARCHIVAL DELAY
AND "SECONDARY VALUE"

Twentieth-century black counterarchiving is illustrative of a shifting postwar democratic landscape that continued to lag in ascribing value to black lives; it stands as a pledge to a speculative posterity that such archives would one day help make a reality. In the sense Derrida outlines in *Archive Fever*,[40] shadow archivism is at once a promise and a "wager" that the generation of the New Negro movement, perhaps best symbolized by Arturo A. Schomburg's personal collection, effectively made amid continued inequality. Of course, for African American authors, delay not only is built into the temporality of the archive but is also a structural facet, if not the architectural logic, of freedom and equality across the twentieth century. As the now infamous phrase from the *Brown vs. Board of Education* (347 U.S. 483 [1954]) Supreme Court decision puts it, desegregation comes "with all deliberate speed," vague words that were used to justify deferment across the U.S. school system.

Yet, in a more prosaic sense, the strange temporality of literary papers is also an inevitable result of the delay that comes with the author's active years, subsequent demise or death, and the final acquisition of those papers by an institution—which then has to process their contents (what is called "physical control" in archival science) and prepare the front matter (a process called "intellectual control") in order to make the papers accessible to users. As a result, many midcentury authors are being rediscovered in the new millennium as the majority of their papers finally become ready for the public. In one very real sense, *archive* is a synonym for *delay*. Yet, in another way, as Toni Morrison suggests in *Beloved*, the archive reminds us that "everything" is contemporary: "It is all now."[41] Literary papers are unwieldy, sprawling, even postmodern texts that unhinge our sense of the past and force us to reinterpret, redescribe, and rewrite whole biographies. The date an archive is made available to researchers acts upon literary studies like the release of a previously unknown work by the author—and, in a way, it is.

Brent Hayes Edwards's use of the French term *décalage* in *The Practice of Diaspora* brings a resonant set of connotations to the prolepsis that defines the archive's intervention. As Edwards points out, *décalage* has many subtle meanings but broadly refers to a "gap" or displacement in time or space or both, one implying an "interval," and it is commonly the term French speakers use to translate "jet lag,"[42] even though the full French phrase meaning "jet lag" is *décalage horaire*. *Horaire* literally means "schedule" but in this case refers back to *fuseau horaire*, the French term for "time zone," an English phrase that pithily fuses time and space together. Spatiality is chiefly what interests Edwards in the practice of diaspora; he clarifies his use of the term *décalage* through the meaning of its inverse, *caler*, which, he says, means "to prop up or wedge" something in space in order to restore or give it an evenness. Equipped with this European significance for *caler*, Edwards elegantly suggests that *décalage*, as the opposite of *caler*, thus "indicates the reestablishment of a prior unevenness or diversity; it alludes to the taking away of something that was added in the first place, something artificial, a stone or a piece of wood that served to fill some gap or to rectify some imbalance."[43]

For a French Canadian reader such as me, Edwards's etymological exercise conjures further protean associations. In Québec, the verb *caler* holds distinct additional meanings, the most common being to chug a beer in one swig (*caler sa bière*) and to be growing bald (*il cale*)—neither of which, admittedly, offers a very edifying vision of my people. But *caler* can also refer to the disappearance of the ice crust over a lake in the spring just as it can refer to the descent of an object into a liquid or some other porous substance (say, quicksand—but a common use among Québécois children is the equivalent of dunking cookies into milk). We can also say, "*Se caler*," which is something French Canadians do well: to be the architect of your own demise, to put yourself in a disadvantageous position or humiliate yourself, basically to dig yourself into a bigger hole. And *recaler*, of course, in Québec as in France, means to fail a test or flunk a year of school and in effect to be pushed back in time, forced to begin again. Here we reencounter the effects of *décalage horaire*, of jet lag: a disturbance to an arbitrary schedule, a scrambler of ordered time, implying the movement of an object or a lifeform from one time zone to another, all of which further inform how I understand the lifecycles of documents and how I approach the archival as a proleptic pastness to come.

The supplementary Québécois connotations of *caler/décaler* extend the joint movements authorized by Edwards's diasporic articulations, notably because of these movements' association with natural ecosystems as opposed to artificial constructs such as props and wedges: the melting of ice over a lake, the gradual loss of male cranial fur—both organic signs of the passing of time and mortality. Thus, if *caler* can also mean to submerge something until it is no longer visible, a process reminiscent of the archiving of documents, then in such a scenario *décalage* would be to retrieve the sunken record, to break though the icy crust of time and plunge one's arm in the depths (*fonds*), grab hold, and unwedge the desired fossil back above the surface. Rescued from this disadvantageous position, the fossil, its youthful head of hair regained, may begin its belated (*recalée*) life again. Or those that had never really started living can begin their lives in earnest.

In a way that is both tragic and inspiring, the posthumous—literally "born after death"—is an intimate and integral part of the history of African American letters, as this book's opening anecdote regarding

Richard Wright's oeuvre suggests. Many of the works penned by black writers—from *The Bondswoman Narrative* by Hannah Craft (written in the mid–nineteenth century but not published until 2002) to *Amiable with Big Teeth* by Claude McKay (written in 1941 but not published until 2017)—had to languish in darkness before seeing the light of day. In consideration of the *longue durée* trajectory of black special collections, I propose that African American authors developed a unique relation to preservation and archiving, one that hoped for release but planned for delay. As such, African American letters are suffused with a spectral poetics of anticipation that gestates in and through archivism. As one historian puts it, the "grammatical tense of the archive is thus the future perfect, 'when it will have been.'"[44] Shadow archivism is an Afrofuturist pledge—an affirmation made in the face of the "wreckage upon wreckage" of centuries of violence.[45] Despite a lack of futurity lived as a systemic lack of equal opportunity and partly in response to the institutional appreciation of literary papers, African American writers nevertheless began preserving and fashioning their own files in anticipation of an eventual acquisition. Such is how the archive moves: "Not like an arrow, but a boomerang," as Ellison says of history. This black boomeranging archival sensibility not only structures self-understanding and self-representation but also becomes the means through which ideas are thought and expressed. Sensibilities, after all, cannot be reduced to ideas, and each strikes its own sound, akin to a quarter tone vibrating in the interstices of the archive.

The creation of a document, its preservation by the author, and its repurposing into a new temporality, often through a new vessel (a novel, a story, an essay, a song, a photograph, a letter, a statue), suggest the ways in which literary archives are both "being and becoming"—a temporality that Margo Crawford persuasively ties to blackness or, rather, the "rhythm" of blackness in time in her recent book *Blackness Post-blackness*. Crawford's discussion of the serial "circularity of black aesthetic traditions" identifies, via Nathaniel Mackey and Kamau Brathwaite's idea of "tidalectics," a "tension between pacing back and forth with a sense of stasis (a 'failed advance') and pacing back and forth" as a staccato form of forward propulsion. For Crawford, this back-and-forth temporality lies at the center of the "black radical tradition of continuity *and* rupture" that both defines her theory of black postblackness and marks the historical period between the Black Arts Movement and contemporary black aesthetics.[46] Crawford's meticulous unpacking of tidalectics as a bridge between moments in time that are both distant yet near, radically different yet so similar, may also stand as a model for the complexities of archival delay in African American studies. When an archived literary artifact washes up on the shores of the present, it inevitably brings something from the sands of the past, from the *fonds*; it washes over us toward a future thanks to the propulsive force—"in the wake," as Christina Sharpe puts it—of the old tide. Yet in archival tidalectics the past's landfall into the present further anticipates a new horizon upon which yet another wave will one day come to strike.

The future, unpredictable itinerary that archival documents travel while in the hands of novelists (or scholars), partaking of both the aesthetic and the political, lies at the heart of this book. Some form of peripatetic reactivation, "secondary value," or repurposing of a document is featured and unpacked in each of the chapters that follow—whether within the novelist's career or beyond his or her biological lifespan. Literary lifecycles become an intergenerational process that traces what Stoler calls the "*mutating assignments of essence*" in documents.[47] Stoler's phrase is yet another way of understanding what archivists mean when they use the shorthand term *lifecycle*: it refers to the protean and multitudinous functions all records possess, lose, regain, and adopt.

The "secondary value' is often regarded as a "second" lifecycle, a kind of afterlife, akin to a secular resurrection. Interestingly, this supplemental value appears to be perpetually latent; a record may lie dormant indefinitely until it is suddenly brought back to life by a new administration, a wandering scholar, an accidental traveler, or a conscientious archivist. "It's never too late!" is the archive's version of the modernist's "Make it new!" In a Benjaminian sense, excavating the dead conjures the messianic tradition—the occult relation, akin to a séance, fostered by the lifecycles concept. The "death of the author" is precisely what authorizes his or her revival—as Stephen Enniss points out, "The one person we most want to find in the archive is, after all, the one person we can be sure we will not find." We nevertheless persist, in a desperately human desire "for some transubstantiation of pen and paper that may yet fill that unfillable space."[48] Though "the archive" is often used in the service of the disciplinary embrace of the institutional and quantitative, it would be foolish to deny the intensely affective, even otherworldly aspect of the "psychic link," to use David Greetham's phrase,[49] of the archival encounter. Beyond the messianic, the concept of "secondary value" further invokes the gothic or even a certain Herbert West reanimator. Much of genre fiction reminds us that the realm of the occult, which seeks to contact immaterial spirits lying in wait through ancient material vessels, is an archival practice. Far from representing the triumph of the empirical in literary studies, the archive therefore might hold sway in that discipline in part because of the way it taps into basic fantasies of immortality and offers a balm against the threat of loss and impermanence. In seeking the dry bones of evidence, we have, like Henry Dumas's Headeye, stumbled upon spirituality, even if we, too, prefer to deny it.

As Mbembe underscores, the "live" dialogue between past and present that the archive facilitates is privileged because it usually happens in specific, designated, protected locations that have "something of the nature of a temple and a cemetery."[50] His metaphors, rooted in voodoo, refer to places in genre fiction where priests or wizards can concentrate their powers through a nexus of ley lines or villains can revive the army of the dead with the *Necronomicon* and the blood of a king or a virgin—perhaps the most glaring difference being that we (Lisbeth Salander aside) can't go to an archive at night, under a full moon, but are forced to go there during business hours, (presumably) without vials of blood, and face bored security guards rather than otherworldly guardians of Asgard. And scholars of all kinds flock to congregate there, united in the heroic notion that they are "engaged in a battle against this world of spectres," perhaps without admitting the extent to which they are sharing in a spirituality that masquerades as "the inescapable materiality of the archive."[51] Let's turn, now, to how this materiality is made manifest.

THE ARCHIVESCAPES OF BLACK
LITERARY PRODUCTION

In his oft-cited essay "In the Author's Hand: Artifacts of Origin and Twentieth-Century Reading Practices," Stephen Enniss, former head librarian of the Folger Shakespeare Library and now director of the Harry Ransom Center in Texas, estimates that one of the archival profession's "most dramatic success stories" has been the "growth of our institutions' literary collections in the century just past—and the increasing professionalization in our stewardship of them."[52] The story of this growth, sketched in chapter 1, reveals how entwined the fields of archival profession and literary studies are and how they have mutually influenced not only each other's pragmatic strategies but also each other's values and methods of appraisal. As Enniss puts it, the systematic swelling of literary collections has "helped to shape twentieth-century literary studies even as our practices of collecting have, in turn, been shaped by them."[53]

Literary criticism over the past decade has become richly attentive to the conditions that underwrite literary professionalization, yet the crucial role played by literary collections in "making this professionalization possible" remains obscure.[54] This obscurity is all the more surprising when we take into consideration the fact that the proliferation of literary archives represents an upheaval in American letters that rivals the spread of university creative-writing programs so skillfully exposed by Mark McGurl in *The Program Era: Postwar Fiction and the Rise of Creative Writing.*[55] From a historical standpoint, in the United States literary archives coalesced as a cultural and monetary value in the wake of modernism and the Depression and thus on the heels of New Deal reforms such as the Works Progress Administration as well as on the paradigm-shifting turn in archival science brought about by the publication of Schellenberg's manual *Modern Archives* in 1956. In the midst of such convergence, authors increasingly considered the status of their lives essentially as occasions for an archive.

The case studies in this book revolve around African American authors whose personal archives were forged precisely at this time when the literary papers of established white writers emerged as a valuable commodity and as a means of refashioning the personal into cultural capital. Although the profitable commodification of black literary archives was delayed, black counterarchiving was already inscribed as part of a tradition and legacy of Afromodernism. Midcentury African American authors such as Claude McKay, Richard Wright, Ralph Ellison, Gordon Parks, and Ann Petry, among others, were among the first adoptees of this institutionally informed archival sensibility; they acted as bridges to a past just as they pointed to a future beyond their grasp. As the pressure point that both transformed and transferred tradition, the mid–twentieth century stands as that liminal moment when the "indignant generation," to use Lawrence P. Jackson's phrase,[56] absorbed the triumphs and failures of the New Negro movement and established new methods of resistance that laid the groundwork for the Black Arts Movement of the 1960s.

Attending to the lifecycles of literary archives—the archaeological sediment of novelistic craft—can make visible both authors' aesthetic engagement with the novel form and their otherwise opaque political commitments. All of the novelists I consider incorporate archival concepts into their aesthetics—namely, use value, evidentiary truth, access, authenticity, provenance, and original order. Thanks also in part to the upheavals in paper-reproduction technologies, as Lisa Gitelman traces in *Paper Knowledge*, the midcentury was stamped with what Hal Foster calls an "archival impulse": to "make historical information, often lost or displaced, physically present."[57] For African American novelists, the logic of such an impulse often proved to be a two-pronged affair: it manifested itself in their idiosyncratic archiving practices performed behind closed doors, and their novels frequently positioned "the often lost or displaced" at the very center of the story as a mirror of the black experience in the United States. This new focal point—plucked from the periphery—recuperates a slew of historical information that otherwise would remain invisible. Thus, new histories and lives become "physically present" at once in both literary and archival form.

These dynamics are precisely those I explore in chapter 2, where I trace the lifecycles of the "special research work" McKay did as part of the

Federal Writers Project to write his nonfiction book *Harlem: Negro Metropolis* (1940), work that he then later repurposed into novel form as the long-lost *Amiable with Big Teeth*.[58] The latter not only brings the Italo-Abyssinian conflict of 1935 to the foreground—an event largely "lost or displaced" by mainstream history—but further revives heroic African American figures in the service of group unity. McKay is also careful to ground his novel in key documents—an imperial letter, photographs, newspapers, and ledgers—and thus insists on a materiality that demands to be confronted and questioned. Similarly, I investigate a corresponding concern in chapter 5 when I turn to the important role played by dismissed ephemera such as comic books in Ellison's novel *Invisible Man*, a relation I explore through a genetic analysis of Ellison's drafts as well as of his research into Harlem's children and American mythic fantasies.

Likewise, Ann Petry's novel *The Street* (1946) opens with a meticulous inventory of all the different kinds of papers—flyers, ticket stubs, sandwich wrappers, envelopes, newspapers, and so on—that populate, surround, and practically attack the protagonist, Lutie Johnson, as she walks in Harlem. Petry not only emphasizes this kind of materiality on a thematic level but also, like Richard Wright does with *Native Son*, composed her novel out of a careful study of emerging socioeconomic statistical data. Both Petry and Wright bend their naturalist fiction to "explain the statistics that regularly confused people and seemed to support the hoary notions of biological inferiority."[59] Where Wright merges his fiction, memoir, and photojournalistic practice to expose the "reality of the Negro problem" for young African American men at midcentury, Petry allows for the neglected positionality of motherhood, womanhood, and blackness to become the dominant perspective in the defiant figure of Lutie. Despite manifesting a distinct archival sensibility unique to their individuality, each of the midcentury authors in my project displays a personal commitment to combining record building with aesthetic practice as a means to ensure group survival.

Undergirding the formation of black personal archives is the constantly shifting, ever-widening cultural battle over who is valued and what is valuable. The dual tasks of novel writing and archiving converge in the act of transvaluation—and literary papers, a subset of "personal papers," become a privileged site that maps on a granular level the countercultural hopes of a present to come. It follows that the mutability of what is considered valuable, which the lifecycles concept lays bare, is a governing concern of this book. This contingency of use value is what makes the archival profession so challenging and the work of novelists, artists, literary scholars, and cultural historians so vital. Although scholars have long been able to address and celebrate the ability of African American literature to articulate and embody functions we associate with the archive—recuperation, memory, preservation—the actual access to authors' private collections has been fraught with natural and institutional delays. Even after acquisition, a collection can remain in the backlog for years until the repository's resources allow for processing. Yet for literary collections to exist at all, authors need to have preserved their papers in the first place. By necessity, therefore, this book turns to major midcentury black novelists whose papers are (mostly) now available to researchers. Literary papers offer scholars the opportunity to track the different forking paths of documents or artifacts preserved in these authors' own files, journeys that sometimes span several lifecycles, including ultimately that of posthumous publication. As a result, modern literary archives emerge as new assemblages to be reckoned with as we attempt to rebuild the past. A single author's papers are never singular—they are always polyphonic: at the same time that they complicate and enrich our understanding of a given writer, they offer new perspectives onto countless figures, events, institutions, and relationships that can be read from myriad disciplinary approaches. As Terry Cook says, there are always "*fonds* within *fonds*."[60] If a human being's life can contain Whitmanesque multitudes, then a single literary collection can potentially refashion an entire field's underlying architecture.

This book uses the tools of literary criticism to closely read and unpack the richly suggestive language of archival science, and, in turn, it also applies the governing prisms and paradigms of archival practice to our discussions of the literary. The role of the archive in my work is therefore both methodological and thematic: first, I deploy material-text tools by incorporating these authors' caches of research materials, correspondence, drafts, diaries, and aborted, undisclosed, or unpublished pieces, obtained during my visits to their various repositories. Second, I extricate how the political and aesthetic stakes of research, documentation, artifacts, ephemera, curation, and classification practices are foregrounded within their novels and other works. Set against the historical background of the rise of modern literary papers, I further explore how black literary archives smuggle radicalism into traditional sites of cultural and national authority—such as the Library of Congress and the Ivy League—and thereby destabilize incumbent identities while opening the door to new systems of value.

I am interested in thinking about the novel's role in what Henry James calls a "perpetually provisional" democratization:[61] how novelists enter democratic discourse by celebrating certain marginal types and institutions, by including neglected artifacts and documents, and thus by dramatizing the struggle for historical legibility not just in their artistic output but also in their private archival practices. In other words, the act of arrangement performed by the living writer—both within novels and through personal archives—carries meaning beyond the item being singled-out for "filing"; arrangement transforms the item's meaning and ascribes it new value. Similarly, so does the scholar's excavating work; as the historian Carolyn Steedman suggests, the object under investigation is "altered by the very search for it."[62] In other words, the nomadic artifact, once caught, takes its place within a system of thought and literary production that allows it to be put into relation to the creator's larger oeuvre. The work of archivists in processing the collection's contents performs analogous functions; in giving further definition and shape to the author's archive, archivists guide—or, perhaps one should say, manipulate—scholarly practice. As a subset of the personal, they reflect the idiosyncrasies of individuality and excesses of circumstance that confound any "critical consensus."

I am thus concerned with analyzing both the *archival function* novels serve—the way they can stand as alternative, expanded, or even counterfactual sites of historical preservation—and the roles that novelists have played as archivists and record creators. I explore these authors' own appraisal strategies and record-creating processes and, at times, their own research practices to uncover how their archival sensibility informs their novelistic practice. The papers that novelists amass and create offer ways for them to negotiate civic, social, and national estrangement; how and what they choose to document and record in the world reflect the kind of nation they are working to redefine, both in the present moment and for posterity. In this respect, these authors are appropriating for themselves the strategies usually reserved—and originally conceived—for imperial governance.

Although in *Along the Archival Grain* Stoler is speaking exclusively of colonial archives—the Dutch colonial archives to be more specific—she parses how the documents produced by administrators continue to have varied uses even after "the moment of their making has passed." In Stoler's words, these archives represent "an arsenal of sorts" that can be "reactivated" at a moment's notice "to suit new governing strategies." "Documents honed in the pursuit of prior issues could be requisitioned to write new histories," she explains, "could be reclassified for new initiatives, could be renewed to fortify security measures against what were perceived as new assaults on imperial sovereignty and its moralizing claims."[63] Within Stoler's portrait of discourse control, of governance rooted in its materiality, we may also glimpse—in an admittedly radically different context—a description of how novelists make use of the documents they create and gather for subversive political ends. In other words, how a novel chooses to be historical is an argument about history, preservation, and the archive. Yet literature, or the literary, is not just a substitute archive; it is both a symbolic engagement with and a material critique of governmental and organizational record management.

Steedman suggests that "in the Archive, you cannot be shocked at its exclusions, its emptinesses, at what is *not* catalogued, at what was—so the returned call-slip tells you—'destroyed by enemy action during the Second World War.' . . . Its condition of being deflects outrage: in its quiet folders and bundles is the neatest demonstration of how state power has operated, through ledgers and lists and indictments, and what is missing from them."[64] But unlike the acquiescing, presumably white historian, the black novelist must go against the grain of what Steedman describes. Nor can any Jamesonian waning of affect be tolerated for most black historians, as Michel-Rolph Trouillot's seminal recuperative history of the Haitian revolution,

Silencing the Past: Power and the Production of History, demonstrates.[65] To regard the archive's "condition of being" as what "deflects outrage" stems from the historical privilege of having successfully silenced the past. In contrast, here is what a twenty-eight-year-old Ralph Ellison wrote to Richard Wright after having consulted the Farm Security Administration photographic record collected in Wright's book *12 Million Black Voices*: "The trauma of passing from the country to the city of destruction brought no anesthesia of unconsciousness, but left our nerves peeled and quivering. We are not the numbed, but the seething. God! It makes you want to write and write and write, or murder."[66] For Ellison, the communal experience of blackness brought a necessary outrage that compelled him toward both violence and repeated acts of writing. Both were means of filling in the emptinesses, and we must be thankful that Ellison channeled most of his energies into literary acts and a lifelong accumulation of personal records.

The filling of "gaps" with "fiction" is precisely what some historians, notably Arlette Farge, find most objectionable in the novelist's use of archival materials—and, by extension, the literary scholar's use of a novel as a historically valid resource. In her sublime little book *Le goût de l'archive*, translated as *The Allure of Archives*, Farge disagrees that "fiction is the ideal way to free oneself from the constraints of the discipline [history] and make the archive live again." "The argument that the novel resurrects the archive and gives it life," Farge declares, is "not a real argument at all," and writing novels "has nothing to do with 'writing history.'" Yet for all of her reticence to accept fiction as an ethically valid filler for history's gaps, even when the work in question is steeped in a "knowledge of the archive," Farge, like all historians, is also in the business of telling stories. Indeed, she intersperses her chapters on eighteenth-century French history with anecdotes from her research visits to various repositories, using her own "gift for writing to captivate readers and take them on a very specific adventure." Did she include these stories to subtly (and paradoxically) keep open the door to narrative as another possible ethical means "to do right by these many forgotten lives"?[67] Or was it simply, and humbly, to further inscribe her own fallible self as a historical subject? Nevertheless, even if we disallow any consideration of the novel as history, we cannot escape the fact that the formation of special collections can become a means of writing history. Moreover, if, as count-less historians such as Steedman have shown, public archives "came into being in order to solidify and memorialize first monarchical and then state power"[68]—in other words, as a prosthetic of state power—then private archives can serve a similar purpose for the private citizen.

THE PARALLAX OF THE REFERENCE DESK

There are two temporalities to keep distinct here: that of novelistic creation—stretched over a varying number of active years and accompa-nied by idiosyncratic record production and record compiling—and that of the literary collection being acquired, processed, and made available to researchers, its contents released once more upon the world via scholarship, museum exhibitions, posthumous publications, and more. These two over-arching lifecycles are interrelated, and they mutually, often retroactively transform each other. The writer's archive is the perpetually unfinished text, spanning decades, amassing successes and failures, speaking back to a multi-plicity of fixed temporal moments upon which scholars can alight, sometimes even deceiving themselves into believing that it just might be possible to step into the same river twice.

At the same time, literary scholars need to be more cognizant of the ways in which the history of archival science has come to affect the very arti-facts at the center of our profession. To that end, chapter 1 is a concerted look at how archivists have conceived of personal papers over the past cen-tury and how such evolving conceptualization necessarily affected both the kinds of materials that were preserved and how they were arranged. Works of literary criticism based on "the archive" too often fail to engage with the labor and scholarship produced by archivists, those who have been acquir-ing, cataloging, appraising, controlling, and curating the collections that have become essential resources in the revitalization of the discipline. The elasticity of the term *archival* in criticism today represents both a challenge and an opportunity: as an opportunity, it allows us to think about history, memory, documentary, record keeping, and other related concerns as part of a cross-disciplinary network; as a challenge, it threatens to become so diluted a concept as to be practically devoid of meaning and can, in fact, prevent true interdisciplinary conversation.

A survey of recent archival criticism reveals some distinct and overlapping analytical trends. One branch, spearheaded by Suzanne Keen's book *Romances of the Archive in Contemporary British Fiction*, investigates the surge of narratives that feature archives at the core of their plots, usually by having the protagonists perform archival research in libraries or other repositories. A central example would be A. S. Byatt's novel *Possession* (1990), but Stieg Larsson's Millennium trilogy and even films such as *Indiana Jones and the Last Crusade* (Steven Spielberg, 1989) also fall within that category. For Keen and for the British tradition she examines, romances of the archive are often successful; in these romances, "characters are transformed, wrongs righted, disasters averted, villains exposed, crimes solved."[69] On the American side, however, success or closure remains persistently elusive— artifacts are rarely found, answers are withheld, evidence is destroyed—and this is doubly true for the African American tradition.

Perhaps the quintessential African American postwar "archive" novel is David Bradley's *The Chaneysville Incident* (1981), whose protagonist, John Washington, is a historian by trade who spends most of the novel doing extensive research, scouring an imposing array of artifacts, and creating piles of notes on index cards, desperate for clues to both his father's demise and the "incident": the apparent ritual suicide of thirteen fugitive slaves. Early on, the novel revels in the historian's forensic excitement in the face of mystery. Entering his father's office in the attic, the hidden site of his family archive, Washington recounts: "It was almost as if the chair, the table, the book, the lamp, the empty fireplace, were items under glass; they were the keys to a man's mind, laid bare to me, clues to a mystery, the answer to every question there. All I had to do was interpret them. It was the greatest thrill I had ever known."[70] In the end, however, he must confront the fact that he will always be left with speculation, uncertainty, and absence— the polar opposite of the positivist fantasy Keen ascribes to the British tradition. Washington has to learn "to accept the idea that we will never know everything," that there is no such thing as a "Historians' Heaven: a firmly fixed chamber far removed from the subjective uncertainties of this mortal coil, where there is a gallery of pictures of the dinosaur taken constantly from every angle, and motion pictures, and cross sections." What frustrates Washington, as it frustrates novelists and literary scholars, is the fact that despite having gathered an impressive array of facts and despite having taken careful chronological notes on index cards, he has ultimately just "help[ed] order events." The notes and cards provide "no suppositions or connections. No cause and effect." As a historian, Washington refuses to allow "imagination" to fill in the gaps—there can be "no imagination in it," he says, adding, "You can't create facts. But you can discover the connections . . . there's a point where all the facts just come together and the ideas come out. It's like a fire, smoldering, and then it catches, and the flame catches other things, and then it's like a forest fire."[71] Alas, this fire both purifies and destroys the very edifice of evidence that was erected through the archive. Fittingly, the novel ends not on a note of triumph but rather of equanimity as the historian literally sets fire to his own research, precisely on the original site where the slaves chose death rather than recapture. However, he does, I would like to underscore, restore his family's attic archive and leaves it open for the next (re)searcher.

The Chaneysville Incident is a prototype of Saidiya Hartman's "critical fabulation": the novel intends "both to tell an impossible story and to amplify the impossibility of its telling."[72] Formally structured around zigzagging dates, the novel presents an encyclopedic hodgepodge of generic styles in the tradition of *Moby-Dick* (1851), grafting academic prose to imaginative fiction, shifting between thrilling adventure sections and abstruse jargon that drastically slows down the pace. Epistemic disappointment repeatedly befalls the historian who can never gather enough "facts" to solve the mystery of his family, of the "incident," and, ultimately, of slavery. The novel's material ties to slavery come via the artifacts preserved by the family, notably the unfinished journal of John's great-grandfather, C. K., an escaped slave. Through nonlinear intergenerational time hopping, the novel enacts the collapsing temporalities of the archive that define so much of postwar African American literature. Washington uncovers "horror stories" populated by "ghosts" yet retains a scholarly distance that appalls his girl-friend, who sees such professionalism as a lack of empathy. She shouts, "You just sit there on top of all this . . . I don't even know what to call it. Death. Horrible things. And you make notes on little cards and then you ask for another cup of coffee." But Washington's veneer eventually breaks under the weight of his archival excavation: "I fell prey to one of the great-est fallacies that surrounds the study of the past: the notion that there is such a thing as a detached researcher, that it is possible to discover and analyze and interpret without getting caught up and swept away."[73] As in the case of McKay's final novel, the consultation of notes and newspapers—archival research—both politicizes the tale and irrevocably affects the human being doing the excavation.

As "critical fabulation," Bradley's novel is thus an example of what Linda Hutcheon calls "historiographic metafiction," a mode whose popularity arose precisely alongside the increased proliferation of literary papers in the university. African American masters of the genre such as Ishmael Reed weaved modernist and postmodernist elements with folk tales, creating dia-logic polyphonies that usually involved collapsed temporalities, and often represented the living communing with dead ancestors, finding their spirit embodied in material objects or sites. Perhaps the nearest white counterpart to *The Chaneysville Incident*—aside from Stephen King's *The Shining* (1977)—may be Don DeLillo's novel *Libra* (1988). Released seven years after Brad-ley's novel, *Libra* exemplifies the archive's failure to provide any kind of closure, producing instead an elaborate paranoid conspiracy. Even Nicho-las Branch, the CIA's own archivist, who collects, processes, and analyzes all documents and records related to the Kennedy assassination, never "solves" the case, never knows the truth. "Some stories never end," DeLillo states in the opening sentence of his introduction to the reissue of *Libra* in 2006, and he goes on to speak of Branch—a name that implies being sim-ply a part, a limb of the whole—as the voice that "maintains that facts are brittle things. He maintains that the past is changing even as he sits and thinks about it."[74] Branch's relation to the past, here expressed by DeLillo years after completing *Libra* (Libra[ry]), is a compelling articulation of the archive's ideological underpinning—it is the site where the past changes at every sitting. As in *The Chaneysville Incident*, in *Libra* we have accumulation without grand narrative, correspondences without clear connections, excess defined by gaps.

An approach related to Keen's considers what Marco Codebò calls "narrating from the archive," a practice "where the narrative stores records, bureaucratic writing informs language, and the archive functions as a semiotic frame that structures the text's context and meaning." These "archive novels" usually contain an archival theme woven within their plots and produce "the same kind of meaning-making operations executed by the records, files, and inventories that characterize bureaucratic archives' practices."[75] Whereas Keen restricts her analysis to postwar Britain, Codebò discusses examples from both nineteenth- and twentieth-century European and American fiction (Manzoni, Balzac, Flaubert, Perec, DeLillo). The authors of these archival romances, in a reflection of the authors studied here, often performed their own behind-the-scenes archival quests in order to craft their narratives, thereby creating layers of archival *mise-en-abime*.

Another prominent trend in current criticism is simply to consider literature—usually the novel but poetry as well—as an alternative site of historical preservation, a counterpoint to official or "major" history. Fiction thus becomes a historical corrective or supplement, a trove of otherwise unobtainable sets of historical data that were considered "too obscure for learned classification," to use Ellison's phrase,[76] yet nevertheless contain objectivity gaps resulting from levels of fictionalization. When applied to twentieth-century—especially postwar—texts, this branch of criticism usually demonstrates in often illuminating ways how such historical fiction, in flaunting its status as speculative, can thus act as a "statement" on historiography and the meaning-making processes we impose on the past. As Linda Hutcheon observes, such "postmodern novels scrutinize the process of 'event becoming fact,'"[77] a statement that also aptly describes what McKay is doing in *Amiable with Big Teeth*. A related aspect of this kind of criticism tackles those kinds of experiences that never or rarely leave a "record" behind. The body of African American literature, perhaps more than any other in the American tradition, imposes itself as a counterarchival imaginative documentation that allows such "nonevents" to become history, reflecting the "historical pluralism" Hayden White describes.[78]

A fourth trend in archival literary criticism emerges out of the nineteenth-century epistolary novel: the *Archivroman*. The term was first applied to Johann Wolfgang von Goethe's *Wilhelm Meister's Journeyman Years* (1821), a "novel" composed of a mishmash of shorter narrative pieces, letters, poetry, aphorisms, and so on, creating generic chaos. In other words, this novel form seems to be a raw archive in disarray, a "special collection" of disparate genres not yet arranged but bound together between two covers as a means of stretching novelistic boundaries—in short, novels of this type, such as Theresa Hak Kyung Cha's *Dictee* (1982), Jack Kerouac's *Visions of Cody* (1972), Max Frisch's *Man in the Holocene* (1979), and John Keene's *Counternarratives* (2015), to name a few, have an undeniable "archival poetics."[79] A subset of this approach doubles down on the novel form in its materiality to consider bibliographic aspects of the book and its production process—from dust jackets to changing covers for various or foreign editions to matters of typesetting and the typography of the page.

The four types just described, in addition to more purely theoretical engagements inspired by Derrida and Foucault, are common rubrics under which literary scholars are choosing to think of the archive and literature together. Although by no means exhaustive and certainly overlapping, they represent the chief taxonomic prisms through which archival criticism operates. Taken together, concerned with both form and content, they demonstrate how novels, as Aarthi Vadde elegantly puts it, "reflect upon history as a mode of writing and a pattern of assembly."[80] One of the most interesting features of this contemporary criticism is that literary scholars, historians, and archivists are producing it. Although they are rarely working collaboratively—and are, in fact, often working in isolation for separate audiences—a nascent interdisciplinary network is emerging. This book navigates all these critical approaches, guided by the needs and the natures of the lifecycles under investigation.

Much of my own thinking about literary papers has come from two distinct yet mutually informative experiences: first, the time I spent as an intern processing publisher and literary archives in Columbia University's Rare Book and Manuscript Library and, second, my trips from one repository to another for research. This book is thus a product of the parallax of the reference desk: shuttling between the scholar's usual position in front and the hidden world in back. Although literary archives are often jarringly distinct from administrative records in both form and formation, they have nevertheless often been processed by individuals trained in record management. Though processing archivists assigned to personal collections today may be more cognizant than archivists of yesteryear when it comes to the unique features of literary papers, the fact remains that the majority of extant literary collections were handled by professionals without specialized knowledge of literary history, just as many literary scholars are untrained in the ways of the archivist.

Indeed, as the work of Senior Archivist Catherine Hobbs has made clear, the area of personal archives—of which literary archives are a subset—was utterly undertheorized until the turn of the twenty-first century.[81] Not only has archival theory "done a terrible job of accommodating the particular needs of individual people's archives," argues Hobbs, but it has "also made little effort to accommodate adequately the particular exigencies of literary archives."[82] Literary papers are a special breed; the archivist David Sutton describes them as "the most volatile and unpredictable type" of personal papers.[83] Like Hobbs, Sutton calls for a better understanding of how most already-accessible literary collections have been handled. Such insider knowledge of the archivist's oft-misunderstood profession can clarify why the archivist imposed intellectual control on personal and literary materials, a clarification that in turn can be of both practical and theoretical use in helping scholars reckon with the changing values assigned to the literary.

In recent years, perhaps without realizing, literary scholars and archivists have been moving in similar directions through their mutual shift away from an understanding of archival records as *product* toward a sense of them as *process*. For archivists, this invisible resonance has taken place as part of a larger effort to grasp the nature and role of archival *fonds*.[84] Much like some of the latest trends in literary criticism, recent archival "macroappraisal" theory has called for "a shift away from the records themselves to the social context in which the records are created."[85] For archivists, this shift is yet another, more refined means of following *respect des fonds*, the single most important guiding principle of the archival profession. In general terms, emerging out of the European tradition and the "Dutch Manual"—the colloquial name given to the book *Arrangement and Description of Archives* (1898) composed by the Dutch trio Samuel Muller, Johan Adriaan Feith, and Robert Fruin—to respect the *fonds* is to uphold the twofold dictums of provenance and the "sanctity of original order"—namely, "the maintenance of which focused on preserving the logical structure and internal arrangement of the records of each creator," as Terry Cook puts it. To be more precise, Cook explains, the *fonds* is the "theoretical product of both creation (provenance) and arrangement (original order)" and is thus a manifestation of "both a logical and a physical reality." The battles and difficulties over how *fonds* is ultimately conceptualized, let alone practically applied "to descriptive or appraisal practice," thus rest on "a central contradiction in archival theory": documents are inevitably both product and process.[86]

Put another way, the *fonds* is the Schrödinger's cat paradox of archival physics. Like the cat in the famous thought experiment, records are in a kind of stasis—akin to what Jacques Derrida calls *survivance*, perpetually suspended between life and death, partaking of both.[87] In archival quantum mechanics, explains Cook, "the essential describable unit of archives" acts both as a wave and as a particle; it is simultaneously "a function, a process, a dynamic activity on the one hand, and a concrete product, an artifact, a record on the other."[88] Such definitions of archival *fonds* in many ways uncannily reflect how literary studies has come to understand novelistic and bibliographic practices. As Catherine Hobbs puts it, "Literary archives have a particular resonance for archivists" because "acts of documentation blend very closely (in space and time) with acts of literary creation."[89] The literary artifact encountered in the reading room becomes, according to Tyler Walters, the "physical expression of personal interactions and organizational processes"; this artifact reflects the tidalectical ebb and flow of the discipline's evolution, its alternating desire for hermeneutical interpretation and textual forensics.[90] In short, literary scholarship and the archival profession have a singular affinity.

As Cook makes clear, it is incumbent upon the modern archivist to have "a clear understanding of the nature, scope and authority of the creator of the records involved and of the records-creating process."[91] The evidential power—the traditional raison d'être of archives—to be gleaned from the papers of creators involved in the business of literature and art (from authors to publishers to booksellers) can thus be increased only by the close involvement of related professionals at the archival-processing level. Put another way, training literary scholars in archival and library science or, alternatively, training archivists in literary criticism and methods would mutually benefit each profession in ways that are congruent with the changes each group is facing and will continue to face. Most curators in charge of repositories were traditionally trained as historians.[92] Although this is a logical background for an archivist to have, the kinds of preparation and intellectual formation given to historians are distinct from the sensibilities honed through the study of literature. As I address in chapter 1, these differences inevitably affected the ways in which collections were appraised—both in terms of which collections were selected as worthy of preservation and in terms of how they were internally policed—over the course of the twentieth century. Interestingly, recent scholarship by archivists on literary archives has indicated the need to diversify the disciplinary background, not to mention the biopolitical diversity, of incoming librarians. Only those archivists trained in the latest literary methods, familiar with book history and, for example, the unreliability of the best-seller list as indicator of posterity, will be in a position to address the complexity of determining "the importance of the writer" being appraised for possible archivization.[93]

This is especially important for minority authors whose works struggle to have visibility both to the public and in the academy. Hiring literary scholars trained in minority literature as acquisition directors or at least as consultants can go a long way toward redressing the diversity pool of available data for posterity. Scholars trained in African American studies and in the studies of other minority cultures (Latinx, LGBTQ, Indigenous) bring a salutary alternative perspective to potential targets of acquisition through their expertise in the new emerging vessels of value of the past century. Take, for instance, the establishment of the Hip Hop Archive and Research Institute at Harvard University in 2002 under the pioneering direction of Marcyliena Morgan or the Hip Hop History Archive founded by Johan Kugelberg at Cornell in 2008. Since the late 1990s, through his company Boo-Hooray, Kugelberg has helped organize, consolidate, and place close to one hundred unique collections of postwar radicalism in the United States. From Afrika Bambaataa to Ed Sanders, punk rock to the Amsterdam News Photography Archive, Ed Wood's pornographic pulp fiction to the Living Theatre, Kugelberg has been an architect of salvation for many unique, endangered, marginal postwar collections.

As a corollary, an increase in archivist and librarian positions, or postcustodial roles, for persons of color and members of the communities whose materials are being preserved would be ideal to aid the continued transformation and reclamation efforts of literary history. Even when the creation of new staff positions remains prohibitive, a potential immediate measure would be to establish collaborations between those responsible for new acquisitions and the literary scholars already present at a given institution. Just as an acquisition director can consult with faculty about future accessions, a processing archivist could invite a leading scholar in a given field to be present during the initial survey phase of a collection or to peruse the extent of relevant materials at some preappraisal point. Ideally, the scholar could be accompanied by students during this survey visit, thereby demystifying much of the process and allowing further collaboration. Though the logistics of this process may not always be feasible, its implementation may prove uniquely valuable.

The tenets of "minimal processing" that have taken hold since the popularity of Mark A. Greene and Dennis Meissner's essay "More Product, Less Process: Revamping Traditional Archival Processing" inadvertently invite this kind of involvement on the part of researchers because less material, generally speaking, is thrown out.[94] Thus, in the new economy of "more product, less process," the onus of time is now on the researcher: there is just more paper to look through to find the few golden nuggets. In turn, when something "new" or noteworthy is found nestled within a given folder or notebook, researchers can in turn inform the archivists about the find—through such microcollaborations, the collection's finding aid may be amended to alert future researchers (essentially enlisting scholars as fellow processors).

Such collaborations between researcher and archivist mirror those that take place in the reading room during the communion between record creator and scholar. Within that quantum space materialized by the encounter, that place where future hands brush the pages of the past, we receive the transformative transmission. In preserving their records, authors allow for that materiality to be welcomed as an integral part of their oeuvre. This is the pledge and promise of shadow archivism, where the preservation of records anticipates a future when the dream may once again grow young, where the vicissitudes of blackness, the split and fragmented, the delayed and deferred, the incomplete and undecipherable nature of these archives become the message. Product and process, these archives are portraits of unwritten, removed, lost lives that the conditions of white supremacy have sundered. Hurled into darkness, these hibernating boomerangs are about to come up for breath. Keep a steel helmet handy.

1

BLACK SPECIAL COLLECTIONS AND THE MIDCENTURY RISE OF THE INSTITUTIONAL COLLECTOR

"The historical development of special black collections that have been assembled and subsequently housed in American libraries would make interesting study [*sic*]," wrote Jessie Carney Smith, the longstanding dean of the library at Fisk University in 1990.[1] It would indeed, and although this book is above all a literary study, it shares Smith's conviction. This chapter takes a closer look at the neglected yet crucial history of the rise of contemporary literary papers in the United States across the twentieth century through a focus on black special collections and their struggle for acquisition by university and college libraries as well as other institutional collectors. It would be impossible to cover the entirety of this complex and moveable scene, let alone the fate of every player, so I concentrate on representative cases involving major institutional collectors and on the novelists most prominently featured in this book, Claude McKay, Richard Wright, Ann Petry, and Ralph Ellison.

For African American authors, the postwar institutional love for literary papers was far from universally distributed. Unlike today, outside of historically black colleges and universities (HBCUs), only a few repositories—notably Yale University and the Harlem branch of the NYPL (now the Schomburg Center for Research in Black Culture)—were actively interested in acquiring their papers. More often than not, such acquisitions also had to be in the form of gifts and donations on deposit rather than purchases. In contrast, living white authors, British and American alike, enjoyed an intensifying and increasingly aggressive attention from the rare-book and manuscript market in the postwar period—as exemplified by the acquisition record of the University of Texas library (now the Harry Ransom Center)—marking a paradigm shift in value that turned the living writer's waste basket into a potential goldmine.

Regardless of race, the "institutional collector," to quote Stephen Enniss, the current director of the Harry Ransom Center, played a tremendous role in altering the literary landscape. At midcentury, the rabid acquisition program of these collectors—mainly university and college libraries—increased the value of literary artifacts, introducing fierce competition in the market (which always favors repositories with deep pockets) that led to "a shift toward contemporary collecting."[2] Professional writers' archival practices, therefore, matured in the institutional collectors' shadow; a swelling number of authors began to preserve rather than throw away, establishing a trend that has now come to include born-digital records. In turn, literary study was altered once access to a larger number of literary collections changed what was possible to know and assess of the writing business. As more and more literary scholars became de facto historians thanks to these collections—which further affected the where and the how of literary study, privileging the sizable holdings of elite institutions—living writers and their heirs regarded their personal archives as another means of revenue. Families and estates were enticed by the potential promise of financial rewards down the line; they consulted literary appraisers, who assisted them in setting base prices, in isolating certain items that could fetch higher prices at auction, and in recommending repositories that might be potential buyers.

Though my focus in this book is not the role of literary collections as gatekeepers to what Jim English calls the "economy of prestige,"[3] it is essential to examine the postwar upsurge of interest in literary collections and to do so through the perspective of the archivists who have also seen their profession altered by this shift. As with Richard Wright's case at Yale, the specific custodial repository can be "the difference that makes a difference." Secured within what looks like a gigantic Asgardian hammer supported by vibranium, Yale's prestigious Beinecke Rare Book and Manuscript

Library houses one of the largest collections of African American materials on the globe: the James Weldon Johnson Collection. The establishment of this collection, founded in 1941 by Carl Van Vechten, has played an especially central role in the future of modern African American letters: it has allowed for the delayed recuperation of numerous previously unpublished texts, enabled thousands of new scholarly projects to emerge, and made it possible, as archives do, to discover new voices for the first time and old voices anew. This collection, which is deservedly the subject of a rising number of studies in modernist and African American literary history, is also directly tied to each author considered in this book and so warrants some attention.

PROVENANCE:
THE JAMES WELDON JOHNSON EFFECT

Along with its many other considerable achievements in the worlds of literature and the arts, the New Negro movement, later known as the Harlem Renaissance, also brought about a "revolution in the act of saving and collecting the black past," as the Beinecke curator Melissa Barton puts it.[4] By midcentury, I suggest, that "revolution" came to alter what it meant to be a professional black writer and was one of the major factors in establishing archivism as an entrenched practice. This archival sensibility can in part be traced back to interwar modernism, but it also stems from an evolving ideological shift taking place in the American scene in relation to the preservation of documents and records and in the postwar competition for literary artifacts by living writers. As Jeremy Braddock makes clear in his book *Collecting as Modernist Practice*, the "collecting" revolution is a modernist staple that reaches beyond race, even though Afromodernism operated within a distinct set of stakes and conditions of possibility.[5] The foundation of the James Weldon Johnson (JWJ) Collection at Yale University in 1941, as Braddock describes, represents a key moment in this ideological and practical revolution. In addition to Braddock's book, Emily Bernard's invaluable biography *Carl Van Vechten and the Harlem Renaissance* and Michele Birnbaum's critical assessment of the JWJ Collection's importance and far-reaching implications yield a comprehensive account of how Van Vechten helped orchestrate the establishment of this archive.[6]

Carl Van Vechten, perhaps the most prominent white member of the Harlem Renaissance, remains a polarizing figure, even though today he is often remembered more as a portrait photographer than as a writer in his own right, despite the tremendous literary fame he enjoyed in his heyday. Regardless of what one makes of him as a person, Van Vechten was a major figure in the arts of the interwar years, and he used his privilege and contacts in the publishing world (notably Alfred Knopf, a personal friend) to boost the careers of many writers, black and white, from Mina Loy to Nella Larsen, Wallace Stevens to Langston Hughes.[7] His relationship with Hughes ran deep, and the two were lifelong friends and collaborators. Yet as a growing body of scholarship is demonstrating, Van Vechten's ultimate importance may be his all-consuming passion for collecting and archiving writ large, a passion that proved to be particularly instrumental for African American letters even though it ran across the color line.[8] The founding of the JWJ Collection, plus the decades of solicitation for black materials that came in its wake, was a watershed moment.

Sometime in 1939, the Library of Congress approached the recently widowed Grace Nail Johnson to inquire about the papers of her late husband, James Weldon Johnson, with the intention of making his archive "the nucleus of a new poetry room."[9] Major upheavals had been afoot at the nation's library ever since President Franklin Roosevelt had appointed poet-bureaucrat and champion of literature Archibald MacLeish as librarian of Congress in July 1939, a post he occupied until 1944. MacLeish was a supporter of Roosevelt's New Deal initiatives throughout the 1930s, and his tenure at the nation's library brought tremendous administrative changes and a pointed increase in the value and presence of literary artifacts, including poetry readings and a fellowship for writers and scholars. By 1941, MacLeish had undertaken a general restructuring of the library's operations, revising its "cataloging, acquisitions, personnel, and budget policies."[10] The following year he formed the Librarian's Council, a group "composed of distinguished librarians, scholars, and book collectors who would make recommendations about collection development and reference service."[11] This council, in short, helped determine whose voices would be included in the nation's growing heritage and thus boosted the value of certain collections over others. It was at this early pivotal moment of remarkable change that the Library of Congress attempted to obtain the James Weldon Johnson archive, a request that was progressive enough to attract the attention of close Johnson family friend Carl Van Vechten.

Van Vechten became consumed with the idea of placing his own impressive collection, one he had been amassing diligently for years, in a renowned institution. In fact, he was determined to expand it beyond anything the world had ever seen by soliciting items through the vast network of black writers, teachers, librarians, artists, reporters, intellectuals, and dilettantes he had nurtured for more than two decades. In terms of site, Van Vechten settled on Yale because, as he told readers of *The Crisis* in 1942, it was ideally located between major urban centers Boston and New York, and its librarian, Bernhard Knollenberg, had confessed, "We haven't any Negro books at all."[12] So enthusiastic was Van Vechten at striking this deal with Yale that he believed the collection would soon bring about the creation of a chair of African American literature at the Ivy League institution—a position that, in reality, was not created until decades later.[13]

Even though "Yale was the first white college to lobby for black materials," extending this inclusion to the level of the library staff in the form of "a living, breathing Negro," as Bernard puts it, let alone a chair of black studies, "became a different matter altogether."[14] Despite strong support from Van Vechten and Knollenberg's self-professed wish that he "should like very much to try the experiment of having colored people on our staff," both Harold Jackman and Dorothy Peterson were denied a position at the library.[15] Even Hampton University's Lillian G. Lewis, a young African American student who lobbied to join the Yale library staff for a summer job, was turned down for "her lack of library training." When Lewis replied that she would "do anything to be close to the collections," even take a position as charwoman, Knollenberg was "touched by the offer but did not want to hire another black person in a menial labor job."[16] A year later, the young Farm Security Administration photographer Gordon R. Parks would take his iconic photograph of Ella Watson, U.S. government charwoman, holding mop and broom framed by the American flag in one of the federal buildings she cleaned in Washington, D.C. The image, known as *American Gothic, Washington, DC*, forcefully captured the prejudice and level of racial discrimination permeating the country, especially in the nation's elite institutions. The Double V campaign of World War II, "victory abroad, victory at home," was aimed precisely at this kind of injustice.

Like Van Vechten, Harold Jackman felt that therein lay part of the importance of the JWJ Collection—that it could "be made an open wedge for a capable Negro at Yale."[17] The first step in this journey, it seemed, was to admit the "talented tenth" in paper-surrogate form as part of the collection. Van Vechten, Jackman, and Peterson knew that once these black counterarchives became academically sanctioned, they would essentially smuggle radical blackness into traditional sites of cultural and national authority. And word was spreading; as the century entered into its second half, an increasing number of writers realized how diligent archivism could be a means of creating "a permanent register of their careers and weaving them into the recalcitrant fabric of American culture," as Morris Dickstein puts it.[18] Archiving was a way to break through this recalcitrance from the inside, a challenge black authors faced in every aspect of their sociopolitical lives. In a few short years, having welcomed its very own Trojan horse, if you will, Yale was suddenly brimming with black texts, yet the trepidatious Ivy League continued to keep actual black lives at bay.

This initial resistance to African Americans on the payroll at Yale, along with the reality that the great majority of white colleges and libraries were not interested in acquiring black materials, reminds us all the more of the importance of HBCUs as repositories for African and African diasporic artifacts. For instance, under the pioneering librarianship of Dorothy Porter Wesley, the first black woman to graduate in library science at Columbia University, Howard University purchased Arthur Spingarn's collection in 1946, appending it to the Moorland Collection to create what eventually became the world-renowned Moorland-Spingarn Research Collection. During her forty-three-year tenure as Howard's chief librarian, from 1930 to 1973, Porter, who is now also enjoying a renaissance, radically expanded the collection while establishing a new classification system and essentially helped lay the groundwork for what became black studies.[19] Van Vechten, who took a series of portrait photographs of Porter in 1951, was cognizant of this institutional imbalance between the Ivy League and HBCUs, so he purposefully decided to place his substantive George Gershwin Memorial Collection of Music and Musical Literature at Fisk University as a means of encouraging whites to visit this historically black university, just as he hoped the JWJ Collection would lead black scholars to Yale.

Another aspect of Van Vechten's contributions were his continued efforts in the final decades of his life to donate substantial materials to multiple black special-collection repositories across the country, notably the Countee Cullen Memorial Collection (now the Harold Jackman–Countee Cullen Collection) at Atlanta University. Even as late as 1961, the year Harold Jackman passed away, and three years before Van Vechten died, the Atlanta librarian's report for that year concluded: "The death of Harold Jackman, long time donor to the library, was felt by us. His sister contributed over 300 titles to the library from his estate. The Negro Collection continues to grow. Carl Van Vechten continues to send photographs and playbills to the Countee Cullen Collection."[20] What the librarian's report also makes clear is that black collections were growing via donations, not purchases, through the coordinated efforts of multiple collectors, not simply Van Vechten— thanks to his marketing flair, his "private" collecting was frequently turned into a "public" announcement, a visibility rarely afforded to the thousands of black donors who remained anonymous.

Porter's and Van Vechten's efforts are in fact a concentrated reflection, perhaps a continuation, of a long-standing black tradition; after all, "for as long as black people have lived they have preserved their history and culture in one form or another,"[21] a practice tied to literal and figurative survival, as the full significance of the word *preservation* implies. Arturo Schomburg's influential essay "The Negro Digs Up His Past" from the March 1925 issue of *Survey Graphic*—edited by Alain Locke and the precursor to the *New Negro* anthology—had forcefully expounded on the need for digging, excavating, and self-archiving for peoples of African descent.

"The American Negro must remake his past in order to make his future," Schomburg had boldly declared in his opening sentence,[22] and in so doing he not only inspired generations of black historians and storytellers but also pointed to some potent new weapons in the cause for equality and freedom.

A generation after Schomburg, the interest showed by such hallowed institutions as the Library of Congress and Yale University indicated that a larger ideological and sociopolitical shift in relation to black culture had begun to take hold in the United States. The foundational labor of these early-twentieth-century black bibliophiles—including Schomburg, Arthur Spingarn, Charles F. Heartman, Charles Seifert, Clarence Holte Charles Blockson, Daniel Alexander Payne Murray, Henry Proctor Slaughter, Alexander Gumby, Hubert H. Harrison, Arna Bontemps, and many others—bolstered the value of collecting the black past though their singular archival sensibilities. Part of the revolutionary feature of the new midcentury archiving enterprise was the value it ascribed, more visibly than ever, to the living black *present*. In fact, the library world in the United States as a whole was undergoing a veritable paradigm shift that gradually brought a focus onto contemporary record creators rather than those from the distant past. Though these institutional upheavals would be slow in bearing fruit, they irrevocably transformed what it meant to be a living writer in the mid–twentieth century.

As Porter's career arc demonstrates, the resources created through black bibliophiles' collecting efforts further helped clear the way for the establishment of black studies in the 1960s. "Some uninitiated Americans," writes Jessie Carney Smith, "have assumed that black studies and supporting collections began with the advent of the civil rights in the 1960s,"[23] but these radical developments were first made possible by the collective adoption of private collecting practices. Indeed, the archivism of these pioneers represents a meeting of tradition and radicalism that went on to define and establish the field of African American or black studies. As Smith goes on to say, "The development of black private collections helped give impetus to the founding of public ones," as the former became the "nucleus around which public collections were built." More often than not, "the private collector was the architect for the collections now found in libraries."[24] The personal, in other words, is institutional, an insight that early African American collectors had presaged in their archival wager.

TO DONATE OR NOT TO DONATE?
ENTER THE RECORD CREATORS

Many of the seminal figures who were associated with the New Negro movement and for whom collecting became a vocation had intimate and professional ties to the library world: Nella Larsen was a librarian at the Harlem branch of the NYPL; Arna Bontemps was longtime librarian at Fisk University, where he founded the Langston Hughes Renaissance Collection and watched over the Jean Toomer Papers at a time when Toomer was forgotten; Schomburg was the collector and bibliophile who sold his impressive collection to the NYPL in 1926 and for whom the Harlem branch is now named. And those who weren't librarians more often than not had teaching positions and regularly made use of libraries.

This context perhaps helps to explain why Claude McKay decided to turn bibliophiles and collectors into the unlikely heroes of his final novel, *Amiable with Big Teeth*. McKay composed the novel in 1941, the very year in which Yale and Carl Van Vechten struck a deal to bring the JWJ Collection to New Haven as well as the year that saw the implementation of the special Librarian's Council by Archibald MacLeish at the Library of Congress. It was also in 1941 that MacLeish became supervisor of the federal government's newly established Office of Facts and Figures, an office to which an out-of-work McKay unsuccessfully applied for employment shortly after his last novel was rejected by the publisher. And by December 1941, of course, the United States had officially entered into World War II.

Given the mobilization toward collecting, building, and preserving archives in 1941 and thereafter, it seems even more surprising that McKay's novel slipped through the cracks in utter silence, unnoticed and unmentioned. As Brent Edwards and I note in our introduction to the novel, Carl Van Vechten—then consumed with the launching of the JWJ Collection project at Yale—even took a series of photographs of McKay in the days following the novel's submission to a publisher. Less than a week after the photo session, McKay wrote Van Vechten in support of the collection project; the letter's language suggests that the archive had been a topic of discussion at their meeting: "I want to congratulate you again for the idea of a JWJ Collection." This letter was accompanied by what McKay called "the rarest of my few literary items": "the salesman's dummy for *Home to Harlem*."[25] Six days later, McKay would learn that the publisher E. P. Dutton had rejected his latest novel manuscript, then titled "God's Black Sheep."

Though sympathetic to Van Vechten's collection project, McKay had not decided, as the former erroneously assumed, to eventually donate all his papers to Yale, a misunderstanding that upset McKay. As the Jamaican exile explained to Van Vechten, he had by then already received requests for his manuscripts from the Schomburg Library, the 115th Street Library, and Henry Proctor Slaughter of Washington, DC. What would the "Negro intelligentsia" think, McKay wrote, "if I gave two or three manuscripts to a white person and none to colored collectors, who asked first!"[26] The misunderstanding was in part due to a small machination on McKay's part; even though the cash-poor McKay had promised Van Vechten a manuscript, he intimated that he might be able to sell the rest of his manuscripts rather than donate them. The last few months had proved especially hard for McKay financially; not only was his final novel legally forced to remain unpublished unless he could pay Dutton back a $500 advance, but twenty days before he sent this explanatory missive to Van Vechten, a check from Samuel Roth for an aborted ghostwriting book project titled "Descent Into Harlem" had bounced.[27] The problem in McKay's latest plan, as he confessed to Van Vechten, was that he "had been lazy about getting back the manuscripts" from his various publishers and thought he "would use you [Van Vechten and Yale] to get them for me."[28] The scheme worked; Van Vechten and Yale dispatched inquiries to Harper & Brothers (for *Banana Bottom*), Lee Furman (for *A Long Way from Home*), and Dutton (for *Harlem: Negro Metropolis*), which promptly sent Yale Library the manuscripts in question. McKay then demanded the prompt return of all his manuscripts save for *Harlem: Negro Metropolis*, which he allowed Yale to keep.

In fact, the retrieval scheme had worked better than he could have hoped; Harper's uncovered not only the manuscript for *Banana Bottom* but also an eighty-eight-page unpublished story titled "Lafala" (a.k.a. "Romance in Marseilles") that McKay "had forgotten about."[29]

However, like most black writers of his generation, McKay was unable to turn a profit from any of his materials. Ironically perhaps, the majority of McKay's papers did eventually end up at Yale, "including, of course, the record of his ambivalence over where the material should be housed," as Bernard judiciously points out.[30] The actual acquisition, however, took place posthumously two decades later; the Claude McKay Collection finding aid notes that Yale obtained its McKay materials "primarily by purchase and gifts from Ruth Hope McKay Virtue, McKay's daughter, from 1964–1991."[31] This story is common enough: though the deferred value of black literary materials came too late to aid the record creator himself or herself, it might have eventually provided modest compensation to those who succeeded him or her. Indeed, in his correspondence with Van Vechten in 1941 McKay seemed to predict what eventually happened: since "my possessions of any value are so few," he wrote, one day "my daughter might say, Well, he did leave me an old m.s."[32] McKay's daughter, Hope Virtue, sold the Claude McKay Collection to Yale in 1963 and a few other items to the Schomburg Center in 1992. The materials in question had been shipped from Chicago— where McKay died in 1948—to Miss Virtue, who stored the "large traveling bag" and "a trunk" in the Brooklyn apartment that Carl Cowl, McKay's last literary agent, used as an office.[33] The manuscripts, correspondence, notes, and books contained in the bag and trunk were the "literary remains" that McKay had somehow managed to hold onto after his move to Chicago in 1943.[34]

Unlike McKay, whose vagabondage and penury prevented the careful preservation of all his papers in a single, secured location, Langston Hughes "carefully self-edited and curated" his own records with a conscious concern for posterity. He maintained a close relationship with co-conspirator and collector Van Vechten, who helped provide him with archival assistants via funds generated by Yale.[35] As the work of Bernard, Birnbaum, and Braddock has shown, the letters between Van Vechten and Hughes provide an

especially educational window onto the ramifications of such conscious con-
struction of private archives. In *Race, Work, and Desire in American Literature, 1860–1930,* Birnbaum argues that the epistolary exchanges between
Van Vechten and Hughes accentuate the self-attributed role the two played
as the "era's historiographers," turning their correspondence into "a historical artifact" that will be secured for posterity through its institutionalization at Yale.[36] Through a revealing set of confessions and statements in their
letters—for example, Hughes telling Van Vechten in 1941, "You really should
not tell me you are going to give all my letters to Yale . . . because now I
will become self-conscious"[37]—Birnbaum demonstrates "how they [Hughes
and Van Vechten] constructed themselves in relation to history and to each
other."[38] Though this Hughes–Van Vechten exchange marks a rather pivotal moment of literary meta-archivism, such a practice was taking hold
among a growing number of authors, who were now choosing to maintain
careful records.

That said, some writers neglected to do so, whether through disinterest,
an ideological rejection of this form of professionalization, an overwhelming schedule, or a lifestyle on the run. In some cases, it should be stressed,
keeping detailed records was also flat out dangerous due to surveillance by
U.S. intelligence agencies, as William Maxwell's recent book *F.B. Eyes*
compellingly reveals, particularly with respect to African American writers.[39] Indeed, though I don't have the space to parse this relation further
here, the boom in archiving corresponds to the boom in surveillance and
identification technologies. Even those who kept records (regardless of the
danger they faced) did not necessarily do so with any clear cataloging system. The long-standing leader of the National Association for the Advancement of Colored People (NAACP) Walter White, who helped Van Vechten obtain materials from an impressive number of black writers, "never got
around to assembling his papers," Bernard relates. Consumed by his duties
at the NAACP and other secretive, undercover missions passing for white
in the South, White kept but never organized his own papers. After years
of hounding White for his collection, Van Vechten at last "did receive them
after White's death in 1955," through his widow.[40]

In *Collecting as Modernist Practice*, Braddock touches on another instructive example of a living writer who did not adopt archivism as a practice: African American poet Anne Spencer, who, in contrast to Hughes, lamented her failure to save her manuscripts, writing to Harold Jackman that during her youthful poetry-writing days she had not yet learned to "save the sheets" as part of "author-practice."[41] Spencer's case brings a noteworthy gender dimension to the archiving business: when we look at the number of extant collections, we must note that an overwhelming number belong to male authors. Thus, as I address in my chapter on Ann Petry, there is an added layer of invisibility surrounding the work of black women writers at mid-century. Due to a lopsided penury of collections, the state of archiving the papers of black female writers is precarious; it is not simply a matter of a smaller number of writers being women but also a reflection of the lack of opportunities for women, who for the most part could not afford the luxury of this kind of care for one's affairs—a reality that is a significant theme in Petry's novel *The Street*, which chronicles all the sacrifices and relocations Lutie Johnson has to make as a working mother abandoned by her husband. Even women writers whose work we today consider essential reading, such as Zora Neale Hurston, often had to contend with limited resources and a lack of interest in their lifetime. Hurston donated a few select items to the JWJ Collection during her career, but the bulk of her manuscripts was almost completely burned outside her Florida home following her lonely death in 1960. Only the quick actions of friend and local law officer Patrick DuVal prevented the fire from consuming the rest of the literary documents.[42]

It is also imperative to note that even though archivism was spreading as a practice among living writers, not everyone was willing to cooperate with Van Vechten and his collecting project. In other words, a given author's refusal to contribute personal materials to Yale specifically did not preclude said author from nevertheless developing an archival sensibility. Further, regardless of an author's ambiguous relation to Van Vechten, a reticence to part with one's personal papers can also be explained by the visceral break of privacy such a donation represents, a reality that haunted Ann Petry.

When we take a quantitative look at the number of different repositories that house black literary archives as well as *when* such acquisitions took place, the numbers suggest that a large-scale archiving enterprise had indeed been set in motion by midcentury but had often been privately undertaken behind closed doors so that an individual collection was made public only after the author's passing. At this point, with archivism now part of black author practice and with a speculative posterity in mind, many up-and-coming African American authors were wary of Van Vechten as the funnel through which their records should ultimately flow.

In a letter written in 1959, Van Vechten expressed frustration at the realization that so few members of the current generation of black writers "make any attempt to assist the collection."[43] Ralph Ellison notoriously refused to pose for Van Vechten's camera—as did actor Sidney Poitier—unlike many of his famous contemporaries, such as Richard Wright (whom Van Vechten photographed in 1945 and whose own papers eventually became part of the JWJ Collection), Chester Himes (1946), Ann Petry (1948, who later donated some manuscripts to Yale), and James Baldwin (1955). Ellison's reaction to Van Vechten and the building of the JWJ Collection is particularly instructive and suggests that Ellison may have been at his most radical and political when it came to the archive.

Even though Ellison was ultimately uncooperative in terms of donating his whole archive to Yale, he is listed as one of the close to two hundred donors in the booklet accompanying the official opening of the JWJ Collection in 1950, titled *Exercises Marking the Opening of the James Weldon Johnson Memorial Collection of Negro Arts and Letters, Founded by Carl Van Vechten*. Although "the records for these gifts are often difficult to track down," as the current Yale curator Melissa Barton reports[44]—in part because they are intermingled with the Yale librarian's records—the JWJ Collection files list two folders of materials by Ellison. Both are related to his short story "The King of the Bingo Game" and together include the original draft typescript with corrections, the revised draft ("Draft 2"), and a note in Ellison's hand. The materials are dated October 22, 1943, and beneath the folder titles the finding aid adds: "Gift of the author through Langston Hughes and Carl Van Vechten, 1943." These dates, however, are puzzling.

"King of the Bingo Game" was first published in the November 1944 issue of *Tomorrow*, thus more than a full year after Ellison appears to have donated the materials. It was Ellison's last story to appear before the "Battle Royal" section of *Invisible Man* came out in October 1947.[45] Adding confusion to this timeline is the fact that it is only in a letter from August 1944 that Langston Hughes first mentioned Ellison to Van Vechten as a potentially interesting donor for the latter's ongoing collecting effort at Yale. Hughes's enthusiastic description is of a still unknown but dedicated writer: "Mr. Ralph Ellison, 306 West 141st Street, New York, 30, is going to be a good writer, I believe, so why don't you ask him to give all his drafts to Yale, as he is writing all the time, and likes to write so well he won't do any other kind of work if he can help it, and will probably in due time pile up a great big lot of stuff, which you-all might as well have."[46] Five days later, Van Vechten wrote back to Hughes to confirm that he had "asked Ellison for his manuscripts."[47] Since "King of the Bingo Game" appeared in *Tomorrow* less than three months after Van Vechten's request, it seems more likely that Ellison decided then and there to donate the materials related to that recently completed story. Thus, as Yale's acknowledgment of receipt to Ellison proves,[48] the gift was made in 1944, not in 1943, and Ellison never again donated any of his materials to Yale during his lifetime.

As Hughes predicted, Ellison did indeed "in due time pile up a great big lot of stuff," but he had no desire for Van Vechten and Yale ("you-all," as Hughes puns) to have it. In his biography of Hughes, Arnold Rampersad reveals that Ellison confessed in an interview in 1983 that he not only "despised [Van Vechten's] photography" but also "didn't care for the whole Van Vechten influence." For Ellison, that influence had "introduced a note of decadence into Afro-American literary matters which was not needed. The literature had not earned its decadence."[49] When Ellison refused to be photographed by Van Vechten after the successful release of *Invisible Man* in 1952, a frustrated Van Vechten wrote to Hughes: "In spite of Ralph Ellison's professed distaste for the camera, his photographs continue to appear everywhere. Perhaps he has a distaste for *me*, or for *YALE*."[50] For Ellison, however, perhaps the "distaste" was also for being lumped into a "Collection" with "you-all," an undifferentiated mass of other "Negro" materials, as the JWJ Collection's name then included. After all, much of Ellison's career as a writer and intellectual was devoted to defending individualism and transcending racial categories. Combined with Ellison's own tremendous ambition, this early interaction with Hughes and Van Vechten nevertheless alerted Ellison to the importance of preserving his drafts and materials even as it seems to have awakened in him a determination to do so on his own terms. He would build the Ralph Ellison Papers, not a mere list of donated items from the "author" in a collection bearing another man's name.

This anecdote is also useful in suggesting how practically any up-and-coming black writer at the time would likely have received a personal invitation to donate his or her materials to Yale. There is no exaggerating the impact of the sustained solicitation campaign undertaken by Carl Van Vechten, Harold Jackman, Dorothy Peterson, Walter White, Langston Hughes, and others. In what must have acted as a constant reminder of the potential value of their works in progress—if not of their very lives—the 1940s and 1950s were marked by the forceful, even appropriative, solicitation of materials from black writers and artists for the growth of "the Collection"—as exemplified by Van Vechten's insistent letters to Ann Petry showcased in chapter 4. In other words, as the United States was entering World War II, African American authors, artists, musicians, and intellectuals across the country were encouraged to see figurative and literal value in their work. The age of the black archive had been set into motion, and the word was out: keep your stuff. However, for many African Americans in the up-and-coming generation, this did not necessarily mean "give it to Yale."

In the end, for Ellison, there was only one proper house for his papers: the Library of Congress. Despite the fact that Ellison had taught at Yale and resided there on occasion, and even though he had lived in or near Harlem for the majority of his life, he selected the Library of Congress over the Beinecke or the Schomburg Center, where a "spirit of place," to use David Sutton's poignant phrase,[51] made them logical choices. The Schomburg Center, while under the directorship of Howard Dodson, in fact approached Ellison to acquire his papers in the late 1980s, but the novelist "deflected" their attempt, Rampersad reports. He instead told his friend and future literary executor John Callahan, "The Library of Congress, in

Washington, D.C., is the nation's library. I want my papers there."[52] And so they are. Ellison's decision offers an interesting historical reversal, we might even say a "corrective," to the "whole Van Vechten influence" that Ellison lamented. After all, following James Weldon Johnson's tragic death in 1938, it was the Library of Congress that first expressed interest in acquiring his papers, and it had been this very gesture that had inspired Van Vechten to come up with the plan for Johnson's collection to go to Yale.[53]

By the 1980s, the Ellisons' Riverside Drive home was a "crowded old nest . . . bulging in boxes and full filing cabinets that clogged passageways" thanks to years of "hoarding, ordering, filing, clipping, and pruning."[54] Bart Auerbach, the literary appraiser who evaluated the collection after Ellison's death in 1994, reports that one room was so full of boxes that he could take only one or two steps inside during the appraisal.[55] As Rampersad details in his biography, Ellison and his wife, Fanny, had "collected his papers assiduously," and Fanny had made a further point "to preserve the complete evidence, unflattering as well as flattering, that went with Ralph's greatness."[56] Thanks to this proleptic ethics of care taken by Fanny to preserve her husband's papers, the Ellison collection has already led to a growing number of revisionist studies of the ever-complex Ellison, not to mention candid biographies and the release of previously unseen writings and photographs, including those discussed in this book. Fanny's custodial care further points to another overlooked yet central aspect of the history of black literary archives: the behind-the-scenes labor performed by women to ensure the posterity of their famous spouses or relatives. Indeed, the acquisition files of literary collections are brimming with the names of unsung women.

As was the case with Grace Nail Johnson, Poppy Cannon White, and Hope McKay Virtue, widows, sisters, daughters, and nieces played a neglected role in the preservation of black special collections. The Frederick Douglass Papers at the Library of Congress received "significant additions" in 1975 from Douglass's great-granddaughter, Mrs. Ann Weaver Teabeau, and Alice V. Coffee and Opal M. Pollard gave still more materials in 1978. Although Arna Bontemps gave some of his own materials to both Fisk and Syracuse during his lifetime, his spouse, Mrs. Alberta Bontemps, gave a significant portion to Syracuse in 1998. As I recount in more detail later, Marjorie Content Toomer facilitated the transfer of Jean Toomer's papers to Fisk in the early 1960s and then their relocation to Yale in the 1980s. Horace Cayton's niece, Susan Cayton Woodson, donated his papers to the Chicago Public Library in 1983 and 2008, and his first wife, Bonnie (Branch) Hansen, gave them more materials in 2002. Regarding specifically the authors prominently featured in this book, their papers would never have survived without the efforts of Fanny McConnell Ellison; Ellen Poplar Wright and Julia Wright (Richard Wright's widow and daughter, respectively); Louise Bryant, with whom McKay entrusted much of his papers in the 1920s; Hope Virtue, McKay's only daughter (one he tragically never met in person); and Elisabeth Petry, Ann Petry's daughter, who oversees her late mother's literary estate and continues to care for how the materials are used. Indeed, in a majority of cases, women were the ones who administered the sale or donation and transfer of literary papers to specific institutions. As the twentieth century unfolded, these rights holders had to learn to navigate the turbulent waves of the changing rare-book and manuscript market writ large, a state of affairs that came to affect the state and status of black literary collections.

THE MIDCENTURY RISE OF CONTEMPORARY (WHITE) LITERARY COLLECTIONS

Near the end of the Victorian period and into the interwar heyday of modernism, the interest in and acquisition of literary artifacts were chiefly a private collector's game. Men such as Henry Edwards Huntington, Elihu Dwight Church, A. S. W. Rosenbach, John Quinn, J. P. Morgan, and Henry Clay Folger—most of whom are now better known for the major libraries named after them—competed and collaborated to build significant literary collections. Transatlantic modernism also brought an increased interest in American materials—because the United States was such a young nation, British artifacts had historically been more prized in the English-speaking world. But as Charles Hobson reports in *Great Libraries*, "the 1920s saw the addition of Americana in large numbers."[57] The focus of these new large additions was still on the past—the older the better—but the savvy marketing of the modernists had awakened the marketplace to the value of collecting the works of living writers such as James Joyce and Gertrude Stein. Comparatively, however, the financial value of contemporary artifacts remained low.

As Jeremy Braddock reports, in the mid-1930s Charles Abbott of Buffalo was able to obtain for free, with a clever yet simple solicitation campaign, a large collection of discarded drafts from living poets. Similarly, Van Vechten and company were tirelessly beseeching donations from black writers for the JWJ Collection—like Abbott, Yale was not offering payment for these materials. Such stirrings slowly began to create waves of fluctuating value, but most accounts seem to agree that the landscape did not really change until the late 1950s, when Dr. Harry Huntt Ransom burst onto the literary-acquisition scene. Ransom's idea was to move away from the rat race for the oldest and rarest artifacts and instead to enter "a new field, where competition was less intense and it was possible to achieve a preeminent position—the twentieth century in England and America."[58] He convinced the president of the University of Texas, Logan Wilson, as well as the state legislators to vote for the necessary funds and made a deal with wealthy oil men ("friends of the library") to give "$9 for every $1 of state money, a rate that will yield at least $4,000,000 a year."[59] "By the autumn of 1956," the same year as the publication of Theodore Schellenberg's manual *Modern Archives*, "the programme was ready to take off." With these funds, Ransom launched "a programme of acquisition such as had not been seen in the USA since Henry E. Huntington's death" in 1927.[60] In 1958, a single major purchase elevated "the collection to the level of international importance"—namely, the papers assembled by the Pennsylvanian collector T. E. Hanley. Hanley's library was filled with items by white modernist royalty such as D. H. Lawrence, Joyce, Pound, Eliot, Shaw, Yeats, and Dylan Thomas.[61] Texas was quickly becoming what *Time* magazine then called "the terror of the book market."[62]

In 1960, Ransom hired Lew David Feldman, from the House of El Dieff, Inc., and sent him to the big auction of nineteenth- and twentieth-century materials at Sotheby's.[63] As the story goes, Feldman got up late the morning of the auction and spent the day at Sotheby's looking like a spook in his buttoned-up raincoat and hat to hide the fact that he was still wearing pajamas underneath. The University of Texas representative stood out, though, not because of his appearance but because of "the amount he was willing to pay and for his habit of buying every lot he bid for."[64] He purchased items by Oscar Wilde and D. H. Lawrence and had already acquired the previous month "every lot of a T. E. Lawrence collection" as well as the manuscript for E. M. Forster's *A Passage to India*.[65] The price paid for the latter item, £6,500, "was nearly three times the previous English record for a modern manuscript," an amount that was not lost on other living writers. Contrast it to J. R. R. Tolkien's sale, just four years earlier, in 1956, of his manuscript collection (including the entire *Lord of the Rings* trilogy, *The Hobbit*, and other works) for a mere £1,500, the equivalent of his yearly teaching salary at Oxford. Milwaukee's Marquette University director of libraries, the savvy and appropriately named William Ready, negotiated this deal, though now almost unthinkable, at a time when "no other institution had shown interest in the author's literary papers."[66]

By 1962, *Time* was reporting on "the growing competition among U.S. universities for rare books and manuscripts" and announced that a major institutional shift had taken place: "universities have almost completely replaced private collectors as lavish buyers." Even though some of the highest library book budgets in 1961 predictably belonged to Yale ($993,400) and Harvard ($926,500), more than twenty-eight American libraries had purchasing budgets of greater than $300,000. "Most voracious of all," *Time* reported, "is the University of Texas, which has not only $966,000 budgeted for books, but a torrent of cash gifts from anonymous 'friends of the library.' Last year it acquired perhaps $2,000,000 worth of rarities, and probably topped all other universities."[67] Texas's "huge programme of acquisition" of the papers of recently deceased or still living British and American writers was affecting the market from top to bottom: "prices rose sharply," states Hobson, and other institutions feared missing out on all the latest collections.[68]

As competition between universities raged on, word reached professional writers from both sides of the Atlantic. In a marvelous satirical piece for the *Sunday Times* in April 1962, Cyril Connolly took stock of what he called this new "largely benevolent" process. Noting how the gap "between the value set on pictures and the written word" had historically been "enormous," Connolly advanced that now "there are signs the gap is closing." Whereas "up to the end of the last war hardly any writer would have expected more than £60 for the manuscript of one of his books, nor more than a pound or two for any of his first editions," the postwar literary marketplace had changed dramatically. "The best American universities," Connolly wrote, "will not only pay for what an author has written but what he has tried to throw away; his note-books, correspondence, false starts; they will sort it all out for him and accept material which is never to be shown and provide him with copies and even resident facilities for writing his autobiography. His waste-paper basket becomes as precious as the late Aga Khan's bath-water. . . . It is probably the best thing that has happened to writers for many years."[69]

Connolly went on to parody this voracious acquisition impulse by relating the invented tale of Victor Galbraith (a name made famous through Longfellow's eponymous poem about the Rasputin-like bugler who takes a long time to die from bullet wounds and returns as a wraith), who is renowned for his long poem *The Bunns of Macaroon* and whose entire archive—indeed, his entire being—was being acquired by the "boyish President of Chincoteague, that small but powerful university with an estimated budget of (approximately) one million pounds a minute." Connolly mockingly lists the extent of the university's acquisitions: "the notebooks, the rough drafts, the finished drafts, the typescripts, the carbons, the galleys, the corrected galleys, the page proofs, the corrected page proofs, the seven issues of the first edition with seventy copies each, the seventy other editions, the paperbacks and translations, the correspondence with his publisher and agent, the Braille edition," and so on. Taking this totalizing preservationist compulsion to fantastic extremes, Connolly then imagines that a recording device has been "sewn" inside the living writer to record "all his conversation" and reports how the president of Chincoteague laments that "the man himself," whom the university is trying to conserve as well, is unfortunately in a constant state of deterioration due to aging. The article ends with a speculative fantasy: the university has somehow miniaturized and purchased whole sections of major cosmopolitan literary centers, where "Lilliputian scenes" are enacted, including "Ford with his sea-lion face and Pound throwing back his head and Joyce reading from a midget book in the magical voice of his Anna Livia recording."[70]

As can be deduced from Connolly's choice of authors in his satire, the modernists were the new chic for libraries with big budgets in this postwar moment. Indeed, as the 1960s rolled on, Ransom continued to voraciously acquire the manuscripts and corrected typescripts of authors such as Joseph Conrad, Aldous Huxley, W. H. Auden, Samuel Beckett, Arthur Conan Doyle, William Faulkner, Graham Greene, Arthur Miller, Jack Kerouac, and many others. By 1964, the library had enough to put together a major exhibition of the work of one hundred contemporary writers titled *A Creative Century*, celebrating its already impressive collection of twentieth-century materials. The selected authors are a sobering reminder of the overwhelming dominance of white male writers in the literary canon in this period and the ways in which institutional initiatives such as the programmatic purchasing of literary papers consolidated their status for posterity. Ninety-three of the one hundred featured writers were white males. Pearl S. Buck, Lillian Hellman, Marianne Moore, Katherine Anne Porter, Edith Sitwell, and Eudora Welty were the six white women to make the cut. James Baldwin, who had sold the autograph manuscript and corrected typescript for *Another Country* to the University of Texas, is the only African American writer in the lot. No black women are included, not to mention any Latinx, Asian, or Native authors. Even today, although the Harry Ransom Center has diversified its acquisition targets, it remains a predominantly white archive of canonized masculinity, with more recent acquisitions including David Foster Wallace, Norman Mailer, Denis Johnson, Tim O'Brien, Andre Dubus, and Arthur Miller. In 2003, the center also purchased Carl Bernstein and Bob Woodward's Watergate papers for a hefty $5 million—the same price paid by Harvard for John Updike's papers in 2009—a move that once again sent waves of disturbance through the rare-book and manuscript market. "To my mind, that's one of the most absurd things I ever heard," rare-book dealer John Wronoski stated after hearing the purchasing price of the Watergate papers. "A large number of Nobel laureates' papers sold for less than that."[71]

Due to the common use of nondisclosure agreements drawn up in the acquisition process between estates and repositories, the purchasing price of collections can be difficult to ascertain, though some are made public. The highest price paid for a single literary artifact from the twentieth century is $2.43 million for Jack Kerouac's original scroll for *On the Road*, purchased in 2001 by Jim Irsay, owner of the Indianapolis Colts. In 2005, the *Chicago Tribune* reported that the average price for a contemporary author's entire collection stood between $200,000 and $500,000, though some "high-profile authors' collections" can "reach the millions."[72] Also in 2001, the Harry Ransom Center purchased Norman Mailer's papers for $2.5 million, and actor Johnny Depp paid $3 million for Hunter S. Thompson's archive.[73] Clearly, the literary marketplace—like most Western institutions—is a good place for white males, including both the writers themselves and the booksellers and antiquarians who appraise their value.[74]

Yale's initial purchase of the Claude McKay Collection, made the same year as the *A Creative Century* exhibition at the University of Texas in 1964, provides an instructive glimpse into the depreciated value of black special collections at the time. Though publicly undisclosed, the purchasing price as well as the appraisal report were shared with Carl Van Vechten by Yale librarian Donald Gallup. Van Vechten had been trying to get the collection since the founding of the JWJ Collection in 1941, and when McKay died in 1948, he had redoubled his efforts by ingratiating himself with the late writer's daughter, Hope McKay Virtue.[75] Busy with her own studies in California and perhaps sensing that her father's collection might increase in value over time, she promised to eventually "offer some worthwhile material," but her first goal was to release her father's poems.[76] She waited fifteen years before arranging for the sale of the materials, beginning with an appraisal of the collection.

The mere fact that McKay's papers had to be professionally appraised indicates that the general increase in the market value of contemporary papers was beginning to affect African American materials as well; even though the numbers remained comparatively smaller for black collections, donation was no longer the de facto means of placing one's collection in a repository.[77] The McKay papers were appraised by Walter Goldwater, bookseller and owner of the famed University Place Book Shop specializing in African diasporic artifacts and whose records, held at Columbia and the University of Delaware, document the rise of interest in African American materials in this period. Goldwater's appraisal report to Gallup, the Yale librarian who paid for the appraisal, is among the first he ever performed—the novel nature of the appraisal enterprise is evinced by Goldwater's self-conscious concluding line: "I hope I have done properly."[78]

In May 1963, Goldwater went to the Brooklyn office of the literary agent Carl Cowl—Cowl now represented Mrs. Virtue—a fifth-floor walk-up apartment where "of course the temperature was close to 101 degrees," and "got right to work."[79] Openly admitting his admiration for McKay, Goldwater concluded his report thus:

> As I have no ax to grind in the matter, and you did not ask for my literary opinion, the following few words may be of no interest to you; but my opinion has been and remains this, about Claude McKay: of the four Negro poets of the Negro renaissance (say, 1915–1940), viz., McKay, Hughes, JWJohnson, Cullen, I think McKay is by all means the most important both as a poet and as a person; and if this is true or even largely true, this collection is something you ought to have. I have put a figure on it of $2,000.00, which is somewhat more than I would pay for it as a dealer, but somewhat less than I would charge for it if I had paid what I ought to pay, worked on it to put it in some order, and then offered it to a library. I have not indicated anything about the figure to Cowl, but my guess is that he and McKay's daughter will be pleased if they get anything like that much.[80]

Ranking McKay as "the most important" poet of the Harlem Renaissance, Goldwater clearly saw the cultural and research value of the collection, yet he put its price tag at $2,000, adding that Cowl and Virtue "will be pleased if they get anything like that much." As the figures cited earlier prove, collections and even single literary artifacts by white writers of McKay's generation were selling for much, much more than this by the mid-1960s.

Perhaps even more revelatory of the institutional acquisition landscape for African American collections is a detail Gallup dropped to Van Vechten in their exchange regarding the McKay collection. After Mrs. Virtue agreed to sell for $2,000, Gallup told Van Vechten that he was able to secure $500 from the James Weldon Johnson Fund and hoped he "shall be able to find the rest of the money" before next year—"I warned Mr. Cowl that we might have to spread the payment out over a year," he added.[81] In his follow-up letter, Gallup confirmed the year-long arrangement but again underscored how uncertain additional sources of funding for the purchase stood: "We are paying $500 from the JWJFund [sic] on 1 July and have promised to pay the remaining $1500 on or before 1 July 1964. I think we shall be able to find the money somehow."[82] Despite Yale's overall library budget of roughly a million dollars per year in 1963–1964, the letter makes it clear that Gallup had to scrounge to purchase materials by black writers destined for the JWJ Collection. The fact that even Yale University would not allocate more funds per annum for acquisitions to its black special collections paints a stark picture of the institutional roadblocks African Americans and their literature faced.

As the University Place Book Shop records held at Columbia demonstrate, Walter Goldwater went on to appraise several African American collections for universities up to his death in 1985. As the practice became routine, his appraisal reports, unlike his improvised letter regarding the McKay collection, began to exhibit a formula aimed at legitimizing the process: he opened with a paragraph stating his professional expertise in the subject matter (whether it be black materials, chess, or, later, architecture) and listed some of the other institutions for whom he had performed this task. An appraisal he made for the Schomburg in 1979 provides an example:

For some forty-six years I have been engaged in the buying, selling, and appraising of books, pamphlets, periodicals, and other printed and written materials. I have appraised many collections of such materials, for university libraries such as those of Yale, Harvard, New York University, and Columbia University; also for institutions such as the New York Public Library and the Library of Congress, and also for many other institutions and private individuals. During that whole period, my chief field of specialization has been that of Black Studies in all their aspects.[83]

Based on the extant records, even by the end of the 1970s—when fervent interest in black collections and titles had waned—the dollar value assigned to the collections remained in the low thousands. For more than fifty years, Goldwater, one of the founding members of the African Studies Association, also stocked his book shop with the best and latest in African diasporic holdings; in that time, he issued more than a hundred catalogs of material and "handled something over a million books and pamphlets," as his records show.[84] Not only was the book shop a favorite hangout among the black intelligentsia, but his booklist went on to supply several libraries in the United States and Canada once black studies began gaining traction in the late 1960s. "We have helped largely in developing not only the Schomburg collection," Goldwater reported in 1978, "but also the library at Atlanta University, the Howard University Moorland Collection, and in fact almost every substantial such collection in the country."[85] The shop's records include a letter sent to Goldwater announcing Dorothy Porter's retirement as head librarian at Howard in 1973 and the Howard acquisition librarian's hope that Goldwater would provide "continued help in locating Black Studies materials."[86] In short, not only private collectors such as Arthur Spingarn or acquisition librarians such as Porter but also booksellers such as Goldwater formed an oft-invisible yet crucial segment of what Robert Darnton calls the "communications circuit" of book history.[87] In the late 1960s, the *Africa Guide* recognized Goldwater's work and University Place Book Shop: "the store is an eloquent example of the cultural importance of booksellers, who often do the work of libraries and museums well before these institutions are persuaded to follow suit."[88] Indeed, the folders of correspondence and invoices from the 1970s in the shop's records attest to a spike of sales of African diasporic titles from around the globe to university and college libraries, even though, as Goldwater admitted in a letter from December 1974, "some of the hyperenthusiasm has waned."[89]

BLACK SPECIAL COLLECTIONS: FROM ACQUISITION TO PROCESSING

In an essay in the collection *Black Bibliophiles*, published in 1990, renowned archival sleuth and editor Robert Hill provides an assessment of which collections related to black radicalism were then currently available to researchers. Out of the one hundred or more black radicals he and his colleagues identified as active during the New Negro movement, he estimates that "the number of black historical figures for whom manuscript collections are currently available or are likely to become available is less than nine percent of the cohort of identifiable radicals for the entire interwar period." W. E. B. Du Bois, Hughes, and McKay are three of the nine named, and Hill notes that although the A. Phillip Randolph Collection had been acquired by the Library of Congress, it was not expected to be processed "for some time to come." "What kind of history is being written," Hill asks, "when the basic documentary pool of data from which a historian or researcher is drawing constitutes no more than roughly four percent of what existed?"[90]

In Hill's question we may discern much of what is at stake in the archivism of African American authors and, I argue, a key to why the literary itself becomes a means of providing an alternative "documentary pool of data" regarding black lives. As this book demonstrates, the gaps in institutional archives were in part being filled in by novelists (and booksellers), both through the performativity of the literary and through their private archiving that would one day come to redress the penury of available materials. It is precisely in this convergence of concerns and praxis that we should apprehend how African American literature at midcentury developed its institutionally aware archival sensibility, with the authors explored in this book among the pioneers of this development. To underscore how this institutional awareness works, let me turn to a gap in historical knowledge that Robert Hill underscores in this same piece.

Hill laments the fact that even though we have successfully documented the speeches given by the many soap-box street orators "who emerged on Lenox Avenue in Harlem" in the interwar years, such documentation remains devoid of its living context. In other words, Hill says, "we have no history of the audience" who stood on those sidewalks, walked the Harlem streets, and crossed paths with these exhorters, "picking up something here, picking up something there, and moving on," "the same people who moved on later that night to a dance, to their lodges, or to some other important black activity." [91] The scenario Hill here imagines is precisely one that so much of midcentury African American literature dramatizes in its pages, thus restoring some of the gaps in the history of black radicalism and its "audience."

Specifically, the scenario is imagined in the work of Claude McKay, whose final novel, *Amiable with Big Teeth*, stages major clashes between street orators during the mid-1930s and whose archive today preserves some of the flyers that were circulated by orators such as the Sufi Abdul Hamid, nicknamed the "Black Hitler" (see figure 1.1). In the work of Ann Petry, whose protagonist in *The Street*, Lutie Johnson, is repeatedly seen walking the Harlem streets as she goes home from work, taking note of every possible kind of denizen—and scrap of paper—that roams the ghetto's sidewalks and alleyways. And in the work of Ralph Ellison, who through his novel *Invisible Man* and his work as a photographer took special care to document the Harlem streets and its myriad characters, including the memorable Ras the Exhorter, standing high on his soapbox before turning into Ras the Destroyer. Or consider Richard Wright's *Native Son*, a novel that brings us to Chicago yet nevertheless captures the neglected perspective of the audience—the tenants, the chauffeurs, the moviegoers—through

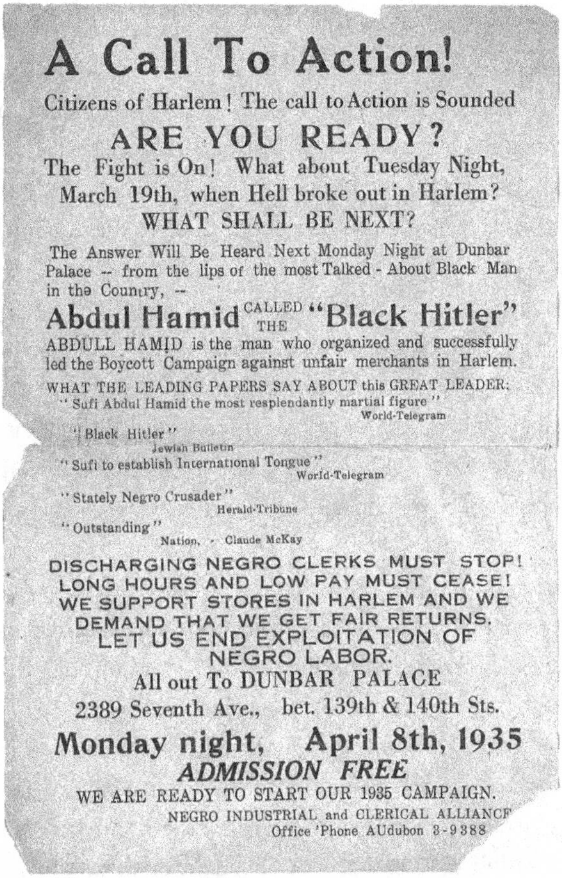

A Call To Action!

Citizens of Harlem! The call to Action is Sounded

ARE YOU READY?

The Fight is On! What about Tuesday Night, March 19th, when Hell broke out in Harlem?

WHAT SHALL BE NEXT?

The Answer Will Be Heard Next Monday Night at Dunbar Palace -- from the lips of the most Talked - About Black Man in the Country, --

Abdul Hamid CALLED THE "Black Hitler"

ABDULL HAMID is the man who organized and successfully led the Boycott Campaign against unfair merchants in Harlem.

WHAT THE LEADING PAPERS SAY ABOUT this GREAT LEADER:

" Sufi Abdul Hamid the most resplendantly martial figure "
World-Telegram

" Black Hitler "
Jewish Bulletin

" Sufi to establish International Tongue "
World-Telegram

" Stately Negro Crusader "
Herald-Tribune

" Outstanding "
Nation, - Claude McKay

DISCHARGING NEGRO CLERKS MUST STOP! LONG HOURS AND LOW PAY MUST CEASE! WE SUPPORT STORES IN HARLEM AND WE DEMAND THAT WE GET FAIR RETURNS. LET US END EXPLOITATION OF NEGRO LABOR.

All out To DUNBAR PALACE

2389 Seventh Ave., bet. 139th & 140th Sts.

Monday night, April 8th, 1935

ADMISSION FREE

WE ARE READY TO START OUR 1935 CAMPAIGN.

NEGRO INDUSTRIAL and CLERICAL ALLIANCE
Office 'Phone AUdubon 3-9388

FIGURE 1.1. "A Call to Action!" flier for an event with Sufi Abdul Hamid, 1935.

Source: Box 9, folder 302, Claude McKay Collection, Collection of American Literature, Beinecke Rare Book and Manuscript Library, Yale.

Bigger Thomas's troubles. In short, these novels stand as some of our best sources for putting a spotlight on otherwise invisible aspects of African Americans' quotidian realities in this period.

The power of the literary to act as a counterarchive to mainstream history has long been celebrated in scholarship. However, it is only once the personal archives of their creators are made accessible to researchers that we are able to see the extent of these creators' preservationist and historiographic labor. Only once their collections are open, as I demonstrate in the following chapters, may scholars attend to the lifecycles of specific documents, tracing their origins and their eventual deployment in novelistic form. Such textual archaeology at last becomes evidence of how their novelistic practice is inseparable from their archivism. It is through the parallax of the reference desk, therefore, that we may uncover the reciprocity and seductive power of literary archives, where the counterarchiving content of novels is shown to be founded upon diligent archival practices. Yet much of what was produced by African American authors across the twentieth century had to wait until its last decade to have those literary products' (financial) value recognized—a reality that is confirmed when we look at *who* was acquiring the collections of contemporary African American writers and, most importantly, *when* such acquisitions occurred.

Perhaps even more instructive than identifying the years of acquisition is tracing what happened to the record creators' paper surrogates once they finally made it inside the archive. Put another way, how long does a collection sag like a heavy load in the backlog before it is processed? To ask when a collection is processed is to ask when the repository has been able to dedicate the necessary internal resources to assign an archivist (or a team of archivists) to arrange the collection, prepare the finding aid, and make it physically accessible to researchers or the public or both. The moment such resources are assigned to a collection is the moment said collection is recognized as having a high enough value to justify the expense. All repositories, even the wealthiest among them, ultimately function on finite resources (time, staff, labor, space) and therefore use internal ranking systems—sometimes known as the "Research Value Rating"—to prioritize which collections will be processed first. Mirroring the concomitant fight for civil rights in the United States, black special collections outside of HBCUs usually struggled, when they were considered for preservation at all, to reach high value ratings and thus faced longer internal delays before being processed. A perplexing example of this standard is the small collection of Ann

Petry manuscripts currently still in Yale's backlog—a full account of which I offer in chapter 4.

In the compilation of processing dates for major black manuscript collections, a rather fascinating correlation emerges between the sudden access to a significantly larger number of collections and what has been deemed the "archival turn" in literary studies, a shift that began its ongoing domination in the American academy in the 1990s. Put simply and perhaps unsurprisingly, the archival turn corresponds to an ascending growth of available collections. Many collections of twentieth-century African American literary materials—held at large repository centers such as Emory, Howard, Fisk, Yale, NYPL, Syracuse, the Chicago Public Library, and the Library of Congress—were not made available en masse (relatively speaking) until the final decade of the twentieth century. Out of a sample of the collections of roughly forty of the most famous and studied black authors, only fifteen were processed in the 1990s. In the chronological list given here, I provide the year the collection was processed and then the acquisition date in parenthesis:

- J. Saunders Redding, Brown, initial sort 1991; arrangement and description 1997–1998 (gift acquired 1988)
- Julian Mayfield, Schomburg, 1992 (first materials acquired 1985–1986)
- Alain Locke, Howard, 1993 (first acquired in 1956; finding aid finalized 2016)
- Claude McKay, Yale, 1993 (acquired piecemeal from 1964 to 1991; revised finding aid 2014)
- Claude McKay, Schomburg, 1999 (purchases in 1973, 1974, and 1992)
- Richard Wright, Yale, 1994 (original finding aid 1975–1977; additions 1996–1998; revised 2014)
- Booker T. Washington, Library of Congress, initial process 1958, reprocessed 1994 (initial acquisition 1943–1945)
- Zora Neale Hurston, Yale, 1996, revised 2017
- Wallace Thurman, Yale, 1996 (based on an initial manuscript inventory, date unknown; acquired ca. 1934)

- Frederick Douglass, Library of Congress, first processed 1974, portion of materials acquired after 1975 processed in 1997
- Melvin B. Tolson, Library of Congress, first processed 1976; expansion and revision 1997, revised again 2009
- Ralph Ellison, Library of Congress, 1997, revised 2006, part 2 additions 2010, revised again 2015
- St. Clair Drake, Schomburg, 1998 (initial gift 1989)
- Arna Bontemps, Syracuse, 1999 (initial gift 1965–1973, additions 1998)

And the following collections were not processed until the current millennium:

- L. S. Alexander Gumby Collection of Negroiana, Columbia, 2000 (initial acquisitions 1950–1960, additions 1982)
- Frank P. and Helen Chisholm Family, Emory, 2001 (acquired 1994)
- Matt N. and Evelyn Graves Crawford, Emory, 2001 (acquired 2001)
- Audre Lorde, Spelman College, 2002 (acquired 1995)
- Horace Cayton, Chicago Public Library, ca. 2003 (initial gift 1983)
- Willard F. Motley, Chicago Public Library, ca. 2003 (initial gift 2002)
- Harold Cruse, New York University, 2003, with addenda in 2011 and 2014 (first acquired 1993)
- Lorraine Hansberry, Schomburg, 2006 (acquired 1998)
- Gwendolyn Brooks, University of California at Berkeley, 2006 (acquired 2000)
- Michel Fabre Archives of African American Arts and Letters, Emory, 2007 (acquired 2002)
- Hubert H. Harrison, Columbia, 2007 (acquired 2005)
- Alice Browning, Chicago Public Library, 2008 (acquired 2000)
- James Weldon Johnson and Grace Nail Johnson, Yale, major additions processed in 2008–2009, original process 1973 (initial acquisition 1941–1976)
- Countee Cullen, Amistad Research Center, Tulane, first processed 1975, reprocessed 2009 (initially acquired 1970, with additions in 1970, 1976, and 1986)[92]

- Alice Walker, Emory, 2009 (purchase 2007); born-digital materials processed 2014
- Dorothy West, Harvard, 2011 (initial acquisition 1985)
- John Oliver Killens, Emory, 2011 (acquired 2003)
- C. L. R. James, Columbia, 2011 (acquired 2006–2009)
- Richard Bruce Nugent, Yale, 2012 (acquired 2012)
- Lisbeth Tellefsen, Yale, 2013, revised 2017 (acquired 2012)
- Dorothy Porter Wesley, Yale, 2013 (acquired 2012)
- Gwendolyn Bennett, Yale, 2013 (acquired 2013)
- Amiri Baraka, Columbia, 2014 (acquired 2009)
- Toni Morrison, Princeton, 2015–2017 (purchased in 2009); born-digital materials processed 2017
- Albert Murray, Harvard, 2017 (acquired 2016)
- James Baldwin, Schomburg, 2017 (acquired 2017)
- Ann Petry, Yale, still unprocessed (acquired 1949)
- William M. Kelley, Emory, still unprocessed (acquired 2006)

Note that even though I do not have the precise dates, the collections of the following authors were also processed sometime between 1990 and the present day: Alice Dunbar Nelson at Delaware; Chester Himes at the Amistad Research Center (acquired 1990); John Henrik Clarke at the Schomburg (additions kept coming until 1999); and C. L. R. James at the University of West Indies (initial purchase in 1997, with additional purchase in 2006).

When we compare the year(s) acquired with the year(s) processed, it is clear that a collection can linger in the backlog for years before it is finally processed. As my research on Ann Petry unearthed, Yale has been in possession of the manuscripts of her first two novels, *The Street* and *Country Place*, since 1949, yet the collection has sat in the shadows, uncataloged for all these years—a telling reflection of the ways in which the work of black female writers has been and continues to be invisible, inaccessible, and neglected. Even major figures such as Alain Locke, whose papers were acquired by Howard in 1956, took thirty-seven years to be processed. For the McKay materials at the Schomburg, there was a twenty-six-year gap between initial purchase in 1973 to processing in 1999. Dorothy West's papers also took a quarter-century to be processed at Harvard, waiting from 1985 to 2011. The J. Saunders Redding Papers at Brown may have received an "initial sort" in 1991, three years after acquisition, but the collection was not arranged and described until 1997—indeed, to this day the finding aid for the collection remains preliminary.[93] The Arna Bontemps Collection at Syracuse began receiving materials in 1965 but was processed thirty-four years later, in 1999. When we take a closer look at the latter, however, we see the collection kept receiving additions up to a final shipment from the estate in 1998. This delay reflects another common occurrence with literary papers: repositories often wait for the collection to be complete to begin processing.

In many cases, a collection will undergo a significant reprocessing— either to reflect an addition or new processing guidelines—creating another "break" in the evolving life of the collection. Thus, another towering way in which archival delay and deferment come into play for black special collections are the very mundane vicissitudes of library science. I should also note that perhaps the most "mundane"—that is, all too human— reason behind delayed access is simply that in most cases the author usually has to die for the papers to be acquired in the first place. Moreover, it can take time for a finding aid to be made public, a process that further complicates when the public can gain access to the totality of a collection; indeed, some material deemed sensitive will oftentimes remain restricted for years.

Thus, as Robert Hill underscores, a reality of archives is that "over the years the classifications are changed so that one may find a subject under one classification but then it disappears and sometimes you have to look very hard to see where it's being moved."[94] In other words, the evolving practices of library science continue to have a direct effect on scholarly projects and thus on the history of literature. Collections of some longevity usually address such changes in classification on the latest finding aid. Yale is particularly diligent in this department, and many of its finding aids in the JWJ Memorial Collection candidly outline the nature of the changes brought to the arrangement.[95]

A remarkable example are the Langston Hughes Papers, as I address soon in relation to the problem of "split collections," but other examples are equally telling. For instance, the "Processing Notes" in the finding aid to the James Weldon Johnson and Grace Nail Johnson Papers explains that the bulk of the collection was processed in 1973 and accompanies this information with a reminder of that era's outdated cataloging policies: in "the 1970s priority was given to correspondence and writings. As a result, other material, such as photographs, personal papers, objects, and artwork, were left unprocessed." We also learn that a cluster of "unprocessed correspondence was found in 1999" and then "integrated" with the extant correspondence series—a phenomenon that occurs more often than one might think. Moreover, the many additions acquired since the passing of Mrs. Johnson remained unprocessed until 2008–2009. After her death, the papers' title was changed to incorporate both Mr. Johnson and Mrs. Johnson, and several internal changes were subsequently imposed.[96]

When we turn to Yale's initial purchase of the Richard Wright Papers, which took place in 1976, sixteen years after his death, we learn that the "original finding aid," as Yale's website calls it, was created from 1975 to 1977 but that the collection underwent significant rearrangement, so a new finding aid was produced in 1994 (thus in the wake of the excavating work performed by Arnold Rampersad and the Library of America, who had perceived anomalies in the initial arrangement).[97] Such irregularities were likely the result of the fact that, as is often the case with a famous author, the Wright Papers received several additions after the collection was first processed. Among the major changes imposed following the accretion of materials were the introduction of a new Subject Files series in 1996 and in that same year the lifting of the restriction that had originally been put upon the manuscript for "Island of Hallucination" (in 1998, these formerly restricted documents were also entirely rehoused in a new box). The finding aid was revised once more in 2014. The Wright materials held at the Schomburg Center in New York were purchased at auction in 1969 and processed in 1971. Through this purchase, the Schomburg also received research materials related to Wright from Constance Webb, who had just published the first biography of Wright in 1968.

The latter detail brings up an important facet of manuscript collections, notably among black special collections. A number of scholars who work on and with black archives subsequently donate the research materials they have accumulated at the conclusion of their projects. For instance, Alan McLeod, who edited Claude McKay's book *The Negroes in America* in 1979 (which includes the English translation of the Russian translation of McKay's speech in the Kremlin in 1922) gave a substantial collection of photocopies and facsimiles of records related to McKay, including samples of material available only at other repositories.[98] Such additions facilitate future scholars' research and are often welcome by repositories seeking to consolidate their strengths in a given author or topic. In the case of Constance Webb, whose second husband was the radical Trinidadian intellectual C. L. R. James, not only did she supplement the Schomburg's Wright materials with a donation from her research into Wright's life, but her own papers at Columbia today contain rare items she was able to obtain in the early 1960s when she was working on the biography.[99]

In a letter from Horace Cayton to Webb in May 1969—both of whom were working on books about Wright—Cayton brought up the importance of such gestures for the future of black studies. After thanking Webb for a copy of her recently published book and for privately sharing some of her research with him, Cayton wrote: "I am making a duplicate of every bit of evidence that I have on Dick and will donate it to some black college in the south. Probably Atlanta University, as it seems to be a cultural center. I believe firmly that black students should have access to their hero's [*sic*] and learn to do research." Cayton then asks Webb to do the same with her own duplicates, if she can.[100] In the end, sharing Cayton's spirit of communal pledge to posterity, Webb sent to the Schomburg the materials she had collected while doing her research for the Wright biography. Indeed, David Bradley's novel *The Chaneysville Incident* alludes to such a tradition when he underscores how the protagonist's grandfather had donated his impressive library of African American literature to Howard University in his will—"books by Langston Hughes and Countee Cullen and William Melvin Kelly and Paul Laurence Dunbar and all the rest . . . a first-edition copy of *Cane* by Jean Toomer . . . a copy of *The Souls of Black Folk* with a personal inscription from W. E. B. Du Bois."[101] Cayton's own papers now reside in the Chicago Public Library and were processed sometime after 2003 as part of "Mapping the Stacks: A Guide to Chicago's Black Hidden Archives," a groundbreaking project spearheaded by Jacqueline Goldsby that sought to "identify and organize uncatalogued archival collections that chronicle Black Chicago between the 1930s and 1970s, in order to increase their use by researchers and the general public."[102] Thus, the New Negro movement's "revolution in the act of saving and collecting the black past," to quote Melissa Barton again, the Yale curator who was on the "Mapping the Stacks" team as a graduate student at the University of Chicago, is an intergenerational project that reinforces itself across time, across projects, and across repositories.

"Mapping the Stacks" is thus an initiative that recognized and sought to rectify how longer holding times in the backlog have historically been an overarching institutional factor that has contributed to the systemic inequality faced by minorities in the United States. When we assess the acquisition and processing dates of African American authors' collections, these long holding times further emerge as a reflection of a comparatively young field slowly consolidating itself through such institutional means. In this context, pioneering projects such as "Mapping the Stacks" are crucial to the advancement of knowledge about the (African) American experience in the twentieth century. Even some of the most celebrated authors of the African American canon must wait years before their papers are finally made accessible (the finding aid of the Frederick Douglass Papers at the Library of Congress shows that these papers were not processed until 1974).[103] The work of many lesser-known figures continues to dry up in the basement stacks of numerous repositories; indeed, without insider access, the public would be hard-pressed to obtain a list of such extant but back-logged collections. Legend has it, for instance, that a Charles S. Seifert collection of more than one hundred boxes has long been held in limbo at Langston Hughes's alma mater, Lincoln University (Seifert was one of the real-life bibliophiles upon whom McKay based the character of Professor Koazhy in *Amiable with Big Teeth*).[104]

Should such delays look egregious to Twitter-trained eyes, we should first be grateful that any such material is preserved and housed safely. So many shadow collections have never even had the chance to wait in the darkness of the backlog, and others have been decimated by attrition, accident, and carelessness. For some—too many—the valuing of black lives tragically came too late, and the private-archiving enterprise, tied as it is to a sense of self-worth and racial kinship, was cut off at the root. In yet another affront to scholarship, collections that do exist are in fact rarely kept in the same repository but have rather been "split" among various owners, each seeking a relic of the sacred dead. Indeed, split collections are the most common and the most significant problem for the study of literary collections. It should be clear by now that with respect to most literary collections—plagued by splitness and assailed by additions, rearrangements, extractions, restrictions, and relocations—the idea of "original order" is more often than not an illusion far removed from the truth.

(DIS)RESPECT DES FONDS: THE ILLUSION OF ORIGINAL ORDER

For more than a century, archival science's dedication to *respect des fonds* has emphasized the need to observe and preserve two central concepts: provenance and original order. Though consensus on what original order truly means has remained stubbornly elusive, even more problems arise when these archival precepts, forged largely in respect to administrative records, are applied to literary papers. Precisely because archivists adhere to provenance and original order when they process a collection, the methods authors have used to preserve and classify their own records take on additional—sometimes crucial—importance. These practices are a message to posterity so long as the gatekeeping archons who acquire the materials respect that spectral transmission, an approach otherwise referred to as *respect des fonds*.

As Catherine Hobbs has suggested, respecting original order not only honors the record creator but also reflects facets of his or her personality.[105] Through an assessment not simply of "what" is being collected but also of "how" it is being filed, we may further discern unique aspects of the creator's tastes and political commitments. A scrapbook, for instance, is never only the data inscribed on the clippings collected but also the curated juxtapositions, Dadaesque poems that aesthetically emerge on the page layout. For instance, in his graduate seminar "The Black Radical Archive" at Columbia University, which involves having access to uncurated and semiprocessed collections, Brent Hayes Edwards reported such an experience with the Hubert H. Harrison Collection. In an interview, Edwards addressed how such privileged access to uncataloged materials allows scholars to ask new types of questions. Opening up boxes from the Amiri Baraka Collection, newly arrived at Columbia, and assessing its contents and juxtapositions, students could ask, "Why did he decide to keep 24 copies of that particular photo of Maya Angelou? Why was that Malcolm X research material on top of the letters from Nina Simone?"[106] In terms of the latter, the question does remain whether this particular juxtaposition occurred at the time of packing and shipping or was truly the way Baraka stacked these documents. For Edwards, however, the point is that such questions are "exactly the facets of the collection that disappear from view once the processing archivist organizes it according to logical categories like date, genre, and subject matter."[107] An archivist who is particularly diligent, however, and attuned to the unique challenges of personal papers could include such idiosyncratic information as part of the metadata in the finding aid.

As archivist Jennifer Douglas reminds us, more transparency regarding the "legitimacy" of any claim to original order as well as the processing archivist's arrangement decisions is essential. Traditionally speaking, original order is, as Douglas explains, either "the last order the archive assumed in its creator's care" or "the order in which the archive is eventually received by the archivist." Yet as the lifecycles model underscores, "different types of order . . . manifest in archives over time," and the "last order" may not necessarily reflect the order in which the records spent most of their lives—it just happens to be the one we encounter at acquisition. It may be the "packing or shipping order," how the materials were packed to be transferred from the home or office to repository, which is also known as "received order." In some cases, the received order can "provide clues about the manner in which materials were created," but in some cases where other hands (such as heirs) have significantly shifted the arrangement and even the contents of a collection, "received order" is deemed to be not original and thus any responsibility over its preservation is potentially lifted. The processing act can nevertheless become an opportunity for the archivist to "recreate a writer's creative process through arrangement and description" rather than to undertake any physical rearrangement. In some rare cases, such a "creative order" has remained intact, and the collection comes to the archivist in the order it was in when the writer was active. Yet most of the time, the arrangement at acquisition is really the "first-sight physical order"—namely, how the collection was arranged in the writer's workspace at the moment of death, presuming it was not then subsequently altered (and it almost always is). Boiled down, according to Douglas, archivists usually either consider original order as "an encountered physical order"—the timing of the encounter then determines precedence—"or an imagined or inferred logical order" based on the archivist's understanding of the author's life. Ultimately, every processed collection ends up with an "archival order"—no matter how closely the arrangement remains to the available "creative" order, the phenomenological act of processing, the transfer into acid-free folders, and the subsequent reboxing always mean that "archivists themselves impact the final shape of a fonds."[108]

In a way, even if only as an exercise, all literary archives should be apprehended as a kind of experimental collaboration between creator and archivist. Seeing archiving from this perspective, scholars making use of literary papers are well served by taking the time to apprehend the whole of a collection rather than focusing solely on their predetermined targets or keywords. As a rule, the best means of viewing the whole is through a careful reading of the finding aid—archivists devote a great deal of knowledge and labor to the composition of such front matter, where they justify the intellectual arrangement of the collection. Even though we have only so much time to consult an archive and must usually prioritize what materials we consult, a thorough reading of a finding aid can provide vital information in much the same way that we read the biographies or the bibliography of the authors we are researching. Arrangement remains, in part, an interpretive act on the part of the archivist; if the personal archive of a given literary figure already had an arrangement of its own, then that in itself becomes an interpretable text—the collection becomes a kind of collage open to deciphering. By maintaining as much of the creator's original arrangement as possible—and indicating this arrangement in the finding aid—archivists safeguard otherwise unknowable aspects of literary figures. It is through such fidelity to provenance that traces of the author's agency and appraisal practices are preserved.[109]

That said, it should already be abundantly clear that the picture being painted here is more utopic than realistic. The fantasy we crave is that an acquired collection represents a complete snapshot of the writer's living workshop. In truth, however, layers of loss have already taken place—not only has the author often curated her files to eliminate anything deemed undesirable, but even valued artifacts were inevitably also lost over the course of a busy, vagabond life. For instance, when McKay was asked to donate some of his manuscripts to the Schomburg in 1941, he told librarian Catherine Latimer that "many of the original ones are lost and others scattered here and there. . . . I have not been careless about them," McKay added, "but one loses manuscripts in packing and moving, sometimes one makes the mistake of throwing out valuable items with trash."[110] That same year McKay explained to Van Vechten how the difficulties of the Depression further worked against the timely return of manuscripts to authors: "After the Depression set in, publishers were not so generous and prompt about returning manuscripts and there are about three of mine that were never returned. Banana Bottom at Harper's, A Long Way From Home at Lee Furman's and Marlem [sic], Negro Metropolis at Dutton's."[111] In a letter to his last agent, Carl Cowl, in July 1947, McKay lamented the loss of his book contracts: "I put them in storage when I was in New York. And when Dorothy Day sent the books to me here all the contracts (even the one with Dutton's) had disappeared and some other valuable items."[112] In the case of authors who happen to become famous or recognized within their lifetimes, their archives run an additional risk of being stolen or raided by desperate scoundrels and opportunists.

Successful writers can have the means to hire assistants or archivists to help them sort and organize their papers before they are eventually sold.[113] If such arrangements were not made prior to a high-profile author's passing, that author's literary estate usually consults with appraisers to evaluate and organize the collection in anticipation of a sale. Such was the case for Lorraine Hansberry, a leading inspiration of the Black Arts Movement who arrived on the literary scene at the exact moment when literary archives were aggressively increasing in value; as a consequence, Hansberry is one of the first professional black women writers for whom we have a large collection. After her passing at the young age of thirty-four in January 1965, the Lorraine Hansberry Estate had her papers arranged by archivist Matthew Lyons before authorizing the transfer to the Schomburg Center. "In most instances," the Hansberry Papers finding aid states, "the Schomburg archival team has adhered to this initial arrangement,"[114] indicating that the Schomburg largely respected the principles of original order—yet in this case because this order had already been altered prior to donation, the collection's arrangement is more a reflection of Hansberry's status at the time of her passing than a reflection of her personality. Both outcomes remain informative in their own way.

Thus, whether due to an author's controlling, posterity-minded disposition or to the actions of the succession or simply to the attrition of life, a certain amount of arrangement artifice has always already been introduced into a collection even before an archivist comes into the picture. In fact, *original order* is something of a misnomer; it actually refers to "order at acquisition." Prior to this order at acquisition, there may have been an order at death that was subsequently altered by the succession, and prior to the order at death these same records passed through all sorts of orders during their lifecycles under the record creator's custodianship. For instance, the Samuel Roth Papers, in which was ensconced the manuscript for *Amiable with Big Teeth*, was partly rearranged by Roth's daughter, Adelaide Kugel,

FIGURE 1.2. Samuel Roth's office after a police raid, 1954.

Source: Box 47, folder 8, Samuel Roth Papers, Rare Book and Manuscript Library, Columbia. Courtesy of the Samuel Roth Estate.

following his passing. She intended to write a book about her father's life and imposed a new arrangement on the collection in an effort to assist her in this task. Prior to that, though, these records had already seen their share of upheavals and rearrangements in the wake of police raids and relocations to Roth's many business addresses during the years he operated as an independent publisher (see figure 1.2). When such shifts in arrangement prior to acquisition are known, archivists (should) make note of them in the collection's front matter.

Due to the comparatively long-standing status of the JWJ Collection at the Beinecke as a major hub for contemporary literary collections, it presents an instructive overview of changes in the archival profession's evolving relation to handling personal papers. The Beinecke is also one of the most diligent when it comes to publicly disclosing the past processing history of its holdings. As a means of showcasing the archival profession's enduring awkwardness in knowing how to deal with literary papers and of underscoring once again the illusion of "original order," the Langston Hughes Papers offer an ideal case. At the same time, the processing history of the Hughes Papers shows a determination, if not a dedication, on Yale's part to repair the "errors" of the past in the service of posterity.

Over the past thirty years, the Hughes collection has been reprocessed "at several points," which eventually prompted a procession intervention project in 2000–2002 "to clarify problematic listings of materials and incorporate previously unprocessed materials, including some groups formerly classified as 'printed' (such as newspaper clippings, postcards, and photographs)." The statement stands as evidence of the procedural changes in classification used by archivists, something Robert Hill observes in his experience returning to the same collection over the course of many years (there is, in other words, no such thing as "the same collection"). In a nod to this revisionist process, the Hughes Papers finding aid notes that "researchers familiar with older versions of this finding aid will find that many names have been added, as letters were taken from 'letter general' folders and listed separately." The document further warns that in an effort to standardize subject headings to match those generated by the Library of Congress, some "names may be missing, due to efforts to regularize authoritative names of correspondents."[115]

For all its intricate detail and exemplar of archival labor, the Hughes Papers finding aid nevertheless goes on to admit that the collection has failed in its sacred duty to maintain original order: "Due to the number of times the papers were rearranged," it states, "much of the original identification and arrangement of materials was lost, making it difficult to recreate associations (such as photographs that were once enclosed in letters to Hughes)." What is remarkable about this particular finding aid is that it features an extended "Processing Notes" section where it inscribes the history of its own institutional lifecycles and in so doing acts as a window into changes in postwar archival logic. For instance, because many of the series "were inherited" from earlier processing lifecycles, they have "been kept intact" even though current archival techniques now recommend that the material nestled within a series—such as "Personal Appearances"—"would have been more logically broken into individual components (writings, printed ephemera, clippings, etc.)."[116] In its reparative effort, the Beinecke has further elected to break up some inherited series and rearranged them in what it calls "appropriate" series. This statement is made without irony—in other words, without acknowledging the fact that this entire finding aid proves how one generation's "appropriate series" can be the next one's reparative burden.

Yale's wholesale twenty-first-century reprocessing project has also restored some aspects of "original order": small clusters of material that had not come directly from the Hughes Estate but that had nevertheless been integrated are now extracted and cataloged separately, "per standard library practice." With such a restorative move, the rhetoric of the arrangement, so to speak, more closely reflects how such material lived farther away from Hughes as epicenter.[117] Even though, as a rule, archivists are professionally bound to make note of such disruptions—or of phases in the collection's lifecycle—researchers may also come to the realization that what they are seeing represents only the latest order of a given artifact—novels included. Close attention to a literary collection's processing history, therefore, is a form of genetic criticism. As a consequence, the literary geneticist's understanding of archival science can help reconstruct the sedimented past lives of texts. Such research moments—when one literally pieces together an earlier order for a certain specific set of records—are discoveries in themselves. The idea of a "restored" text—such as the Wright novels Rampersad was able to edit for the Library of America—partakes of this reparative work made possible by the retracing of an original or intended order. Similarly, the sudden realization that what are now separate files in a collection were once "living" together in the writer's workshop and that, when reunited, make up an entirely new story is the stuff of which genetic critical dreams are made. Discoveries of previous literary lifecycles enter the imagination almost like grainy found footage of the novelist at work. In chapter 3, the tracing of the lost "Harlem Is Nowhere" photographs and accompanying captions from photo-essay to novelistic passages furnishes an elaborate example of this phenomenon.

SPLIT COLLECTIONS, SPLIT CENTURY: THE FRAUGHT HISTORIES OF LITERARY PAPERS

Archivists can work with the collections they acquire only in the order in which the collections are received and according to the principles active in the era of their acquisition. The intellectual arrangement imposed on the material in a collection is intended to make the collection intellectually logical and easier to navigate. And yet, alas, the lack of proper training in the idiosyncrasies of personal archives has led to decades of sometimes poor decision making in matters of appraisal. As archivist Phillip N. Cronenwett underscores, "The collection of manuscripts, particularly literary manuscripts, by institutions is a relatively new phenomenon." Literary manuscripts have been "acquired on a systematic basis" only since the late nineteenth century, a practice that grew rapidly a century later. Yet even as literary collections were acquired at an accelerating pace, the archival profession did not immediately adjust to the unique challenges personal archives represent. As a consequence, states Cronenwett, the "appraisal of literary papers is an even more recent phenomenon." Even by the mid-1980s, little progress had been made in the area, and archivists increasingly deplored the fact that there was "little or no literature in the field that treats the collecting, accessioning, appraisal, or disposition of literary papers."[118]

Only over the past twenty years or so has there been a forceful, organized effort on the part of a few archivists to establish new and better parameters for the processing of personal archives. As I stated earlier, perhaps the most damaging reality of the literary archival market is the phenomenon of "split collections."[119] Split collections have become "so common that it is often surprising to find an author's papers in a single location," and they are thus one of the defining characteristics of literary papers.[120] Every archivist who has written on literary papers, from Cronenwett to Michael Forstrom to David Sutton to Catherine Hobbs and many more, attests to and agrees that the phenomenon of split collections "poses a serious problem for both users and the curators"; because the latter have to make "permanent decisions regarding the appraisal of institutional holdings," being unable to assess the whole severely hampers the task.[121] As a result, both original order and provenance, hallmarks of the archival profession, are acutely jeopardized with respect to literary papers.

The plague of split collections stems from the aforementioned uneven history of collecting and the removal of specific items deemed especially valuable in a given collection. Repositories have therefore been known to acquire one or two items at a time or sometimes one large but specialized chunk—for instance, only photographs or only materials pertaining to one specific novel—and ignore any other materials. Such practices obliterate any semblance of *respect des fonds* and turn literary heirs and acquiring repositories into what Cronenwett calls "cannibals in the guise of manuscript curators."[122] If the writer enjoyed any kind of fame, it is practically guaranteed that the collection will be archivally "split." In fact, a common practice today now has authors selling their papers at midcareer, locking down deals that will involve scheduled shipments over their lifetime. Some repositories "are so competitive," Breon Mitchell, the former director of the Lilly Library at Indiana University, stated in 2005, "that they 'gamble' on young writers, securing early works in hopes of future greatness and the proportionate scholarly enthusiasm."[123]

Some libraries find the idea of open bidding for an author's collection to be "distasteful," yet it has become a common means for literary estates to maximize the monetary value of their holdings by selling various segments to interested parties.[124] That said, library directors are well aware of this problem and usually advise estates to first approach any institution that may already have a collection by the same author, though this does not always sway those in search of a potentially larger score. Prominent recent examples involve Arthur Miller and Michael Ondaatje: in 2017, Yale surprised the Harry Ransom Center with an "aggressive" offer for the archive of

Arthur Miller, an author who had already donated materials to Texas during his lifetime, so Texas was forced to match Yale's price to ensure retention and completion of its Miller holdings.[125] Conversely, that same year, by putting a higher sum on the table, the Harry Ransom Center wrested away the rest of the Ondaatje archive from Library and Archives Canada, which had been accumulating his papers across several installments between 1985 and 1993. With this purchase, the Ransom Center thereby created an egregious split.[126]

Some writers independently resist the temptation of a bigger payday in favor of "spirit of place," the notion that one's papers can have a sense of belonging to a specific site based on personal aspects of the record creator's biography. When Toni Morrison opted to sell her archive to Princeton in 2009, for example, some saw this choice as a rebuke to her alma mater Howard University, even though Morrison had been faculty at Princeton for close to thirty years. At the time, Greg Carr, then chair of Afro-American studies at Howard, lamented the "loss" of Morrison's papers and those of many other African American authors that end up in Ivy League repositories: "We've left much of our institutional memory at non-black institutions."[127] In 2017, bell hooks decided to bequeath her archive to Berea College in Kentucky, despite Harvard University's, among others', active pursuit of the collection.[128] A native Kentuckian, hooks allowed a "sense of community and identity," as she said, rather than financial gain to ultimately guide her choice. Conversely, West Coast and University of California system stalwart Angela Davis elected to sell her archive to Harvard, where it fetched a lofty sum, in 2018. In some ideal cases, the two—spirit of place and bigger payday—can be obtained from the same repository, such as the James Baldwin Papers finally landing at the Schomburg Center in Harlem, the very same library that was so formative to the young Baldwin.

In the postwar years in the United States, before most African American collections had attracted this kind of monetary interest, many established living writers were able to make an indirect "profit" by divesting themselves of chunks of their archives through yearly donations listed as tax write-offs. Following a pattern of solicitation that had arguably been pioneered by Charles D. Abbott at the State University of New York at

Buffalo starting in 1935, Howard Gotlieb, the curator at Boston University, was throughout the 1960s one of the most adept at convincing a wide array of writers and other notable figures—such as Martin Luther King Jr.—to donate parts of their collections to the university.[129] As I discuss in more detail in relation to Ann Petry's archive (one of Gotlieb's coups) in chapter 4, a change in the tax code in 1970 effectively put a stop to this practice. Although the sending of pieces of an archive "in small increments and almost invariably as deposits," where they often remain dormant "until the creator dies and the estate can benefit from the bequest,"[130] represented a major disruption in original order, it at least had the benefit of preserving materials that might otherwise have been destroyed.

Nevertheless, because of this pattern of sending small increments of an archive to a repository, a great number of postwar literary collections were "divided artificially" and, as a result, the "chronological development of a collection"—traces of original order—becomes increasingly difficult to assess.[131] After the change in tax law, all American repositories saw their literary acquisitions drop significantly—those that could not compensate via purchases suffered the most. Although this sea change affected all writers regardless of color in the United States, it had an immeasurably deleterious effect on the safekeeping of African Americans' collections because they remained undervalued on the rare-book and manuscript market. In other words, most black writers could rarely profit from selling their papers, but without the possibility of a tax relief they also had no incentive to donate them aside from a kind of nebulous, altruistic idealism. However, it should be noted that some writers, depending on their archival practices, never even considered parting ways with chunks of their archive because the ability to consult their own growing records was part of their novelistic practice—Ralph Ellison, who ceaselessly revisited and revised, as the chapters in this book make clear, was of this ilk.

Yet even though "splitting" or fragmentation usually begins during the writer's lifetime and career—and thus much earlier than acquisition—the most damaging way in which literary papers are dispersed occurs when the same author's papers are partitioned and sold to different repositories—usually at different moments in the writer's career or posthumously. Ammiel

Alcalay, the literary archaeologist and director of the City University of New York "Lost & Found" archival project, tackles the problem of split collections from a more intimate and editorial perspective in his book *a little history*. Alcalay underscores the fact that because the same record creator's papers are housed "in disparate institutions," literary collections exist in an "unedited, unlinked, and out of touch with each other" status. This distance inevitably introduces "distortions" depending on which pieces "are seen, and where,"[132] distortions that affect—invisibly, insidiously— not only the scholar's argument, whatever it may be, but also the reality of the original scene; the living provenance of the literary. Writing in 2013, Alcalay articulates the many registers upon which this distortion operates:

> The record of the work, as well as of the coming together of people in common endeavor and friendship, is atomized, pulled apart, stored in separate containers, making it much harder for us to inhabit coherent stories, to make sense of ourselves, our history, and the times we live in. Properly preserved, these materials offer context that is absolutely essential and provides an invaluable legacy—readings, classes, public discussions, correspondence, and other encounters with many of America's most important writers of the past fifty years.[133]

Alcalay is pointing precisely to parts of literary collections that in many instances were targeted by archivists for deletion.

For example, in essay included in the anthology *Archival Choices: Managing the Historical Record in an Age of Abundance*, the archivist Phillip Cronenwett sets down what he considers to be the "best practices" for the "appraisal of literary manuscripts." Even though Cronenwett is cognizant of the fact that "many writers are also educators," he suggests that "papers that relate to their teaching function tend to be voluminous and of small consequence." Thus, he recommends that "much of the material can be deleted" unless the teacher/writer in question happens to have taught other "influential" writers. He cites Richard Eberhart as an example of someone whose teaching papers are worth preserving on the grounds that Eberhart's "prize pupil" was "Robert Lowell, later recognized as a great poet."[134] Obviously, Cronenwett did not anticipate Alcalay's "Lost & Found" project or Rachel Buurma and Laura Heffernan's recent study of the teaching papers of early-twentieth-century literary critics.[135] Alas, he is not alone in making such depreciatory assessments of what constitutes a modern literary life.

Much of the appraisal problem in literary papers has to do with how an author is valued at the time of acquisition. As Cronenwett baldly puts it, "Decisions regarding retention of manuscript drafts and their copies depend on the importance of the writer" or the "importance of the text" in question. Many writers "amass quantities of materials" related to works that are considered minor or works reflecting nonliterary projects, so "much of this material can be deleted from the author's papers with little or no loss to the integrity of the collection." We must be thankful that Cronenwett more or less contradicts himself—or, rather, unwittingly shows how hard it is to determine exactly what can be thrown out: "it may not be easy to identify the source of information in or inspiration for creative writing. Material that was clearly the basis of a creative work is best left in the collection."[136] The "clearly" in Cronenwett's sentence is perhaps the most obscure challenge of appraising a literary collection.

From lines scribbled on the back of a receipt to variant drafts of a novel, as the British cataloger, indexer, and scholar David C. Sutton underscores, the primary value ascribed to literary papers is the "insights they give into the act of creation."[137] Depending on how removed a collection is from its "creative" original order, let alone how many times it has been split across disparate repositories, determining the exact chronology of drafts can be one of the greatest challenges facing the processing archivist. Without dates or other distinguishing temporal indicators, the precise chronology may never be determined or requires careful, dedicated research by a scholar. Indeed, this kind of task can be exhilarating for a scholar, and we should not realistically expect archivists to have already done this kind of labor for us.

As I noted at the end of the introduction, since the spread of Mark A. Greene and Dennis Meissner's seminal essay "More Product, Less Process" beginning in 2005,[138] the division of labor between cataloger and researcher is tipping toward the latter. As archivists spend less time processing and listing item-level information, more collections become accessible to researchers at a faster pace. Largely as a response to the overwhelming amount of paper accumulated with recent and contemporary collections and to the ever-increasing backlog, numerous repositories almost immediately implemented the alterations in processing practices suggested by Greene and Meissner. Literary scholars would thus be well served by familiarizing themselves with the practical consequences of "more product, less process"— the biggest boon is that less material will be thrown out, but the biggest drawback is that each sought-after item then becomes that much more of a needle in a haystack.

Thus, looking back to the ways archivists used to handle literary collections before the turn of the millennium brings into relief the towering importance of recuperative projects such as Jacqueline Goldsby's "Mapping the Stacks" and Alcalay's "Lost & Found" chapbook series, which make "available to the public in accessible and stable formats" many of the vital encounters and dissemination of knowledge and art that took place over a writer's lifetime.[139] Through "Lost & Found," for instance, we can discover Ted Joans's travel logs and reminiscences from his Greenwich Village days and Kathy Acker's homage to Leroi Jones (Amiri Baraka); we can access Langston Hughes's letters to Nancy Cunard during the Spanish Civil War or read the correspondence between Baraka and Ed Dorn. The danger of appraising what an archivist may consider "ancillary" or just some heartless side hustle for writers—such as *teaching*—is that without the material produced in this "side hustle," not only is the living provenance (the "social history of the text") distorted, but we can also only ever produce a Photoshopped archive, evacuated from the "dense literary, poetic, and social culture" world from which it was taken.[140] As Alcalay shows, these missteps have introduced an illusion that dulls our historical sense of the literary and gives us make-believe fantasies masquerading as fact.

In some more unusual cases, an entire collection can be processed in one location and then later transferred to another institution, whereupon it can be subjected to further rearrangement. The unique journey of the Jean Toomer Papers from Doylestown, Pennsylvania, to Fisk University and then to the Amistad Research Center at Tulane and finally to Yale paints an instructive portrait of what can happen behind the scenes. In 1959, Jean Toomer—the African American novelist and poet most widely known for *Cane* (1923)—who by this point had stopped writing literary texts, was beginning to fall into obscurity. Sensing the need for a revival, Arna Bontemps, the long-standing Fisk University head librarian and fellow Harlem Renaissance stalwart, wrote to Toomer at his Doylestown residence in an effort to inquire about his archive. In ill health, Toomer never replied to Bontemps, but Bontemps was finally able to reach Toomer's wife, Marjorie Content, in 1962. Although Mrs. Toomer "had not heard of Fisk University," she appreciated Bontemps's initiative to safeguard her husband's archive and obtained Toomer's agreement to have his papers shipped to Nashville in December 1962 as long as "he would not be asked to do anything about it," as the story goes. Fisk could not afford to purchase the papers, but it did pay for the packing and shipping—a total of $71.29.[141]

As head librarian, Bontemps accepted the collection on Fisk's behalf with the understanding that it would be available for his own use and "that Fisk would attempt to order and arrange the papers." In 1968, three years after Bontemps stepped down and was replaced by Jessie Carney Smith as Fisk's head librarian, the Toomer Collection was transferred to the Amistad Research Center, which was then on Fisk's campus,[142] where the bulk of it was processed and microfilmed under the curatorship of Clifton Johnson. It is at this stage of their journey that the Toomer Papers were "stamped, numbered, labelled, and annotated with dates and names at Fisk University."[143] The amount of labor that ordering the Toomer archive necessitated was one of the reasons why Mrs. Toomer was eager to send the papers to Fisk; as she explained in a letter to Smith in 1969, "Jean Toomer's papers were sent originally to Fisk University library without any conditions, stipulations, strings, or what-have-you because of Arna Bontemps's urgent desire to have them, and because I couldn't possibly put any order into them." By 1970, Bontemps, who, though retired, "continued to handle all matters involving the Toomer Collection," had spearheaded two publications that helped revive interest in Toomer's work: Harper and Row's reprint of Toomer's masterwork *Cane* and a new publication, *The Poetry of the Negro, 1746–1970* (1970), coedited with Langston Hughes. In his introduction to the former, Bontemps positioned *Cane* in a trajectory that led directly to Richard Wright, Ralph Ellison, and James Baldwin. In the latter, Bontemps included a previously unknown poem by Toomer that he had found in the collection. Throughout the years of Fisk's custodianship of the Toomer Papers, Bontemps diligently sought permission for use and consultation of the material and implemented Mrs. Toomer's requests or suggestions regarding the collection. When Bontemps passed away in 1973, Fisk continued to honor this practice.

Then in February 1980 Mrs. Toomer informed Fisk of her decision to donate the Toomer Collection to Yale. Although any financial details regarding the transfer remain undisclosed, one can easily imagine that Yale made her an offer she couldn't refuse. Officially, among the reasons Mrs. Toomer listed for having the collection removed from Fisk was "the fact that the manuscript collections of many of Toomer's literary contemporaries were at Yale,"[144] demonstrating some of the centripetal force of Van Vechten's Ivy League initiative. Archives, after all, like to build on their strengths—what Thomas F. Staley, the notorious former director of the Harry Ransom Center, used to call "nodal collecting."[145] A legal battle ensued between Fisk and Yale that lasted for five years.

The investigation concluded that, legally speaking, the Toomer Collection had not been sent to Fisk as "an outright gift" but rather had been put there "on deposit," a phrase that signifies the collection "is on loan to the library, as distinguished from a collection owned by the library as a result of a purchase" or gift. It seems that Bontemps had never sent Mrs. Toomer an "acknowledgement of gift form" and had always considered the papers to belong to Mrs. Toomer ("these belong to you," he had written to her in 1967). Yale's legal team argued that Fisk had never treated the collection as their property but had rather followed the procedures associated with collections that are merely on deposit. No document proving any transfer of ownership of the papers to Fisk could be produced—only the original letter to Bontemps from 1962 in which Mrs. Toomer told him that her husband had agreed to have the materials physically moved to Nashville. In contrast, Yale had Mrs. Toomer execute a "deed of gift" in 1983. The following year Mrs. Toomer passed away. And finally, in 1985, despite Jessie Carney Smith's best efforts, the court recognized Yale University as "the owner of the Toomer Collection and the literary rights therein." In the wake of the court's decision, the collection was transferred to Yale, where it was (re)processed at the Beinecke in 1987–1988. Jean, Arna, Marjorie—everyone was dead, and Yale had come away, once again, with the spoils.[146]

What the journey of the Toomer Papers further demonstrates—aside from sadly reiterating the dispossession of HBCUs in favor of the Ivy League—is how, in the absence of a standardized set of practices for processing literary papers, different kinds of intellectual control are imposed depending on the repository in charge. Once Yale took possession of the Toomer Papers, it tweaked the processing work performed by the Amistad Research Center and thus further altered "original order" through additional microsplits. Thus, the manner in which a given collection is (re)arranged depends on the acquiring repository's sanctioned internal practices. For instance, the Harry Ransom Center exclusively followed a card-catalog system to describe its extensive collections before introducing new archival cataloging procedures in 1990. Prior to this change, it had organized all of its literary collections into four categories: works (by author), letters (outgoing), recipient (incoming), and miscellaneous (manuscripts and correspondence by others). Whenever an item "did not fit into these categories, such as art, photographs, books, and near-print materials such as newspaper clippings," the center's website notes, it was "dispersed to other Ransom Center collections for cataloging and storage."[147] Without a record of what was originally an organic part of a given collection, such dispersion is a great loss for future scholarship.

The finding aids of Yale's most recent additions to the JWJ Collection—such as the Richard Bruce Nugent Papers and the Lisbet Tellefsen Papers, both acquired and processed in 2012—include a generic "Processing Notes" section that is fascinating in its own right. Incidentally, the fact that these two collections were processed immediately upon acquisition is a clear indication that black literary collections are now considered to have a much higher financial and research value than at any other time in book history. Yale's current standardized note on processing is less a description of a collection's postacquisition history than a manifesto of contemporary archival logic at an elite institution—it is the "fine print" often invisibly appended to every literary collection in the age of "more product, less process": "Collections are processed to a variety of levels, depending on the work necessary to make them usable, their perceived research value, the availability of staff, competing priorities, and whether or not further accruals are expected. The library attempts to provide a basic level of preservation and access for all collections [as they are acquired], and does more extensive processing of higher priority collections as time and resources permit." The "Processing Notes" section of the finding aid goes on to add that the materials are rehoused and that the description of a collection's contents is "drawn from information supplied with the collection and from an initial survey of the contents." Whenever possible, folder titles are "based on those provided by the creator" and have thus "not been verified against the contents of the folders in all cases. Otherwise, folder titles are supplied by staff during initial processing." Though it may seem strange, retaining the creator's titles regardless of appropriateness necessarily ensures more fidelity to original arrangement. The manifesto ends with a forewarning: "This finding aid may be updated periodically to account for new acquisitions to the collection and/or revisions in arrangement and description."[148]

In sum, as this overview of the upheavals fundamental to the history of twentieth-century black special collections—and of literary collections *tout court*—reveals, the archive is never a stable, fixed repository but rather a dynamic, ever-shifting city whose arrangement largely depends on our—readers', creative writers', scholars'—"psychogeographic" mapping, to use Guy Debord's situationist term (see this book's coda for more on Debord). In the end, "split collections" is perhaps a metaphor for the practice of diaspora: vanishing itineraries, literary migrations, families separated, the search for a new life and new home, perpetual threat of relocation, failure to live up to expectations, the experience of being discarded, being "lost," being forgotten even by one's own creator—the very scattered materiality of black special collections is an integral part of the story.

2

CLAUDE MCKAY'S ARCHIVAL REBIRTH

Provenance and Politics in *Amiable with Big Teeth*

Put everything in it, yourself and everything else.

—MAX EASTMAN TO CLAUDE MCKAY, APRIL 20, 1941

Two years before the publication of *Ulysses* in 1922, James Joyce famously claimed that it would contain "a picture of Dublin so complete that if the city suddenly disappeared from the earth it could be reconstructed out of my book."[1] The claim not only helps position the novel form as an alternative, essential site of historical preservation but also suggests literature's recuperative powers for what would otherwise be lost. The modernist motto to "make it new" is an implicit means to make it last. Joyce's encyclopedic approach to literature has enjoyed a wide influence, notably on the Jamaican American poet, Claude McKay, who stayed in Paris shortly after *Ulysses* was published in 1922. In his autobiography, *A Long Way from Home* (1937), McKay acknowledges Joyce as "*le maître* among the moderns" yet considers *Ulysses* to be "greater as a textbook for modern writers than as a novel for the general public." In *Ulysses*, McKay finds "the sum of two thousand years" woven into "the ultimate pattern," and in a letter to Max Eastman he calls Joyce "a Don Quixote of contemporary literature," part of a few "crusading revolutionists against the dead weight of formal respectability under which modern literature is buried."[2] Although McKay—who fought his fair share of windmills over the years—certainly had other contemporary modernist influences, his privileged relation to *Ulysses* as a "textbook" manifests in his novelistic attempts to reconstruct a lost world, one buttressed by a similar Joycean fidelity to the history out of which it emerges. As McKay's biographer Wayne Cooper has underscored, his depiction of Marseilles's *vieux port* in his second novel, *Banjo* (1929), "was thorough, unsparing, and accurate," and in light of the quarter's complete destruction during World War II "McKay's description of its congested alleyways, dark habitations, seedy bars, and sinister denizens has become for some French a classic evocation of the quarter as it was between the wars."[3] Thus, the ability to "give a picture so complete" that the reader can "reconstruct" what has "disappeared" directly aligns the literary with other forms of preservation, most notably the archive. This preservationist strain, particularly pronounced within modernism, reflects a desire to accumulate, process, and conserve experience not as a means for dusty repose or historical exactitude but rather as a way to retrieve the past for the living— thus embodying what I call an "archival sensibility."

McKay's writing career is marked by contradictory forces; his dedication to careful study and factual accuracy ran against his most staunchly defended values: individualism, independence, and the creative freedom of art. At the height of the Harlem Renaissance, these inner struggles usually manifested in his ubiquitous issues with plot and continued to be a challenge for him as he set out to write what would turn out to be his last novel, the recently published work *Amiable with Big Teeth*, first composed in 1941.[4] In our introduction to the novel, published in 2017, Brent Edwards and I gather the material fruits of the archival research we undertook to authenticate the novel after its initial discovery—the preserved materials we encountered in multiple repositories across the United States uncovered an almost overwhelming array of correspondences between historical figures and events as well as the characters and scenes found in McKay's novel. The process led me to reflect on the many ways in which late McKay increasingly grounded his writerly practices in material traces of the past; he was both relying on and building new archives.

This chapter traces the evolution of Claude McKay's late career as it relates to the writer's archival strategies as a means of understanding how he came to craft his final novel. In the years following his return to the United States, what McKay called his "special research work," the work he had begun as part of the Federal Writers' Project (FWP), gave him a new writerly lease on life. An FWP writer from 1936 to 1939, McKay contributed a significant amount of research and spent considerable time consulting the work of his colleagues, activities that the mature writer found inspiring. In fact, McKay eventually wrote two books based on this research, first a history of Harlem, *Harlem: Negro Metropolis* (*HNM*), published in 1940 (the last book he would see appear in print in his lifetime), and then a work of fiction, the long-mummified *Amiable with Big Teeth.* This chapter explores two intertwined notions of McKay's archival "rebirth," as the chapter title states: on the one hand how the archive's recuperative power can induce a belated rebirth via posthumous publication—*posthumous* literally meaning "born after death"—and on the other hand how McKay's own archival practices as a mature writer led him to return to prose fiction for the first time in close to a decade.

Exposing the ways in which *Amiable* fictionalizes the hard-won archive undergirding the novel, I want to understand what was at stake for McKay as a black intellectual and novelist in the early years of World War II and to reflect on what these "alternative facts," to use the now infamous phrase, do in the novel form. As my research shows, McKay gave himself the right to compose his final "fictional narrative as an alternative site of archival imagining," with a trademark boldness that both empowered the black community for which he was writing and challenges our "assumptions about material 'truths,'"[5] giving rise to what Ann Laura Stoler terms "epistemic uncertainties."[6] Although my work here lies outside the strict context of colonial records that Stoler describes, I am similarly interested in following the vagabond itineraries of documents, in this case those McKay gathered and wielded for his own literary purposes.

McKay fashioned *Amiable* as a roman à clef, a genre that is dedicated to the embedding of sociohistorical facts but that nevertheless resists the tyranny of "actual" history—in that way, he was able to offer a more empowering speculative history. In this chapter, I read "along the archival grain" to highlight the ways in which the "minor" history McKay crafted runs *against* the historical grain as a means of disrupting the power dynamics threatening black autonomy. Ostensibly about the complex world-historical dynamics involved in the emergence of the Aid to Ethiopia organizations in Harlem during the Italo-Abyssinian crisis, which stimulated "new racial solidarity,"[7] *Amiable* is McKay's most realized literary expression of his desire for greater group unity among African Americans. His archival sensibility was shaped by his ethical ideals of black self-reliance rather than by a strict adherence to historical truth. In this respect, the political, speculative, and archival are intertwined.

When McKay returned to the United States in 1934 after twelve years abroad in Germany, France, Spain, and North Africa, he confronted a

FIGURE 2.1. Claude McKay, July 25, 1941, the day after he submitted the manuscript "God's Black Sheep" (*Amiable with Big Teeth*) for publication. Photograph by Carl Van Vechten.

changed nation that was just as broke as he was. An earlier return would have been too risky for the surveilled Jamaican; as William Maxwell has brilliantly shown, McKay's vagabondage on the other side of the Atlantic was in part a direct result of FBI surveillance and the fact that for more than a decade he could have been seized at most port of entries. As Maxwell puts it, McKay's overseas journey "was both a chosen bohemian adventure and a compulsory Black Atlanticism."[8] It was only through the assistance of long-standing acolytes from the New Negro movement such as James Weldon Johnson and Walter White, who "intervened with the State Department on McKay's behalf," that the British subject was able to reenter the United States in 1934.[9] With the Depression and partial decline of the New Negro movement, McKay shifted away from poetry and fiction and wrote his memoir, *A Long Way from Home*, as well as an unsparing work of nonfiction, *HNM*. During this time, however, he also penned numerous essays for various publications, including *The Nation*, *New Leader*, *Opportunity*, *Amsterdam News*, and more. He tried to found a new magazine called *Bambara* and almost took over the editorship, with Countee Cullen, of *The African: A Journal of African Affairs*.[10] With the recent discovery of *Amiable with Big Teeth*, we now know he was also writing a novel in this period.

As I show in this chapter, for his return to prose fiction McKay tapped into the same archive of events and facts he used in his journalistic pieces. That fiction provides an occasion to reassess late McKay's goals as a socially responsible novelist as well as to revise most narratives of the evolution of the Harlem Renaissance by extending its reach into World War II. With its unique archival history, *Amiable* further reinforces the importance of the relation between archival and aesthetic practices in his oeuvre. Critical accounts of late McKay have concentrated largely on his fervent anticommunism, his Catholic turn, his queerness, and his inability to get his Cycle poems published, but encountering him through the archive revises our understanding of his career path. Having outgrown his status as *"enfant terrible* of the Negro Renaissance," as Alain Locke infamously labeled him,[11] McKay turned to the novel form to remix the archive he gathered in writing what Maxwell calls his "party-bashing Baedeker *Harlem: Negro Metropolis*."[12]

The resulting roman à clef underscores the singularity of his mature aesthetic principles and his trajectory as a transnational novelist.

McKay's literary imagining of the archive preserves a watershed moment in African American diasporic history in a way that a purely documentary account could not. Just as McKay preserved Marseilles's *vieux port* in *Banjo* through accurate yet fictional depiction, *Amiable with Big Teeth* transports the reader back to a tumultuous time when Harlem's streets stirred with fervor for Ethiopia's cause. The novel not only becomes the final key to McKay's Joycean "reconstruction" of a lost time and place but also presents an ambivalent engagement with the necessary "fabrication" that fiction entails. As his final published works, biography, research notes, correspondence, and work in the FWP make clear, McKay was occupied—from the moment he set foot back in Harlem in 1934 until his passing in 1948—with a quest to foster "a group spirit and strong group organization [among] Aframericans."[13] As I argue in this chapter, the uneven plot and factual inaccuracies of *Amiable* are guided by McKay's didactic motive to share the unique perspective of his years abroad, erudition, and experiences with the Communist International (Comintern) in a way that would empower his community. As Cooper puts it, McKay returned from North Africa "convinced that American blacks had much to learn from studying, as he had done, the lives of minority groups in Europe and North Africa."[14] The joint failure of international communism and rise of fascism in Europe now posed an immediate threat to what McKay considered an overly credulous African American minority lacking in leadership. "McKay feared that," amid these looming dangers and lack of cohesive group life, "blacks lagged behind in comprehending the international forces that threatened them."[15] His sense of urgency in transmitting this knowledge is manifest in the variety of genres he resorted to in attempting to communicate his fears and solutions: memoir (*A Long Way from Home*), reportage and nonfiction (*HNM*), and novel (*Amiable with Big Teeth*). By combining and falsifying characteristics of historical figures, fudging exact dates, casting doubt on extant records, tampering with official documents, and manipulating other "facts," McKay reveals an archival sensibility guided by an ethics that transformed his late aesthetic principles. Not only by transporting the reader back to a forgotten moment in time but also by relying on the literary as a refuge for an author's desperate, passionate political ideals, he demonstrates how novels can outperform the archive's forensic task to tell "the story of a past event that remains otherwise unknown and unexplained."[16]

THE EYE OF A POET AND THE EQUIPMENT OF A SCHOLAR

The major historical events wedged between the Second Italo-Ethiopian War (October 1935–May 1936) and the eruption of the Spanish Civil War (July 1936) provided McKay with a rich tapestry onto which he could fictionalize his political agenda while exposing what Brent Edwards calls "the transnational contours of black expression between the world wars."[17] When McKay returned from North Africa—five years after the market crash of 1929 and the so-called end of the Harlem Renaissance—he was bursting with potential writing projects but devoid of a source of steady income. Given the fact that McKay was abroad both during and after Harlem was "in vogue," any staunch periodization of the Renaissance—what Lawrence Jackson calls its "truncated chronology"[18]—continues to be misleading in relation to his career. After all, like his contemporaries Langston Hughes and Zora Neale Hurston, McKay continued to produce major prose works throughout the 1930s. But the disappearance of the old circuits of Renaissance patronage during the Depression did lead him to seek assistance from institutions that would prove instrumental to African American writing in years to come—namely, the FWP, the Julius Rosenwald Fund, and the Guggenheim Foundation. Today, these institutions' records can cast an invaluable light on twentieth-century African American letters— indeed, many emerging scholarly projects center on the histories of such institutions.

When McKay was back on U.S. soil for the first time in more than a decade, his mind teemed with plans for crafting a new novel out of his vagabond experiences but wavered regarding how best to communicate that

knowledge. In his advertisement for *Bambara*, his intended new literary magazine, he wanted contributors to uphold three main standards:
"SINCERITY OF PURPOSE / FRESHNESS AND KEENNESS OF
PERCEPTION / ADEQUATE FORM OF EXPRESSION."[19] We can
detect in this statement the same standards he imposed upon himself in
composing his final works, with the third standard, form, clearly giving him
the most trouble. Shortly after plans for *Bambara* fell apart, he applied for
a grant from the Julius Rosenwald Fund in 1935 and explained in his application to director Edwin R. Embree that he "had originally planned a fictional version of his years abroad" but now felt that a straightforward autobiographical account would suffice.[20] As it turns out, his fictional project
was merely postponed by the completion of what became *A Long Way from
Home* and, after his years working for the FWP, the writing of *HNM*.
Coming in the wake of all this, *Amiable* bears the fruits of both his transnational reflections and his diligent research on Harlem.

It seems McKay never really abandoned the idea of doing a novel: in his
application for a Guggenheim fellowship in 1937, he explained that the
scholarly work he was doing was too time-consuming to let him "complete
a new novel of the Negro section of Harlem." "I should like to give up to
devote my time to a creative novel of Harlem life," he stated, "but at present I am employed in research and rewriting on the Harlem section of the
Federal Guide Book."[21] To Lewis Gannet, who had written a letter of rec-
ommendation for him, McKay confessed: "I crave to get away from the
enervating atmosphere of the Federal Writers' Project . . . and plunge into"
the new novel, though he did admit that it was largely thanks to his work
at the FWP that he had already "piled up a lot of material for a new story."[22]
Although the particular novel he had in mind in 1937 was likely the unfinished *Harlem Glory*, this same material would eventually make its way into
the complete *Amiable*.[23] Despite McKay's wish to "get away" from the FWP
atmosphere, the time he spent in it nevertheless inspired his idea for a literary project.

McKay's agenda thus never really deviated from the one he outlined to
Embree in his grant proposal in 1935: he wished to set down his "views as
to what an intelligent American Negro may gain from travelling, how he

may use his experiences in perspective to see and understand more clearly and broadly the social and cultural position of the American Negro and also in adjusting himself to American life."[24] Although his autobiography and nonfiction do convey some of the richness of his experiences, *Amiable* stands as his most mature expression of this sentiment because it so directly dramatizes his stated concerns. After all, McKay's "first objective," as Cooper asserts, "had always been to experience life directly in order to communicate the truth of his experience in his art."[25] Yet although McKay claimed that the artistic calling trumped any other—political or otherwise—his art increasingly required tremendous amounts of research and archival acumen.

McKay was clear about his allegiance to the artistic over the political, explaining his position in *A Long Way from Home*: "In any work of art my natural reaction was more for its intrinsic beauty than for its social significance . . . my social sentiments were strong, definite and radical, but . . . I kept them separate from my esthetic emotions, for the two were different and should not be mixed up."[26] These sentiments are what had set him apart from his communist colleagues during his days at *The Liberator*, especially modernist-basher Michael Gold.[27] Unlike Gold, McKay felt that "there were bad and mediocre, and good and great, literature and art, and that the class labels were incidental," but he could "not be convinced of a proletarian, or a bourgeois, or any special literature or art." He granted the possibility of a "proletarian *period* of literature" but firmly believed that "whenever literature and art are good and great they leap over narrow group barriers and periods to make a universal appeal."[28]

Yet by the time McKay wrote *Amiable* in 1941, he seems to have forced his aesthetic hand to adopt a more "mixed" approach. In a letter to his friend Max Eastman discussing his progress on *Amiable*, McKay confesses that his arduous archival research has affected his novelistic practice:

I took your advice (half-way) and spent a month, not two, pottering with the plot, characters and aim of the novel. And it has worked out a little differently from the first draft I showed you. The main thing is that it has some politics in it and we had thought it expedient to keep politics out. But after building up the Lij into a really sympathetic character (albeit weak) and consulting notes and newspaper stories of the period (early 1936) in which the tale begins, I discovered that it was impossible to keep politics out, for the Aid to Ethiopia was the jumping-off of the Popular Front movement in the United States. Of course, I am keeping the political stuff in its proper place, so that it may not be a handicap to the straight tale.[29]

After spending time on problems of plot and characters, McKay admitted that his own research notes and clippings made it "impossible to keep politics out" of the novel. This was a conscious metamorphosis on McKay's part, something he tried in vain to explain to E. P. Dutton president John Macrae after the publisher rejected the novel. "I had the idea of breaking with my former performance in fiction," he wrote, and "attempted to do a contemporary historical tale of local conflict with an ethical basis."[30] So although he may still have felt that matters of "social significance" must be "kept separate from [his] esthetic emotions" rather than "mixed up," this segregation, so to speak, of radical politics and aesthetic sense proved untenable in his late, post-FWP novelistic practice—an aesthetic potentiality awakened by his conjoined "ethical basis" and archival sensibility. Put another way, his diligent research strengthened the ethics that led him to break with form.

McKay's notebooks from this period, now held at the Beinecke, are filled with dates, names, quotes, and other factual details on subjects discussed throughout *HNM* and become the tapestry of *Amiable*, such as Marcus Garvey, Father Divine, Faithful Mary, Sufi Adbul Hamid, Willis Huggins, Casper Holstein, Jews, communists, Ethiopia, and so on. Even a listing of the titles of the Subject Files series in the McKay Collection at the Beinecke shows the range of interests and topics in his research notes: economics, France, Germany and Nazis, health and medicine, Jews and Judaism, labor, literature, the Middle East, North Africa, politics, race, religion, Russia, Spain, and the Spanish Civil War. In the "Miscellaneous" folder, clippings range from articles on eccentric domestic issues such as old men marrying preadolescent girls to articles on shark attacks, Louise Bryant,

Charlie Chaplin, communism, and, crucially, Ethiopians after the fall of Ethiopia as well as a short piece that apparently caught his interest: "Idle Writers Get Jobs Analyzing History."[31] In other words, by the time he was honing his novelistic skills with *Amiable*, the "distilled poetry of [his] experience"[32] was wedded to a form of literary archiving—the collapsed temporalities of what he called the "contemporary historical tale"—that served his roles as social activist and artist. But how had his archival practices led to such a politicization of his novelistic practice?

The truth is McKay had been consistently moving toward deploying his abilities as a creative writer in the service of his political convictions. His articles from the late 1930s and early 1940s—the period that informs both *HNM* and *Amiable*—provide a glimpse into his evolving notions on this issue. In distancing himself from what he considered to be George S. Schuyler's sloppy journalism, McKay declares: "I believe that the approach of the writer and artist to social problems is radically different from the approach of the politician,"[33] a statement that nevertheless acknowledges that writers and artists *do* engage with social problems. Two years later in the *New Leader*, McKay pithily encapsulates his new ethics: "When creative writers become politically-minded, they owe it to the public to dig down to the facts and interpret them."[34] The metaphor of digging down as archival practice recalls the famous essay "The Negro Digs Up His Past" by McKay's friend Arturo A. Schomburg, wherein the act of digging—researching, collecting, excavating, recuperating—becomes the scientific key to historical correctives that promise to put an end one day to any illusions about race superiority. With such an archival practice, Schomburg argued, we shall have "less of the sand of controversy and more of the dust of digging."[35] Unlike the politician, the radicalized creative writer is faced with the public responsibility to hone his archival skills because, as McKay put it, "the public expects more from [creative writers] than from ordinary politicians."[36] A fiction writer armed with an archival sensibility to dig up the past can thus embody a new form of politics and in doing so point to an alternative futurity.[37] In another article, where he now attacked the communist-led League of American Writers, McKay again put a premium on investigative acumen: "Instead of promoting scientific social enquiry and research, the League of American Writers prefers to vilify and silence those who adhere to such principles of free inquiry."[38] For the late McKay, therefore, the freedom of the writer goes beyond the constraints of the political, yet "political-mindedness" nevertheless calls for an assiduous archival aesthetic that the creative writer "owes" to the public.

Let me be clear: McKay was diligent about researching "facts" throughout his career, stressing the importance of firsthand experience in his reportage and documenting, as *Banjo* attests. For instance, in *HNM* he reveals giving "much of my time to acquiring information about the trade union movement" during his stay in Great Britain in 1919.[39] When he returned to Germany in 1923, he was warned beforehand that the Germans were now badly mistreating blacks, but McKay, as always, "wanted to authenticate that . . . sentiment for myself."[40] But it was his stint with the FWP that allowed him to truly hone his archival practices, a faculty he not only felt was necessary but also enjoyed. In a letter to Schomburg, McKay notes: "I am working all day every day," both at home and "at the big library digging things up."[41] To Orrick Johns around the same time, he writes: "I like that research work, and I have been privileged to suggest the items I like to work on."[42] Crucially, McKay admits in *HNM* that he "preferred" doing the "special research work" asked of the FWP "Negro group" "because the facts we unearthed were of intrinsic value to those of us who were writing about Negro life in our off-project time."[43] As a result of his digging, McKay became a fearsome investigative journalist, publishing incendiary articles and editorials in the late 1930s that laid the groundwork for much of his later work. He was proud of his archaeological excavations of facts and relied on them when he was forced to defend himself publicly after other black intellectuals began to criticize his anticommunist articles and those on the labor situation in Harlem.

Notably, both Adam Clayton Powell Jr. and George Schuyler attacked McKay for his article "Labor Steps Out in Harlem," published in *The Nation* in 1937.[44] They claimed that he had either made up or exaggerated many of his statements and, in an echo of the criticism he later received for *HNM*, considered his plea for black autonomy as a form of segregation. In response, McKay composed two distinct rejoinders in the *New York Amsterdam News*, where he defended his status as an independent thinker based on the accuracy of his facts. He retorted to Powell that the man "marshals no facts to refute the statements contained in my article."[45] In his reply to Schuyler, he underscored that "there has been no challenge of the facts marshalled [sic] in my article. I got them straight before I wrote." "I stand by my article," McKay concluded, because he was confident in his archival practices. In fact, his reply to Schuyler contains a short-order archival tour de force; he showed off his research skills—a form of reprimand and victory over Schuyler the investigative journalist—by deciding "to consult the Schuyler dossier." He read all the pieces written by Schuyler in his regular column in the *Pittsburgh Courier* since 1930 and was "amazed to discover that almost every important point in my radio debate had been advocated much more forcibly by George Schuyler himself a few years ago." McKay then proceeded to quote extensively from Schuyler to show how "Schuyler's inept attempt to slander me merely discredits himself." He was thus able to turn the table on Schuyler by exposing his accuser as the "falsifier of the truth."[46] This use of the archive as defensive tactic—where careful research unearths evidence that can protect you—displayed during this public debate with Powell and Schuyler later takes central stage in *HNM* and *Amiable with Big Teeth*.

Although some reviewers of *HNM* felt the book was not always objective, McKay declared it a pure "examination of the facts."[47] Today, the repositories housing McKay's correspondence bear proof that he sent numerous letters to experts seeking their testimonies on various matters, covering important questions dealt with in *HNM* as a means of double-checking his information.[48] McKay also received high praise from prominent figures for his abilities as a researcher; Zora Neale Hurston applauded his knowledge in her *Common Ground* review; Grace Nail Johnson, James Weldon's recent widow, admired McKay's "fact-finding study" and its "fool-proof comprehension," adding that the "Negro needs this study tremendously."[49] A. Philip Randolph also thought the book "brilliant, penetrating, and constructive" and echoed McKay's convictions regarding black self-reliance.[50] John Dewey thought it "a model for all studies of its kind" and felt that it had "enough detailed information presenting hard solid work to justify half a dozen

Ph.D. degrees." In a statement that nicely encapsulates McKay's late archival aesthetic, Dewey concluded his letter to McKay by expressing how impressed he was with McKay's ability to combine "both the eye of a poet + the equipment of a scholar."[51] Indeed, McKay had become so adept at handling and filing records that he repeatedly sought employment with the U.S. Office of Facts and Figures in 1941, once the publication of *Amiable* fell through.[52]

Factual exactitude backed by material evidence had come to define McKay's journalistic articles and *HNM*, and his papers demonstrate that he continued to apply his archival practice when he crafted *Amiable*. In the final months of writing the novel, McKay sent a letter to Simon Williamson, his former FWP colleague and a reliable source of information on the Ethiopian situation, asking him to confirm "whether the Spanish Civil War broke in June or July of 1936." "I want to dovetail the Fascist conquest of Ethiopia into it," he explained, "but I need to be certain about the facts."[53] In the acknowledgments in *HNM*, McKay thanks Williamson for having "generously made available his considerable collection of Negro material, consisting of pamphlets, excerpts from various articles and newspaper cuttings."[54] Indeed, his reliance on Williamson for material evidence and exactitude is reminiscent of James Joyce's repeated requests to his "dear aunt Josephine" for various details about Dublin while writing *Ulysses*.

Thanks to helpers such as Williamson and Grace Campbell, to the growing FWP archive, and to his own fieldwork in and around Harlem, McKay was able to investigate Harlem's community life and prominent denizens with a level of thoroughness that had been materially impossible earlier.[55] This research also allowed him to study the increasingly entrenched presence of the Popular Front in African American organizations, which led him to mobilize his energies into promoting autonomous black solidarity. Much of this research eventually made its way into *HNM* in a rather straightforward fashion, but it also animates the backdrop for *Amiable*'s melodrama. What emerges, above all, when one consults McKay's records and writings of this period is how his archival sensibility is intimately tied to his desire for greater group unity among Aframericans, which is perhaps best expressed in his wish to form an all-black Negro Writers'

Guild.[56] In "Circular Letter for the Creation of a Negro Writers' Guild," sent out in October 1937, McKay stressed the need for "Negro writers to draw closer together in mutual fellowship." Such a group, McKay continued, "would be beneficial to all our writers and especially to those younger and potential ones who may look to the older for inspiration" and would allow Negro intellectuals to explore the "universal aspect of group culture." In a striking comparison, he added: "We think that it is possible to establish through intellectual fellowship something like a *living counterpart* of the unparalleled Schomburg collection of Negro books in the domain of scholarship."[57] McKay's wish for the guild, therefore, was that it would be nothing less than a living archive.

When the guild fell through due to too much in-fighting, McKay still gravitated toward using the literary as a politicizing and culturally enriching tool. By 1938, McKay and Countee Cullen had agreed to take over the editorship of *The African: A Journal of African Affairs* with the intention of renaming it, tellingly, *The African: A Journal of Literary and Social Progress*. In a letter to James Weldon Johnson asking him to be one of two "Honorary Editors"—the other was to be W. E. B. Du Bois—McKay explained that the journal was to be "an organ of group culture." The May–June issue announced McKay and Cullen's subsequent editorship of the journal, but the venture never took place. Though it is difficult to ascertain exactly why the project was abandoned, it is clear that disagreement over the journal's new focus—from the baldly political to the socioliterary—lay at the root. A letter to McKay from Cullen, who was in Paris at the time, July 1938, suggests as much: "I am very anxious to know what finally transpired in connection with *The African*. It was a great disappointment to me that we could not make a go of it, but it was impossible to work with such narrow-minded people. They were interested in propaganda only."[58] Now that both collaborative endeavors, the Negro Writers' Guild and the editorship of *The African*, had failed—just as his effort to create the *Bambara* magazine had floundered in 1934—McKay had to find yet another solution to achieving group unity. He first wrote the nonfictional work *Harlem: Negro Metropolis* to expose with facts and figures the reality of black life as he saw it. Yet once he perceived what he called the "conspiracy of silence" against *HNM* in the press,[59] he returned to his artistic calling in a last-ditch effort to demonstrate how his dreams of strong black unity and leadership would work out in (fictional) practice through the crafting of a novel, *Amiable with Big Teeth*.

SELF-RELIANCE AND GROUP UNITY

Both McKay's unique experiences vagabonding across the pond and his excursions as an FWP researcher informed his commitment to the uplift of the Aframerican community. While abroad, McKay had "observed that the people who were getting . . . anything were those who could realize the strength of their cultural group; their political demands were considered and determined by the force of their cultural grouping."[60] As a consequence, he wrote to James Weldon Johnson, "I am certain that Negroes will have to realize themselves as an organized group to get anything."[61] As reflected in *Banjo*, while in Marseilles McKay relished living "among a great gang of black and brown humanity" and felt firsthand "the strength and distinction of a group and the assurance of belonging to it."[62] After returning to the United States, he saw the establishment of a similar sense of belonging as essential for the future benefit of black America.

According to his biographer, Wayne Cooper, McKay felt "that blacks had to develop a stronger group spirit in order to overcome their disadvantages, while at the same time disavowing any political role for himself either as a socialist or a black."[63] In other words, McKay paradoxically vacillated between downplaying his own political role and engaging with the day's most burning political issues in the many articles he wrote. His usual stubborn claim to being, at bottom, an apolitical poet who had "nothing to give but my singing" was difficult for his critics to understand—or believe. This disbelief was not surprising, given that he constantly advocated "social consciousness," "practical education," and "group orientation" and attacked communists at every turn, only to then hide behind his role as "troubadour wanderer."[64] Alain Locke, whom McKay had roundly mocked in his

CLAUDE MCKAY'S ARCHIVAL REBIRTH

autobiography, criticized McKay (at the behest of a young Richard Wright[65]), calling him a "spiritual truant" who was "caught in the egocentric predicament of aesthetic vanity." Locke deplored what he perceived as McKay's segregationist stance, the result of having "repudiated all possible loyalties," which amounted "to a self-imposed apostasy," and naturally considered it hypocritical of McKay to advocate greater group unity among blacks while he himself remained notoriously independent, if not isolated.[66]

Others criticized McKay for his suspicion and rejection of communism. At the time, it should be noted, many young black intellectuals were embracing communism—a relationship McKay's novel subtitle describes as "a love affair"—notably two future superstars of American literature, Richard Wright and Ralph Ellison, both of whom also worked in the FWP with McKay at the midtown branch. James Weldon Johnson, however, remained sympathetic to McKay's position regarding communism, and a letter from Johnson may have helped to inspire the novelist's portrayal of the character Newton Castle in *Amiable*: "These Negro near-Marxists are often quite amusing, if not ridiculous. You, of course, know many times more about Russia and Communism than all of them put together."[67] McKay represented a particular affront to these young black communists, for he had been to Russia in the 1920s, serving as the unofficial African American representative to the Fourth Congress of the Third International and giving an address in the Kremlin Throne Room. Now that he was utterly disillusioned with communism more than a decade later, most radical leftist intellectuals of the day feared and misunderstood him.

Naturally, this contention made the FWP—with Ellison and Wright in their pro-Left phases popping in and out—an "enervating" and "faction-riven" group. McKay felt that Aframericans should learn to become autarkic, without the help of whites or Reds, as a first step to establishing greater dignity and confidence. The greatest threat to the possibility of such group unity, McKay came to believe, was the "chicanery and intrigue" of communism, combining "a perfect technique of overt and covert propaganda."[68] Accordingly, the villain of *Amiable*, Maxim Tasan, is a secret agent of the Comintern who employs just such methods, and the black intellectuals associated with him are eventually shown to be unstable fools.

But it was often what was perceived as McKay's segregationist stance that proved to be most problematic for many black intellectuals. The Helen Boardman affair is illustrative of this conflict. At a preliminary meeting for the formation of the Negro Writers' Guild in the summer of 1937, McKay vigorously opposed the membership of a white woman, Helen Boardman. Even the most sympathetic whites, McKay tried to explain, could inadvertently inject "subtle inhibitions," as Wayne Cooper puts it, into the guild's operations, and he regarded temporary segregation as necessary to enable the group's "consolidation."[69] McKay argued that in order for African Americans to achieve a "sustained communal self-improvement," as Cooper puts it, "blacks needed to start thinking about organizing both locally and nationally,"[70] and for the Writers' Guild to take a step in that direction it could not allow any white members. McKay took the time to write to Boardman directly, apologizing for making her into the unfortunate "goat" of the guild meeting, even adding: "I am certain that intellectually I may have more in common with you than any member of the Guild." But, he explained, "my attitude in the Guild is merely part of a plan I hope to formulate for intensive group work and consolidation." Even if "65 per cent or more of Negro Americans will disagree with me at first . . . the Negro group badly needs self-confidence, self-reliance and group unity . . . to build itself up on a sound foundation."[71] Boardman didn't buy any of what he claimed and, echoing McKay's many critics, responded by accusing McKay of expressing himself with too much "vituperation" and arguing that his ideas "would lead to self-segregation, narrow ethno-centrism, and isolation."[72]

These charges were still being thrown at McKay three years later in the reviews of *HNM*. With this reconstructed backstory in mind, it seems logical that McKay's last resort was to put his ideas into novel form—no other "Form of Expression" seemed "adequate," as the *Bambara* advertisement advocated. *Amiable* can thus be read as McKay's final effort to reply to these critiques; through the characters Pablo Peixota, Dorsey Flagg, Sufi Abdul Hamid, and Professor Koazhy and his Senegambians, the novel dramatizes the ways in which peoples of African descent can be successful in overthrowing the nefarious influence of communists and whites, sympathetic and otherwise, thanks to the methods of bibliophiles—such as "digging," collecting and scrapbooking, authenticating, and taking active interest in

CLAUDE MCKAY'S ARCHIVAL REBIRTH

cultural heritage. McKay, as usual, was basing his ideas of black self-reliance on his own experiences and research: "It is a clear historical fact that different groups have won their social rights only when they developed a group spirit and strong group organization."[73] He called for Aframericans "to develop their own banks, co-operative stores, printing establishments, clubs, theatres, colleges, hotels, hospitals and other social service institutions and trade unions."[74] It is to the desired establishment of such institutions that much of *HNM* is dedicated, and in his subsequent novel he shows some of these possibilities at work, functioning together via a semispeculative narrative.

In short, there is no question that McKay intended *Amiable* to play a role in political action; it seems meant as a literary rallying cry, a Deweyesque "art as experience" example of black coalition successfully uniting and defeating threats from within and without—here are the big teeth of the amiable communist, McKay is saying, and this is how we, united Aframericans, can deal with this Red trash. The time had come to dash the Communist Party's "brains among the garbage of the neglected Harlem pavement," to cite the novel's dark final sentence.[75] Returning to the archive he built, turning it into a "generative system," as Brent Edwards puts it, animates McKay's novelistic craft.[76] McKay also used this occasion to reassess his past contributions as a fiction writer; he was well aware that in the past he had often been criticized for providing reductive or primitive representations of African American life. Taking another crack at the novel form offered him an opportunity to write back to some of this criticism and to portray "group pride and strength and self respect [*sic*]."[77] But how could the literary bring about such group unity?

"MAKE THE CANVAS AS BIG AND SIGNIFICANT AS IT CAN BE"

As the novel tries to make sense of the intense ferment of enthusiasm gripping Harlem in 1936, McKay takes any opportunity to insert history lessons into *Amiable*, ventriloquizing his own views through its sympathetic characters and articulating threats via its villains.[78] With the fascist incursion into its sacred territory, Ethiopia emerged "on the horizon as an embarrassing new Canaan," igniting a "vague religious sentiment for Ethiopia" among Aframericans.[79] At the time, Ethiopia was only one of three independent black nations, along with Liberia and Haiti. The events of the previous two decades, encompassing the Great War and Marcus Garvey's Back-to-Africa movement, had awakened many Westerners to Africa's presence as a tangible and reachable territory. Ethiopia, the novel reminds us, had "swung into the international spotlight when it was admitted to the League of Nations in 1923, after its abolition of slavery," and once again in 1930 when Haile Selassie was crowned emperor (28). *Amiable* opens at the precise cultural moment when "the biblical legendary Ethiopia and earliest Christian state was revealed as a reality with a new significance in the minds of Aframericans" (28). As in *HNM*, in *Amiable* McKay gives us a Harlem in turmoil: it had just suffered through a major riot in 1935; it was plagued by unemployment, labor strikes, occultists, and mystics of all kinds; and it was festering with a growing number of communists, all wanting their share of "God's black sheep" (110). McKay's novel is at every turn acutely aware of this troubled history and uses any opportunity to remind the reader of events that are now, for twenty-first-century audiences, sometimes obscure.[80] What is perhaps most remarkable in McKay's didactic tactics against the "credulity of the Aframerican masses" (27) is the novel's dedication to a multitude of transnational perspectives, combined with its global historical knowledge. As the narrative unfolds, Ethiopians look upon Aframericans with surprise, disappointment, admiration. In turn, Aframericans look upon Soviets, Italians, Frenchmen, Chinese, Ethiopians, and other native Africans with a similar range of puzzlement, curiosity, suspicion, and amiability.

Often through the character of the self-taught Professor Koazhy, with his early Lenin-inspired cry "Learn, learn, and more learn" (10), and through the example of the reformed gangster turned philanthropist Pablo Peixota, McKay continually stresses the importance of historical and global political knowledge as the ideal way to combat gullibility. Clarifying the root causes of political conflict, exposing the real financial backers of various organizations—sometimes in order to cast them as villains or reveal them as quiet heroes—tracing the genealogy of certain movements, and outing prominent figures such as Father Divine as traitorous communists are among the main goals of McKay's twin works of the early 1940s, *Harlem: Negro Metropolis* and *Amiable with Big Teeth*. Whereas the former throws a great deal of information at the reader, the latter, as literature, is concerned with how to put that knowledge into narrative form and thus into practice. For example, early in the novel Pablo Peixota tries to educate the young Newton Castle about the need for blacks to organize without the aid of whites: "Your fathers and mothers didn't learn to organize their benevolent and protective societies from drinking cocktails with bohemian white folks. They learned it cleaning the white man's W.C. and over the washtub in the kitchen. And they learned their lesson hard enough to use it to give you an education. Yes *you* who are using that education now to destroy the things which your parents worked so hard to build " (30–31, original italics). Not surprisingly, "Newton Castle looked uncomfortable" (31) after this lecture, yet he stubbornly refuses to change his ways, eventually leading to the tragic death of one such white bohemian girl and the temporary breakup of his marriage. The narrative voice tips McKay's hand when it blames the Left for Castle's weakness: "Shrewd evaluators of personalities, the Marxists found Newton Castle malleable material, a type of intellectual that could be dominated and disciplined, and who once converted would remain faithful to their cause" (87–88).

The novel contextualizes historical knowledge regarding important facets of African American life by creating correspondences between the local and the global. We are reminded, for instance, that the first Harlem riot was on March 19, 1935—less than a year before the events of the novel—and that it was started because of a rumor that police had beaten and killed a Puerto Rican boy. This information is carefully juxtaposed with the fact that World War I was precipitated by the assassination of Archduke Ferdinand. McKay weaves in the rich history of Aframerican life and culture, using the novel form to move from politically significant details to culturally relevant ones. We hear of the Jubilee Singers (86) and learn that the very first Harlem Fashion Show had recently taken place (we find this out because Seraphine Peixota's ensemble is described as having been purchased by her stepfather, Pablo, at that exhibition). Notably, however, it is through the fictional club the Airplane that McKay relocates all sorts of African American trivia onto an international stage.

In the Airplane club, the owner, Buster Quincy, has hung a painting above the bar depicting "an airplane in the sky and a parachute jumper descending, who was caught up in a tall tree" (69). Most people who came into the club "thought that this picture was intended to represent the exploits of the notorious Aframerican Hubert Fauntleroy Julian, who had visited Ethiopia at the time of the coronation of Emperor Haile Selassie and by whom he was decorated and made a colonel of aviation" (69). There are many reasons to believe it might be Julian, including the fact that he *did* crash into a tree during this very same coronation ceremony.[81] But the painting's artist claims that he was really thinking of Charles Lindbergh's famous flight over the Atlantic. Quincy originally intended to call his club the Lindy Hop, but once he learned of Lindbergh's racism, he changed his mind. Lindbergh's reason for detesting Aframericans, we are told, is that "they had desecrated the sublimity of his glorious hop across the Atlantic by immortalizing it in a popular dance" (70). This episode is noteworthy not only because it reminds us of the dance name's origin but also because it reminds us that it was a black man who found the infamous Lindbergh baby's decomposing corpse, a fact that apparently "incensed" Lindbergh (70).[82] Through an anecdote about the evolution of a bar's name and its mysterious painting, McKay inserts the provenance of a popular dance, exposes the racism of the most famous white aviator of the time (Lindbergh the "Lone Eagle"), and subsequently showcases Lindbergh's black counterpart, Hubert Fauntleroy Julian (the "Black Eagle"), a man who actually fought alongside Ethiopians.[83] McKay is here employing a novelistic "strategy of reinscription," to use Aarthi Vadde's phrase, as a means of "deciphering global collectivity."[84] Nevertheless—and this is an important effect of the scene—the epistemic uncertainty as to whether the painting depicts the Lone Eagle or the Black Eagle dramatizes the struggle for historical legibility and the recognition of Aframerican involvement in both local and world events.

It is in this same chapter, "The Tower and the Airplane," that McKay most explicitly expounds on his reasons why Aframericans should develop independent archival practices as a means of extricating themselves from communist and other disingenuous influences. A group consisting of Newton Castle, Delta Castle (Newton's wife), Lij Tekla Alamaya, Seraphine Peixota, Bunchetta Facey, and Mrs. Witern runs into Professor Koazhy in the Airplane (where they will also eventually encounter Dorsey Flagg, Castle's rival). Their "serious social discussions" over the merits and pitfalls of democracy are followed by a complementary discussion of art, where education and reliable provenance are key to both exposing communists' falsifications and gaining a greater appreciation of art. Koazhy believes that his students "could be good artists only by serious research in African anatomy and physiognomy and hard apprenticeship to the execution of African and Aframerican form and figure. When colored artists painted Aframericans, he said, they turned out to be white people dyed in dark tints. Some white artists did a better job with Aframerican material" (78). When Castle retorts that colored artists should follow the Soviet example, Koazhy shows his superior knowledge of Soviet literature, stating that the "best" of it was produced during the czarist regime, and concludes: "Today the Soviet is just a prostitute of the pen for the Communist party." The outwitted Castle lashes out with insults and a threat: "When we Marxists take the POWER, I hope they make me Commissar of Education and I'll clean out the stinking academic niggerati renegades like you" (81). Unimpressed, Flagg tells Castle to be quiet, and McKay mocks Castle through a cartoonish description: "Bantam-sized Castle was right up against the powerfully built Flagg and beating his fists against his breast" (81). Indulging in a bit of slapstick modernism, as William Solomon would call it,[85] Flagg picks Castle up by the seat of his pants and then drops him to the floor. While Flagg most closely resembles McKay in build and disposition, the "teacher" of the novel is undoubtedly Koazhy: the professor literally becomes the undisguised mouthpiece for McKay's didactic wishes, announcing, "You must know the truth and Professor Koazhy is here to teach you" (10).

Importantly, this scene also depicts Koazhy as having the same desire for factual accuracy as McKay; when Koazhy is presented with the opportunity to meet a native Ethiopian, Lij Alamaya, he asks whether the young man would be willing to "tell me whether [the objects in his (Koazhy's)

Ethiopian collection] are genuine" (79). Factual authentication is raised yet again by an extended observation about the Airplane's guest book, a document filled with a series of "exciting international signatures" (70). Rather than simply including the log book as material proof of Harlem's international reach, McKay goes on to say that in the neighborhood the rumor is that "many of the signatures in the [bar]'s log book were fake" (70–71). In other words, McKay always seems to present the potential unreliability of any archival records as an inherent threat to the kinds of histories we can confidently write. As a result, the evidentiary challenges surrounding authentication become a prime concern of the narrative. Indeed, most major plot points in *Amiable* hinge on testing the authenticity of documents and people, questioning and qualifying declarations of fact, and figuring how to act in the face of fraud, propaganda, and "fake news," from this log book to the truth behind Alamaya's stolen imperial letter to the exposure of "Ethiopian Princess" Benebe Zarihana as a fraud.

The novel's opening scene stages an example of this kind of suspicion by pitting varying levels and sources of knowledge against one another, culminating in the "professor's" lesson. Even though Professor Koazhy comes to the parade uninvited, the audience demands to hear him once Peixota, Reverend Trawl, and Alamaya have spoken. Koazhy has a remarkable capacity to insert himself into the important affairs of the Harlem community; his timely interventions usually involve an important lesson to be learned, and his first speech is no exception. The professor explains to the crowd that he is wearing the uniform of an Ethiopian warrior and implores them to understand the significance of having an official "Prince of Africa" such as Alamaya in their midst. He underscores the importance of African history, of knowing the "real Ethiopia" in order to properly help her, and corrects some of the misconceptions that have already been uttered by the other speakers: "I have just heard these learned speakers inform you that the kings of Ethiopia are descended from Solomon. I am sorry to correct them, but that is not true, my friends. The dynasty of Ethiopia is older than Solomon; it is older than the Bible" (9). He then turns to Alamaya and apologizes to him, for "even the Ethiopians themselves today do not know their great history. They imagine that their Emperor is the Lion of Judah because he was descended from the Queen of Sheba. But that is history turned upside down. The Emperor of Ethiopia extended to Egypt across Judea into Persia and India" (9). Koazhy concludes by telling the crowd that "what you all should know is also what the Ethiopians should know about themselves" (10); in other words, he implores the peoples of African descent to unite through collective knowledge of their mutual provenance. Koazhy's lesson is thus directed not simply at the Harlem congregation (or the novel's readers) but also at the young Ethiopian who suddenly finds himself in North America learning about his native land.

This encounter with an educated Aframerican he considers so "extraordinarily well-informed" has a profound impact on Alamaya, who reflects that Koazhy "had made apparently authoritative and profound statements about Ethiopia of which, he, the Lij himself, was ignorant" (14). Alamaya emerges from the event feeling "that it was incumbent upon him to open his mind to study more" (14). It is significant that the novel is bookended by such a lesson; the story concludes with the suggestion that detailed knowledge of African lore ultimately proves to be a matter of life and death. Maxim Tasan's ignorance of the ritual of the Leopard Men prevents him from realizing that the white feather attached to his costume designates *him* as the blood-sacrifice victim. McKay thus positions extensive study, skepticism, and authentication as imperative ("dig down to the facts and interpret them") to foster "group survival," as given in the title of one of McKay's articles of the day.[86] The protective function of such material text-based archival practices is thereby made manifest, as it was during McKay's debate over "facts" with Powell and Schuyler, a move that further suggests the archive's multivalent status as a means of "preservation"—preservation of material and of life itself.

Although Alamaya is taught a lesson in the opening scene, his specialized knowledge and perspective as a native African often proves the most educational to others. At the first welcoming dinner for him, the conversation quickly turns to world politics. In a scene that echoes the Helen Boardman affair, Newton Castle, acting under orders from Tasan, tries to push the idea of including whites in the Hands to Ethiopia organization. Peixota objects, explaining that "the common people feel that Ethiopia was betrayed by the white nations" (19). Castle retorts that the League of Nations is, on the contrary, "joined in sanctions against Italy." But it is the Ethiopian who reveals what the sanctions really entail, schooling Castle with a vivid simile: "The sanctions are like passing a lot of resolutions and not acting on them. . . . Italy is importing all the essential things she needs. The League of Nations is like those curious creatures that I hear exist in Haiti—the zombies. Dead nations which act as if they were living without knowing they are dead" (19). Alamaya's reference to Haitian zombies is a trademark McKay moment of diasporic flair: he has an Ethiopian tell an Aframerican that the League of Nations is akin to creatures out of Caribbean folklore. When Castle tries to single out Soviet Russia as an exception, Flagg retorts, "Russia is selling more war goods to Italy than any nation" (19), echoing what McKay writes in *HNM*.[87] McKay always positions the utterances of Peixota, Flagg, Alamaya, and Koazhy—the heroes of the novel—as the most well researched, whereas the villains, Castle, Tasan, and Bishop, have misinterpreted—misread—the current political turmoil fermenting in the years leading to World War II, poisoned as they are by communist rhetoric.

The interplay between divergent political perspectives and levels of knowledge are juxtaposed with similar clashes at the cultural level, often when each side exposes its ignorance of the other. In one scene, Seraphine Peixota admiringly comments on the "lovely wine color" of Lij Alamaya's pajamas and asks if they were made in Addis Ababa. In a humorous moment tinged with orientalism, the Ethiopian replies, "No, they are your father's" (29). Attire is in fact a preferred vehicle for McKay's exposure of the cultural misconceptions held by his transnational characters. For instance, even though Alamaya is the genuine Ethiopian, he is eclipsed by Koazhy when the latter attends the parade "bedecked in a uniform so rare, so gorgeous, it made the people prance and shout with joy" (4). The "saluting dignitary," Koazhy, channels Marcus Garvey as he displays his "mailed shirt extravagantly covered with golden gleaming arabesques and a wonderfully high shako, white and surmounted by a variegated cluster of ostrich plumes," and unsheathes his sword, "brandish[ing] it at heaven" (4).[88] Immediately, "the mass roared in a frenzy" (4). In contrast, the envoy, an actual Ethiopian, dressed "in formal clothes distinguished only by a red slash aslant his breast," is given only mild applause. Alamaya is incredulous as to the behavior of "these Aftramericans," wondering why Professor Koazhy chose "to wear this barbaric fantastic costume" (6). As it turns out, Koazhy's uniform *is* authentic Ethiopian yet anachronistic, the kind "old tribal kings" (17) used to wear before Emperor Selassie's modernization of Ethiopia. The newspapers subsequently heroize Professor Koazhy for his dramatic performance, which surprises Alamaya. The young man, who is quickly being educated, uses this occasion as a lesson about the power of ornament over authenticity in the United States, a dynamic that mirrors the novel's overarching concern with the problem of authentication. Indeed, as I explore later, Alamaya's use of the imperial letter implies that he has already learned the power that anachronism can wield upon an unsuspecting public.

As an Ethiopian, Alamaya is unfamiliar with many features of African American culture; this ignorance offers McKay a dramatic and didactic occasion to look at America from a foreigner's perspective. For instance, Alamaya later learns even more about the peculiarities of attire and politics in the United States. The scene heats up when Newton Castle, sitting onstage with other members of the two Aid to Ethiopia organizations, loudly and repeatedly accuses Dorsey Flagg of being a fascist Trotskyite. In defiance, Flagg throws "off his coat and stood out conspicuously in his white shirt" (96). As the situation escalates and the angry crowd seems poised to rush the stage, Alamaya stands up and speaks in defense of Flagg, concluding his speech by "suddenly divesting himself of his coat" in order to stand alongside the equally coatless Flagg, in unity. Although some of the remaining whites in the audience utter a few "hesitant hisses," they are "immediately suppressed by the mighty applause, which broke like a thunder-clap" (97). The women rush the stage to kiss Alamaya and Flagg in "joyous demonstration" (97). Alamaya is pleased with the result of his speech, but he is puzzled as to why it received such thunderous approval. Peixota explains to the Ethiopian "that it was the unexpected gesture, throwing off his coat to shake Flagg's hand, which had fired the enthusiasm of the people" (98). Although Alamaya's gesture was done "merely from politeness," he unwittingly tapped into "one of the pillars upon which rested American diplomacy"—namely, as Peixota calls it, "shirt-sleeve diplomacy" (98).

But the cultural and racial lessons learned by the *lij*—and those he in turn gives to others—are not always welcome. For instance, Alamaya doesn't understand the American concept of "passing" and is upset when Seraphine tells him they are light-skinned enough to "pass" successfully (165). Rather than apprehending passing as one of the tactics used by some ethnic Americans to navigate sociopolitical constraints, the African's perspective exposes the irrationality and inequality enveloping the United States. In McKay's novelistic scheme, Alamaya's inability to "understand the American point of view" (165), as Seraphine puts it, is precisely why his presence can become a source of pride and hope for Aframericans. For Bunchetta Facey—Seraphine's intellectual friend—Alamaya represents the "human point of view" and, as such, "more important than the American point of view" (165). Bunchetta pushes her transnational humanism further, lamenting the blinders of nationalistic perspective: "It is the American point of view, the German point of view, the British point of view and all the different nations' point of view that makes a mess of the world" (165). Her statement echoes what McKay wrote to Langston Hughes years before he wrote the novel: although "I write of America as home," he said, "I am really a poet without a country. Maybe that is why I have an international mind."[89]

One of the novel's richest transnational scenes is the party held by Mrs. Witern in honor of Lij Alamaya, gathering as it does a wide array of foreign nationals in the same room. Among them is a thoughtless white British man named Aubrey Pickett—friend to the novel's chief antagonist, Maxim Tasan. Pickett accuses Alamaya of suffering from "C.P.T." because the latter doesn't arrive to the party until midnight. Pickett says, "I see, already you are keeping C.P.T. . . . Well, it wouldn't be strange for an African" (39). Alamaya has no idea what the abbreviation C.P.T. stands for, but interestingly neither do two of the Harlemites present. Pickett is forced to explain it and does so "with an amused expression as if he were imparting some special knowledge of Aframerican similarity to Africa: "C.P.T. is Colored People's Time, of course, because as they say, 'Colored people are always late'" (40). Alamaya is "surprised and nettled by the stress Pickett put on 'Colored'" as he "had not been long enough in America to think in terms of being 'colored'" (40). Alamaya thinks of himself as "an Ethiopian, and African," as opposed to "colored," so he is here receiving an American lesson he does not wish to learn, one that points to the systemic oppression suffered by the Aframerican minority in the United States. The Ethiopian's reply not only positions his African perspective as an advantage but demonstrates his superior historical knowledge: "Perhaps *colored* people are never early, because they can afford to be late. They have nothing in the world to hurry about. But you English have everything. Yet you were late in Asia in 1931, you were late in Africa in 1935 and perhaps you will soon be late in Europe and in Britain itself" (40, emphasis in original). In a brilliant move, Alamaya takes Pickett's racist stereotype of ethnic time and through the invocation of historical facts turns it into a critique of the British Empire's poor timing.[90] Japan seized Manchuria from China in 1931, and the year 1935 saw Mussolini's invasion of Ethiopia. Composing this scene in 1941, McKay had the advantage of knowing the development of events leading into World War II and could thus give his Ethiopian envoy what seems like perspicacious wisdom and clairvoyance. Again, historical knowledge is tactical, deployed as protection from oppression and ethnic profiling.

Pickett is saved further embarrassment by the arrival of Seraphine, Bunchetta, and three German refugees—a doctor, a professor of anthropology, and a young artist. The scene continues the theme of misconceptions regarding the African diaspora when Bunchetta relates that Fischer, the anthropologist, said that "the Ethiopians are not really an African people in the sense that Aframericans are, that they are a Semitic people like the Arabs" (41). Alamaya's response to this statement is final: "Ethiopians don't think so. We call ourselves a black African nation" (41). In a moment that recalls the four photographs by Martin Smith and Marvin Smith gathered under the caption "Types of Harlem Women" in *HNM*,[91] the girls then proceed to theorize about which peoples of the diaspora their bodies most look like. Bunchetta insists that she "could pass for a typical Ethiopian girl," but Seraphine embarrassingly reminds her that since Bunchetta is already "passing as a Balinese in the village," she wants "to be everything"

(41). Pressed to weigh in, the lone African in the room says that Ethiopia boasts "various types [of women], just like in Harlem," but that another girl present at the party, Miss Gloria Kendall, "could be a typical Ethiopian girl" (41). This moment, unbeknownst to the reader, plants the seed of later chicanery perpetrated by Tasan—who is present during this conversation— in which Gloria will be turned into the fake Ethiopian princess Benebe Zarihana. The scene also foreshadows the romantic union of Alamaya and Gloria that occurs in the novel's concluding sections.

The presence of German Jewish citizens in the novel, "some of the first refugees from Nazi Germany" (39), attests to McKay's notion that "the Jews of Germany are being systematically reduced to the status of Negroes in America," as he wrote in a piece for the *Jewish Frontier* in October 1937.[92] McKay felt that Aframericans had much to learn from Jews in matters of group unity and expounded on that notion in *HNM*: "Jewish intellectuals . . . saw the unconscionable suffering and economic disadvantage of the members of their own group. . . . They went to their own people and helped to organize them into unions."[93] In *Amiable*'s party scene, one of the refugees, Dr. Schmidt, uncomfortably observes that "a colored person is as rare as a red Indian" (43) in downtown Manhattan and wonders whether there is any "popular resentment" against the fact that black Americans are more or less ghettoized in Harlem. He asks whether Harlemites feel "cut off from the fuller life of the city" and reminds them of "what is happening to the Jews in Germany" (43). The ghettoized status of Aframericans in the United States becomes a matter of international political significance, specifically as a point the communists use to gain the black community's loyalty. Maxim Tasan explains to Claxon, the black director of the Interlink,[94] that "Aframericans are like a small foreign nation within the United States. As foreign as the Chinese in China and Eskimos in Alaska. Did you ever think of that?" Claxon concurs, adding that "Aframericans have become so matter-of-course among us that few white persons realize they are practically strangers among us" (170). McKay here casts the invisibility of Aframericans as a particularly American defect of perception. That Aframericans are "a colony of subject people within the nation" (170) is a point the novel makes on numerous occasions, significantly both by the sympathetic heroes of the novel and by its main villain, Maxim Tasan.

Underscoring an important difference, the perspicacious Peixota is convinced that "short of exile or extermination, what the Nazis are attempting in Germany is to reduce the Jews socially and politically to the level of colored people in America," and he provocatively wonders whether "the Nazis have made a secret comprehensive study of the laws and customs covering the status of the Aframerican minority" (254). On the one hand, Peixota is "excited to think how closely the problem of Ethiopia and Europe parallels the Aframericans in America," but on the other he is saddened when "liberal whites" tell Aframericans that they are "better off than Jews in Germany" simply because of their ability to "organize and protest." This kind of thinking, he argues, also belongs to "the big guns of the Popular Front" and misleads "well-meaning whites" into weighing "Aframerican minority problems by a European standard. They quite forget that our group position has never approached the high estate of the Jews in Germany" (254). Peixota's comment provides the necessary distinction that balances the other characters' more naive forms of equating Jews and Aframericans and is a means of fleshing out McKay's own position.

Earlier in the novel, when Tasan stresses that "the white man also can be sincere in his attitude towards the colored man," Peixota's response further echoes McKay's own convictions: "I have never doubted that a white man can be sincere towards the colored man. Many are as individuals. But we are all subject to limitations. Our views are influenced by our training and environment" (59). For black men such as Peixota and McKay, white communists such as Tasan only "wanted power over the life and thought of people, to turn their mind to Soviet Russia as a Promised Land." For this reason, Peixota is "convinced that the man [Tasan] cared little about Ethiopia" (61).[95] Although Peixota's streetwise instincts allow him to size up Tasan right away, Tasan remains a mystery to most Harlemites, as hard evidence about him is scarce yet rumors abound: "Some said he was a Russian and agent of Stalin; others thought he was an agent of Trotsky and still others believed he was agent at large of the Communist International.

An anti-Communist Indian Nationalist said that he had seen Tasan in Shanghai and that he had arrived in the United States by way of the Pacific" (90). Many find it strange, we are told by the narrative voice, that such an important person hangs out almost exclusively with the "comparatively insignificant Aframerican group" (90). This key observation provides a two-fold portrait of the time: on the one hand, McKay suggests that Aframeri-cans have a cripplingly low opinion of themselves, and, on the other, Tasan's interest in Aframericans implicitly underscores how the Popular Front real-izes the power Aframericans potentially have and how instrumental they might be in world affairs should a strong communist foothold be obtained in Harlem.

Yet despite the Peixota clan's best efforts, Maxim Tasan, that "Commu-nist hyena disguised as shepherd dog," is successful in wreaking "havoc in the sheepfold under cover of darkness," as McKay described the actual sit-uation in Harlem in an article for the *New Leader*.[96] By exposing the extent of Tasan's machinations, the novel ultimately and with the mercilessness of satire exposes the many nefarious ways in which the Comintern and its unwitting supporters ceaselessly undermine black self-determination. By the end of the novel, a string of false publicity forces Pablo Peixota to step down from his role as president of Hands to Ethiopia; Professor Koazhy is evicted from the home where he held free classes for local students and where he kept his prized collection of African artifacts; and Dorsey Flagg is fired from his teaching job. Tasan engineers this chain of misfortunes, a trick enabled by his theft of Alamaya's imperial letter. Having stolen the precious document the night he met Alamaya, Tasan leaks a story to the press that Emperor Selassie never sent an envoy to the United States to speak on his behalf. Since the letter is the only material evidence that can refute these emerging media reports, Hands to Ethiopia is disgraced. Peix-ota is forced to step down as its president, and Tasan swoops in to coerce Alamaya into joining White Friends of Ethiopia, the organization that now represents the last and best hope to continue raising funds for the cause. Amid this deception—which, I would like to underscore, revolves around documents, an imperial letter and printed media—comes the central hoax of the novel: the sudden appearance of "Princess Benebe Zarihana" of

Ethiopia. Alamaya, whose presence as an Ethiopian lends a necessary authenticity to the spectacle, is forced to act as her "interpreter" in return for continued, Comintern-funded financial assistance. McKay, however, does not provide conclusive evidence of Tasan's elaborate scheme until late in the novel, when Seraphine Peixota, the daughter of the former president of Hands to Ethiopia, finds a secret cache of documents—a hidden archive—in a safe inside Maxim Tasan's apartment.

In the wake of Ethiopia's defeat, and having been tricked, as part of Tasan's ongoing efforts to humiliate Pablo, into marrying "Dandy" Nordling, a moronic white Communist Party member, Seraphine has now finally begun to grow suspicious of Tasan. Left alone at his apartment and having fortuitously come into possession of his lost set of keys, Seraphine digs around until she eventually finds and unlocks the chest where Tasan keeps his secret documents. Once Seraphine opens the safe, she discovers "a lot of cancelled cheques, many letters and various business papers fastened together with clips," as well as "a large thick envelope marked 'Ethiopia'" containing "half a dozen photographs of Princess Benebe in different costumes and poses and four of Gloria Kendall, the young woman to whose job Seraphine succeeded at the office of the Friends of Ethiopia" (208). Seraphine immediately realizes that Benebe and Kendall are the same person; hard to believe such "an elaborate trick," she thinks, "but the evidence was right there." On the back of one of the photographs, she finds a note in Alamaya's handwriting, reading, "This costume is Persian—unsuitable" (208). Sifting further into the "Ethiopia" envelope, Seraphine finds Alamaya's stolen imperial letter, and the extent of Maxim Tasan's "vile frame-up" is finally revealed. Not only is Tasan responsible for the fall of her father's organization, but he has also manipulated Alamaya into going along with the princess deception and is using him as a consultant to make sure they get her costumes right. On a wider register, McKay is also demonstrating how those Aframericans who have had "a love affair" with the communists have been duped.

What I also want to stress here is, first, the co-opting of black intellectuals and, second, how McKay as a novelist opts to expose the degrees of factual deceit the communists have perpetrated: Seraphine's unearthing of material evidence. In having Seraphine finally take control over her own life at this juncture in the novel, McKay suggestively ties agency to archival practice. Further, in needing Alamaya's specialized knowledge of proper Ethiopian dress to weed out the bad costumes, Tasan implicitly reveals his own cultural ignorance, a flaw that will literally lead to his downfall in the final chapter when Koazhy's Senegambians throw him off the top of a building in a dark Harlem alleyway. And yet what comes to complicate Seraphine's discovery and the novel as a whole is that the evidence she unearths is at once authentic and fabricated.

As it turns out—and here is the real kicker—even Alamaya's imperial letter, retrieved by Seraphine and later taken back to the Ethiopian, proves problematic as material evidence. Though the narrative makes the letter seem "the most authentic thing of all," Alamaya later reveals that it was not altogether "genuine" (251). At the end of the novel, after Ethiopia has been defeated and interest in his homeland seems to have disappeared from the sidewalks of Harlem, Alamaya finally reveals the true provenance of the letter. The document is in fact a remnant of the pan-African movement, written at the height of the Harlem Renaissance when the government of Ethiopia was convinced by "prominent Africans, Haitians, Cubans, Aframericans and others . . . in the idea of sending a mission" to America (251). Although the "plan was abandoned just before it was put into execution," Alamaya eventually got hold of the letter that was meant for "one of the originally designated members of the postponed mission" (251). As Alamaya humorously explains, because "so few people can read the official Amharic language of Ethiopia," he decided the letter might still work twelve years after it was issued, even though he knew that "it couldn't stand close scrutiny" (251)—just as Koazhy, in the novel's opening scene, dons an anachronistic Ethiopian costume so as to better dazzle the crowd. In other words, through an undisclosed deceit, Alamaya appropriates the document and belatedly reendows it with what archivists would call its primary value by forcing it back into a new lifecycle or, perhaps, the lifecycle it was always meant to have.

Because this belated reendowment goes to the heart of what I mean by "archival," what I wish to stress here too is the *delay*, the twelve-year delay, in making use of the document and the black intellectual's ability to remain authentic—to his goals, his true purpose, his ethics—while simultaneously being disingenuous. For McKay, the fight waged over Harlem's "poor black sheep" (110) hinges on the use and close scrutiny of archival documents as well as the realization that these documents are always vulnerable to exploitation.

ROMAN À CLEF: INSIDE MCKAY'S SECRET CACHE

Tasan and Alamaya aren't the only ones who have been tampering with material evidence; McKay, too, played with the historical record. In real life, the man who presented a fake Ethiopian princess to the Harlem world was not a Comintern secret agent but rather a former baseball star turned public-relations man named Chappy Gardner. Gardner, "the black PT Barnum,"[97] was an original member of McKay's Negro Writers' Guild, one of the few who agreed with McKay that whites should be banned from the guild (see figure 2.2).[98] He worked as an arts critic for the *Pittsburgh Courier*, writing on film and theater, but in his youth he had been an important early figure on the black sports scene, something he capitalized on later when he entered showbiz. The FWP writers composed portraits of Gardner and traced the arrival as well as the subsequent exposure of "Princess" Heshla Tamanya in the local newspapers (see figure 2.3).[99] In the FWP's *Almanac for New Yorkers 1938*, the entry for July 20 reads: "Harlemites chuckled this day in 1935 when it was learned that Chappy Gardner, Negro press-agent, had hoaxed the entire metropolitan press with his story of an 'Ethiopian Princess.'" For *Amiable*, why did McKay make this hoax the handiwork of a communist secret agent rather than that of a black entrepreneur, as in the actual story? The move might not be "genuine," to quote Alamaya, but it becomes the novelist's best means of providing "authentic" reality of life as he saw it. Through this plot twist, McKay is able to lend credence to much of what he had denounced about the Communist Party

FIGURE 2.2. "Negro Writers Guild of New York City in Conference during Strike May 25, 1937. L. to r. Chappy Gardner, Ted Yates, Floyd Snelson, Wilford Bain." As inscribed by Claude McKay on the back of this photo. Photographer unknown.

Source: Negro Writers Guild, May 25, 1937, box 18, folder 579, Claude McKay Collection, Collection of American Literature, Beinecke Rare Book and Manuscript Library, Yale.

in his previous book, *Harlem: Negro Metropolis*, where he writes: "Communists can stage some of the most spectacular affairs and could bring obscure Negroes into the spotlight to speak in splendid halls before huge audiences."[100]

Just as McKay alleviates Aframerican guilt by planting the public deception onto guilty white (Red) hands, he also idealizes and synthesizes the qualities he admires in creating his novel's heroes. As Edwards and I touch on in our introduction to the novel, Lij Tekla Alamaya is a composite character that seems based largely on Dr. Malaku Bayen, a friend of McKay's who was an Ethiopian emissary and who acted as director to the organization Harlem United Aid to Ethiopia (later named Ethiopia World

FIGURE 2.3. "Princess" Heshla Tamanya (*seated*), whose real name was Iselyn Harvey (née Smith), with two unidentified companions, 1935.

Source: Associated Press.

Federation). Bayen was the man who took the pilot Hubert Fauntleroy Julian over to Ethiopia in 1930.[101] He and McKay shared the same opinion regarding black group unity; William Scott writes that, as a spokesman, Bayen "was careful to stress the importance of international black unity and the responsibility of black people to each other."[102] McKay praises Bayen in *HNM*, mentions that he is "recently deceased" (he died in May 1940), and includes a photo of him taken in 1937, in which he is accompanied by another Ethiopian named Lij Araya Abebe.[103]

The character of Professor Koazhy is likely a hybrid of Dr. Willis N. Huggins and Charles C. Seifert. Dr. Huggins was a notable yet controversial African American historian and public intellectual "who opposed the Communists in the Aid-to-Ethiopia Campaign." In *HNM*, McKay thanks

Huggins and meticulously provides material evidence of communist propaganda circulated against Huggins.[104] Huggins's body was found on July 5, 1941, after a six-month disappearance, likely due to foul play; although the authorities declared his death a suicide, many at the time believed that unknown assailants killed him. This scandal took place *while* McKay was writing *Amiable*; after he asked his friend Simon Williamson to interview Mrs. Huggins, he received the following reply: "She seems difficult to find at home since the disappearance of the professor. I can't say I blame her for that."[105] This event may have helped inspire Tasan's "final fate" in the novel, which reverses history: this time, the "unknown assailants" (the costumed Senegambians) get rid of the white communist.

As for Charles C. Seifert, even though he "published no books and very little was published about him while he lived . . . his impact among influential people in Harlem was great."[106] As Robert Hill reports, Seifert was "one of the most renowned of the early black bibliophiles and pioneers in the recovery of African-American history."[107] A member of the Universal Negro Improvement Association, he, like Professor Koazhy in the novel, was a collector of African memorabilia, a historian, an antiquarian, and a local mentor to young intellectuals, opening the Ethiopian School of Research History in a building that also housed his large collection. One of his pupils was none other than Marcus Garvey, whom Seifert met shortly after Garvey's arrival to the United States. Hill suggests that it was Seifert "who gave Garvey the idea for a black merchant marine line in late 1918 that would become the Black Star Line."[108] The respect Seifert enjoyed can be seen in Elmer Wendell Dean's story "An Elephant Lives in Harlem." Dean dedicates the story to Seifert "because his thoughts are set to shake loose many logs of error, ignorance and prejudice that clutter the river of life. . . . He is considered by at least one to be the greatest thinker of our times."[109] Thanks to McKay's correspondence with Max Eastman, we know that in August 1934 McKay was living in the home of what he called "an eccentric old Negro who titles himself Professor" in return for "doing part-time work writing history to prove that African blacks were the founders of civilization." That man was likely Seifert, and although the work and research proved to be interesting for McKay, he confessed to Eastman that he nevertheless deplored the arrangement because "the old fool" was "always butting in on me with senile talk about ancient African glory."[110] Clearly, McKay did not share young Dean's high regard of Seifert.

Yet in *Amiable* Professor Koazhy is portrayed wholly positively and in fact turns out to be the quiet hero of the entire tale, always showing up at crucial times or waiting behind the scenes for the right moment to say or do the right thing. His league of Senegambians is an example of "behind-the-scenes" group unity put to work in protecting the interests of the Afra-merican community. Again, the literary manifestation of Huggins/Seifert points to historically active members of Harlem's intelligentsia and suggests that, given the right circumstances, these bibliophiles could and perhaps should rise as leaders. In point of fact, McKay inserts a fantastic scene in *Amiable* where Professor Koazhy and the real Sufi Abdul Hamid collabo-rate to stop a group of picketing communists led by Newton Castle.[111] At this anti-Italian gathering based on an actual riot that took place in 1936, Koazhy and Sufi Hamid whisper to each other, then suddenly the profes-sor "clapped his hands and boomed, 'Senegambians! Senegambians!' as the Sufi shouts, 'Any Sufists in the crowd, step forward!'" (111–12). Their respec-tive secret societies, united and unafraid to rumble, snuff out the demon-stration. Through such speculative literary reimagining of the archive, McKay shows what his political and cultural ideals would look like in practice.

Alongside Koazhy and Abdul Hamid—who needs no embellishment and appears as himself in the novel—the Honduras-born character Pablo Peixota is McKay's manifestation of a mature Harlem leader. Peixota is in part an idealized version of Casper Holstein, the reformed gangster fondly represented in *HNM* and in part an evolution of protagonists from McKay's previous novels. Holstein was "a wealthy Harlem Negro" who had made his fortune in the numbers game of the 1920s but now "dealt in real estate," just like Peixota.[112] According to McKay, Holstein was "outstand-ing and upstanding in the community" as "the only" Harlem philanthro-pist donating money "to Negro colleges and charitable institutions" and "scholarships for brilliant Negro students, who were too poor to enter high school and college."[113] Holstein also provided financial assistance to destitute individuals and families and often did so anonymously.[114] McKay further admired the "artistic side" of "Holstein's extraordinary activity," for he supported writers, artists, and even established a "fund for literary prizes" through *Opportunity*, a magazine to which McKay contributed articles. Holstein's political involvement came in the 1930s when he helped organize the Virgin Islanders—he was a native of the Virgin Islands—to "change from military to civil administration." But as a result of "his aggressive part in Virgin Isles politics," McKay tells us, "Holstein drew the enmity of powerful politicians" and was eventually imprisoned in 1937 for being a numbers operator, even though "he had long since quit the racket." Since his release from prison, McKay regretfully adds, Holstein had become "more withdrawn than ever."[115] One can thus detect in McKay's fictional handling of Peixota his fantasy of Holstein's continued political involvement.

On a literary register, Peixota represents McKay's answer to those critics who saw him as giving debased portraits of criminal and working-class Aframericans. Like Holstein, Peixota has risen from a past as a numbers-game boss to become in middle age a respected community leader and philanthropist. As such, Peixota is a recasting of the vibrant and rugged truant street criminals who are the protagonists of *Home to Harlem* (1928) and *Banjo* (1929), where the criminal becomes a mature and wise family man. As Cooper puts it, "For McKay, the true exemplars of the [black] race were uprooted but self-sufficient urban drifters," and McKay was convinced that "only by wedding themselves to such men in their natural, unself-conscious striving for fellowship could the educated 'leaders' of the race achieve genuine liberation for themselves and their people."[116] In McKay's early fiction, the prominent example of an intellectual leader learning such lessons in black autarky is Ray, the Haitian intellectual who tramps around with Jake Brown in *Home to Harlem* and later with Banjo in *Banjo*. *Amiable*'s relation to this major vein in McKay's novels is the education of Alamaya under Pablo Peixota, who in his youth embodied the Jake Brown type but has since then grown into a respected businessman. In Peixota, McKay synthetizes the qualities he most admires and desires in black leadership: streetwise flair, philanthropic generosity, internationally informed political savvy, an anticommunist stance, and problack self-reliance. In a mirroring of the Haitian Ray's union with Jake Brown and Banjo in McKay's early novels, the Ethiopian Alamaya ends *Amiable* by taking a job under Peixota's wing. The joining of a homeless African intellectual with a reformed American gangster is indicative of McKay's evolution as a politicized novelist, a development also manifested in the character of Dorsey Flagg.

The misunderstood Flagg is notably Peixota's closest acolyte and just happens to be the character closest to McKay himself. Through Flagg, McKay erects his defense as an independent intellectual and clarifies his position in relation to communism and the racial aesthetics inherited from the New Negro movement. Like McKay, Flagg is accused of being a fascist and Trotskyite and defends himself from these accusations, explaining that he is neither a fascist nor a communist nor a friend of Leon Trotsky, but, "as a democrat, he had defended [Trotsky's] right to express his opinions. He had opposed the Popular Front and its drive among Aframericans, because it was promoted by the Soviet Dictatorship" (76). Adam Clayton Powell had similarly tried "to label [McKay] a Trotskyite" in his response to McKay's article "Labor Steps Out in Harlem."[117] In retaliation, McKay had reiterated that he was not a Trotskyite or any kind of communist and fearlessly added that he did "have a high respect for Trotsky as a thinking man [but] none for Stalin."[118] Powell wasn't alone in his view of McKay; as Cooper explains in his biography of McKay, "many believed that McKay had gone to Russia in 1922 with the American Communist delegation as a party member," and others "thought he had become a follower of Leon Trotsky," but, of course, "both views were wrong, and McKay was anxious to set the record straight."[119] Because both *A Long Way from Home* and *Harlem: Negro Metropolis* had failed to "set the record straight" to McKay's satisfaction, the Flagg character in *Amiable* seems to represent his continued effort to clarify his exact stance. Both Peixota and Flagg are noted for their "deep detestation of the Communists from observation of their propaganda tactics in the Aframerican community" (77) and their equal contempt for the fascists because of their attacks on Ethiopia, their "proscribing [of] the Jews as colored people were proscribed" (77), and Hitler's statement in *Mein Kampf* "that black people were half apes"—a quote given three times in *Amiable* (77, 149, 230).

It is also through Flagg that McKay voices his opinion on the urgent question of the relation between "art and race" in a chapter that stands out from the rest of the novel and demonstrates how the core debates of the New Negro movement were still very much in play in the late 1930s and early 1940s. Indeed, Alain Locke's imposing book *The Negro in Art: A Pictorial Record of the Negro Artist and of the Negro Theme in Art* (1940) was released the year before McKay composed *Amiable*. In the chapter "Art and Race," which serves overall as a critique of white patronage, the Popular Front sponsors a meeting to honor the work of the Aframerican artist Dèdé Lee to which Flagg is invited by mistake. Early in his career, as a way of breaking into the art world, Dèdé Lee—née Dixon Davis Lee—had been advised by a white critic to "make your Aframericans brutal and bloody and big with life—'bawdacious' as they say in Harlem." The critic encouraged him to "do caricatures of the better-known Broadway sepians, so that the public can guess who they are without their names being mentioned" (220). As a result of applying this method, "Lee overcame the unconscious habit of making his Aframerican features appear like 'stereotype whites,' but he could not make them look human. Upon the powerful energetic bodies he invariably placed gorilla-like heads, with incredibly vacant, vicious and depraved faces" (221). But the final masterstroke to Lee's work was how he also included "a white figure as a foil to his black, in which he reverted to his originally unsophisticated manner: the white faces were always rose-pink sweet" (221). The white art world praises Lee's work as possessing a "profound social significance," and the powerful art critic Magnus Chetwind declares that in Lee's "miracle of achievement" one can find "the hidden qualities, the unknown soul of a people" (226). Tellingly, the praise Lee receives from white critics mirrors the praise *Home to Harlem* enjoyed in 1928. Chetwind's argument is that because Aframericans are "a humiliated and crushed minority in our midst," their soul is "violent, bestial, and monstrous," features vividly portrayed in Lee's paintings. Chetwind's assessment is followed by Prudhomme Bishop's own lofty words on art: "Art is the glory of success and a tribute to the visibility of intelligence and the germs of culture in the crucible of common understanding. It is the yardstick to measure the test of achievement and the honey that sweetens the precious nectar of the beautiful life, when we partake of the melodious wine of the sacrament of human fellowship" (226). For Bishop—a black associate of Tasan's in his role as president of the Equal Rights Action and thus a rival to Peixota—black artists have been raised "to attain the benevolent standard" of "the common culture of our American heritage," and in Dèdé Lee they have for the "first time" approached America as a whole "with the burnt-offering of a perfected artist, an expert in the execution of the general character of a race" (227).[120]

Hearing this assessment from his place in the audience at the meeting, the irate Flagg cannot resist voicing his disagreement and forcibly takes the stage. His speech reads like McKay's apologia for the motivations behind the writing of *Amiable*. With the rise of fascism in Europe, Flagg declares, "These are times when minority problems which are always grave have become acute," and they affect not only "the social and political status" of minorities but also "their special artistic and literary contributions" (228). He goes on: "The rise to power of National Socialism has focused the mind of the world on the words 'minority' and 'race,'" and Aframericans represent "the largest minority and the greatest problem to the American nation." "Against the threat of Nazism," Flagg declares, "all minority groups in this country are taking stock of themselves," and it is in this highly charged context and volatile times that Dèdé Lee's drawings "are held up to national opprobrium by a member of their own group." Although Flagg hopes Lee "makes plenty of money," he "cannot agree with Mr. Chetwind that these graphic delineations of certain Aframerican types represent the soul of my people." "What soul?" he asks. "It is not the soul of myself or any of the Aframericans here in this gallery. It is not the soul of our brothers and sisters who work for you white folk as porters, errand boys, elevator operators, waiters, cooks and chauffeurs" (229–30). Flagg proceeds to describe how he interprets Lee's Aframerican figures, and his assessment is reminiscent of some of the criticism McKay's early novels received, especially in the black press:

These drawings are violent, bestial and monstrous. They represent the extreme of depravity, imbecility and criminality. I cannot say they are

immoral, for to be moral or immoral one must be human. But these Aframerican types are all inhuman. Look at them again and see as I see:
colored persons snarling like hounds, posed like baboons in the chain
gang, working like zombies in the cotton field, crazy with unreasonable
anger. . . . [Y]ou expect my people to accept this distorted exhibition of
their race as human. We will not accept it. If we do, then Hitler is right
when he says in *Mein Kampf* that Negroes are half-apes. And the South
would be certainly correct in its attitude, for such types as these should
be quarantined. . . . We refuse to accept this exhibition as the interpretation of the Aframerican soul. It is if anything an assault upon the sanctuary of our soul. Praise the work of Mr. Lee for its power, its originality and artistry. But do not try to convince us that of such is the black
man's soul.

(230–31)

Just as McKay explained in his letter to Max Eastman, he discovered in
1941 that the consulting of "notes and newspaper stories of the period" made
it "impossible to keep politics out" of an aesthetic project that addressed
"minority problems." Flagg is here stressing the exact same point by invok-
ing the recent rise of fascism in Europe as the main reason behind his
objections to the wide appraisal of Lee's monstrous representations of
Aframericans.[121]

The black press had criticized McKay's early novels for their animalistic
portraits of certain black types and for, according to Tyrone Tillery, their
"treatment of lower-class black life as a slanderous attempt to glorify the
lowest class of Negro life." This point of contention among black intellectuals
and artists, Tillery underscores, "struck at the heart of one of the fundamental themes of the Renaissance: the relationship between art and society,
and most particularly at the problem of defining a writer's obligation—if
any—to society."[122] In *Amiable*, McKay reenters that debate, though with a
radically different contribution. Flagg's added qualification that Lee's work
should still be praised for "its power, its originality and artistry" suggests
that McKay was not apologizing for his earlier works; he still believed in
total artistic freedom (and certainly the need for artists to get *paid*).

Flagg's improvised speech on racial art, therefore, is the strange fruit of the politicization of McKay's own mutable aesthetic at this late stage in his novelistic career.

"TO BE CONTINUED"

McKay's unpublished essay "Group Life and Literature," written toward the end of his stint in the FWP, can guide us through this morass of literature's relation to minority group life, politics, and society. Here, McKay confirms his belief that writers who primarily treat questions of prejudice, disenfranchisement, discrimination, and segregation are only creating a "literature of protest" and that "such subjects are not suitable for literary treatment."[123] Although he admits that "the literature of protest requires a special passion and outlook," he quickly warns—recalling Ralph Ellison's later essays—that "colored writers should bear in mind that despite demarcations and barriers their group life is not a gesture of eternal protest. Our life follows the common pattern, even like that of other groups or nations of people who have existed under oppression, such as: the Irish, Greeks, Jews, Indians, Chinese." In the essay, McKay then proceeds to group different creative writers according to basic genres, differentiating between whites and blacks. First, he names the "field of manners and customs," then "the psychological" novel—in which he includes modernists such as Proust, Joyce, Henry James, and Lawrence. Next comes the "sociological field," which has "attracted the elite of the Afro-American group as investigators," but sadly—in a typical McKay dig at fellow writers—a "real novelist" has yet to "emerge from among them." For McKay, the "great field of literature vaster than any is the romantic," and he names his friend Countee Cullen, the "charming poet of our group," as its shining example. He then moves to the "field of the lower depths of rural and urban life," naming Zola and Gorky as European exemplars and none other than himself as the only "colored" writer "truly representative of this field. My novels, Home to Harlem and Banjo belong to it." His next statement reads like a later maturation of his piece "A Negro Writer to His Critics" (1932) and sees a steadfast McKay still refusing to back down: "It is not my intention to explain or defend my own works. I do not think there need be any apology for a novel about the submerged world of the colored man. For the fact stands that the great majority of colored people live in the lower depths."[124]

Interestingly, McKay ends "Group Life and Literature" with an appeal for the "minor field" of "the historical romance," announcing that "our group has need of a great novelist in the historical field. A novelist who could depict the enthralling romance of the lives of the towering figures of the colored world."[125] Just a few years earlier, he had proposed a few such projects to Nancy Cunard as possible contributions to her anthology *Negro*.[126] He concludes his essay with a list of such towering historical figures of black diaspora, followed by the enigmatic teaser "(to be continued)."[127] *Amiable with Big Teeth* is not a typical example of historical fiction—it chooses the immediate past as its historical context rather than a *longue durée* throwback; it is instead something McKay somewhat paradoxically describes in a letter as "a contemporary historical tale."[128] Yet as a roman à clef it employs the same archival tactics, using historical figures and material evidence gathered through extensive research to weave a dramatic tale. In that sense, McKay did follow through in his handwritten postscript, "to be continued," when he depicted "the enthralling romance of the lives of the towering figures of the colored world" of the Harlem of 1936 in *Amiable* and tried his hand at becoming the novelist he felt his group so sorely needed. In such a context, it is not surprising that McKay, a writer who once seemed to thrive on heated conflicts and disagreements, was left "chagrined and depressed" when Dutton editor John Macrae brutally and without proper explanations rejected the novel.[129]

So what happened to Claude McKay? What had life, communist hyenas, and his archival practices wrought upon the beleaguered novelist? Had he forgotten Louise Bryant's advice, "Don't try to force your stories with propaganda. If you write a good story, that will be the biggest propaganda"?[130] Or did McKay, having realized "that the Communists manipulate real issues to promote their propaganda,"[131] now want to enact his own revisionist retaliation, to manipulate the issues as an independent fiction

CLAUDE MCKAY'S ARCHIVAL REBIRTH

writer? If we think back to the Joycean declaration that opens this chapter, the Harlem we could rebuild out of the protean blueprints of McKay's oeuvre would be both historically faithful and counterfactual. Its archival quality depicts a pastness that never was, one that would be refuted by documentary evidence, yet that nevertheless feels true and somehow seems to reflect the zeitgeist of its moment. Despite McKay's investment in factual accuracy backed by material evidence, he litters his novel with forgeries: when the *lij*'s official letter proves to be a "fake," we are reminded that archival material also depends on narrative and is thereby ceaselessly contaminated by what Marilyn Booth calls the "interested pressures that shape narrative."[132] Alamaya's use of the imperial document is the quintessential example of McKay's own archival sensibility, guided as it is by his own sense of morality regarding group unity and suffering from outdatedness. McKay's urgent revisionist history of 1936 Harlem suggests that the archive of "available historical narratives" was "codif[ying] moments of political failure and weakness"[133] and that his novel was meant to recodify them into triumphs and strength. As McKay wrote to the director of the Julius Rosenwald Fund, Edward Embree, just prior to undertaking *Amiable*, "I believe that the Negro minority stands in need of a new orientation of positive thinking in relation to its adjustment with the forces of labor and the majority in general."[134] By 1941, the picture looked grim: Huggins, Bayen, and Sufi Abdul Hamid were dead; Holstein was just out of jail; and Seifert was sort of a crank. Instead of depicting a series of actual leadership tragedies, McKay's revisionist history put a positive, empowering spin on these facts—his novel becomes an answer to the question posed by Saidiya Hartman: "How can a narrative of defeat enable a place for the living or envision an alternate future?"[135]

As McKay observed in his working notes for *HNM*, "Behind the headlines lies the real throbbing life of Harlem";[136] in other words, the archive can provide only a skeletonized version of life, hence the need for the literary. By ultimately redeploying his carefully compiled records in the service of an alternative history, McKay's novel provides the necessary narrative to make a new, recuperative diasporic archive accessible. As Laura Winkiel suggests in the context of Cunard's anthology, such an archival sensibility "depends on the recontextualization and revision of a hidden past in order to construct a new kind of future."[137] By giving living form to the events of 1936 in his novel, McKay approaches the archival as a state of hibernation in an Ellisonian sense, as a "covert preparation for a more overt action,"[138] and thus fashions his novel, as his FWP colleague Ralph Ellison would say, "as a raft of hope."[139] The nonfictional *HNM* could go only so far in fulfilling McKay's vision; without a novelization, the intensity of forces, the human interplay, the savory characters would be lost to history, invisible, relegated to the "unprocessed" archive.

For McKay, therefore, the archive is not a positivist repository of *facts* that then become history but rather a source of *clues* that can position the reader in an empowered relation to past and future, lending itself to aesthetic interpretation. I have in mind here the sense Franco Moretti gives to clues in *Signs Taken for Wonders*, where he argues that despite both being grounded in materiality, "*clues* are not *facts*, but rather rhetorical figures; clues represent a moment of multiple possibilities of signification and semantic ambiguity."[140] Or, as Arlette Farge puts it, "the reality of the archive lies not only in the clues it contains, but also in the sequences of different representations of reality. The archive always preserves an infinite number of relations to reality."[141] Though Farge would surely disagree, the literary metamorphosis of facts into clues points to an archival morality where material evidence is shown to always be manipulated, made malleable by poetic *and* deceitful political hands, and thereby takes "advantage of the novel's capacity for telling the truth while actually telling a 'lie,'" as Ellison puts it.[142] It is in this sense that McKay's late archival aesthetic is really a hidden ethic, a responsibility he felt toward his readers. McKay goes beyond the edges of critical fabulation, as Hartman defines it, yet forges "a narrative of what might have been or could have been . . . a history written with and against the archive."[143] In reconstituting, reactivating, reclassifying, and rewriting his own vagabond archive, McKay appropriates for himself and in the service of his community the strategies usually reserved for institutional or imperial governance. Indeed, as Jeremy Braddock puts it, "McKay's late aesthetic practices suggest that he may have deemed the archive—taken in both the institutional and the Derridean senses—as the most hopeful location for long-term political action."[144] Ultimately, we can read the archival practices that led to the crafting of *Amiable* as a methodological schooling in what we can do with "facts," a didactic impetus that was always latent in McKay. "I am very very disappointed after working so hard on a novel of ideas about Aframericans," McKay wrote Eastman in the wake of the novel's rejection by E. P. Dutton.[145] His inability to get the novel published stung beyond a wound to his artistic pride because *Amiable* was the "ethical basis" of his "contemporary historical tale" that he had most hoped to convey. The novel's failure to find favor in the publisher's eyes can also be seen as a reflection of the difficulties radical black voices of this period faced when they attempted to be heard by a receptive public.

For all these reasons and more, it is unfortunate that *Amiable* was not published the year it was written, 1941—just a year after Wright unleashed *Native Son*—because it might have solidified McKay's status as one of the foremost black prose writers of his day and clarified his dedication to his own group. In a letter to McKay in June 1941, at a time when McKay still thought the novel would be published by E. P. Dutton, his former FWP colleague Simon Williamson shared these high hopes for *Amiable*, telling McKay that the publication would come

at an opportune time of social change, development and disillusion of the Negro,—(of the peoples of the world). . . . In the meantime, all we can do is organize, educate and reorientate the lives of our people into channels of self-respect, economic improvement and social and cultural development. They must be given a determination to overcome obstacles and continue to survive. In so many words; the black man must create his world out [of] the debris and mess the white peoples are making of the present.[146]

Williamson's letter today feels tragically timely, and the novel, though seventy-five years late, nevertheless seems to come "at an opportune time." *Amiable with Big Teeth* is a late novel in more ways than one: not only does it come from McKay's late phase, what we might call his late style, but it also comes to us late, much later than its initial lifecycle was ever devised or designed. Yet herein lies the essence of the archival; for what is the "archival" but "a dream deferred," a pastness to come, *un passé à venir*, a belated form of timeliness? Perhaps not what McKay had in mind, but a most welcome rebirth nonetheless.

3

"AT ONCE BOTH DOCUMENT
AND SYMBOL"

Richard Wright, Ralph Ellison, and
the Lafargue Clinic Photographic Archive

*Maybe the history of the Clinic is a more important experiment than
the Clinic itself.*

—FREDRIC WERTHAM TO RICHARD WRIGHT, MAY 12, 1953

The back cover of the June issue of *'48: The Magazine of the Year*
advertised that "next month's" edition would include a "photo-
report by Ralph Ellison and Gordon Parks" titled "Harlem Is Nowhere"
and offered the following tantalizing preview and caption: "'A thousand
clinics could not cure the sense of unreality that haunts Harlem as it haunts
the world.' A brilliant writer and a distinguished photographer, with a sensitive comprehension of their own people, examine New York's troubled
Negro city as a laboratory for universal problems."[1] What is particularly
striking about this back-cover announcement, aside from its naive phraseology, is the fact that this intended collaboration between Parks and Ellison was never published in the magazine. Ellison's essay wasn't published
until sixteen years later, in 1964, when it was included as the penultimate
piece in his first nonfiction book, *Shadow and Act* (1964)—but nowhere to
be found were Parks's photographs. After decades of being considered lost
and ten years after Parks's passing, they were finally unveiled to the world
at the exhibition *Invisible Man: Gordon Parks and Ralph Ellison in Harlem*
at the Art Institute of Chicago in 2016.[2] Although the exhibition and

accompanying catalog at last allow us to assess the full force and scope of the collaboration between Ellison and Parks in 1948, we must recall that the collaboration was lived by these two creators as a loss, an unfulfilled promise. Their inability to give life to "Harlem Is Nowhere" in its original form turned into a productive haunting, its shadowy absence proving transformative over the course of their careers.

"Harlem Is Nowhere" is Ellison's piece on the Lafargue Mental Hygiene Clinic, a grassroots psychiatric facility he famously called "an underground extension of democracy" and "one of Harlem's most important institutions."[3] This clinic, as a small yet growing body of scholarship shows, played a key role in Ellison's professional development as both writer and photographer, but it also exerted a profound influence on Ellison's friend and former mentor Richard Wright.[4] In fact, as with so much of midcentury African American culture, Wright was at the center of it all. He not only served on the clinic's board of directors but also intimately collaborated with the clinic's founder, Dr. Fredric Wertham, in making the doctor's dream of a free psychiatric clinic in Harlem come to life. In yet another fascinating historical convergence, whereas Ellison was unable to publish his photo-essay on Lafargue, Wright successfully released his own essay, "Psychiatry Comes to Harlem," in *Free World* magazine in 1946, where his text was accompanied with photographs "specially made" by Richard Saunders.[5] By then, Wright was an old hand at combining his prose with pictures, having published *12 Million Black Voices* in 1941, the book that Parks referred to as his "bible."[6] Although both Wright and Ellison were primarily prose stylists, it is important to remember that they were also photographers, experimenting in collaborative yet competitive ways throughout the 1940s as Wright continued to cement his legacy and Ellison sought to make a place for himself on the writerly and photographic scene.

Tracing the trope of visuality as it emerges in both Ellison's and Wright's writings allows us to appreciate the extent to which the two authors differed in their contrasting visions of the Lafargue Clinic and of its aesthetic—and political—relevance. And yet, despite their divergent aesthetics, both Wright and Ellison insisted on approaching this psychiatric facility with photography, that emblem of documentary truth. The photograph's cachet as wedged shrapnel of the real, what Roland Barthes calls its "evidential force,"[7] is precisely what drew Wright to photography and what troubled Ellison. Where the elder relied on photography's power to document the "reality" of "the Negro problem," the younger sought to preserve the fragmented "sense of unreality that haunts Harlem as it haunts the world." To that end, Ellison devised a complex shooting script for Gordon Parks—who was also a writer—that complicated photography's claim to objective reality, convinced as he was that Harlem was not simply a pictorial opportunity but rather a "pictorial problem," as given in the title he attached to this shooting script. Put another way, whereas Ellison saw a "pictorial problem," Wright found a solution in the pictorial.

Wright turned to photography as a tool that would lend power to his ongoing efforts to document the clinic and thus "prove" its existence in the first place. Throughout his entire oeuvre, it could be argued, Wright is concerned with making his Doubting Thomas audience see and believe; not only does he use the latest psychological and sociological studies to buttress the accuracy of his claims, but he further enlists photography as additional source of evidence. In her recent excavating work of Wright's late-career work as a photographer, Sara Blair demonstrates the ways in which Wright held a complex and "mixed understanding of his own imaging practices."[8] Even during his travels across the Atlantic in the 1950s, when he dabbled in more expressionistic image making, his relation to photography remained primarily a documentary one as a production and recording of evidence.

Ellison, in contrast, was more seduced by the subjective, artistic perspective photography can tease out through careful technique. More importantly, as he explained to his friend Albert Murray during a discussion on photography, he needed a camera to mediate the intensity of the real: "You know me, I have to have something between me and reality when I'm dealing with it most intensely."[9] There was something hidden beneath the surface of Harlem for Ellison, where "the real and the unreal merge, and the marvelous beckons from behind the same sordid reality that denies its existence."[10] I argue that with "Psychiatry Comes to Harlem" (1946) and "Harlem Is Nowhere" (1948), both Wright and Ellison used what were on the surface promotional pieces for the Lafargue Mental Hygiene Clinic as a means to experiment with and validate their distinct relation to documentary evidence.

The convergence of each writer's selection of the same subject of investigation, the Lafargue Clinic, and same genre, the photo-text, becomes a unique opportunity to explore the disparities between their aesthetic and political commitments. The resulting juxtaposition, I argue, suggests the emergence of what we might call a postwar shift from the documentary to the archival. In the context of this book, I understand the difference between the two chiefly in terms of their temporality: the documentary is an urgent practice that records and is deployed for immediate use, whereas the archival is a practice performed in the same urgent present yet in a way that already relates to the contemporary as past, a past to be unveiled in posterity, wherein its true power can be unleashed. If the archival is a pastness to come, then an archival sensibility thirsts for the timeless rather than the timely. Moving beyond the documentary's concerns with the "real" and the "moment" yet nevertheless tied to it like a phantom umbilical cord across space–time, the archival is inevitably entrenched in a practice of "critical futurity," as Paul Saint-Amour puts it, where record creation functions as an Ellisonian "hibernation," a "storehouse of dormant possibilities that might be reactivated in the present."[11] As always when one deals in collapsing temporalities, this relation is complex, and it is not my intention to establish the documentary and the archival as firm categories, nor do I wish to pigeonhole Wright or Ellison strictly into one or the other; rather, I want to limn the ways in which documentary practice can become archival, how uncanny their family resemblances sometimes are—indeed, the term *reincarnation* would perhaps be more precise—and how the latter needs the former as a child needs his mother or a pupil her mentor.

From a more traditional disciplinary standpoint, the juxtaposition between Wright and Ellison dramatizes a core debate at the heart of the twentieth-century American novel: Did the African American writer of this period have a duty to write timely "protest" novels, or did his allegiance lie elsewhere, in another, more universal, atemporal artistic realm? The didacticism of naturalist or social realism is one of the ways novelists use documentary evidence, deploying data as a claim to legitimate their political message. Wright's writings on Harlem and the Lafargue Clinic as well as his other sociological pieces concerned with poverty, delinquency, and crime—notably his forceful introduction to St. Clair Drake and Horace Cayton's book *Black Metropolis: A Study of Negro Life in a Northern City* (1945)[12]—appeal to the evidentiary prestige of statistical work and photographic representations. Though James Baldwin famously accused Wright of writing "everybody's favorite protest novel," I argue that Wright was dedicated to providing a counterarchive of social facts in his fiction and relied on sociology and psychiatry to do so. In short, he deployed his lifelong social-realist commitments in the service of immediately rendering visible those few institutions favorable to the uplift of African Americans.

Ellison, however, focused on the individual psyche and used his own aborted photo-essay on the clinic to depict the "unreality" that plagued the postwar African American, an atmospheric excess obscured by historical fact and documentary record. At the same time, his attempt to offer "something new in photo-journalism," as he put it in a letter to Wright,[13] was informed—and authorized—by Wright's pioneering efforts. "Harlem Is Nowhere" borrowed much of its imagery from Wright, who afforded Ellison with an opportunity to go beyond the clinic's actual confines to explore the larger environment. When read in the light of a highly suggestive, unpublished set of notes located in the "Lafargue Clinic" folder in the Ralph Ellison Papers at the Library of Congress, the archival journey of "Harlem Is Nowhere" documents how the way Ellison *looked* at the clinic became integral to his evolving conception of invisibility and to his overall aim to be a socially responsible novelist. Not only did Ellison see Parks's photographs as an integral part of his planned essay on Harlem and the clinic, but, as his papers reveal, he also conceived of the clinic itself as a "special kind of camera" on the problems of the day. Although he was unable to use Parks's photographs in 1948, he brought them back to spectral life when he transformed them into prose images and repurposed them in his novel *Invisible Man* in 1952. Even further, in what has to stand as one of the most fascinating examples of a recurrent lifecycle, Ellison later resurrected "Harlem Is Nowhere" twice in 1964, first in *Shadow and Act* and then in *Harper's*

Magazine, where it appeared with a different set of photographs that seem to reflect his second novel-in-progress, *Three Days Before the Shooting*, and the changing social landscape of the 1960s.

THE LAFARGUE CLINIC

How did an obscure clinic, which opened on March 8, 1946, and closed its doors in 1959, come to have such importance for Harlem and for the trajectory of African American literature? As unlikely as it may sound, the Lafargue Clinic was the first mental-hygiene clinic ever established in Harlem—where about 400,000 African Americans were packed 1,600 per acre. Hilde L. Mossé, the clinic's physician in charge, characterized it as form of direct social action and contextualized its emergence in her unpublished recollections on the clinic preserved in the Schomburg Center for Research in Black Culture: "Discrimination was so intense that it was almost impossible for any black person to get psychiatric care anywhere in New York except in city and state hospitals where the care was minimal. Those who could afford private care also had great difficulty finding psychiatrists because many of their [the psychiatrists'] leases had a clause which said that they were forbidden to treat black patients."[14]

The clinic came into existence mainly through the collaborative efforts of Richard Wright, Ralph Ellison, Earl Brown, Reverend Shelton Hale Bishop, and Dr. Fredric Wertham—who later became infamous for his relentless crusade against crime and horror comic books in the 1950s (see chapter 5). Wertham was then a well-respected psychiatrist in charge of the mental-hygiene branch of Queens General Hospital and president of the Association for the Advancement of Psychotherapy when he also adopted the title of Lafargue's director. He had been attempting to open such a free clinic for more than a decade but had been unable to convince either the City of New York or private philanthropists to provide financial backing. Upon Ellison's suggestion, Reverend Bishop, the rector of the St. Philips Protestant Episcopal Church, offered two dingy rooms in the church's basement for the clinic, rent free. Father Bishop was an influential and active member of the Harlem community; he had personally acted as mediator between two large rival juvenile gangs, the Sabers and the Slicksters, by gaining the respect of their leaders.[15]

One of the clinic's immediate aims was in fact to counter the growing violence and criminality perpetrated by Harlem's staggering number of juvenile delinquents. Because this particular demographic was targeted, and because Father Bishop already enjoyed the respect of Harlem's youth gangs, it was not uncommon to see these youths come to the clinic, first out of curiosity and then for treatment. Dr. Mossé recalled that "one of the gang leaders became a patient of the clinic. He came to the clinic accompanied by two bodyguards who stood in front of the door of the parish house. He was afraid that a member of a rival gang might stab him. . . . [T]his boy had a severe reading disorder and almost never attended school."[16] The entire staff of the clinic worked as volunteers and received no remuneration. There was a charge of twenty-five cents to those patients who could spare it, fifty cents if they required a member of the staff to provide court testimony (these funds went largely to postage and carfare for those who could not afford it).

The clinic's program was outlined in a small pamphlet that was made available around Harlem: "The Lafargue Clinic is a clinic for the treatment of all kinds of nervous and mental disorders and behavior difficulties of adults and children. Its emphasis is not on testing and retesting, but on practical, intensive and if necessary prolonged psychotherapy. The diagnostic and psychotherapeutic methods employed are in accordance with the highest scientific standards."[17] According to Mossé, there "was no dearth of volunteers," and every member of the staff was "highly qualified."[18] The clinic was able to secure the services of mental-health workers, social workers, psychologists, psychiatrists, psychiatric nurses, special-education teachers, speech and reading therapists, and secretaries. The clinic abolished segregation not only of their clientele but of the working staff as well. Dr. André Tweed—who is prominently featured in the photographs for Wright's piece on the clinic—was the first black psychiatrist employed by a mental-hygiene clinic in New York (and one of only eight African

American psychiatrists working in the United States at the time). He had been brought to the clinic through Dr. Wertham's influence.[19] What the clinic's first patients revealed was that most of the problems suffered by the community members stemmed from a lack of elementary social care and generalized neglect by the state, not to mention the larger psychological wounds created through segregation. The facts that the federal government was unwilling to subsidize the clinic and that most social agencies or philanthropists were reluctant to finance it are emblematic of the difficulties confronting African Americans in postwar America.

The clinic quickly became a lively democratic center of social, psychological, political, and artistic action, even though the community did not always understand its intentions. As Ralph Martin's piece "Doctor's Dream in Harlem" (1946) stressed, Wertham was careful to prevent misunderstandings of his work: "I don't want anybody to get an idea we're specializing in some interracial project, because we're not. . . . We're here in Harlem because this is where the need is greatest. And we're not here to make a study of the Negro, because the Negro's problem is just an exaggeration of what happens to all other people anyway. Only here it's so much more naked and obvious."[20] This statement seems to accord with Ellison's view of Harlem as a metonym for the world, as the "next month" preview of "Harlem Is Nowhere" quoted at the opening of this chapter attests. Moreover, given that in Harlem the "Negro's problem" was "so much more naked and obvious," the clinic seemed to call out for a pictorial treatment; in Harlem, the problem was ready for its close-up, and photographers swarmed upon it like moths to a flame.

Wertham called his treatment and approach "social psychiatry," which meant that the psychiatrist had to "understand a patient's economic and community life, as well as his sex life" before providing the correct treatment.[21] This desegregated institution not only provided direct relief for the immediate Harlem community but also led to a reinforced front in battling racial inequality in the United States. Dr. Wertham and the research he conducted at the clinic were instrumental in the Supreme Court decision to abolish school segregation in *Brown v. Board of Education* (347 U.S. 483) in 1954. In 1951, Thurgood Marshall, then chief attorney for the Legal Defense Fund of the NAACP, had asked Wertham for help in winning a lawsuit brought by a group of children—represented by their parents—against the State of Delaware to contest the state's school segregation statute. Wertham had the children brought to Lafargue with the idea of framing the problem in a new way: he asked whether school segregation was injurious to the mental health of children and whether it constituted a public-health problem. Crucially, he also made sure to study the effects of segregation on both black and white children, which "revealed the possibility that white children, too, may be harmed by school segregation."[22] Wertham's court testimony was the very first instance of psychiatry being used in a case of this kind, and it had considerable impact. As James Reibman recounts, "Wertham's presence and his cogent argument detailing the results of his research so persuaded Chancellor Collins Seitz that in his legal opinion he both quotes and paraphrases Wertham's testimony."[23]

The doctor's testimony in the Delaware cases was incorporated into the legal argument used in *Brown v. Board*. Thurgood Marshall wrote Wertham: "I hope that you and the members of your clinic will have satisfaction in knowing that your great efforts contributed significantly to the end result."[24] As Reibman puts it, the Lafargue Clinic, "which began so modestly, had now achieved major national recognition."[25] And yet, in spite of tremendously favorable publicity, the clinic closed its doors in 1959, "when," according to Mossé, "circumstances had changed in such a way that it was not possible for this type of free clinic to survive."[26] Chief among these circumstances was the opening of a mental-hygiene branch within Harlem Hospital, even though, as Mossé put it in a letter, this new facility was "not able to take care of the needs of the community. Our long waiting list proves this conclusively."[27] Yet in its heyday the clinic benefitted from a fair amount of publicity and documentation from multiple well-respected media outlets: newspapers, magazines, journals, and even television when it was featured in an NBC program titled *The House I Enter: A Portrait of the American Doctor*.[28] African Americans such as Richard Wright, Richard Saunders, Ralph Ellison, and Gordon Parks participated in this historical and pictorial record of the Lafargue Clinic, eventually integrating the clinic's approach to desegregated psychotherapy into their aesthetic and practices in ways that reflected their distinct political and artistic agendas.

BLUEPRINT FOR WRIGHT WRITING

By the time Richard Wright wrote "Psychiatry Comes to Harlem" to celebrate the clinic's opening in 1946, he was at the height of his fame and stood at a crucial crossroads in his career as an artist and intellectual. That same year, he would expatriate with his family to Paris, France. The past year had been momentous; his autobiography, *Black Boy*, was published, as was his introduction to St. Clair Drake and Horace R. Cayton's seminal sociological treatise *Black Metropolis*. It is difficult to understate the latter text's significance for our understanding of Wright's intellectual trajectory. Wright wrote the introduction to *Black Metropolis* while vacationing with his family for a few months in "French Quebec," Canada, where he was seeking refuge from communists, American racism, and what he now considered the toxic, competitive atmosphere of New York's artistic scene. The trip also afforded him an opportunity to test his French-speaking skills before his upcoming secret move to France.

Wright confirmed the importance of this introduction in a letter to his friend and patron Ida Guggenheimer in July 1945: "I've been working hard on the introduction to a book called *Black Metropolis*. . . . In this introduction, I'm coming out and saying some things I've wanted to say for a long, long time."[29] The fresh change in location, language, and atmosphere seems to have provided Wright with a new way to look at the "interpretation of Negro life." During his first trip to Québec a year earlier, in the summer of 1944, he had told Guggenheimer, "Really, if you want to see how foolish and wrong the policy on the Negro is, look at it from the point of view of a foreign country."[30] Wright's return to Québec in 1945 once again underscores the power of a new perspective—of literally seeing things from a new vantage point—and he wanted his introduction to *Black Metropolis* to provide that salutary novelty, as he explained to Guggenheimer in July 1945:

> Only when a concept has been forged can the Negro problem be seen, can its relation to the nation be shown, etc. That is my objection to the Liberals, too. . . . But they do not have any place from which to see the Negro problem in all its complexity. The Negro can be the true yard stick to measure the depth of any political program.
>
> I do hope that introduction I wrote for *Black Metropolis* will help to clarify some of the problems facing Negroes; and I think that the book will too. In this introduction, I take issue with both the political Left and Right on the issue of the Negro. I'm showing that both want to convert the Negro problem from a race, cultural, economic, political, and national problem into something which they can control and handle.[31]

Wright's belief that the "Negro can be the true yard stick to measure the depth of any political program" recalls Wertham's statement, cited earlier, that "the Negro's problem is just an exaggeration of what happens to all other people anyway." Wright's language is further framed by visuality: he emphasizes the need for the "Negro problem" to "be seen" and for a "place from which to see [it] in all its complexity," which becomes an underlying rationale for his use of photography.

Wright's language also revolves around sight throughout his introduction to *Black Metropolis*, an interdisciplinary text that blends currents from history and psychology under the auspices of the burgeoning urban sociology that would define the Chicago school. Wright's introduction exposes the reciprocal relationship between his own aesthetic project and the work being done by prominent sociologists and psychiatrists of the time; the relation between literature and social sciences substantiated the one through the other. Besides the fact that Drake and Cayton's book lent scientific credibility to his own oeuvre, Wright admired it because he felt it outlined "the facts of urban Negro life" and "thus rendered visible" what "whites do not see and do not want to see."[32]

Wright opens his introduction by calling the book both "a landmark of research and scientific achievement" and a work with which he "personally identified."[33] The scientific and the personal, here stressed, are the two poles animating not just Wright's introductory essay but arguably also his entire oeuvre. The central subject of *Black Metropolis* allowed Wright to ruminate on the formative impact that the city in question, Chicago, had on this Mississippi boy. In a suggestive passage, Wright confesses how the metropolis forced him to feel "those extremes of possibility, death and hope" and had instilled in him a "yearning to write, to tell my story." He goes on: "But I did not know what my story was, and it was not until I stumbled upon science that I discovered some of the meanings of the environment that battered and taunted me." Wright's vagabond experiences crystallized as narrative once he encountered science, his naturalist muse. After meeting the new scientists who were "amassing facts about urban Negro life," Wright was able to articulate his documentary aesthetics: "I found that sincere art and honest science were not far apart, that each could enrich the other." In other words, "the huge mountain of fact piled up by the Department of Sociology at the University of Chicago gave me my first concrete vision of the forces that molded the urban Negro's body and soul."[34] Wright even lists how facts had "enriched" all of his artistic accomplishments to date:

It was from the scientific findings of men like the late Robert E. Park, Robert Redfield, and Louis Wirth that I drew the meanings for my documentary book, *12,000,000 Black Voices*; for my novel, *Native Son*; it was from their scientific facts that I absorbed some of that quota of inspiration necessary for me to write *Uncle Tom's Children* and *Black Boy*. *Black Metropolis*, Drake's and Cayton's scientific statement about the urban Negro, pictures the environment out of which the Bigger Thomases of our nation come; and it is the environment of the Bosses of the Buildings; and it is the environment to which Negro boys and girls turn their eyes when they hear the word Freedom.[35]

The passage lists all of Wright's published works at the time he wrote the introduction and gives one the impression that his method was simply to sift through the newest compiled data available and immediately make his fiction match the fact. As in the case of his contemporary Ann Petry, his large-scale research practices became both source of material and source of inspiration. Here in this introduction as well as in the autobiographical book he had just published, *Black Boy*, Wright strangely skips over the fact that Chicago is also where he first became a member of the FWP and where he began tapping into its statistical and folkloric archives, even contributing to its growth. In *Black Boy*, he more or less dismisses his years on the FWP, casually referring to it without emphasis: "From the Federal Experimental Theater, I was transferred to the Federal Writers' Project, and I tried to earn my bread by writing guidebooks."[36] Much as he would have liked to present it otherwise, therefore, his "stumble" into "science" involved a meticulous trajectory.

The impetus behind Wright's approach has to do with revealing, exposing, picturing: in short, a photographic process of proof, of documenting the real with material evidence as a means for the public to apprehend his message as truthful. The sociologists' and psychiatrists' work imbued his artistic—and "personal"—documentation with the objectivity of science. Yet in the introduction to *Black Metropolis* what Wright particularly commends in the Chicago school of sociology is that its leading members also relied on "their feelings for a situation or an event, were not afraid to stress the role of insight, and to warn against a slavish devotion to figures, charts, graphs, and sterile scientific techniques." In short, he adds, the resulting works are "scientific volumes brilliantly characterized by insight and feeling."[37] The latter, we might say, is precisely the balance Wright seeks to achieve in his own literary output, if somewhat reversed: insightful and affective literature brilliantly characterized by scientific research.

In "How Bigger Was Born," a lecture Wright first gave in New York on March 12, 1940, he had already expressed something similar: "An imaginative novel," he explained, "represents the merging of two extremes; it is an intensely intimate expression on the part of a consciousness couched in terms of the most objective and commonly known events." The novelist's imagination, Wright added, is "a kind of self-generating cement which glued his facts together, and his emotions as a kind of dark and obscure designer of those facts."[38] Here the imaginary merges with emotion—two facets of the human condition usually seen as threats to objectivity—to generate "facts," the building blocks, if you will, of objective, rational statements. Yet for Wright it was this combination, as opposed to a contradiction, that could create a "place from which to see the Negro problem in all its complexity," as he wrote to Guggenheimer. Thus, the force of Wright's art stems from his talent for infusing the viscera of raging life through a clinical documentarian treatment.

In a way that today seems to anticipate the potential dangers of doing digital humanities devoid of insight and feeling, Wright agreed with the Chicago school's warning against having "a slavish devotion to figures, charts, graphs, and sterile scientific techniques," and yet he was quick to rely on such gathered data to prove the accuracy of his own works. In a remarkable passage in the introduction to *Black Metropolis*, he declares: "If, in reading my novel, *Native Son*, you doubted the reality of Bigger Thomas, then examine the delinquency rates cited in this book; if, in reading my autobiography, *Black Boy*, you doubted the picture of family life shown there, then study the figures on family disorganization given here."[39] The passage almost contradicts his earlier reservation against rates and figures, so eager is he to claim the evidentiary power of science for his art.

Wright follows this embrace of science's enrichment of his art with a comparison that belies the naturalist's fatalism (even though he preferred to think of himself as a "psychologist" rather than a "naturalist"[40]). "After studying the social processes in this book," he declares, "you cannot expect Negro life to be other than what it is. To expect the contrary would be like expecting to see Rolls-Royces coming off the assembly lines at Ford's River Rouge plant!" Wright takes this determinism further: "The imposed conditions under which Negroes live detail the structure of their lives like an engineer outlining the blue-prints for the production of machines."[41] This assertion is in stark contrast to the famous statement made by the founder of the Chicago school, Robert E. Park, when first meeting Wright: "How in Hell did you happen?" In an unpublished lecture given in Paris, "The Position of the Negro Artist and Intellectual in American Society," Wright delighted in this anecdote because it marked him as an anomalous, independent monad among the conditioned African American masses—the lone, unexplainable flower in the desert. In that lecture, under the influence of Jean-Paul Sartre, whom he cited, Wright ascribed to himself independence from philanthropy, institutional education, and any other forms of ideological conditioning imposed upon black artistic and intellectual life.[42] It is almost as if he needed the vantage of his state of exception, independent from other African Americans, to present the "reality" of the "Negro problem" on their behalf.

Wright is thus uniquely suited to guide his readers toward a novel understanding of these difficult new facts of modern life. He aligns *Black Metropolis* with modernism's common characteristics of difficulty, novelty, and shock, calling it a book that will "wrench your mind rather violently out of your accustomed ways of thinking." The directness of the book's factual exhibitionism is key to its power: "There is no attempt in *Black Metropolis* to understate, to gloss over, to doll up, or make harsh facts pleasant."[43] Narration, if narration there be, should now serve the harsh fact, not couch it or bury it within its fictionalized layers.[44] With the advent of World War II, understatement became a technique used by the old guard, a remnant of the Harlem Renaissance that Wright openly derided in *New Challenge* in 1938. In this context, Drake and Cayton were part of the modernist avant-garde of black writing precisely because "the facts of urban life presented here are in their starkest form. . . . To have presented them otherwise would have been to negate the humanity of the American Negro."[45] The latter sentiment suggests the reasoning behind Wright's own documentary impulse in his novelistic practice. It also points to that other important mode of presenting urban life in its "starkest form" at play in Wright's professional development: photography. Indeed, Wright admires the way in which *Black Metropolis* "examines the social structure as though it were frozen at a moment in time,"[46] a formulation that recalls a commonplace definition of the photograph.

As Wright forcefully hammers home in *Black Metropolis*, the main problem is that for the ruling ideology "the lives of the dispossessed are not real to them . . . the men who run our industrial world cannot see what really *is*."[47] He had already proved in *12 Million Black Voices* that photography can be an unparalleled tool in such a documentary project of exposure. Tellingly, Wright frames this invisibility as a problem of the archive: "a society that recognizes only those forms of social maladjustment which are recorded in courts, prisons, clinics, hospitals, newspapers, and bureaus of vital statistics will be missing some of the most fateful of the tell-tale clues to its destiny."[48] The repositories Wright names amount to what we might call the visible archive, the state-sanctioned houses of record. These repositories are tragically incomplete and, he suggests, blind the nation to its future. In this introduction, Wright, as he does in *Native Son* and *Black Boy*, seeks to correct America's blindness by exposing what public archives do not yet recognize, using the unflinching realism of his documentary mode to promote the counterarchives of initiatives such as the Chicago school and the Lafargue Clinic. In other words, for Wright, it is not simply the "Negro problem" that threatens to persist unperceived but also any works or enterprises that could be part of the solution to that problem. In the racial struggle for equality in the United States, the province of the artist is to "dwell upon these imponderables."[49]

In *Native Son*, Wright addresses this invisibility through scenes that share the theme of a failure to recognize what is right in front of you. The narrative is invested in tracing moments of recognition and usually does so with visual language in which seeing is equated with knowing. For example, Jan Erlone insists that Bigger give him and Mary Dalton a tour of Chicago's black neighborhoods, admitting that he wants to "just *see* how your people live . . . I just want to *see*. I want to *know* these people."[50] Seeing is likened to acquiring a new set of epistemological data through which to understand "these people." Bigger's escalating violence propels him toward greater clarity of vision regarding the world in which he lives. After murdering Mary, dragging her corpse into the basement, cutting off her head, and putting her body in the furnace, Bigger returns to his broken-down apartment and "looked round the room, seeing it for the first time. There was no rug on the floor and the plastering on the walls and ceiling hung loose in many places. . . . This was much different from the Dalton home"

(105). Bigger now notices the physical manifestations of inequality, whereas his sleeping family and everyone else only "yearned to see life in a certain way; they needed a certain picture of the world and they were blind to what did not fit" (106).

The new sight does reinvigorate Bigger, who is soon described as "a man reborn" (111), a man who "had shed an invisible burden he had long carried" (114). Ironically, Bigger's new superior vision seems to consist in seeing the ubiquitous blindness—"the whole blind world" (135)—around him; He see everyone as "simply blind people, blind like his mother, his brother, his sister, Peggy, Britten, Jan, Mr. Dalton, and the sightless Mrs. Dalton and the quiet empty houses with their black gaping windows" (173). In that wonderful passage, the city's infrastructure is now blindly "gaping" at Bigger; he suffers from the implied oppressive force of its gaze despite its sightless eyes. And sure enough, as the buildings blindly gape at Bigger, he suddenly "saw a sign on a building: THIS PROPERTY IS MANAGED BY THE SOUTH SIDE REAL ESTATE COMPANY" (173, capitalization in the original), and realizes that this company was owned by Mr. Dalton. Through his new sight, Bigger is making important connections about who owns and operates these Chicago slums in which he and his family reside. It is at this epiphanic moment that Bigger resolves to send the kidnapping note, hoping to "jar them out of their senses" (175), just as Wright later warns readers that reading *Black Metropolis* will "wrench your mind rather violently out of your accustomed ways of thinking."

As is the case for many of Wright's protagonists, Bigger is described as the symbolic "picture of reality" that can rectify the vision of the ruling ideology: "he wished that he could be an idea in their minds; that his black face and the image of his smothering Mary and cutting off her head and burning her could hover before their eyes as a terrible picture of reality which they could see and feel and yet not destroy" (130). Like "the man who lived underground," Bigger "was the statement" trying to "force the reality of himself upon them."[51] Put another way, Wright creates Bigger to "loom as a symbolic figure of American life."[52] This impulse informs Wright's choice to follow *Native Son* with his own autobiography, allowing Wright himself to become that symbolic figure of American life.

William Faulkner addressed Wright's trajectory from novelist to memoirist—from fiction to autobiography or, as Wright called it, a "record" of his past[53]—in a telling letter written to Wright soon after the publication of *Black Boy* in 1945. Faulkner praised the book yet also admonished his fellow Mississippi native on questions of form: "I have just read BLACK BOY. It needed to be said, and you said it well . . . as well as it could have been said in this form. Because I think you said it much better in Native Son. I hope you will keep on saying it, but I hope you will say it as an artist, as in Native Son."[54] For Faulkner, the novel form takes precedence over memoir, and he cast *Native Son* as a superior blending of "sincere art and honest science," as Wright puts it in the introduction to *Black Metropolis*.

When Fredric Wertham read *Black Boy*, he wrote Wright a letter along the same lines as Faulkner by questioning the power of nonfiction to successfully transmit its intended message:

> "Black Boy" describes certain bad features in our society. Pointing these things out in the way in which you do is an act that has revolutionary implications. It should arouse the reader to the wish and perhaps the deed of changing these things. Now the paradox comes in in the fact that hundreds of thousands of people buy and read this book. The vast majority of these readers are of course the persecutors themselves, and not the persecuted. . . . Maybe they give these people, the readers, the wrong impression that they are actually doing something just by reading about these things, which gives them the satisfaction of leaving everything as it goes and feeling at the same time that they are righteous.[55]

Like Wright, Wertham hoped that the nonfictional treatment of reality carries a revolutionary potential but ultimately felt that words alone are not enough to bring change. It is not surprising, therefore, that Wright and Wertham collaborated, less than a year later, in 1946, to open a new radical institution, the Lafargue Clinic.

PSYCHIATRY COMES TO RICHARD WRIGHT

Wright praised *Black Metropolis* because it "was written, too, so that Negroes will be able to interpret correctly the meaning of their own actions,"[56] and he saw the Lafargue Clinic as the next logical step in providing correct self-interpretation.[57] In 1945, Wright had already tried to intervene on behalf of the disenfranchised children living at the Wiltwyck School for Boys. Wiltwyck, open since 1936, was located in Upstate New York and was one of the only institutions designed to help African American juvenile delinquents—or as the school's promotional leaflet called them, "New York's unhappiest children"—and sought to provide of "moral and spiritual enlightenment, character development, correction of behavior problems, education and training for good citizenship."[58] In fact, in yet another example of evolving lifecycles, the earliest draft of what eventually became Wright's essay "Psychiatry Comes to Harlem" was not about the Lafargue Clinic at all but rather about the Wiltwyck School. Wright titled the draft "The Children of Harlem" but was never satisfied with it—it lingered in his files until Lafargue became the right catalyst for his ideas. Wright had even visited the school several times, interviewed the "delinquent" boys, and donated money to the school on more than one occasion.

Wright wanted to supplement his essay on Wiltwyck with photography and had asked the school director Robert Cooper if he could bring none other than Gordon Parks to take pictures of the boys and the school's activities; Cooper was elated at the idea.[59] Unfortunately, Parks was ultimately unavailable for the gig, and Wright kept trying in vain to find another "African American photographer who will have free access to the resources of Harlem as well as firsthand knowledge of the subject."[60] Wright eventually reconceived his article to promote the Lafargue Clinic, and he was matched with an up-and-coming young black photographer from Bermuda named Richard Saunders to take pictures for "Psychiatry Comes to Harlem." The assignment was one of the first professional jobs for Saunders, who had arrived in New York in the mid-1940s and began working for the Black Star agency (all of the contact sheets for the "Psychiatry Comes to Harlem" images are stamped *Black Star*). Saunders quickly befriended Gordon Parks, who later helped him secure a job at *Life* magazine as a photographic technician.[61]

With "Psychiatry Comes to Harlem," Wright was enlisting the clinic as part of the progressive program outlined in *Black Metropolis*, and because the clinic represented a maverick endeavor put together by pioneering rebels willing to stare down "the steady, unblinking eyes of American medicine,"[62] he also underscored its radical status as a necessary, underground, "criminal" institution. In trying to explain why and how the clinic came to be, Wright offers the following defiant declaration: "The more our institutions are divorced from the needs of reality, the more urgently will men, responding to the desire to meet the needs of reality, devise *sub rosa*, almost lawless or criminal methods to service the community, to heal the sick, to aid sufferers, to defend the victims of injustice."[63] Just as Drake and Cayton were accumulating a new counterarchive of sociological facts and data on the "Negro problem," the clinic was both responding to the psychological needs of Harlem's population and through its patients' files creating a new interracial psychiatric archive. As Jay Garcia puts it, both the Wiltwyck School for Boys and the Lafargue Clinic represented "institutional variant[s] of the battles [Wright] waged as a writer and intellectual."[64] Wright's own fictional and journalistic output was thus cast as a sub-rosa method that "defend[ed] the victims of injustice"—he had joined the secret underground with his blend of "honest science and sincere art."

In "Psychiatry Comes to Harlem," Wright edges close to how Ellison would later frame the clinic as an underground location for similarly criminal (vigilante) acts that nevertheless "service the community." In fact, Wright's photo-essay on the clinic provided potent imagery and language to Ellison: "Psychologically, repressed need goes underground, gropes for an unguarded outlet in the dark and, once finding it, sneaks out, experimentally tasting the new freedom, then at last gushing forth in a wild torrent, frantic lest a new taboo deprive it of the right to exist."[65] The imagery here recalls how in the prologue to *Invisible Man* Ellison's protagonist goes aboveground only to beat up the racist blond man. In a very material sense,

Wright's earlier essay informs both Ellison's essay "Harlem Is Nowhere" and the symbolic action of *Invisible Man*. Wright declares that "social needs, too, go underground . . . only to reappear later in strange channels and in guises as fantastic as the images of a nightmare."[66] This notion foreshadows the description of the "most surreal fantasies" being lived out on the streets of Harlem in "Harlem Is Nowhere."[67]

In that essay, Ellison plays with the underground location of the clinic, crafting one of his most resonant and quoted lines: "It is the only center in the city wherein both Negroes and whites may receive extended psychiatric care. Thus its importance transcends even its greater value as a center for psychotherapy; it represents an underground extension of democracy."[68] In "Psychiatry Comes to Harlem," Wright uses similar language: "This extension of psychiatry to Harlem must not be confused with philanthropy, charity, or missionary work; it is the extension of the very concept of psychiatry into a new realm, the application of psychiatry to the masses, the turning of Freud upside down."[69] Wright repeats the term *sub rosa* three times in his essay, whereas Ellison's deploys more varied language for the underground—"bowels of the city," "labyrinthine," and so on. Though Ellison's aesthetic would turn drastically away from the staged realism of Wright's photo-essay, his prose clearly relied on the fount of imagery Wright had already articulated.

Alongside this vibrant and provocative language, Wright's photo-essay prosaically outlines why there was a dire need for psychiatric aid for African Americans and lists the administrative, professional, and political obstructions the Lafargue Clinic faced. The "psychological wounding of the Negro personality," Wright pithily states, lay in the "consistent sabotage of their democratic aspirations." Thanks to his diligent research, he delivers a "summarized list of medical objections to establishing a mental hygiene clinic in Harlem" given by the state and then proceeds to underscore the ridiculous nature of these objections. He even uses the vocabulary of these official reports, gathered during his research, to further anchor the veracity of his sub-rosa position: "I take these adjectives from official psychiatric court reports." "It is a matter of record," he states, "that many institutions have closed down deliberately rather than extend equal treatment to Negroes," and in a footnote he cites a *New York Post* article as supportive evidence for his confrontational statements. In an argument backed by material evidence that document the need for psychiatric care in Harlem, the clinic symbolically emerges as a rebuttal, "a complete reversal of all current rules holding in authoritative psychiatric circles,"[70] and its case files form the counterarchival proof of medicine's failure to include African Americans.

In 1946, a forward-looking democratic institution such as the Lafargue Clinic seemed too incredible for most people to believe, and Wright tackles this credulity head on: "Though the Lafargue Clinic does exist, there is a widely prevalent feeling among many people that it does *not exist*; it is apparently almost psychologically impossible for many literate people to believe that a clinic could be built without being backed by renowned committees and financed by well-known millionaires."[71] In this key passage, we again find the pervasive idea of invisibility, one linked to the period's social and economic realities. A little later in the article Wright adds, "Organized medicine has not yet publicly acknowledged the existence of the Lafargue Clinic,"[72] in part because of the New York City Department of Welfare's refusal to process the clinic's application for a license. In other words, the clinic's invisibility was maintained by its systematic exclusion from municipal and state administrative records. Indeed—and this is a point around which Ellison will center his novel—to be forced to remain on the margins of the archive is to be invisible, and, for Wright, what remains unseen does not exist or at least does not exist *enough*. Following his favored documentary means of persuasion, Wright felt that the best way to convince Harlemites that the clinic existed was to take photographs of it. If people could see the clinic in photographs while reading his article, they might have an epiphanic encounter with the actual clinic in the basement of the Parish House.

By the time Wright wrote "Psychiatry Comes to Harlem," the relation between photography and existence was already an operative trope in *Native Son*, where photographic evidence carries more authority than what is actually before one's eyes. Newspaper headlines and articles about the Dalton "kidnapping" become tangible proofs of Bigger's presence in the world; he realizes that what the press says in print becomes the accepted version of reality for the world. When the murder story appears in the paper, "for the first time, [Bigger] saw his picture" (223–24), and it becomes part of the public record. When Bessie asks him how the police will be able to identify him, he simply replies: "They got my picture" (228). In other words, having your picture taken means not only that you exist but also that you can be *found*. Sure enough, when the police and those "vigilante groups" go hunting for Bigger on that fateful Chicago winter night, they are equipped with "photos of the killer" (244).

But in "Psychiatry Comes to Harlem," Wright flips that agency around and uses it in the service of what he wants people to find: not "criminals" but care. He methodically demands to include a picture of the Lafargue Clinic's entrance, its interracial medical and clerical staff, as well as a male and female patient. No longer limiting the photographic archive to wanted black outlaws, he expands the documentary record to include preventative countermeasures against racial inequality, such as the clinic. Through the photo-text, Wright consciously redresses black image making and does so with the same sense of urgency that marks all his works. In total, Richard Saunders "specially made" seven photographs to accompany Wright's text. The photos are very staged; they tell a story that documents the clinic in practice, with a strong interracial emphasis, and are flanked by Wright's didactic captions.

In the foreground of the opening photograph, a black male teenager is seen by a white nurse, while the background shows a smiling older female patient conversing with another nurse (figure 3.1). The same youth returns in the final two photos, where he is seen by Dr. André Tweed and then outside looking at "The Parish House" sign (figure 3.2). In the other images wedged between these pages is a spread showing Dr. Tweed with a female patient (the same one who can be seen in the first image) above another picture of her standing and smiling in front of Dr. Tweed and Reverend Bishop, both of whom are seated behind a desk. The other two pictures show a white nurse in the playroom with African American children and the same nurse handing a lollipop to a black child alongside the caption, "Children's problems are given special attention at the Lafargue Clinic." The captions make a point of celebrating the efforts of Dr. Tweed, Reverend Bishop, and Dr. Wertham, even though the director is never shown, but

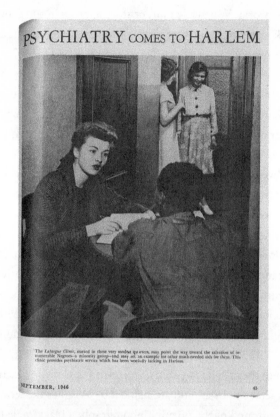

FIGURE 3.1. First page of Richard Wright's essay "Psychiatry Comes to Harlem." Photographs by Richard Saunders.

Source: *Free World*, September 1946.

they do not name the patients or even mention them as "patients." All these images are procedural, focalized snapshots of what happens inside the Lafargue Clinic from a neutral perspective. There are no extremes of behavior being shown, no exaggeration, no "lunacy" or instability; everything is very civil, pleasant, calm.

Notably, we never see the young male patient's face; he is always photographed from the back, and the calculated angle of his head prevents his features from being seen. In the context of the criminalization of black men

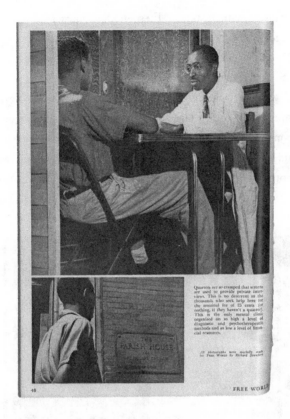

FIGURE 3.2. Final two images in Wright, "Psychiatry Comes to Harlem."
Photographs by Richard Saunders.

Source: *Free World*, September 1946.

that Wright discusses in his essay, these images are literally the opposite of
"mug shots"; the youth remains unidentifiable as an individual and thus cannot be criminalized. He symbolically stands as a representative of a demographic, a "minority group," as Wright states, who may make use of this
free facility. The final photograph is also key to Wright's overall aims; here
the young man is literally standing by the door to the clinic: if the other
photographs provide photographic evidence of the clinic's existence, then
the ultimate image shows readers where to get inside, almost like a call back

to the first caption, which states, "These modest quarters may point the way to salvation for innumerable Negroes."

In the Fredric Wertham Papers at the Library of Congress are two partial contact sheets of the images taken by Saunders that give us a wider glimpse of what Wright wanted to show through the photographs. One includes three of the four images chosen for the published essay and seven that didn't make the cut, notably one of Dr. Tweed in the playroom with children and another of him smiling at his desk in conversation with a black nurse. The other contact sheet contains four images and seems to succinctly summarize what Wright admires about the clinic (figure 3.3).[73]

FIGURE 3.3. Contact sheet with unused images for Wright, "Psychiatry Comes to Harlem." Photographs by Richard Saunders.

Source: Box 215, folder 5, Fredric Wertham Papers, Manuscript Division, Library of Congress, Washington, DC.

The top two bring us just outside the Parish House, where we can see the street and the African American children swarming the entrance of the clinic's steps. The bottom two images are from inside the basement of the Parish House, where the clinic operated: on the left is a picture of the inter-racial staff together, seated in a semicircle underneath a portrait of Paul Lafargue—they all are smiling—and on the right is a white nurse, also smiling, returning to or taking a file out of a filing cabinet.[74] Given Wright's focus on official records in the essay and his plea that sub-rosa counterar-chives like those of the Lafargue Clinic be recognized and sanctioned, this image seems to get to the heart of what was at stake for Wright.

Even though the mental-hygiene clinic had been open for only a few months by the time Wright's article was published in September 1946, it had already had a tangible impact, bringing evidentiary power to Wright's conclusions and beliefs: "One month's intensive operation has proved that Harlem's high rates of delinquency and nervous break-down stem not from biological predilections toward crime existing in Negroes, but from an almost total lack of community services to cope with the problems of Har-lem's individuals."[75] Wright's article, in the end, acted as an appeal for finan-cial backing of the free clinic, and its rigorous use of photography became irrevocable proof of the clinic's existence. By teaming up with Richard Saunders, Wright enlisted photography's help in his quest to document those precious pioneering grassroots projects that constitute the counterar-chive to what the world already "sees." As his letters demonstrate, the clinic was something close to Wright's heart; shortly after his arrival in France in June 1946, he wrote to Guggenheimer, "How is the clinic? Gosh, don't let that idea die. Talk of it, get folks to help it to live; for I tell you that there is nothing over here [Paris] that is as radical and free as that idea we started up there in Harlem."[76]

In the years following the publication of his photo-essay, Wright con-tinued to rely on documentary photographic practice in his nonfiction, such as *Black Power* (1954) and *The Color Curtain* (1956).[77] He also went on to engage with psychiatry in later fictional works such as *Rite of Passage* (1994), *The Outsider* (1953), and *Savage Holiday* (1954), where he used psychoana-lytic theory as an accurate model of the inner workings of his protagonists' minds. For *Rite of Passage*, he even used case files he had consulted at the Wiltwyck School for Boys in creating his protagonist, Johnny Gibbs. Gibbs is a fifteen-year-old boy who begins a downward spiral into juvenile delinquency when the state forces him to change foster families. In essence, Wright creates a narrative that shows not only the need for psychiatric support for Harlem youth but also the state-led neglect that causes psychological distress.[78] To sum up, Wright's documentary impulse was and continued to be wedded to his novelistic practice. Despite what may seem like a more didactic or traditional approach, Wright's pioneering efforts in photojournalism subsequently led Ellison to develop his own unique modernist approach. In other words, Ellison's belated intervention could be erected only on the tangible existence of the clinic that Wright's earlier piece had concretized. Now that the clinic was "somewhere," Ellison's "Harlem Is Nowhere" could "leav[e] the Lafargue Clinic for a while"[79] and look beyond its confines to enter the psychic maze of Harlem.

RALPH ELLISON: THE CLINIC AS CAMERA

In her trailblazing study of the influence of psychological concepts on the writings of African American authors in the 1940s and 1950s, a study framed around the Lafargue Clinic, Shelly Eversley suggests that the perspective shared by both Wright and Ellison, in their mutual commitment to making equality and integration between black and white in America a reality, "depends on the language of psychology and the metaphor of schizophrenia" and "amounts to an assault on the cultural status quo." Eversley further suggests in her discussion of *Brown v. Board of Education* that "in order to win public support for the notion of integration as a bulwark against assaults on American democracy, the antisegregationist position depended on psychological language."[80] In some cases, this dependence was literal, as in Wertham's and Kenneth Clark's court testimonies in *Brown v. Board*. Beyond the law, therefore, Wright and Ellison's invocation of the clinic suggests that psychiatric discourse was viewed as a potential source of support in aiding African Americans to articulate the experience of their social mar-ginalization. Frantz Fanon, writing at the same time, was in agreement: if the black man could be recognized as having neuroses, then this meant he was fully human. In such a context, the clinic was representative of Ellison's conviction that "urgent action" was "the solution for the dire situation in Harlem."[81]

By the time the "Harlem Is Nowhere" assignment came along, Ellison had been living in the neighborhood for a decade and was familiar with the marginalized and sometimes fantastic denizens populating its over-crowded streets; comic-book-reading juvenile delinquents, zoot-suiters with their sunglasses and wide-brimmed hats, little men hiding behind stoves, step-ladder exhorters dressed in animal pelts, and returning veter-ans throwing phantom grenades while talking to themselves. His fascina-tion with marginal types reflects what Robert O'Meally calls his sense of "the significance of black leadership from the periphery."[82] In particular, this sense of cultural dissonance represented by the hipster style "became a con-venient explanation for the astronomical rates of black juvenile delin-quency," which led Ellison to frequently engage in conversations about psy-chology with Wertham, who hoped to deter delinquency.[83] Since living through the events of the Harlem riot in the summer of 1943, Ellison had a febrile interest in sudden acts of violence and had come to diagnose, pace Wright, a kind of figurative schizophrenia enveloping Harlem, where real-ity felt like a dream that produces "surreal fantasies," as he writes in "Har-lem Is Nowhere."

The riot was formative for Ellison, who wrote an article covering it, "Harlem 24 Hours After—Peace and Quiet Reign," for the *New York Post*.[84] Offering insight into these events and perhaps into his first contact with photographer Gordon Parks, Ellison's archive includes a contact sheet of a previously unknown set of four images taken by Parks on what was prob-ably the second day of the riot, August 2.[85] Three of the four frames on the contact sheet show children: an openly gleeful teenager wields a toy rifle whose barrel hides the eyes of the boy behind him; a girl holds her head with a bored or jaded look directed at events occurring outside the frame; and a trio of boys appear seriously absorbed by the action to their left. The children experiencing this race riot in Harlem in the early 1940s will be in their prime by the time of the civil rights era, when a new series of riots would erupt in many American cities—and when "Harlem Is Nowhere" would finally appear in print. Ellison re-created the riot in the concluding chapters of *Invisible Man*, and the novel's prologue hints at the relation between crime, photojournalistic media exposure, and the African American community.

At the outset, the protagonist emerges from his underground lair and brutally assaults a white man who denies his existence. Ellison introduces photography when, the day after the encounter, the narrator sees the white man's "picture in the *Daily News*, beneath a caption stating that he had been mugged."[86] For the newspaper-reading public and for the city and state authorities, Invisible Man is nothing but a criminal. Ellison's narrator even tellingly describes his hole as being lit up like "a photographer's dream night" (6). The reference suggests an awareness of the ideal lighting conditions for night photography and implies that the novel's unnamed protagonist has dabbled in photographic technique. It may even bring a certain twisted logic to his obsession with lightbulbs. Unlike Bigger Thomas, Invisible Man is able to prevent the press from taking pictures of him; he remains invisibly mobile and uncaught as he creates his own record. Nevertheless, even though the narrator admits that most of the time he is "not so overtly violent" (9), his psychological suffering and his aggressive tendencies make him—as they do Bigger, for that matter—an ideal patient of the Lafargue Clinic.

In reality, it is not Invisible Man who has dabbled in photography, but rather his creator, who had been training as a professional photographer throughout the 1940s. As the literary and cultural scholar Sara Blair elucidates in her critical study of Ellison's development as a photographer, he was shooting almost daily, making prints, and studying Henri Cartier-Bresson, Brassaï, Robert Doisneau, and other masters; he even had "Ralph Ellison—Photographer" letterhead.[87] His professional work centered primarily on portraits and street photography but also showed quite an eclectic range—from pictures of art for museum publications to special events such as dog shows.[88]

In July 1947, *Magazine of the Year* first contacted Ellison to propose an "article, probably to be illustrated with photographs, on the Lafargue Clinic."[89] Dr. Wertham had recommended Ellison as the writer and told him that the magazine's idea was "to treat the subject as a community problem rather than as the healing of individual patients."[90] Ellison was attracted to such an approach but knew it would take a great photographer to pull it off.[91] By October, he was able to bring Parks on board as photographer and only then decided to accept the assignment.[92] He sought Parks's help in particular not only because he admired Parks's urban nimbleness and superior skill with a camera but also because he had discerned Parks's staunch commitment to conveying the individual humanity of his subjects as well as his understanding of their environment. Coincidentally, Parks had recently shot photographs for an *Ebony* article on Harlem's other psychiatric facility, the Northside Testing and Consultation Center, founded by Drs. Mamie and Kenneth Clark.[93]

Ellison and Parks dove into the project with remarkable energy and creativity; they wanted it to be a "new departure in photo-reporting."[94] A key set of notes on "Lafargue" in Ellison's archive bear witness to the genesis of their conceptual approach and the centrality of photography to the project. Located at the bottom of the "Lafargue Clinic" folder in the Ralph Ellison Papers at the Library of Congress are two typewritten and one half-handwritten sheets in which Ellison was attempting, through multiple reiterations, to describe how turning to photography—both literally and as analogy—should allow him to illustrate what the clinic represented in Harlem. "Simply by existing and performing its special task," Ellison writes, the clinic formed "a perspective through which many aspects of Harlem reality come to focus" and thus "assumed an importance that is seemingly all out of proportion to the relatively small number of patients that [it] is able to treat." Already, the clinic's very existence—which had been "established" by Wright's earlier piece—was able to bring clarity of vision to Harlem. Following the riff on "focus," the manuscript goes on to iterate hypnotically a series of eight different attempts at conveying the particular qualities and abilities of what Ellison now christens that "special type of camera," the Lafargue Clinic: "Like that special type of camera with which, through a special arrangement of mirrors and filters that split and bend the light rays entering the lense [*sic*] in three directions, it is possible to expose simultaneously three sheets of film which, developed and combined, reproduce a given scene in color."[95] Ellison is describing the exact parallactic process—a modernist favorite—that occurs inside what were then colloquially called "one-shot" color cameras.[96] For Ellison, therefore, the clinic enabled a new perspective capable of piercing through those "three sheets of film" to document a new form of symbolic reality.

Ellison goes on to list these sheets and what they represent: "Let the physical conditions of Harlem stand for one sheet of film; let Negro Americans stand for another; let the color aspects of American democracy stand for the third; and let the clinic stand for the camera"—and here Ellison gives two possible endings—"that brings the three together to the light of meaning" or "in which the three are exposed to the light of understanding."[97] Here, the clinic is the agent capable of superimposing the neighborhood itself, African Americans as a whole, and the tenets of American democracy in a single frame. In other words, the shots that the clinic-camera takes of Harlem portray black subjects who are fully integrated into American citizenry, which suggests that the inner mechanisms of this instrument can solve the discrepancies between the nation's principles and its failure to practice them. The metaphor of bringing "together" the three separate sheets further preserves the interracial spirit of democracy in which the institution was founded. If, for Ellison, photography is an "extension of democracy," for Parks the camera becomes a different kind of instrument that can be used for the cause: a "weapon."[98] By bringing into focus the disparity between the American Dream and the American "reality," this early collaboration between Parks and Ellison confirmed an ethos that would define their respective oeuvres. If we further take Ellison's analogy of the clinic as camera to its logical end, then the specificity of its being a "one-shot" color camera implies a certain urgent precarity; we may have only "one shot" at this delicate national experiment.

Ellison's notion of the clinic as camera confirms Blair's argument that for Ellison "photography was no less than an interpretive instrument, a resource for critical reflection on American cultural practices and norms," yet it positions these interpretations at the Harlem intersection of psychiatry, race, and democracy.[99] Put another way, this notion brings them to the underground, in Wright's sub-rosa basement of the St. Phillip's Parish House. The casting of the Lafargue Clinic as camera in these working notes provides a glimpse into Ellison's creative process that led to the casting of the clinic as the solution, literally the "antidote" to what Ellison calls the "failure" of the current American way of life in the published version of "Harlem Is Nowhere."[100] The clinic's previous incarnation as a camera allows for the possibility of wielding this "extension of democracy" as a portable lens through which to see the world and to take further advantage of photography's capacity to document a democratic vision of America and thus perhaps undertake the building of a new archive.

Herein lies a key to the difference between Ellison's formal and Wright's narratological invocation of the clinic—a difference tied to the nuances in their documentary and archival sensibilities. In Ellison's words, "it is here that lies the importance of the Lafargue Psychiatric Clinic—both as scientific laboratory and as an expression of forthright democratic action."[101] Thus, Ellison's use of the clinic stems from its function as both a means and an end. As an end, according to the published essay, it serves as "antidote" enabling the individual to "reforge the will that can endure in a hostile world."[102] As a means, according to Ellison's archive, it acts as a "camera" exposing "the failure of a way of life" for the disenfranchised African Americans. If an antiracist mental-hygiene clinic can be a camera, then there may be a touch of the therapeutic to photography as well.

For Ellison—as for many others who had worked for the Works Progress Administration—photography was also a way to "go on record." He told Wright in 1946, "I see, I hear, I analyse [sic] and I record."[103] And a few years later, when his friend Albert Murray informed him that he had just purchased a Leica camera, Ellison enthusiastically wrote: "I'm glad as hell to hear that you've taken up Photography; it's dam well time that those curious eyes of yours went on record."[104] Ellison's particular phrase—Murray's "curious eyes" will go "on record"—is a telling indication of how subjectively Ellison regarded photography. It is a means by which, through careful technique and with the right equipment, an individual can bear witness—"go on record"—and preserve that vision for posterity. The "Harlem Is Nowhere" assignment thus represented a particular pictorial problem: Gordon Parks had somehow to put on Ellison's "curious eyes" in order to "go on record."

THE "PICTORIAL PROBLEM"

Unsurprisingly, "Harlem Is Nowhere" became "quite a time-consuming assignment."[105] Unlike Wright and Saunders, Ellison and Parks worked closely on the project, shooting, developing, printing together, even going to the *Photography on Parade* exposition in Rockefeller Center in 1948, all in a dedicated effort to refine their approach and aesthetic goals. "To undertake this writing job," Ellison later explained, "it was necessary to interrupt work on a novel."[106] Over the winter months of 1947–1948, Ellison conducted research, wrote, and directed the shooting script, bringing his own camera along—it was during these excursions that Parks took the portrait of Ellison sitting on a park bench that appeared in Parks's technical guidebook *Camera Portraits: Techniques and Principles of Documentary Portraiture* (1948) and subsequently graced the dustjacket spine of Arnold Rampersad's biography of the novelist.[107] Interestingly, a contact sheet in Ellison's papers shows a variant of Parks's portrait of Ellison on the same bench sandwiched between two shots of Parks taken by Ellison (figure 3.4); at top left, a bespectacled Parks is taken in medium shot at a low angle, solemnly loading his camera, and at bottom left, in a shot taken from farther back and behind, Parks stands on a park bench, using the elevation to look into the camera mounted on the tripod.

Arising squarely amid the early years of *Invisible Man*'s composition, Ellison and Parks's endeavor became—to borrow one of Ellison's own images from an early "Nowhere" draft—"like a sunken log that shapes the currents between a river's banks, remaining to affect the tide of the speaker's moods."[108] Entries in Ellison's appointment calendar for 1948—often

FIGURE 3.4. Detail from contact sheet, Gordon Parks and Ralph Ellison working on the "Harlem Is Nowhere" project, Harlem, New York, 1948. Photographs by Gordon Parks and Ralph Ellison.

Source: PR 13 Call Number 1998:061, container 3, folder 10, Ralph Ellison Papers, Prints and Photographs Division, Library of Congress, Washington, DC. Courtesy of and copyright © The Gordon Parks Foundation.

made by his wife, Fanny, who also was an amateur photographer—outline the intense collaboration between Ellison and Parks in February and March, when the bulk of the "Nowhere" images were taken: February 6, "Parks"; February 10, "Parks by"; February 14, "Took photos"; February 15, "Sewed. Developed. Ralph—Enlarged"; February 16, "Dark room"; February 18, "Downtown with Parks"; February 19, "supposed to work with Parks on Story," then, later that day, "Ralph developed; Parks slept; Wertham called"; February 24, "Clinic"; February 25, "Worked with Parks all day, printing"; March 2, "Clinic"; March 4, "Layout with Gordon & Lauterbach" [a *'48* editor]; March 6, "Ralph took pics—Ralph and Gordon worked"; March 10, "'48 with Parks . . . & Lauterbach 'layout'"; March 16, "Enlarged portrait for Parks."[109] Thus, contrary to what previous scholarship has claimed, the project *was* completed, and by mid-April Ellison had even received from *'48* the final layout of the photo essay so he could begin composing captions for each image.[110]

The fact that Ellison printed their combined negatives—as the calendar further suggests—helps explain the presence of "Harlem Is Nowhere" prints in his own papers at the Library of Congress (such as the tiny print of *Harlem Rooftops*) and suggests a truly collaborative relationship between him and Parks over several months. In his narrative account of the completion of "Harlem Is Nowhere," Ellison blamed the weather and the challenging nature of the subject matter for the lengthy photo shoot—in comparison, the "actual writing" took just "another three weeks."[111] Ellison's explanation of the timeline suggests that he first wrote the shooting script, spent several months taking photographs with Parks, and only then sat down to write the essay; in other words, he wrote the captions, the "Harlem Is Nowhere" essay, as well as much of *Invisible Man* in the wake of the images he and Parks accumulated.

As part of his research for "Harlem Is Nowhere," Ellison frequently visited the Lafargue Clinic and "s[aw] Wertham from time to time."[112] In a letter to Wright written in February 1948, when he was in the thick of shooting and researching, Ellison formulated the clinic's growing power as well as the logic behind both this photo-essay and, subsequently, his novel in progress:

I am working on a piece describing the social conditions of Harlem which make the clinic a necessity. I've worked out a scheme to do it with photographs which should make for something new in photo-journalism—if Gordon Parks is able to capture those aspects of Harlem reality which are so clear to me. '48 is publishing this piece and if successful we should get a few things said. The clinic, incidently [*sic*], is expanding and beginning to have influence in the courts. In doing this piece I've been going through case histories, and though I've encountered nothing that I hadn't conceived, just seeing the stuff in print is terrific.[113]

There is so much to unpack in this letter: Ellison shied away from photographing the actual clinic but rather wanted to capture its raison d'être; his innovative "scheme" demanded an intuitive transfer of vision between himself and Parks the professional photographer; moreover, he underscored the clinic's growing influence at the judicial level, the tangible impact of its existence "in the courts." Of particular note here is that Ellison was doing archival research; he was going through the clinic's case files and was thrilled to "encounter nothing that [he] hadn't conceived." The statement recalls Wright's declaration in the introduction to *Black Metropolis*: "If, in reading my novel, *Native Son*, you doubted the reality of Bigger Thomas, then examine the delinquency rates cited in this book." In Wright's formulation, Ellison seems to be saying, "If, in reading 'Harlem Is Nowhere' (or my upcoming novel *Invisible Man*), you doubted the *unreality* of Harlem, then examine the Lafargue Clinic's case histories." Yet Ellison's own declaration somewhat reverses this logic: rather than have his work proudly align with the archive, the clinic's records are merely a material manifestation of the accuracy of his own fertile imaginary—a position that almost verges on solipsism while at the same time underscoring the logic behind his commitment to transcending the conventions of reportage.

Ellison came to the Lafargue records with a strong background in psychiatric case-history files because a decade earlier he had worked as a clerk and receptionist for the famed psychiatrist Harry Stack Sullivan, where, as he reveals in a letter to Constance Webb, he "had handled, read, and filed case histories of a number of well-known people."[114] As happened for

Wright, who had pored through the Wiltwyck School records, Ellison's encounter with Lafargue's case studies was thrilling for him, despite having read so many case files earlier in his life: seeing what he had already preconceived on record, "in print," was a "terrific" validation of his perspective.[115] Both writers recognized the evidentiary power of such records to support their vision; Ellison even further remarked in his preparatory notes that "as far as possible all points relating to mental difficulties of Negroes to be illustrated with material from clinic case histories."[116]

The "scheme" Ellison "worked out" is outlined in an elaborate shooting script he entitled "Pictorial Problem," accompanied by a few loose sheets of brainstorming notes, now preserved in his papers. As Sara Blair demonstrates in *Harlem Crossroads*, much of midcentury African American photography was deployed as a means of exposing the nefarious effects of segregation. The broader project of documentary photography, Blair adds, was "a way to make claims for experience rendered forcibly invisible, to relocate the meaning of social experience within everyday spaces—the tenements and alleys and basements."[117] Couched in its historical moment, Ellison's "scheme" suggests that he wanted to divorce these "everyday spaces" from the familiar by transposing them into shifting angles that reflect "the more or less 'normal' violence of Harlem folkways, the desperate attempts to respond to the symbols of American success and well-being," and, as a result, to capture the anomic sense of being "nowhere." The script sketches "the social conditions of Harlem which make the clinic a necessity," casting Harlem as "a ghetto area inhabited by a people undergoing all those blasting pressures which, in a scant eighty years, have sent the Negro people as a whole hurtling." It then describes the upheavals typically associated with modernism—the moves "from log cabin to city tenement, from the white folks fields and kitchens to factory sweat shops and assembly lines"—and underscores the fact that these changes have largely taken place between the two world wars. "This is," Ellison admits, "a part of the rapid growth of the United States as a whole, and thus of the general upheaval of the world; yet it has its own particular features, and it is these which give Harlem its individual character."[118]

Although African Americans' exclusion from proper institutional care was endemic to the nation as a whole, in Harlem it had "increased and

become a special problem through the failure of those in authority to provide for its correction, either by admitting Negroes to existing institutions,
or providing such institutions in the Harlem area."[119] Ellison presents
Wertham as a maverick pioneer combating the democratic sabotage in
Harlem and the nation with his clinic. In these respects, the ideology
behind the article remains in perfect intellectual compatibility with Richard Wright's agenda for his own photo-text. The difference between the
two only really begins to emerge once Ellison challenges photography's
ability to go beyond mere documentation through a modernist "scheme"
that aims to achieve "something new in photo-journalism." Ellison intended
to surpass not just Wright's take on the photo-essay but also all of the
other promotional pieces of photojournalism on the Lafargue Clinic that
had already appeared.[120]

Notable phrases from Ellison's notes match up strikingly with the
images Parks produced in 1948 for both "Harlem Is Nowhere" and "Harlem Gang Leader"—indicating that Parks was indeed up to the task Ellison devised. "Maze, Decay, Filth," the notes begin and go on to conjure a
series of locations and themes: "tripping on garbage cans," "start argu-
ments, fighting," "dope pad," "narrow broken stairs," "undertakers in Harlem," "strange walk by Parish House" (in whose basement the Lafargue
Clinic was located), "Rebirth & transcendence," "repititions [sic] of symbols & ritual, clash between private rites and public situations, comic
books, horror stories," and, written upside down on the sheet, "Symbols
of Authority; shot of Cop while at low angle."[121] Another sheet of holograph notes reveals Ellison's awareness of photographic technique and
his desire to go beyond documentary practice in favor of a more expressionist form:

1. Stairway shot from extreme angle, distorted to give sense of danger, mugger might appear lurking upon it.

2. Area way with its passages shoot with wide angle lenses to get door-
ways. Shoot slow, have figure running through it so as to smear movement across negative.

3. Effect of woman (or child) falling down stairs, blurred, a swirl of
clothing.[122]

Peril and impending criminality at every turn, tenement housing with swift figures "smearing" the texture of reality, falling women and children in a "blur" and "swirl" of clothing—in Ellison's notes as in Parks's photographs and in a way that prefigures the later chapters of *Invisible Man*—Harlem emerges as a schizophrenic maze zigzagging between filth and rebirth, decay and transcendence, powerlessness and agency.

The shooting script Ellison wrote for Parks directly articulates the "pictorial problem" they were facing. Put simply, "prints must present scenes that are at once both document and symbol; both reality and (for the reader) psychologically disturbing 'image.'"[123] "The problem for the camera," Ellison continues:

> is to approach material in this twofold manner: It must present the negative sociological aspects of Harlem, the crowding, delinquency, family disorientation, unemployment, while at the same time it must be alert to those aspects of the Harlem scene that appear in the dreams of the individual as symbol (underground tunnels, mazes, basements, broken stairways, long narrow hallways, [rats, roaches; empty, unprotected elevator shafts; fire traps; violence], burning buildings; white policemen; decay; chimneys emitting black smoke that sweeps low into the street, crowded pawn shops on Monday morn, etc.).[124]

These instructions reflect the content not only of "Harlem Is Nowhere" but also much of *Invisible Man*. Indeed, the concepts underlying Ellison's efforts to forge "something new in photo-journalism" are precisely those that inform his experiments with the novel form. As Blair puts it, the power of photography to "wrest the fullness and mystery of experience out from under the rubrics of poverty, delinquency, and oppression" came to have "particular novelistic uses" for Ellison.[125]

Ellison was never able to use the Gordon Parks photographs, so the absence of the accompanying images left him with part of the story untold, which may have provided an incentive for their subsequent translation into *Invisible Man*. His novelistic prose had somehow to communicate what the prints—as both "document and symbol"—were meant to evoke. When Ellison collaborated with Parks again in 1952 to create an experimental photo-essay for *Life* magazine promoting the publication of *Invisible Man*, he again pointed to the difficulty of having photographic documents capture his aesthetic sense. In a letter to Wright, he commented: "Being a photographer and a writer, you will appreciate the tremendous difficulty of translating such intensified and heightened prose images into those of photography."[126] The sentiment reframes his postwar novel as a repository of "intensified and heightened prose images" in need of remediation: "the transformation of lived experience into narrative, of social fact into aesthetic possibility—and vice versa," as Blair puts it.[127] Nowhere is this reciprocal relation between photography and Ellison's novelistic practice more evident than in the shooting script and captions he prepared for "Harlem Is Nowhere."

CAPTIONS: DIRECT READER'S EYE TO FACTS

We must be thankful that most of the lost "Nowhere" images were recently found intermingled with the contact sheets, negatives, and prints belonging to the "Harlem Gang Leader" files now in The Gordon Parks Foundation holdings.[128] Ellison's working drafts for the captions, preserved at the Library of Congress, were among the essential clues that allowed the identification, from within Parks's archive, of the specific pictures that were meant to be used in "Harlem Is Nowhere" for *'48: The Magazine of the Year*.[129] The editors of *'48* had assigned a key letter to each picture, from A to M (although L appears to have been skipped), a system Ellison followed in drafting captions and one adopted for the *Invisible Man: Gordon Parks and Ralph Ellison in Harlem* catalog and exhibition at the Art Institute of Chicago in 2016. Thus reunited with Ellison's captions, Parks's photographs are given a chance to resume their intended lifecycle and are startling in their ability to grapple with the complex, allegorical goals of Ellison's script and subsequent novel.

Because the Lafargue Clinic could be reached only by zigzagging "through a disturbing narrow maze-like series of halls and stairways," Ellison wanted to "play on the irony of its being located in a basement," where

FIGURE 3.5. *Harlem Rooftops*, Harlem, New York, 1948. Photograph by Gordon Parks.

Source: Courtesy of and copyright © The Gordon Parks Foundation.

its "friendly social workers and psychiatrists" "had to go 'underground' to carry out their work," and he initially hoped to have the "opening shot to be one of the general community, leading into [a] shot that will emphasize the maze-like aspect of ghetto living."[130] The image chosen to illustrate this first idea was likely *Harlem Rooftops* (figure 3.5), which was later used as the spread opening Parks's feature "Harlem Gang Leader" in *Life* magazine (figure 3.6).

For the final layout, *Harlem Rooftops* appears to have become the third image selected for "Harlem Is Nowhere" because it stands as a perfect embodiment of the "panorama shot" of caption C: "Harlem the largest 'Negro' city in the U.S. A physical ruin that for many represents a psychological maze. Bright spot in photo rises near Lafargue Clinic."[131] The "bright spot" matches the rising white fog emerging from the rooftops close to the center of the frame. Ellison's papers also include several of his own attempts at creating images similar to *Harlem Rooftops*.[132]

This shot of the "general community" was initially supposed to come alongside a shot "emphasiz[ing] the maze-like aspect of ghetto living,"

FIGURE 3.6. Opening spread of Gordon Parks, "Harlem Gang Leader," *Life*, November 1, 1948. Photographs by Gordon Parks.

Source: Courtesy of and copyright © The Gordon Parks Foundation

which was achieved with a print called *Off on My Own* (figure 3.7). [133] This Parks photograph has been widely circulated over the years but never as part of the "Harlem Is Nowhere" project; my research shows that it was the image meant to accompany caption B: "Who am I? Where am I? How did I come to be? Refugees from Southern feudalism, many Negroes wander dazed in the mazes of northern ghettos, displaced persons of American democracy."[134]

Based on the order of the images selected for publication, Ellison ended up reversing his initial idea: he first would bring the viewer down to the ground level to capture the wandering individual in the maze, then pull back into the Harlem stratosphere for the wide panorama shot hovering above the maze. Adding to the evidence that Parks's photograph *Off on My Own* was originally part of "Harlem Is Nowhere," the Ellison Papers contain two contact sheets whose middle frames are three shots taken from

FIGURE 3.7. *Off on My Own*, Harlem, New York, 1948. Photograph by Gordon Parks.

Source: Courtesy and copyright © The Gordon Parks Foundation.

the same narrow passageway but in which the wanderer does not appear.[135] The intermingling of these alternative frames, developed by Ellison and likely taken by Parks, confirms how closely the two photographers worked together.

In the same spirit as caption B, Ellison's script also asks for a "shot of a filthy area way with a confusion of exits, or a shot (preferably from above) of the garbage strewn interconnecting courtyards sometimes found behind the rows of brownstones"[136]—many examples of which can be found in both Parks's and Ellison's files as well as in the work of other Harlem photographers, including Aaron Siskind and Roy DeCarava. These photos obviously share a kinship with *Off on My Own* but also bring us closer to caption D because of the ubiquitous presence of garbage: "Harlem garbage: it's so high you can't get over it; so wide you can't get round it. Children play in it, adults walk through it; it stinks and fouls the inner landscape of the mind."[137] Part of a series of pictures featuring curbside garbage in wintertime found in the "Harlem Gang Leader" files, one Parks print shows five boys playing among the detritus, at the center of which they have set a bushel basket on fire—presumably to help them keep warm.[138] In discussing the kinds of photographs Ellison was taking in the late 1940s, Sara Blair points out that "a significant number of his printed images take children as subjects," but she speculates that this focus was "probably an outgrowth of Ellison's work collecting their oral narratives, riddles, and jump-rope rhymes in Harlem in 1940–41, during his stint on the payroll of the Federal Writers' Project."[139] However, it seems likely that children were his main subjects because "children are given special attention at the Lafargue clinic," as Richard Wright underscores in a caption used for "Psychiatry Comes to Harlem." Further associating this print with Lafargue is the fact that the boy on the left is completely absorbed in the reading of a comic book. Alternative frames of this scene on contact sheets (see figures 5.2 and 5.3 in chapter 5) show that the comic book in question is a horror comic—in one frame, we can clearly make out the head of a ghoul—which Dr. Wertham would have interpreted as yet another factor, on top of the uncollected garbage, that "stinks and fouls the inner landscape" of the boys' minds.

For these images shot outside on location, Ellison preferred "natural light as much possible, using chiaroscuro effects to drive home the psychological nature of the subject matter." "The point photographically," he adds, "is to disturb the reader through the same channel that he receives his visual information."[140] Where Wright wanted to inform and reassure his readers that Lafargue genuinely existed, that it was accessible and free of charge, Ellison instead sought to "disturb" readers and force them to confront the physical and psychological difficulties involved in actually reaching the clinic in this garbage-strewn maze known as Harlem. Only by the end of the essay is the clinic itself to be offered as "the maze . . . through which the individual is helped to rediscover himself; the 'maze' in which he is given 'the courage to live in a hostile world,'"[141] a phrase that echoes the concluding sentence of "Harlem Is Nowhere," while the sentiment as a whole is represented in the photograph associated with the final caption, M: "A patient waiting in one of the cubicles of the Lafargue Clinic. The Lafargue Clinic aims to transform despair, not into hope, but into determination."[142] John Callahan aptly describes the photograph, preserved in the Fredric Wertham Papers at the Library of Congress, as "Harlem's version of Rodin's *Thinker*," featuring an African American man cradling his head in his hands from a seated position.[143] Just like the youth being seen by Dr. Tweed in the Saunders photographs taken for Wright's essay "Psychiatry Comes to Harlem," the man's face is hidden in this photograph for "Harlem Is Nowhere," a move that reflects the privacy of the patient while also elevating the figure to the position of a representative of the human (Harlem) condition.[144]

The caption draft manuscripts further reveal that some illustrations were designed to function via juxtaposition and contrast in the final layout, such as those intended for captions E, F, and G: "Individual failures (E) when taken as proof of inferiority of all Negroes, injure entire group as vitally as man (F) who has been struck by a car. To protect oneself from casual violence and to assert one's individuality, one learns to turn one's head (G)."[145] The "individual failures" of caption E were to be positioned "above" the "man (below) who has been struck by car" of caption F[146] in order to stress how the media's proliferation of "damage imagery" "injures the entire group as vitally" as the car-stricken man. With such an arrangement, the images veer closer to the symbolic than to the documentary, especially in the case of the image chosen to illustrate caption F. Variant frames in the contact sheets containing this particular Parks image reveal that the recumbent man on the sidewalk apparently was not hit by a car but was simply resting—he was using his hand as a pillow. This particular frame—with headlights peeking from within the gloom behind the man, whose body, from this angle, looks twisted, as if broken—adeptly furnishes the implied symbolic context and seems an ideal partner to the image selected to illustrate caption E.[147]

Another pairing was to combine the photographs assigned to captions I and J. Based on the text, the "cynical, furtive, violent" adolescent in the photo for caption I was to be seen "on opposite page" to caption J's image in order to "contrast poignantly with resignation of man still in his prime" found in *Street Scene*.[148] Like *Off on My Own*, *Street Scene* is another example of a Parks photograph that has been in circulation for years but never in the context of the "Harlem Is Nowhere" photo-text. As part of this greater ensemble, *Street Scene* creates the desired contrast with the in-your-face adolescent seen in the photograph of caption I, but the fact that the man sits on a wooden crate by the side of the road also associates him with the comic-book-reading boy from the caption D image, who is also sitting on a crate; the older man becomes a disturbing foreshadowing of what might await the boy.[149]

Other photographs powerfully literalize symbolic experiences—none more so than the frame corresponding to caption H (figure 3.8): "When things take on special significance because you're black. A cold, accusing, unseen eye seems to judge your every act. It makes you feel guilty, hostile, 'nowhere.'"[150] At first, the symbolism is triggered more by Ellison's caption than by the image because painted underneath a giant eye on the wall behind the young boy—a boy bearing a bandage on his forehead in a way that connotes both psychic and physical wounds—are the words "*The* UNSEEN EYE IS WATCHING YOU." Perhaps one of the most "psychologically disturbing" images in the lot, this photo at once represents the boy's subjected status—framed as he is by overshadowing whiteness—and renders the viewer complicit with the "unseen eye" the caption describes. We remain unseen yet are watching him. Although the document invokes the theme of Big Brother surveillance, the black boy suggests that "double-consciousness" W. E. B. Du Bois eloquently describes as "this sense of always looking at one's self through the eyes of others, of measuring one's soul by the tape of a world that looks on in amused contempt and pity."[151] Both the caption and the painted message on the white wall further recall

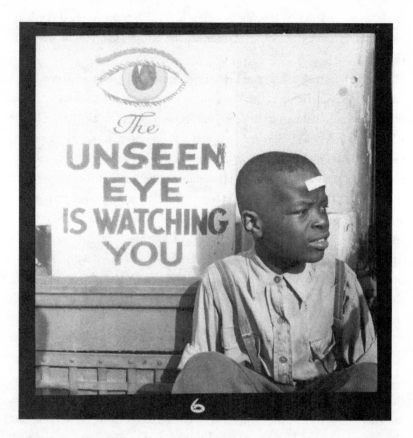

FIGURE 3.8. Detail from contact sheet, untitled, Harlem, New York, 1948; image for caption H, "Harlem Is Nowhere" project. Photograph by Gordon Parks.

Source: Courtesy of and copyright © The Gordon Parks Foundation.

the moment in *Invisible Man* when the narrator first sets foot on Wall Street and imagines "men who looked down at you through peepholes in the ceiling and walls, watching you constantly, silently waiting for a wrong move. Perhaps even now an eye had picked me up and watched my every movement" (165). As Ellison would do for many of these captions and photographs, he found a way to boomerang this particular image back into his novel.

Remarkably, the excavation and reconstitution of the original "Harlem Is Nowhere" photo-text demonstrate that what originated as chiefly a photographic directive—to have "scenes that are at once both document and symbol"—ultimately became the guiding principle behind Ellison's crafting of his novel *Invisible Man*, to the extent that looking at the shooting script today feels like finding the Peter Wheatstraw blueprints Ellison followed as a novelist. That poignant phrase from caption H, "the unseen eye is watching you," ultimately became the disembodied narrative voice that, equally unseen, "speaks for you" from the lower frequencies at the end of *Invisible Man*. That unseen voice flips the "watching" by state surveillance on its head to become a benevolent "watching over," marking an important transfer of agency and power, just as this photograph rises as yet another origin for Ellison's trope of invisibility. Equally fascinating is the realization occasioned by these materials of the extent to which Ellison's collaboration with Parks forged his novelistic vision. Parks's strategies for solving the problem of creating pictures that were simultaneously document and symbol gave Ellison a visual model for his own aesthetic project. In turn, for Parks, this collaboration with Ellison, as historian Erika Doss has observed, "was instrumental in terms of shaping Parks' postwar understanding of race and representation."[152]

Their initial collaboration had gone so well, in fact, that Parks attempted to enlist Ellison in his initial work at *Life* shortly after the "Harlem Is Nowhere" project was completed. "It was a project with Ellison that gave [Parks] confidence to approach the notoriously gruff *Life* picture editor Wilson Hicks in 1948," photo historian Maren Stange has suggested. Parks confirmed this enlistment in an interview: "I had copies of the photographs and took them over to *Life*."[153] In other words, the portfolio Hicks consulted when Parks applied for a staff job at *Life* included the images intended for "Harlem Is Nowhere." What all previous narratives of Parks's entry at *Life* have elided, however, is that Parks initially wanted to continue collaborating with Ellison for the "Harlem Gang Leader" assignment. On August 13, 1948, Ellison wrote to a friend that he had just "had some talks with *Life* concerning a photo-essay assignment with Gordon Parks in which I am not interested and against which Fanny is dead set, although, God

knows, we do need the dough."[154] Given the date of the letter, the assignment referred to could only be what became Parks's first byline at *Life*,
"Harlem Gang Leader," published in the November 1, 1948, issue. We know
that Ellison was ultimately not involved with "Gang Leader," but this evidence does bring "Harlem Is Nowhere" and "Harlem Gang Leader," whose
contact sheets are intertwined, even closer and further helps explain how
"Gang Leader" "inherited" the photograph *Harlem Rooftops* as its opening
spread, thus granting it a new lifecycle.

THE NOVELISTIC LIFECYCLES OF
THE (ABSENT) PHOTOGRAPHS

Four years after the aborted "Nowhere" project, Ellison and Parks collaborated once again to celebrate the publication of *Invisible Man* in 1952 in a
memorable feature for *Life* titled "A Man Becomes Invisible."[155] This second collaboration was a direct attempt to "illustrate specific passages
from the novel," notably concentrating on scenes set in Harlem.[156] Although
only four photographs appeared in the magazine article, the Parks archive
revealed that "more than two dozen verified images" were taken for this
project. Most of the images appear to be staged—they used an actor, John
Bates, to portray the novel's unnamed protagonist—and included "elabo-
rately constructed sets, as well as surreal photomontages assembled by
Parks."[157] The latter were an attempt to literalize the magical-realist elements
of *Invisible Man*—perhaps the most famous images from this series being
the *Emerging Man* photographs that show a man's head peeping out of a
manhole. This moment, though promised in the epilogue, takes us beyond
the events of the novel—the narrator announces that he will end his hibernation, but the actual moment of emergence from underground is not part
of the story.

Although Ellison—in an uncharacteristic move—was involved in helping Parks find ways of translating the "intensified and heightened prose

images [from *Invisible Man*] into those of photography,"[158] in truth he had already performed an analogous process of "translation" in the wake of the "Harlem Is Nowhere" project. Left unrealized and unused, the photo-text "Harlem Is Nowhere" appears to have become so internalized by Ellison that—just as Parks had repurposed *Harlem Rooftops* for "Harlem Gang Leader"—he ended up smuggling some imagery and captions from "Harlem Is Nowhere" into *Invisible Man*, almost, one might say, as an homage to their collaboration. The captions are brought back to life roughly midway through the novel, in the aftermath of the explosion at the Liberty Paints factory.

When the protagonist regains consciousness, his body is ensconced inside a "machine" of some kind, surrounded by doctors/scientists whom he overhears announcing that they have implanted him with a "little gadget." Invisible Man is then tellingly described, like the man in caption M from "Harlem Is Nowhere," as "the patient" (236). Trapped in the machine, he feels himself becoming hostile, "angry, murderously angry," but the treatment—the electric current—prevents him from acting out (237). As he slowly regains consciousness—"rediscovers himself"—his descriptive language recalls the visual effects of photography: "Thoughts evaded me, hiding in the vast stretch of clinical whiteness to which I seemed connected only by a scale of receding grays" (238). Almost as if he can now discern the "unseen eye" mentioned in caption H, he notices that "faces hovered above me like inscrutable fish peering myopically through a glass aquarium wall. I saw them suspended motionless above me . . . seeing them from this angle was disturbing" (239). The latter description matches perfectly with Ellison's directive that "the point photographically . . . is to disturb the reader through the same channel that he receives his visual information." Like any patient entering the Lafargue Clinic for the first time, Invisible Man is asked by a cluster of doctors and nurses a series of routine questions that are isolated and capitalized on the page: "WHAT IS YOUR NAME? . . . WHO . . . ARE . . . YOU? . . . WHAT IS YOUR MOTHER'S NAME?" (239–240, second and third ellipses in the original).

After receiving some kind of treatment, he is declared "a new man" and is taken down a labyrinthine underground path into offices that recall the Lafargue "cubicles": "out of the room and down a long white corridor into an elevator, then swiftly down three floors to a reception room with rows of chairs. At the front were a number of private offices with frosted glass doors and walls" (245). Like the patient in caption M, Invisible Man is told that the "director will see [him] shortly" and seems to be waiting for Dr. Wertham himself, who is "behind a screen of improvised interviewing cubicle." At first, the staff seems to ignore Invisible Man as he "trembled like a leaf," but he is eventually seen by a "tall austere-looking man in a white coat," who watches him with "a calm, scientific gaze" (245). Although their encounter is awkward, the patient does leave comforted by the thought that he is now "no longer afraid" (249). For these reasons and despite the hero's overall need to escape the clinical entrapment in which he awakes, I hesitate to describe this scene, as many critics have done, as a "consistently damning critique of the relationship between psychiatry and race."[159] After all, in "Harlem Is Nowhere," the Lafargue psychiatric facility is literally described as the "antidote" enabling the individual patient to "reforge the will that can endure in a hostile world,"[160] a notion that is symbolically preserved in the novel when Invisible Man is injected with a mysterious substance that courses through his veins and makes his entire body begin to glow: "A huge iridescent bubble seemed to enfold me" (238). Although this substance makes him "sail off like a ball thrown over the roof into mist, striking a hidden wall beyond a pile of broken machinery and sailing back" (238), when the doctor returns to give him another physical examination, he observes that this patient is now "surprisingly strong" (244).

This scene as it appears in the novel represents a significant revision of an earlier iteration of *Invisible Man* in manuscript form. Ellison unveiled in the book *Soon, One Morning: New Writing by American Negroes, 1940–1962* (1968) an excised chapter that once stood in this scene's place. In this unused chapter, titled "Out of the Hospital and Under the Bar," revived from Ellison's dormant files, the place where Invisible Man is held is, according to Campbell, "much more clearly represented as a psychiatric facility."[161] In fact, as Bradford Campbell's reading suggests, Invisible Man ends up in a *psychiatric* clinic because Ellison "had a nervous breakdown in mind for our narrator."[162] The counterfactual chapter casts a wider critical net around the scientific discourses of those who perform their tests upon a helpless narrator caught in an "iron straight-jacket." Mary Rambo—who in this chapter is employed at the facility as a custodian and who frees Invisible Man from its scientific clutches—awkwardly reveals to the protagonist that they "got one of the psychiatristses and a socialist or sociologist or something looking at you all the time." Invisible seems most alarmed by the first of the three types, exclaiming, "A psychiatrist!"[163] Sociology and psychiatry—the two emerging discourses that Richard Wright so openly embraced—are here literally entrapping the hero with their instruments and methods in addition to being subtly associated with socialism. Even though in the unused chapter the narrator does refer to the psychiatrist as "old friendly face,"[164] in the published novel he seems traumatized by "the instruments pointed at [him]" (253) rather than "inspired," as was the case for Wright.

"Out of the Hospital" is a chapter steeped in visuality, brimming with unusual lighting and pictorial details that sometimes read like descriptions of photographs, moments "frozen" in time: "I was in the dark and I could see the freckles on the side of his face that was in the light"; "through the glass door, I could see uniformed men and women caught grotesquely in mid-gesture"; "Several men loomed in the rectangle of light, poised like dancers at the climax of a powerful leap"; "I could see a group of wavering flashlights; then the men above them, their faces skull-like in the shadows shooting from below."[165] The latter description in particular, "shooting from below," recalls some of the directives in Ellison's shooting script for "Harlem Is Nowhere." "Eyes" of all kinds dominate the excised chapter, concluding with the "sightless eyes" of an old blind man whom the narrator tellingly mistakes for his own grandfather. This emphasis extends to visual technology and lenses—from the "microscope" that the white man threatens to hit Invisible Man with to the other "microscope-like instrument" that "two physicians" wield during their observation of "the patient."[166]

The basement location of this mazelike clinic is also accentuated in the chapter as it follows the protagonist's meandering attempts at escape down various corridors, unseen corners, elevators, ladders, a secret speakeasy, and eventually a manhole opening up onto a Harlem street—through which he emerges naked "as ever he come into this world." The narrative twice points to "the labyrinthine pattern of the floor,"[167] recalling the "labyrinthine existence" that comes from dwelling "in the bowels of the city" described in "Harlem Is Nowhere."[168] During his escape in the unused chapter, Invisible Man looks up to the ceiling and wonders: "Were they watching from some hidden peepsight in the ceiling? Testing me like a rat in a maze?"[169] Here, the "cold, accusing, unseen eye" of caption H, judging his every act, symbolically returns to view Harlem's underground as a scientist's mazelike controlled environment in which test subjects scurry about while unseen scientists observe their behavior. Like the wanderer of caption B for "Harlem Is Nowhere," Invisible Man is "dazed in the maze," a "displaced person of American democracy." The narrator even comments that the "basement corresponds to the structure of his mind,"[170] a notion that bookends Ellison's shooting script.

In the published novel, once the narrator has escaped the factory hospital, the narrative continues to follow the cues from the "Harlem Is Nowhere" captions in trickling fashion. As the narrator takes his first steps back above ground, his growing inner doubts lead him to pose the same two questions that were meant for caption B: "Who was I, how had I come to be?" (259), he asks, while the caption reads, "Who am I? Where am I? How did I come to be?" Before the narrator encounters the yam street vendor who will provide him with the answer to such questions ("I yam what I am!" [266]), his eyes focus on a series of artifacts in a store window that closely recall caption K: "Religion and toilet paper, dream books and bobby pins, saints and exotic figures, deodorants and magic incense, piggy banks and belly dancers—the values and yearnings of a civilization in a jumble."[171] As he walks, grazing the passing shops, "a flash of red and gold from a window filled with religious articles caught my eye. And behind the film of frost etching the glass I saw two brashly painted plaster images of Mary and Jesus surrounded by dream books, love powders,

God-Is-Love signs, money-drawing oil and plastic dice" (262). Not only does the content of what Invisible Man sees behind store windows seem based on caption K, but the narrative's focus on his "eye" adds to the photographic effect of this scene. Parks's photograph *Mysticism, Harlem, New York*, used in the *Life* story on *Invisible Man* in 1952, matches this moment perfectly, but Ellison also attempted to photographically capture his own version of caption K, as evidenced by a contact sheet in his papers (figure 3.9).[172] Taken together, these contact sheets and captions demonstrate one of the major ways in which Ellison, in the latter half of his novel, was turning to novelistic practice as a means of giving his archive new lifecyles.

Tracing the genesis of these novelistic scenes back to the "Nowhere" images offers critical insight into the photographic origins of Ellison's craft and into Parks's influence on his novel. For a novel so concerned with invisibility, written by an author who systematically refused that it be adapted into any visual media—such as a film or a comic book—the realization that some of its prose began as literal description of photographs is both baffling and exciting. Following the lifecycles of these captions brings visibility to Ellison's craft—we can map the mobile archivization of photo-textual materials in novelistic form, showing how precisely the Lafargue Clinic became a "camera" through which he could focus the stylistic innovations he "developed" in *Invisible Man*. At the same time, unearthing this archive provides important thematics tethered to a fascinating, largely unnoticed background. It underscores the overwhelming photographic motif of these scenes; it gives potent insight into the interiority of the Invisible Man and new interpretive language with which to understand both him and the postwar moment from which he emerges. In other words, everything the narrator describes during his dazed wandering in Harlem is precisely what Ellison considered to be "photographic documentation of conditions that intensify mental disturbances."[173] His narrator here internalizes, embodies, and verbalizes these exact conditions, and the welling rage he feels—he wants to punch through the store windows—is contextualized by this archive into a larger social critique of the lack of institutional support of African Americans.

FIGURE 3.9. Detail from contact sheet, Harlem, New York, ca. 1948; "Religious Articles and Dream Books," associated with caption K, "Harlem Is Nowhere" project. Photographs by Ralph Ellison.

NOT LIKE AN ARROW, BUT A BOOMERANG

Given the indisputable importance of photography to "Harlem Is Nowhere"—and to *Invisible Man*—why would Ellison choose not to include the photographs when he finally published the essay in *Shadow and Act* in 1964? As fate would have it, less than a month after the photo essay was completed—when it was "actually in the forms and ready to go on the presses"—*'48: The Magazine of the Year* suspended publication and filed for bankruptcy.[174] Its lawyers then kept "Harlem Is Nowhere" as evidence for why the magazine should be allowed to stay in business.[174] In an irritated letter to the magazine's counsel in late September 1948, Ellison requested that his article "and the set of photographs prepared for its illustration be returned to me."[176] The materials remained caught up in litigation until August 1951, and in the meantime Ellison tried to place "Harlem Is Nowhere" in *Harper's Magazine* in late 1948, despite the fact that he no longer had Parks's accompanying photographs. *Harper's* sent a rejection notice four days into the new year: "We are distinctly impressed but not enough to want to run it. The chief criticism has been that the clinic never quite emerges and that the rest is too generalized; I hope it isn't entirely imagination on my part that it is still a 'picture' story and that it suffers the lack of the pictures to pin it down."[177] It was painfully obvious: Ellison's essay was nowhere without Parks's pictures.

"Harlem Is Nowhere" then languished in Ellison's "cluttered files" for years until it surfaced in *Shadow and Act*, the same year James Baldwin and photographer Richard Avedon published their collaborative work *Nothing Personal*.[178] As *Shadow and Act* awaited release, staff at *Harper's*—likely unaware that the magazine had once rejected the essay—contacted Ellison's agency about what they now—surprise, surprise—called his "superb essay on Harlem," wondering whether he would like to devote a whole new essay on the subject. "He could make this one more personal," they wrote, "or he could expand on that section in the Harlem essay."[179] Ellison half agreed; he gave *Harper's* the old essay yet effected some changes that are too consequential to ignore. He removed a few of the opening and closing paragraphs, and at long last the *Harper's* version of "Harlem Is Nowhere" appeared in August 1964 with "pictures to pin it down." But these pictures were not the ones Parks took in 1948. Instead, Ellison chose work by another major photographer—none other than Harlem-born Roy DeCarava.

In yet another twist of this convoluted history, two of the four photographs Ellison selected for the *Harper's* version had already appeared in DeCarava's earlier collaboration with another literary giant: *The Sweet Flypaper of Life*, from 1955, coauthored with Langston Hughes.[180] Although DeCarava's images share a definite kinship—as symbols and as documents—with those Parks produced in 1948, things are not the same. The first image in the *Harper's* version initially seems to be a reproduction of *Man Sitting on Stoop with Baby* (taken in 1952, the year *Invisible Man* was published), which appears in *Sweet Flypaper*, but a comparison reveals that Ellison chose an alternative frame for "Harlem Is Nowhere," one in which the man bows his head and huddles the child closely, whereas in the photo included in *Sweet Flypaper* the father's head is held proudly upright as he looks at the neighborhood (see figures 3.10 and 3.11).[181] Clearly, DeCarava had given Ellison—the two were friends and lived close by to one another—access to his archive of prints and negatives.

This small change, along with the vertiginous three-decade temporal collapse authorized by Ellison's archival practices—prose composed in 1948 frames this man and child from 1952 and brings them into the Harlem of 1964—deepens the symbolic charge of the image. The man who was once part of a happy neighborhood scene—*Sweet Flypaper* tells a warm, dynamic, happy narrative—has now become a lonely father cradling his baby, shielding it from a hostile world. The idea of fatherhood engrained in this photograph is also the central thematic concern in the second novel Ellison was then writing (posthumously published as *Three Days Before the Shooting* [2010]). By 1964, when Ellison selected this image of the father and baby, he had already published a long section from novel manuscript titled "And Hickman Arrives" in a special issue of *Noble Savage* edited by Saul Bellow in 1960. The story introduced American audiences to Reverend Hickman and his adopted foundling, Bliss. In this context, the postmodern reassemblage of these archival materials becomes a timely bridge between Ellison's

FIGURE 3.10. *Man Sitting on Stoop with Baby,* Harlem, New York, 1952. Photograph by Roy DeCarava.

Source: Langston Hughes and Roy DeCarava, *The Sweet Flypaper of Life* (New York: Hill and Wang, 1955), 67. Copyright © the estate of Roy DeCarava.

past—the prehistory of "Harlem Is Nowhere" and his first novel—and his ongoing, future-directed progress on what turned out to be a never-ending novel.[182]

Ellison's decision to (re)create a new photo-text out of his old essay at this particular time is also timely in a more traditional sense: just weeks before this issue of *Harper's* hit the stands in August 1964, James Powell, an African American teenager, was shot and killed by a white police

FIGURE 3.11. Alternate take of *Man Sitting on Stoop with Baby*, Harlem, New York, 1952. Photograph by Roy DeCarava.

Source: Ralph Ellison, "Harlem Is Nowhere," with photographs by Roy DeCarava, *Harper's Magazine*, August 1964. Copyright © the estate of Roy DeCarava.

officer. The following days saw the eruption of the third great Harlem riot, what is now regarded as the precursor to the long, hot summer civil rights riots of the late 1960s.[183] In this respect, the abiding subjection of the African American community nullified the belatedness of "Harlem Is Nowhere"; what the clinic/camera/weapon was able to capture in 1948 still represented by 1964 a vision of an America to come, a "promise" yet to be fulfilled in this laboratory for the realization of national ideals. As the

Harper's editors put it, "Little has changed in the everyday life of the ghetto in the past sixteen years."[184] The following year, as Daniel Matlin contextualizes in *On the Corner: African American Intellectuals and the Urban Crisis*, Kenneth Clark would publish his widely influential work *Dark Ghetto*, a book that Ellison nevertheless considered too mired in "pathologist social scientific oversimplifications."[185]

The other difference Ellison brought to the essay as published in *Harper's* corroborates this point; in the text itself, as Sharifa Rhodes-Pitts stresses in her history of Harlem titled after Ellison's essay, he excised the first four and final three paragraphs of his original essay, thereby gutting mentions of the Lafargue Clinic, which, if you recall, closed in 1959.[186] Although the closing of the clinic was only a small change among so many upheavals in the intervening years, its elision from the *Harper's* version is significant: Ellison had called the clinic an "underground extension of democracy" and a "special kind of camera" that "reproduces in color" the nation's democratic promise. Wright had called it the "way to salvation for innumerable Negroes." Its disappearance both from the Harlem scene and from "Harlem Is Nowhere" was symptomatic of how, between the original intended publication date of the essay and the civil rights movement, the fight for democracy had forcibly shifted aboveground. Parks's images were so instrumental in shaping Ellison's prose in the first place that viewing the Ellison–DeCarava collaboration is like uncovering a palimpsest—or "superimposition" to use Barthe's term—of the essay's earlier, lost manifestations, its invisible and counterfactual past lives. What Ellison's third installment of "Harlem Is Nowhere" ultimately suggests is that what once protected the Harlem community from what he described as the "hostility that bombards the individual from so many directions" had simply vanished. When such institutional presences disappear, Ellison had predicted in 1948, "the results are the spontaneous outbreaks called the 'Harlem riots' of 1935 and 1943," as well as those of the late 1960s, as the *Harper's* version now prophesized.[187] Such a redeployment of his files marks a powerful instance of Ellison's archival sensibility.

Indeed, thanks to Ellison's careful archivism, his papers continue to be a fount of ever timely artifacts. One previously unknown photograph in particular, taken by Ellison around the same time as the "Harlem Is Nowhere" project, approximates the resonant photographic portraiture Parks was noted for, wherein the subjects' individual humanity becomes a means of correcting racial profiling in the mass media of the day (figure 3.12). The image shows a black woman being forcibly seized by policemen on a Harlem sidewalk. She is caught so violently in movement that only a single element of her body is in perfect focus: her anguished yet

FIGURE 3.12. Untitled, woman being arrested, Harlem, New York, ca. 1948. Photograph by Ralph Ellison.

Source: PR 13 Call Number 2010:045, container 5, folder 9, Ralph Ellison Papers, Prints and Photographs Division, Library of Congress, Washington, DC.

defiant face. Her hair is in motion as if from the brusque handling of the officers, whose blurry faces make them blanket representatives of state authority. The blurriness of the image as a whole captures the velocity and mayhem of a street arrest. Because the woman's face is the only section in focus, the viewer's eyes ceaselessly return to her unnerving expression, where we can discern the presence of a diagonal scar, apparently long healed, running from her forehead to her upper lip. The "psychological disturbance"—or "punctum"—of the image is heightened by the presence of bystanders, who seem to be calmly witnessing this capture. The contact sheet where this frame appears underscores the fleetingness of the woman's visibility; in the other shots Ellison took during her arrest, she is already gone or obscured from view. Today, the tear on the left side of the only surviving print of this image embodies the violent materiality of a life roughly lived, damaged yet preserved in time.

As Farah Griffin says of Ann Petry's work in *Harlem Nocturne*, Ellison's photograph gives "complexity to those who remain nameless in official accounts." Petry, whose focus on black women during the Harlem riot of 1943 in the story "In Darkness and Confusion" (1947), brings, as Griffin argues, a necessary corrective to this overwhelmingly male moment in Harlem history and gives "voice to black women who remained invisible to much of American society." In a brilliant move, Griffin suggests that the "too-too girls" in Petry's story are "the female counterparts of [the] zoot-suit-wearing jitterbugs" Invisible Man encounters on the subway.[188] Especially given the dearth of female characters in Ellison's oeuvre, his photograph of the unnamed woman becomes doubly resonant in the larger context that Petry provides. Like "In Darkness and Confusion" and like *Invisible Man*, the photograph is not just a portrait of a black life in distress but also the portrait of a country in distress, a nation tripping over itself, carrying away its citizens into invisibility and incarceration, taking them nowhere. What is particularly painful about encountering this photograph today is that in the intervening decades since it was taken by Ellison, not much has changed. Indeed, as Teju Cole points out in relation to photographs from the civil rights era, "our present moment, a time of vigorous demand for equal treatment, evokes those years of sadness and hope in black American life and renews the relevance of those photos."[189] As such, Ellison's photograph evokes yet another central concept from *Invisible Man*: that "history is not like an arrow, but a boomerang" (6). By carefully preserving their own papers and evidence of their photographic collaborations, African American writers and artists such as Wright, Ellison, Parks, Hughes, DeCarava, and Petry further show us from beyond the grave that the archive is also a worthy "weapon" of choice—"not like an arrow," but indeed like a boomerang.

4

AN INTERLUDE CONCERNING
THE VANISHING MANUSCRIPTS
OF ANN PETRY

The largest Ann Petry collection in the world, coming in at a mere nineteen boxes, is housed in the Howard Gotlieb Archival Research Center at Boston University (BU). Yet until you make an appointment at least two business days in advance to see the material, the size of the collection will remain a mystery. As the center's website clearly states, "The Gotlieb Center does not publish or distribute copies of finding aids." "In some cases," it states, "a scope and content description is published on our website," but it has not done so for the Petry Collection.[1] In fact, something like a shroud of secrecy—or privacy—surrounds most things related to Ann Petry. Born in 1908 (or was it in 1912 or 1909 or 1911 or 1910?), on October 12 (or was it October 20?)—records show that she gave "at least six birth dates"—Petry was a major postwar writer whose first book, *The Street* (1946), became the first novel authored by a black woman to sell more than a million copies.[2] Petry bristled against the limelight immediately upon finding success and sought to safeguard her privacy her entire life. This "rage of privacy," as her daughter, Elisabeth Petry, puts it in her memoir, *At Home Inside: A Daughter's Tribute to Ann Petry*,[3] determined many of her life choices and had a direct impact on what now remains of her archive. And as scholar Farah Griffin puts it, Petry "so feared the possibility of exposure that she destroyed much of her own writing, including letters and journals."[4] Leaving New York in 1947 to seek a more quiet life for her writing, Petry and her husband, George, moved back to her native town, Old Saybrook in

Connecticut, and throughout her career she deflected all inquiries into her life or into her as a person back toward her oeuvre. Publicity campaigns, she wrote in one of her surviving journals from 1992, made her "feel as though I were a helpless creature impaled on a dissecting table—for public viewing."[5]

Appropriately enough, "Keeping Secrets" is the title of the first chapter in *At Home Inside*. As the multiple disclosed birth dates suggest, Petry deliberately "tailored the story of her own life by omitting information, changing details, embellishing the stories she heard as a child."[6] Elisabeth Petry relied on her mother's remaining journals to write her illuminating memoir and carefully explains what materials were left at her disposal at the time of Ann Petry's passing in 1997. Through the memoir, we learn that aside from "the few volumes that she donated to Boston University," thirty-three of Petry's handwritten journals, usually in spiral notebooks, are still in existence. Petry regarded these journals, we are told, "as sacred space where she recorded her private thoughts" and where she would revisit events and experiences from her own life—as she did in earlier drafts of her fiction. Thus, learning that Petry deliberately "embarked on a shred-and-burn campaign" of her archive in the 1980s[7] feels acutely tragic, a figuratively immeasurable loss we can measure quantitatively. In the scholarly confines of twentieth-century American literature, this absence via destruction is tremendous and even more so given the paucity of black women's voices in the archive. As such, the history of the Petry archive is a particularly painful reminder of the many ways—both external and self-inflicted—in which black women writers' archives are scarce. At the same time, Petry's case is instructive on a number of more general points related to the state and availability of twentieth-century American literary archives—notably, the crucial role played by a change in tax law in the late 1960s. Adding yet another layer of mystery and significance to this case, the information I unearthed during my first visit to the Ann Petry Collection at BU seemed to hold the promise of a hidden, undisclosed collection of precious Petry manuscript materials housed at Yale University. But given the facts that Yale does not list any Petry manuscript collection and that the author had conducted a late-career "shred-and-burn" campaign, I had to ask: Was the Yale collection even still of this world?

Ann Petry presents a clear case of an author who "wanted readers to direct their attention to her writing, not to her life."[8] This position raises important ethical questions that archival seekers must wrestle with in their relation with the dead. Are we treating our subject as an automatic "recovery imperative," to use Stephen Best's phrase in *None Like Us*,[9] or is there an ethics of care guiding our curious hands? Should we limit the types of documents we make use of or even consult, or is everything fair game in the name of knowledge production? In life, of course, Ann Petry took control, in part at least, of what she wanted to leave behind as a usable resource. Putting a premium on her work, she concentrated on safeguarding some drafts of her fiction; when it came to correspondence, diaries, and other personal papers, she "thought it was better to destroy this stuff myself than rather than [*sic*] leave it to someone else's tender mercies."[10] When requests to photocopy materials from her archives began coming in, the idea struck her as utterly "repugnant," and she vowed to "oppose all requests made during her lifetime."[11] She admitted in a journal from 1983: "It never occurred to me that in my lifetime people would be poking through that stuff I gave to Boston University, just never occurred to me. Why not? Principally because I tried to disappear. I wanted no part of the celebrity circuit." Indeed, we know all this only because her daughter shares these quotes in her memoir, against her mother's wishes, as she admits in her opening sentence: "My mother did not want this book to exist."[12] In the same journal from 1983, Petry returned to the issue of preservation versus destruction and made her decision: "No reason to give these journals and notebooks to Boston University. Destroy them, journal by journal or else edit them. No. Destroy them."[13] She nevertheless exerted other forms of control upon the materials she chose to save, such as redacting passages, excising certain pages, obscuring names with black markers, altering facts, distorting chronologies, and so on. These actions are a stark reminder, in a fashion complementary to Claude McKay's late archival aesthetic, that what we find in archives can rarely be taken at face value. Each encountered document "must be questioned pointedly," as Arlette Farge reminds us, for "a quotation is never proof, and any historian knows that it is almost always possible to come up with a quotation that contradicts the one she has chosen."[14]

Beyond Petry's alterations and forgeries, her preserved materials were further subjected—as are all papers, those of both the living and the dead—to the mercy of the universe and the laws of thermodynamics. "Poor storage," Elisabeth Petry explains, "resulted in the accidental destruction of other papers."[15] Lack of space in their Old Saybrook home led Petry to relocate multiple boxes to a small building with no insulation in the backyard, where they were exposed to water damage, rodents, and insects. When Elisabeth tried to salvage the "moldy papers" from the building after her mother passed away, "much of it crumbled in my hands," she writes.[16] Only the later material—starting in 1981—had survived, and thus the bulk of materials from the heyday of her writerly career were gone forever. In contrast, it appears Petry decided to keep many of her letters—or at least she "never got around to disposing of them." An atypical journal entry from 1983 seems to offer a little more sympathy for the interest of future scholars regarding her correspondence: "If I were a recorder in the year 2000, I'd be curious, very much interested in what went into letters in the latter part of the 20th century, especially interested in letters written to an author." And then, almost as if to tease these millennial recorders, "I've got stacks of letters."[17] Indeed, in 2012, Harvard University's Schlesinger Library acquired, as a gift from Elisabeth Petry, a collection of letters between Petry and English professor Edward Clark and his wife, Leah R. Caliri-Clark, dated from 1973 to 1997. Even earlier, in 2005, Elisabeth edited *Can Anything Beat White? A Black Family's Letters*, an anthology of personal letters that document the lives of Petry's relatives from 1891 to 1910.[18] In browsing through the Petry Collection at BU, I also noticed that many of the letters therein are indeed "letters written to an author"; they came from, among others, her fans, up-and-coming writers, and high schoolers who had read her young-adult books and sent in questions.

Elisabeth Petry's memoir tantalizes textual-genetics scholars with observations about Petry's own idiosyncratic archival practices, such as the fact
that she often tore "pages from earlier volumes [of her journals] and inserted
them in later ones."[19] Although most of her journals have dated entries,
many of her early journals, "especially the ones containing notes for her novels and short stories," Elisabeth Petry notes, "contain no dates or have a
single date that covered twenty or more pages." One particular journal from
1981, we are told, is part commonplace book, part scrapbook, and part
curated anthology of Petry's own previous journals, containing "pages dated
1974, followed by pages from 1971, 1946, 1970, 1955, and clippings from the
1970s."[20] In short, the journals appear to be a goldmine of converging lifecycles that would surely teach us much about Petry's process, the invisible
steps behind her novelistic craft, and the ways in which sociopolitical concerns merge or clash with her intimate-private beliefs and affect.

We already knew that Petry's fiction was informed by the sociological
data and emerging statistics she had mined during her tenure as the wom-
en's section editor for Adam Clayton Powell Jr.'s newspaper in Harlem, the
People's Voice—notably the "extraordinary rates of domestic violence, alco-
holism, rape and murder," as Lawrence P. Jackson puts it in *The Indignant
Generation*. Petry, he states, "bent her fiction to explain the statistics that
regularly confused people and seemed to support the hoary notions of biological inferiority."[21] According to Farah Griffin, in her weekly column at
the *People's Voice* Petry consistently focused on the realities that most reflect
her early fiction: "housing, segregation, equal opportunity, and the fight
against white supremacy at home and abroad."[22] More than providing journalistic coverage about these pressing issues in her fiction and reporting,
Petry also served on the boards of "as many organizations as seemed to
improve the quality of life for Harlem's most vulnerable: its women and
children."[23] For all these reasons, Petry's personal notebooks and manuscript
drafts would invariably uncover a fount of new knowledge not only about
her novelistic practice and archival sensibility but also about African American sociopolitical history in the wake of World War II from the unique
perspective of a black, female artist-activist. Indeed, as I was to discover
later, Petry often typed her novels directly on the backs of fliers and

newsletters of the activist organizations in which she was a leading member, such as Negro Women, Incorporated. In other words, Petry's literary work is literally inscribed upon her activism, a relation that the materiality of her manuscripts renders inescapable as each typescript page forms two sides of the same coin or, rather, the same sheet of paper (see figures 4.1 and 4.2). We can be thankful, therefore, that Petry decided to donate at least *some* of her archive to BU before her destructive turn. And yet, given her life-long quest for privacy, I began to wonder why she had decided to give any-thing to BU in the first place. After all, this is the author who in an inter-view in 1996 stated, "To be a willing accomplice to the invasion of your own

FIGURES 4.1 AND 4.2. Recto and verso sides of a page from the original typescript of Ann Petry's novel *The Street*, typed on pages of *Negro Women, Incorporated, Newsletter*, October 1944.

Source: Box 1, folder 1, uncataloged James Weldon Johnson MSS Petry Collection, Beinecke Rare Book and Manuscript Library, Yale.

privacy puts a low price on its worth. The creative processes are, or should be, essentially secret, and although naked flesh is now an open commodity, the naked spirit should have sanctuary."[24] The answer to the question of her surprising donation to BU lies, in part and surprisingly enough, in American tax law.

As some archivists have duly noted, one particular tax-deduction law that remained in effect until the early 1970s had tremendous consequences on the state of modern literary papers. Many living writers, archivist Philip Cronenwett notes, would send materials to repositories every year, "in small increments," because at the time they could use such donations as a tax write-off. Most writers "gave only as much as they could legitimately write off on their taxes in a given year."[25] Before 1970, the law allowed individuals to deduct the fair market value of the papers "as a gift to an institution," a practice that Ann Petry, along with a large number of other writers, used to the benefit of both archive and donor. For instance, this tax-deduction option is precisely what first led playwright Arthur Miller to make his first donation to the University of Texas at a time, the early 1960s, when he was "short on cash and facing a big tax bill."[26] But after 1969 the tax code was revised, and "creators of donated works were limited to the costs of the materials that went into the work"—namely, the price of paper, ink, canvases, and paint.[27] Thus, in the wake of what may appear to be a small change, most U.S.-based writers, including Ann Petry, abandoned the practice of selling or gifting papers during their lifetime. Once Ann Petry "learned that she could no longer receive a tax deduction for the full value of her work," Elisabeth Petry relates, "she stopped making contributions" to BU.[28]

Petry was not alone in putting a stop to her contributions; the "impact of the legislation was immediate—and catastrophic. Gifts by artists, writers and musicians to charitable institutions fell radically, and have never recovered."[29] Before the tax revision went into effect, the Library of Congress received an annual average of "over 100,000 literary manuscripts" but saw this number fall "to zero in 1971 and 1972."[30] As a further consequence of the revised tax code, any kind of potential financial gain to be had from one's papers had to come from sales rather than donation. For instance, when Arthur Miller sent another seventy-three boxes to Texas in 1983 "for safekeeping" following a fire on his property, he expressed his interest in "finalizing the transfer" by donation only in the event that the tax reduction be restored. Barring such a restoration, the acquired material would have to be purchased.[31] All repositories saw their literary acquisitions drop significantly, and those that did not have large budgets to make purchases suffered the most. Although this tax reality affected all writers regardless of color in the United States, it became yet another significant obstacle to the safekeeping of African Americans' collections. Many black writers, who already toiled in relative obscurity and without high incomes, were suddenly further deprived of an incentive to donate materials aside from some ideological belief in posterity or similar philosophical altruism. In most cases, compared to their white counterparts' expectations, their prospects of selling their papers at a high price were more or less dire because the few repositories interested in acquiring African American materials had limited budgets and space and thus relied largely on donations. We will never know how many more collections might have been saved had the United States kept this tax deduction, never know how many voices were silenced by a tax code change. We have Richard Nixon's fraudulently backdated and inflated tax return from 1969, in which he lists donating his vice presidential papers to the National Archives, to thank for this amendment.[32]

Yet even before the change, this tax law was really a double-edged sword: although it encouraged living writers to donate their materials—and was thus indirectly responsible for collections that might otherwise never have existed—it also led to the partitioning of larger archives into discrete chunks. As I address in chapter 1, due to this pattern of donation in small increments, a great number of postwar literary collections were "divided artificially," and, as a result, the "chronological development of a collection"— the traces of original order—has become increasingly difficult to assess.[33] The more original order is stripped away, the more crucial information regarding the author's process and personality is evacuated from the archive.

What exactly does the scholar encounter when finally granted access to the Ann Petry Collection in the reading room of the Howard Gotlieb Research Center? First, I should underscore that, almost as a reflection of the author's personality, the fact that BU even has an Ann Petry Collection is information that must first be earned through research. The collection is not listed in WorldCat.org, an otherwise useful database that lists which libraries in the world hold copies of a given item and, in the case of unique items such as archival collections, where the collection is located. ArchiveGrid, a search engine specifically designed to find archival collections, functions by searching through the WorldCat listings (the engine's web address even includes "worldcat," https://beta.worldcat.org/archivegrid/). A search for "Ann Petry" shows that at least three repositories house collections with "Ann Petry" in their name, all of which are among the usual suspects: Harvard, the Library of Congress, and the NYPL. However, these collections are quite small and discrete. The Library of Congress collection consists of fifteen items, mostly correspondence between Petry and her friend Virginia Harrington from 1973 to 1978. Similarly, as mentioned earlier, Harvard's Petry holdings consist of correspondence from the 1970s to the 1990s, along with "an address book, ca.1938; programs, clippings, brochures, and photographs."[34] Each of these two epistolary collections fit into a single box. Finally, the Schomburg Center at the NYPL has an "Ann Petry portrait collection" ("title devised by cataloger"), which are mainly photographic portraits of the author—including some of Petry signing copies of her second novel, *Country Place* (1947)—as well as some "promotional portraits."[35] Thus, based on WorldCat and library database searches, the Petry Collection at BU apparently doesn't exist. Nor do innumerable other unlisted small collections across the globe.

Aside from reading Elisabeth Petry's memoir, one has to look at recent scholarship by Petry scholars and note their sources to reveal the existence of various Petry collections. In *Indignant Generation*, Jackson reliably lists the Gotlieb Center's Ann Petry Collection, as does Keith Clark in *The Radical Fiction of Ann Petry* and Farah Griffin in *Harlem Nocturne*. Griffin in fact recommends four collections that she consulted for her research into Petry, two of which are at New York University and relate to Petry's role in labor unions (and thus do not bear her name).[36] Clark's introduction provides the most information about the Gotlieb collection because he takes the time to recount his astonishment at uncovering "the volume of material Petry had left to BU." He elaborates on what he calls the "cornu-copia of personal and professional artifacts" in the collection: "In addition to handwritten drafts of several works, the twenty or so boxes included a trove of writings and other memorabilia: original versions of nonfiction she'd published in the *Crisis* and *Opportunity* magazines, letters she'd written to politicians (including President Richard M. Nixon), letters from elementary students whose classes Petry had visited, correspondences with members of the literati (Carl Van Vechten et al.)."[37] This account is the closest thing one can find in publicly available outlets to a description of the Petry Collection at BU. But at "twenty boxes or so," this collection is still relatively small compared to the collections of a great number of Petry's contemporaries housed in the James Weldon Johnson Collection at Yale, the Schomburg Center, Emory University, and the Library of Congress (for instance, the Ralph Ellison Papers in the Library of Congress Manuscript Division holds 74,800 items in 314 boxes and 25 oversize containers). A scholar's only and arguably best resource to know anything more regarding what the BU Petry Collection contains is to be handed the actual finding aid, a document accessible only by appointment and only in hard copy, from within the secured and surveilled confines of Howard Gotlieb's lair.

When the day of my appointment at the Gotlieb came, I was at last given the holy artifact: "The Inventory of the Ann Petry Collection #1391." Unfortunately, the document included no description of the collection's arrangement, no bio note, and no list of "related collections." In short, this twenty-two page document was solely a container list devoid of any contextual front matter. Given Petry's history of privacy, I had been looking forward to discover more about the circumstances surrounding the collection's acquisition history: When had the material first arrived? How many deliveries had there been across how many years? Had each donation been a gift, or had any of them been a purchase? And most mysterious of all: Why was the collection here at BU and not in some other repository? Given that Petry was a longtime Connecticut native and resident, and given the presence of the JWJ Collection at the Beinecke, Yale would presumably have been an appropriate site for the Petry papers. Yet Petry is not listed in Yale's inventory of manuscript finding aids, though the Beinecke does have a few autographed first editions of Petry's novel *The Street*. Alas, none of these questions could be answered because the Gotlieb "inventory" provided no processing notes and no acquisition details.

This container list was the only document at my disposal, so I studied it carefully and transcribed it in its entirety for future reference. I noted that there are nineteen boxes in total. The language used in the inventory was that of specialized archival shorthand, full of abbreviations such as TLS (typed letter signed), ALS (autograph letter signed), CTL (carbon typed letter), and so on, with some more personal flourishes that I appreciated, such as "TS [typescript] with profuse holograph corrections." The hand edits in the typescript pages I encountered were indeed "profuse." Because I was most interested in Petry's first novel, *The Street*, I kept an eye out for any mention of the book in the inventory. Alas, it was mentioned only once as being in folder 19 of box 7. Although the folder and box were thrilling to see, only a handful typescript pages in the folder were from *The Street*; the majority of the folder's contents consisted of typescript pages from different works. As I continued my analysis of the inventory, I began to notice something unusual: the same type of material was assigned a different series number at different points in the document. For instance, in the first few pages, I saw "Series I. Manuscripts," but a few pages later I saw manuscript materials nestled under "Series II. Manuscripts." The same was done for correspondence, which was scattered in different, nonconsecutive boxes throughout the collection. Although physical arrangement or "control" (where the stuff actually is) does not need to match the order of intellectual arrangement or "control" (the imposed logic behind the processing), series titles usually remain assigned to the same number in a given collection.

In my efforts to understand why the collection had been processed this way, I noticed that three of the inventory pages boasted a date at the top center. On page 1 was "June 1968," on page 9 "December 1969," and on page 16 "July 1971 and 1988." When I spoke with the archivist, Sarah E. Pratt, on site the day of my visit, she was able to confirm what I suspected: these dates were shipment dates marking the receipt of a discrete amount of materials sent by Ann Petry. I was not allowed to have access to the collection's acquisition file, but based on what Pratt relayed, Petry apparently developed an amicable epistolary relation with Howard Gotlieb, the man for whom the BU archive is now named, and voluntarily sent him these shipments starting in the late 1960s. With this new information, the inventory began to make more sense: the contents of boxes 1–10 had come with the shipment in June 1968, boxes 11–15 in December 1969, and boxes 16–19 in either July 1971 or 1988. The latter two dates still presented something of a mystery because they meant—or seemed to indicate—that Petry had nevertheless decided to make two additional donations after the change in tax law had disallowed deductions for such gifts. Were these "secret" donations that Petry had kept even from her daughter? Had she destroyed the paperwork for these transactions? Or could such dates indicate something more mundane—that is, not just a shipment date but rather the moment this segment of Petry material was actually processed from BU's backlog? According to the Gotlieb archivist, Sarah Pratt, each shipment had been processed as it arrived, likely by a different staff member, effectively creating an independent small collection each time, hence the different numbering of series across the inventory as a whole. In 2006, thanks to a funded program, the Gotlieb Center was able to pay a student intern to redo the collection as a whole and combine the sections into a single inventory—in doing so, the student retained the original arrangement and thus the marks of the collection's interrupted and delayed processing stages.

As a result of all of these actions, it was difficult to tell to what extent the arrangement corresponded to the way Petry had kept this material in her home or office. Could the arrangement be a window into her process, or had she simply slid a bunch of random stuff inside a box and mailed it off, like an Andy Warholian Time Capsule from the Factory?[38] The date range of the correspondence in each box varied wildly and sometimes skipped chunks of years. The folders with typescripts were in disarray and demanded a great deal of attention to decipher. As I mentioned earlier, folder 19 in box 7, for instance, had pages from a draft of *The Narrows* (1953), some from *The Street*, some from short stories, and others that remained "unidentified," all mixed together. The typescript pages were paginated for

FIGURE 4.3. Ann Petry in the midst of composition, 1946. Original caption: "Listening to her own writing helps Ann Petry get the feel of her characters. In the midst of composition, she lights a cigarette and reads a passage aloud to herself." Photograph by Skippy Adelman.

Source: "First Novel," Ebony, April 1, 1946.

the most part but not arranged in consecutive order, and some appeared to be exact duplicates. I wondered whether the wild and unruly, bulging piles, with corners jutting out at various angles, were the result of some frenzied, reckless use of the materials by previous researchers or of careless processing or even of Petry's work habits at home.

When I at last stumbled—the only verb appropriate with folders in such a state—upon a typescript page from *The Street* with "profuse holograph corrections," it stood out for the description Petry had added by hand: "the four corners of the room were alive with silence—deepening pools of an ominous silence." In reading the novel, I had always found this image quietly effective in evoking Lutie Johnson's mood shortly after the murder of Boots Smith. Discovering that this change had come relatively late in the writing process was one of the day's small archival thrills.

The few draft pages from *The Street* marked "TS with profuse holographic corrections" appear random and are sandwiched between draft pages from *The Narrows* and short stories such as "Olaf and His Girlfriend" and "Doby's Gone." The latter set of sheets are more easily discernable because they all are typed on the back of yellow 8½-by-11-inch flyers, "Negro Women Have a Vote," announcing a rally for voter registration in 1944 sponsored by Negro Women, Inc. Copies of this same flyer can also be found in boxes that came in later shipments—Petry, who likely distributed the flyer, clearly still had many copies of it leftover and had found a way to use them, seamlessly incorporating her literary and political commitments.

Encountering such ephemera, in addition to the collection's somewhat chaotic nature, recalled for me the unforgettable descriptions of the multifarious scattered forms of paper littering 116th Street Harlem at the outset of *The Street*, when that "cold November wind" "found every scrap of paper along the street—theater throwaways, announcement of dances and lodge meetings, the heavy waxed paper that loaves of bread had been wrapped in, the thinner waxed paper that had enclosed sandwiches, old envelopes, newspapers. . . . [T]he wind set the bits of paper to dancing high in the air, so that a barrage of paper swirled into the faces of the people on the street."[39] In a way, Petry had become that November wind, putting up a barrage of paper against the angel of history. The novel's opening passage reminded me just how deeply *The Street* paid attention to paper-based artifacts, whether an eviction notice ("a long sheet of white paper stuck under the door"); the rubbish in the stairs of tenements, which are filthy "with wastepaper, cigarette butts, pink ticket stubs from the movie houses"; the products manufactured by Little Henry Chandler's father ("paper towels and paper napkins and paper handkerchiefs"); Mrs. Pizzini's reference letter ("nice neat writing, no misspelled words, careful margins, pretty good English . . . written with a fine pen and black ink on nice thick white paper"); the "fat sleek magazines"; the many pieces of paper Lutie Johnson accumulates in her years of night school learning how to type to become a file clerk; the evidence destroyed by the police officer, who "tore it up into little fine pieces and the pieces drifted slowly out of his hands into a waste-basket near the desk"; or the Harlem garbage, "piled high with rusting tin cans, old newspapers, and other rubbish."[40] As another character, Min, puts it, "The very sight of so much print would only bewilder."[41]

And bewildered I was. As my time spent in the Gotlieb reading room grew, a perplexing set of half-revelations began to unfold through my intermittent encounters with letters from Carl Van Vechten and from Yale. Given Van Vechten's obsession with padding up the JWJ Collection with the papers of as many living black authors as possible and given the fact that Petry had posed for a series of photographs by Van Vechten in 1948, one of my predetermined objectives for this archival trip was to look for correspondence between them. What I found, however, was confounding. In this handful of scattered letters, which range from 1946 to 1964, a narrative unfolds in which another major cache of Petry archival materials might just have survived, even though such a narrative, I knew, was not supported by extant scholarship. And yet there it was.

As was the case for most of the 1940s (and beyond), the Van Vechten of these letters seems obsessed with the accumulation and improvement of the JWJ Collection. His earliest letter to Petry in the BU Petry Collection is dated May 4, 1946, and concerns the manuscript for *The Street*, a novel that had appeared just five months earlier, in January. He wrote:

Dear Mrs Petry, Mrs [Grace Nail] Johnson informed me long ago that you and Mrs Reckling might appear any moment bearing with you the manuscripts, etc. of The Street for the James Weldon Johnson Memorial Collection of Negro Arts and Letters at Yale University. It is a fine book and it will add immediately to the value of the collection.

Now Mrs Johnson tells me that you haven't found time yet to put the manuscript in order (you woudnt [*sic*] have to do this, if you didn't care to, as it is a job to which I have become accustomed). I am hoping there-fore that whether you can arrange to bring the manuscript at an early date or not, you will be able to come in to be photographed for the Collection some day soon. . . . Wont [sic] you telephone me, please, and set an hour for this?[42]

The Mrs. Reckling mentioned is one of Petry's closest friends, whom Petry considered to be her "guardian angel."[43] At the time, Frances Reckling—a composer—owned the Frances Reckling Book and Music Store in Harlem, "which was on the same floor as the *People's Voice* offices," where Petry worked as a reporter.[44] Reckling used the store to host book-launch parties for her friends, including one on September 24, 1947, the day Petry's second novel, *Country Place*, was published, which was attended by Van Vechten and other prominent members of the literary world, such as Langston Hughes.

In his May 1946 letter, Van Vechten was being rather melodramatic in his comment that he had been "informed . . . long ago" regarding the delivery of the manuscript of a novel that had been in print for only a few months, and he appeared to be even more flustered in his follow-up letter from June 22, 1946, where he literally begs Petry to send her material and again speaks of a "long ago" promise:

> Dear Mrs Petry, I hate to bother you again but ever so long ago you promised to call me IN TWO WEEKS to arrange about being photographed, even if the manuscript isn't quite ready for delivery! My anxiety to have everything for the James Weldon Johnson Memorial Collection at Yale added up to PERFECTION is my reason for *re*writing you!. . . I wish too to show you how snugly (and beautifully) the James Weldon Johnson manuscripts are boxed and to get you to inscribe The Street. PLEASE![45]

The "TWO WEEKS" mentioned here had been referred to in the only undated letter from Van Vechten in the Petry Collection, where he wrote: "Dear Mrs Petry, Thank you for your charming letter. I'll be expecting to hear from you in a couple of weeks and Grace Johnson is indeed WONDERFUL!"[46] Evidently, Petry had failed to follow through on this timeline.

Almost a full year passed before the next letter from Van Vechten to Petry, but the subject remains the same—this time, however, despite displaying less anxiety, he sought to deal with a complication he had not expected. On April 30, 1947, he wrote:

> Dear Mrs Petry, Thanks for your charming note. Today I received another letter from Mrs Reckling. I had understood from Mrs. Johnson, and indeed your letter indicates, that you were giving the manuscript of The Street to the James Weldon Collection at Yale, which already includes ALL the James Weldon Johnson Manuscripts, ALL the Langston Hughes Manuscripts, most of the Countee Cullen Manuscripts, and which has been promised the Du Bois Manuscripts (already we have five) and the Chesnutt Manuscripts, but Mrs Reckling writes me that she is LOANING the manuscript. We are of course grateful even for that favor, but I hope she can be persuaded to make her gift complete. In any case I am extremely grateful to you both for this very important addition to the Collection, whether temporary or permanent. As soon as the manuscript is in my possession, I shall have a box made for it, and when eventually it goes to Yale you will receive a receipt from the Librarian there. I will wait, however, until you have sent me the other items from The Street which you say were not included in the manuscript you sent to Mrs Reckling.
>
> As for the photographs, I hope I can get these soon, for the Collections I am forming in various directions. Telephone or write me when it will be convenient for you to have these made.[47]

Based on this one-sided exchange, we can deduce that Petry was apparently feeling some reticence about giving away the manuscript for her first novel to Yale, preferring perhaps a temporary loan of sorts. Van Vechten piled on, in capital letters, the fact that the JWJ Collection already had "ALL" the manuscripts from multiple African American luminaries, but, in fact, he was exaggerating regarding the holistic state of every author's collection he named and, as usual, presumed too much when speculating about future donations.

A few months passed until Van Vechten's next letter—dated September 25, 1947—during which time Petry published her second novel, *Country Place*, and met Van Vechten in person for the first time at the party thrown by her friend Frances Reckling. By this point, Van Vechten seemed to be in possession of the manuscript or part of the manuscript for *The Street*, yet this was still not enough for him. He wanted to have all the ancillary materials related to the novel:

> Dear Mrs Petry, You said there were more notes etc. connected with The Street. Can you possibly get these to me soon as I want to have boxes made to contain this wonderful manuscript which will be one of the gems of the James Weldon Johnson Collection, and boxes take time. And PLEASE save everything from Country Place for the James Weldon Johnson Memorial Collection. It was a great pleasure and privilege to meet you at last and I hope we shall meet more frequently in the future. Try to make an appointment for photography soon: you should be in a dozen of my photographic Collections.[48]

Five days later Van Vechten wrote again, ostensibly to praise *Country Place*, but the praise was really a badly disguised excuse to request that Petry send him the rest of the materials related to *The Street*. He also marked his impatience by implying he would need to photograph her soon, or it might be too late:

> Dear Mrs Petry, I had a wonderful time reading Country Place: it is the kind of period piece I admire and I have a passion for old ladies who are heroines of fiction and who outwit everybody. Do you know Pushkin's story, The Queen of Spades? I have a feeling that you have proved something very definite in this second book: that you are a writer with no limits to your horizon!
>
> Please send me the rest of the STREET manuscript pronto and please come to be photographed *looking serious* before I am too old to use a lens.
>
> Fourteen rose carnations to you and a stalk of larkspur.[49]

Flowers aside, Petry did not heed Van Vechten's warning or share his sense of urgency: she was not photographed by Van Vechten until November 1948, fourteen months after the latter letter from Van Vechten. Had she finally sent him the ancillary materials related to *The Street*? The few letters from James T. Babb, Yale librarian, in the BU Petry Collection provide a partial answer to this question.

In the BU Petry Collection, the earliest correspondence to Petry from Yale are two letters dated January 21, 1949, thus roughly two months after Petry posed for Van Vechten. Babb wrote to acknowledge receipt of gifts by Petry to the Beinecke Library meant for the JWJ Collection, including the "original holograph manuscript of The Street in four notebooks. Each is signed on the cover by the author." The official acknowledgment also lists "First typewritten draft, with many corrections, signed by the author; Page proofs, signed. Carbon of letter to Houghton, Mifflin, with synopsis of The Street, signed. Printer's manuscripts, signed"; and finally, "Letters from Mrs. Reckling and Ann Petry."[50] The other letter, bearing the same date, is another acknowledgment of a gift, this time of materials related to her second novel: "original manuscript of Country Place, in four notebooks. Typewritten draft with many alterations, inscribed by author to the Collection."[51] This document further lists that multiple copies of foreign-language editions of *The Street* were also donated (these editions are indeed still listed on the Beinecke website as part of its rare-book collection). With a more personal follow-up on January 24, Babb invited Petry to come to New Haven and told her that Yale was "delighted to have the manuscripts, books, and other material listed on the enclosed acknowledgement, and it is awfully nice of you to give them to us. They are an important addition to the James Weldon Johnson Collection of Negro Arts and Letters."[52] Almost two years later, in December 1950, Babb wrote again with another "official acknowledgement for your most recent gift to the Library." This time Yale was "very happy to have these inscribed copies of your book *The Street*."[53] As I noted earlier, however, searches indicated that Yale did not boast any Petry manuscript collections, so I had trouble reconciling these letters with that apparent absence. After all, *The Street* is the first novel by an African

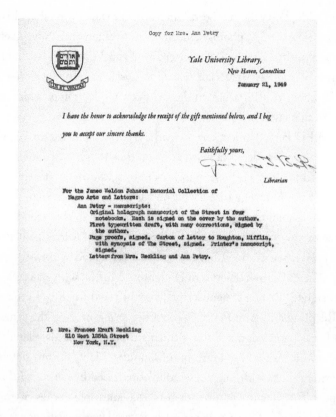

FIGURE 4.4. Acknowledgment of receipt from Yale librarian James T. Babb to Ann Petry, January 21, 1949.

Source: Box 7, folder 2, Ann Petry Collection, Howard Gotlieb Archival Research Center, Boston University.

American woman to sell more than a million copies, so having the original notebooks, let alone the author's own synopsis *and* the manuscripts for her second novel, would represent an invaluable resource.

Something was clearly missing from what these letters appeared to reveal. A lingering unease, perhaps related to Petry's legendary reticence to share her personal records, began to reassert itself in me as I read the later correspondence. On August 16, 1952, the next Van Vechten letter arrived—his last in the Petry Collection at BU—and he seemed perplexed by a recent query on her part:

Dear Mrs Petry, I was happy to hear from you after all these months, but I am not quite clear about your question. If you mean do you have to get consent to use the James Weldon Johnson Memorial Collection in the Yale Library, the answer is NO. Just walk into the Library and ask for Mr. Donald Gallup, the curator, and he will place the collection at your disposal and assist you in any way you want. If you mean that you desire to use the material elsewhere, I am sure this would not be permitted. Why don't you write directly to Mr Gallup and tell him EXACTLY what you want to know?[54]

It appears that Petry wanted to take some of the material out of the Yale collection, but it remains unclear whether her request had to do with her intention to retrieve materials she had donated or was more generally about the content of the collection that she intended to use for research purposes. In 1952, she was writing *The Narrows*, a novel about an interracial couple set in Connecticut, and preparing to write her nonfiction children's book on Harriet Tubman. Throughout her career, Petry was a thorough library and archival researcher—as the presence of her NYPL Manuscript Division registration card for 1963 in the BU collection suggests. Van Vechten's letter from August 1952 does make one wonder: Could Petry have gone down to Yale and forcibly taken back her own manuscripts?

I did not wonder for long, however, because I soon found two other letters, this time from 1964—thus twelve years after Van Vechten's last letter in the BU collection—confirming that Yale still had its Petry materials. On October 26, 1964, Petry's children's book editor at Thomas Y. Crowell Company, Miss Elizabeth Riley, sent her a note after having visited Yale: "My dear Ann: Yesterday I noticed in the Beinecke Library a row of your manuscripts in a glass display case. The manuscripts were all in handsome leather boxes. I can understand why you might not have sent the manuscript for Harriet Tubman—it started out life as a textbook though it has had a distinguished career—but I do hope you are planning to send the manuscript for Tituba. It deserves a place in that splendid row."[55] Petry's children's book on the slave woman involved in the Salem witch trials, *Tituba of Salem Village*, had just been published when Yale curated this display case of Petry manuscripts. Van Vechten, it seemed, had followed through on his promise to have "snug" and "beautiful" boxes made for Petry's manuscripts, and Yale was clearly still in possession of them at this time. Petry must have agreed with Riley's suggestion because in November 1964 the curator of the JWJ Collection, Donald Gallup (James T. Babb was now university librarian), replied to Petry's editor that Yale would indeed "like to have the manuscripts of Mrs. Petry's *Tituba* and *Harriet Tubman*. It is my fault that a specific request did not go to her, but I assumed that she knew that we were and are eager to continue to receive her manuscripts and I hope that from now on she will have them sent automatically."[56]

Insofar as the collection at BU is concerned, this is where the trail of letters between Yale, Van Vechten, and Petry end. I was left with the perplexing, Borgesian problem that all evidence pointed to a Petry manuscript collection at Yale yet not at Yale. Interestingly, much of the manuscript materials for *Tituba* and *Harriet Tubman* are included in the collection at BU, *not* at Yale, so it seems Petry had not, in the end, followed through on Gallup's belated invitation but had opted for Boston University instead. Based on the shipment dates in the Petry Collection inventory at BU, Petry began sending materials to the Gotlieb Center in 1968, roughly four years after this last exchange with Yale and thus after the Beinecke had displayed some of her manuscripts. Among the many questions that remained—chief among them, What happened to those manuscripts at Yale?—I also wondered: Why doesn't Elisabeth Petry mention these manuscripts in her memoir? Could Yale somehow be keeping this collection under wraps, and if so, why? Did those letters from Reckling and Petry mentioned by Van Vechten and by Babb in his acknowledgment of receipt specify something more along the lines of a temporary "loan" to Yale than a permanent gift? And could Petry have later retrieved this collection and then secretly disposed of it? Yet her daughter underscores that her mother did not, as a rule, destroy her fiction drafts but only more "personal" documents, such as diaries and correspondence. If Petry did retrieve the manuscripts at Yale, could she—horror of horrors—have stored them in that little uninsulated outdoor shed where they were devoured by rodents or molded into oblivion after having brushed so close to immortality?

As if to twist the knife in the wound, the next letter I read in the Gotlieb Petry Collection gave a hint of what Petry's writerly practice entailed, what kinds of records she undoubtedly produced over her long career, and thus what the drafts from these two novels, *The Street* and *Country Place*, might look like if they still existed. Dated March 30, 1966, the letter was a reply to a young woman who dreamed of becoming a professional writer in which Petry shared some writing advice and wisdom. After quoting Hemingway twice—who, she commented, "wrote better about writing than pretty much anything else"—Petry got to the "specifics":

Specifics? Well, read, read, read, read—poetry, plays, short stories. Read Flannery O'Connor's "Everything that Rises Must Converge." Write, write, write, write. Keep a journal in a big notebook with plenty of pages and record your reaction to places and to people, write down some of the things that happen to you, things that made you laugh or cry or get angry—this is *not* a diary—it's a kind of record of reactions. Record bits of dialogue, things you overhear, things you make up. Write on only *one* side of the paper. Learn to type.[57]

Reading what she advised in her letter, I was struck by the number of times I had just seen Petry write or take notes on both sides of a sheet of paper. I was also touched by the letter's unwavering assurance, a bluntness somehow wrapped in kindness, and by Petry's insistence to reclaim the notebook as a professional "record of reactions," "*not* a diary," with its connotations of feminization and infantilization. Then, just as suddenly, the letter simply became a painful reminder of the penury of Petry's journals in the BU collection. It made me want to create a record of my own reactions to this collection and this reading room, but it mostly made me want to see the "Original holograph manuscript of *The Street* in four notebooks" in their "handsome leather boxes." Where could they be? Could they actually still exist? To answer these questions, I had to consult the Carl Van Vechten Papers held at the NYPL and the Beinecke.

In the meantime, I sent inquiries to Petry scholars and to the Beinecke asking about the missing manuscripts. No scholar was aware of any collection at Yale or elsewhere that held the manuscripts of Petry's first two novels. My query to the Beinecke's curator of American literature went unanswered, which only served to fuel my curiosity and suspicion. As a result, my motivation was at an all-time high when I finally entered the Brooke Russell Astor Reading Room for Rare Books and Manuscripts on the third floor of the NYPL to consult the Van Vechten Papers. Although Petry's letters to Van Vechten were not here, the correspondence between Van Vechten and Donald Gallup, Yale curator and librarian, recorded further proof, in the form of acknowledgments of receipt and listings of gifts, that Petry had indeed donated materials to Yale.

Ever meticulous, every shipment of materials Van Vechten sent to Yale Library was accompanied by a continuously paginated container list or catalog of its contents—as a practice, Van Vechten would also simultaneously send a letter to Gallup that repeated the list of gifts and provided the corresponding page numbers of the growing JWJ catalog where these materials were listed (James Babb referred to this document as "Carl Van Vechten's catalogue"). Whenever Ann Petry's name was listed among donors, I noted the date of the shipment and the catalog page number. Sure enough, on the same date that James Babb first acknowledged receipt of the Petry manuscripts, January 21, 1949, he also sent a similar receipt to Van Vechten with the following details: "For the James Weldon Johnson Memorial Collection of Negro Arts and Letters: Materials as listed on page 491–494 of Carl Van Vechten's catalogue, and four manuscript boxes." The receipt also informed Van Vechten that Babb had duly sent "acknowledgements for material" to all donors included in this shipment, listing both Ann Petry and Frances Reckling, whose materials would appear itemized "on pages 494–97 of Carl Van Vechten's catalogue."[58] Along with further confirmation, these details were crucial to my next and ultimate stop, Yale's Beinecke Library in New Haven.

Ann Petry's letters to Van Vechten at the Beinecke, combined with the catalog in which Van Vechten kept track of everything he was sending to Yale for the JWJ Collection, proved beyond a shadow of a doubt that she had indeed donated *The Street* and *Country Place* manuscripts, along with other related documents, to the JWJ Collection. The correspondence further lent insight into her author practice: on May 7, 1946, she wrote to Van Vechten, "The manuscript (original) of *The Street* is bundled up just as I picked it up from the floor (I am a sloppy workman) after I finished typing the final draft. So that pages and chapters are completely mixed up." She went on to explain that she had already promised to give Frances Reckling the manuscript—that in fact "there wouldn't have been any original ms. saved except for Frances—she asked me to give it to her—I had planned to throw it away."[59] These details are fascinating in themselves because they point both to friendship between black women as the awakening of Petry's archival sensibility and to the rather chaotic dynamism of her writing process.

"As soon as I can straighten it out so it goes in consecutive order," Petry added, she would ask Mrs. Reckling to forward the manuscript to Van Vechten.[60] As we know from the Van Vechten letters in the Petry Collection at BU, Petry was actually in no hurry, and she "(at long last) turned the original ms of THE STREET, the galleys, the final typed ms, etc., over to Frances Reckling" a year later, in April 1947.[61] It is in this same letter to Van Vechten that she promised to send him additional materials related to *The Street* that had not been included in her package to Reckling. The Van Vechten Papers at Yale also confirmed that Mrs. Reckling initially only wanted to "loan" the manuscript. She wrote to Van Vechten:

Quite some time ago, I was talking with Mrs. James Weldon Johnson about the original manuscript of "The Street" by Ann Petry—and she suggested it would be a valuable addition to the Yale Library. Having been honored with the manuscript as a gift from Mrs. Petry, I hesitate relinquishing it even to such an important collection. How ever [*sic*]—if it will serve as an inspiration to writers and of interest to the public in general I shall be happy to loan it to the collection for say—twenty or twenty five years. Is that selfish? I hope not.[62]

Could this scenario be exactly what happened?, I wondered. Had Mrs. Reckling actually retrieved the manuscript twenty or twenty-five years later? With an acknowledgment of receipt of January 21, 1949, such a delay would bring us somewhere between 1969 and 1974—that is, five to ten years after the last "sighting" of the manuscript by Petry's editor, Elizabeth Riley, under a glass case on display in the new Beinecke building in 1964. If this gift had indeed been a "loan," I was fairly certain that in all likelihood Van Vechten would have noted that fact in "Van Vechten's catalogue." This first catalog is now an integral part of the Carl Van Vechten Papers Relating to African American Arts and Letters at Yale.

With my next archival box request, I rifled through the catalog, looking for pages 491–94, the ones Babb noted as listing the donations by Petry and Reckling. Since Babb's letter, the catalog had been repaginated in ink over the typed numbers, but the original numbers were still visible underneath the ink that now listed these pages as 497 to 502. The catalog more than clarified the matter. In this ledger, Van Vechten carefully documented the status of the Petry manuscripts being given to Yale, noting that they were "gifts of Mrs. Frances Kraft Reckling" after having clearly first written and then crossed out "Ann Petry." The catalog page then states the following for the record: "ALS from Mrs. Reckling in which she offers to loan the manuscript of The Street to Yale, dated April 26, 1947. Later, at a party for Mrs Petry on the publication of Country Place, September 24, 1947, Mrs Reckling changed her mind and *presented* the manuscript to Yale. See Publishers' Weekly, October 18, 1947, Page 2010."[63] At this (ecstatic) point, from the Beinecke reading room, I immediately accessed the online *Publishers' Weekly* archives—all hail the wonders of digitization and access—and hunted down the item mentioned. What I found felt almost like a parody of an overabundance of evidence proving that Yale was indeed supposed to have an Ann Petry manuscript collection: not only did *Publisher's Weekly* state that "the original manuscript of Miss Petry's first novel, 'The Street' . . . was presented to the James Weldon Johnson Collection at

Yale University," but the accompanying photograph shows Reckling literally handing the materials into Van Vechten's hands and Ann Petry herself smiling between the two (see figure 4.5)! Everything had now fallen into place—the one-sided correspondence from Van Vechten finally made sense and even eclipsed the hint of wariness on Petry's part. On February 10, 1949, for example, Petry wrote to Van Vechten: "I have received a downright *handsome* acknowledgement of the ms. etc. you sent to the Yale University Library—and one of these days I'll drop in and look at the Johnson Collection—and glow with pride to think that my ms. [*sic*] are included." In this same letter, Petry announced the birth of her daughter, Elisabeth Ann Petry, "as beautiful as a May morning— and more satisfying than any novel I'll ever write."[64] Her letters to Van Vechten also record that she attended the opening ceremony for the

► FRANCES KRAFT RECKLING, owner of a bookshop on 125th Street in New York City, gave a party for Ann Petry to introduce her latest novel, "Country Place" (*Houghton Mifflin*), to the New York book trade. The party was held at Mrs. Reckling's studio on publication day, September 24.

During the festivities, the original manuscript of Miss Petry's first novel, "The Street," which won a Houghton Mifflin Literary Fellowship in 1945 (*PW*, March 17, 1945) was presented to the James Weldon Johnson Collection at Yale University.

► KELLY & WALSH LTD., 9 Chater Road, Hong Kong, China, officially reopened its bookshop after hostilities in March, 1946. One of Henry M. Snyder & Co.'s best Far Eastern customers, the Kelly & Walsh bookstore, managed by A. S. Abbott, first established itself in Hong Kong in 1870 and has operated continuously since then except for the break occasioned by the Pacific War (*PW*, February 23, 1935 and December 23, 1944).

Frances Kraft Reckling (left) is shown presenting the original manuscript of "The Street" by Ann Petry (center) to Carl Van Vechten, who represented the James Weldon Johnson collection at Yale University. Mr. Van Vechten is the founder of the collection. The presentation was made at Mrs. Reckling's party for Ann Petry's new book "Country Place" (Houghton Mifflin)

FIGURE 4.5. Frances Reckling and Ann Petry presenting "The Street" manuscript to Carl Van Vechten.

Source: From "Shop Talk," *Publishers Weekly*, October 18, 1947. Reprinted with permission of *Publishers Weekly*, permission conveyed through Copyright Clearance Center, Inc.

official launching of the James Weldon Johnson Memorial Collection in January 1950 and extended to him a touching note of thanks: "The exhibit at the Yale Library is magnificent—and I shall always regret that we in the audience at Sprague Hall did not stand and cheer when you were presented with that citation—for it was a memorable occasion. *The Street* items are so beautifully displayed that I felt I ought to say a hearty thank-you—after I looked at the entire exhibit I felt that all of us who are represented there owe you a debt of gratitude."[65] The final two letters by Petry to Van Vechten are from 1952 and 1953, respectively. She wrote the first, dated August 13, 1952, to inform him that she was "working on a biography of Harriet Tubman" and that she intended "to do some of the research for the book in the Yale University Library, making use of the James Weldon Johnson Memorial Collection."[66] Frankly, as I read this letter, I found it difficult to understand why Van Vechten was so confused as to think she intended to take material out of the JWJ Collection, but he was: "I can't make out exactly what she wants," Van Vechten wrote to Gallup just a week later, "but certainly she cannot remove books from the Library."[67]

The folder's final letter from Petry to Van Vechten, dated August 14, 1953, holds a surprising fact; Petry promises to eventually donate the manuscript notebooks of her third novel, *The Narrows*, to Yale. Before then, however, she needed "to use them for income tax purposes." She writes:

> The manuscript of the new book will, of course, eventually join the others in the James Weldon Johnson Collection at the Yale Library. It will be quite a few months before I send it to you, because it is pretty much scattered around in desk drawers, etc., even more important than that I'm going to hang on to some of the notebooks for quite a long time because I am quite certain I shall have to use them for income tax purposes, they're dated and they offer evidence of the fact that I'd been working on the book for six years—but you'll get them eventually—notebooks and all the rest of it.[68]

This letter further marks the growth of Petry's "tax consciousness" in relation to her archive, an indication that the writing business as a whole had become wise to the tax code's significance for professional writers. At the time, as I mentioned earlier, writers could also still claim tax deductions for the perceived market value of their creations, an avenue that closed in 1969. For reasons that remain unclear—though likely related to income tax—Petry never did send the manuscript of *The Narrows* to Yale. Fifteen years later—thus four years after Carl Van Vechten's death in 1964—she instead donated it to BU as part of her first shipment to Howard Gotlieb.[69] Indeed, as I mention at the beginning of this chapter, her late diaries cite only BU as the repository for her papers. When mulling over what to do with the rest of her collection in 1983, she noted, "No reason to give these journals and notebooks to Boston University." And again, when reproduction requests began coming in, she confessed, "It never occurred to me that in my lifetime people would be poking through that stuff I gave to Boston University." Petry seems to have forgotten that some of her papers were at Yale, which suggests the disappearance, unavailability, or overall invisibility of the Beinecke Petry holdings from the late 1960s up to the present day.

Despite the new clarification that reading both halves of the Petry–Van Vechten correspondence yielded, the mystery of the vanishing manuscripts for *The Street* and *Country Place* remained. What had Yale done with them, or what had been done to them at Yale since the exhibition of them in 1964? With all the new additional evidence I had been able to accrue, I decided to contact Yale's curator of American literature again, despite her silence in response to my initial query. This time, Melissa Barton kindly replied, even though she was on vacation: "After a bit of investigation," she wrote, "I learned that we have an uncatalogued Petry Collection that includes both manuscripts as well as some other materials."[70] And just like that, as simply as that, the collection reemerged from the miasma of oblivion.

There had been no heist à la *American Animals*, no accidental loss, no dramatic retrieval from Mrs. Reckling in the 1970s—indeed, nothing other than the miserably dreary ordinariness of the archive. "I believe it has just been in the backlog," Barton concluded in a follow-up email, and she stated that she was unsure whether the collection had ever been cataloged, "though there may have been a catalogue card at some point. . . . [Q]uite a lot of material was described only on cards or minimally and used to be stored in

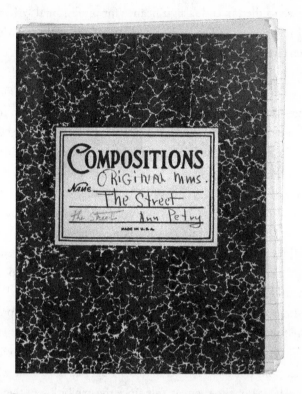

FIGURE 4.6. One of the four original manuscript notebooks of Ann Petry's novel *The Street*.

Source: Box 3, folder 1, uncataloged James Weldon Johnson MSS Petry Collection, Beinecke Rare Book and Manuscript Library, Yale.

the building."[71] Once again, the backlog—Or is it the Balrog?—had reared its ever-growing and fiery head from New Haven's Mines of Moria. What chance do we have, I wondered, when even the collections that have been preserved, donated, put into "snug" archival boxes, and twice exhibited are returned to the depths of the backlog with nary a listing or a note? It was at least comforting to know that these irreplaceable artifacts of twentieth-century American literature were still of this world, safe and sound, and would now likely be processed soon, which meant that more scholars would be able to unearth their secrets and perhaps even, as Tayari Jones hopes for, "ignite an Ann Petry revival."[72] At last, the mystery—though now *mystery* seems much too exciting a term to describe such a banal outcome—was solved. Or was it?

Before Yale confirmed the presence of the uncataloged manuscript collection, but after I had amassed incontrovertible evidence that the manuscripts had been donated to the Beinecke, I also wrote to Ann Petry's daughter, Elisabeth, to see if she might know more about what had happened to the collection. In her generous reply, Liz confirmed that the manuscript for *The Street* had not been in the house at the time of Ann Petry's death in 1997 but confessed that she did not know what had happened to the Beinecke collection. She did, however, add a tiny wrinkle to the whole affair that continues to unsettle me: "At some point my parents were discussing the MS of *The Street*," she wrote, and "after Mother left the room, my father said, 'That one at the Beinecke isn't the original manuscript.' I tried to get more information, but he just gave me a cryptic smile (one of many) and walked away. Since he was in the Army when the book was published," Liz added, "I'm not even sure he would have known."[73] Indeed, it seems none of us will ever truly know.

5

"TOO OBSCURE FOR LEARNED CLASSIFICATION"

Comic Books, Counterculture, and
Archival Invisibility in *Invisible Man*

C omic books are a largely unnoticed presence in Ralph Ellison's life
and work, a critical blind spot that reflects comics' historical status as "the invisible art," as Scott McCloud famously calls them.[1] Their
invisibility associates these cheap, undervalued, and fleeting American
paper artifacts not only with the central conceit of *Invisible Man* but also
with those discursive events Michel Foucault declares, in his discussion of
the archive, "invisible by virtue of being too much at the surface of things."[2]
Yet as the novel's narrator concludes after his encounter with the comic-
book-reading zoot-suiters in the subway, "They'd been there all along, but
somehow I'd missed them."[3] The Ellison archive—both Ellison's papers in
the Library of Congress and his published corpus—reveals that comics have
indeed been there all along. In an interview in 1977, when asked if there
were any popular influences in his work, Ellison replied, "Oh, sure, I use
anything from movies to comic strips."[4] More than two decades earlier, in
1955, Ellison had told a group of writers and publishers that "the individual
man . . . is more apt to get a sense of wonder, a sense of self-awareness and
a sharper reflection of his world from a comic book than from most novels."[5] Echoing that sentiment two years later in "Society, Morality, and the
Novel," Ellison wrote: "The reader who looks here [modern novels] for some
acknowledgement of the turbulence he feels around him would be better
satisfied by a set of comic books."[6] Though obviously committed to the novel

form, he never concealed his sustained engagement with comics and in fact scattered comic-book allusions throughout *Invisible Man*.

On the one hand, Ellison's predilection for indigenous American forms of expression such as jazz as well as his embrace of popular forms render him receptive to the "invisible art." On the other, his allegiance to the novel and his attunement to the violent, hostile reality of what Invisible Man calls the "comic-book world" of Harlem during his funeral oration for the fallen Tod Clifton (458) also indicate Ellison's wariness toward countercultural forces and their relation to black leadership. In their portrayal of violence in defense of a "higher" purpose, both *Invisible Man* and comic books exhibit a troubled relationship to the law and raise the question of whether the American fantasies and myths found in mass culture contribute to an individual's cultivation or lead to unrealistic expectations and a life of crime. Ellison's narrative and superhero comics present vigilantism as both a viable and perhaps an inevitable, extralegal means of achieving justice in an unjust world. These issues are framed by Ellison's work and association with Dr. Fredric Wertham, founder of the Lafargue Mental Hygiene Clinic in Harlem and instigator of a major crusade against comic books throughout the 1950s (see figure 5.1).[7]

Ellison's published writings and those stored at the Library of Congress make apparent that issues surrounding the comic-book culture of the Cold War directly link up with many of *Invisible Man*'s bigger themes: the rapport between violence and heroism, youth culture and leadership, Harlem and urban life. Harlem and comics—in content as well as in their lurid and colorful vividness—seem to be intrinsically linked in Ellison's mind, a relation I parse here by reading the Harlem riot episode in *Invisible Man* alongside Ellison's sociological writings on Harlem, most notably "Harlem's America" and "Harlem Is Nowhere," Ellison's piece on the Lafargue Clinic discussed at length in chapter 3.

This archive enables a reassessment of *Invisible Man*'s narrative arc as one that resembles the type of origin story recounted in early superhero comics—as opposed to the type found in the bildungsroman. The novel traces the episodic metamorphosis of the protagonist from naive Southern schoolboy to urban outlaw living in an underground lair. This "outlaw" promises

FIGURE 5.1. Cover of a brochure produced by the Lafargue Mental Hygiene Clinic in 1949.

Source: Lafargue Clinic Records, Schomburg Center for Research in Black Culture, New York Public Library.

to play a socially responsible leadership role even though he is evidently a man with aggressive tendencies—he beats up that "blond man" within an inch of his life, tries to kill Kimbro in the Liberty Paints engine room, and literally spears Ras through the mouth—a combination of violence and principle that verges on vigilantism. On his way back to the epilogue, the novel will see Invisible Man undergo a strange transformation through a science experiment gone wrong, challenge and thwart a police eviction, run from a mysterious assailant on rooftops, experiment with changes in identity through costumes, and engage in some impressive street fighting using a chain. Is it so surprising, then, that Marvel's Luke Cage can be seen carrying around his own personal copy of *Invisible Man* for most of the episodes in season 1 of his eponymous series on Netflix (2016–2018)?

Invisible Man possesses both structural and thematic affinities with the "ten-cent plague" that changed America in the postwar years,[8] and Ellison's recourse to comic-book allusions offers a new angle for understanding what he calls the "unreality" of the Harlem he is often at pains to depict in his novel and essays. Although he does not unreservedly endorse the influence of comics on American youth, he subtly critiques the reigning midcentury belief that comics mobilize only the nefarious perversities and dangers of mass culture, and in doing so he underscores the imaginative dynamism comics possess as models of urban nimbleness and adaptability. In the process, Ellison takes advantage of literature's own nimbleness in incorporating subjects often left outside "official" history. In that sense, the zoot-suiters of the novel become "history's own revenge," its "big surprise" (441); they elude positivist paradigms of archival conservation. The novel form's status as counterarchive consists in its capacity to accommodate the outmoded and the urgent, the new and the dead, as well as the "fate and promise" of what is to come.[9] Tracing the comic-book allusions in *Invisible Man* in the context of comic books' previous invisibility in scholarship underscores how certain ephemeral aspects of American life resist easy conversion into an "official" archive, even as the novelist nevertheless "gropes" to incorporate them into his tale.[10]

In her introduction to the collected volume *Archive Stories: Facts, Fiction, and the Writing of History*, Antoinette Burton stresses the need to consider "the novel as legitimate archives (that is to say, as makers of History)." Doing so, she suggests, "forces us to confront the limits of the official archive by acknowledging the power of literature to materialize those countless historical subjects who may never have come under the archival gaze."[11] *Invisible Man* adds nuance to Burton's claim by indicating that the issue is not simply a matter of "those countless historical subjects" never having "come under the archival gaze," but of their remaining invisible to that gaze "because of a peculiar disposition of the eyes" (3), as the narrator puts it.

This invisibility is akin to a Foucauldian view of the archive as a method of exclusion enforced by peculiar "configurations of power."[12] Foucault defines his "archaeological" method as "render[ing] visible that which is invisible by virtue of being too much at the surface of things,"[13] so we can speak of the archive's exclusion as an Ellisonian invisibility embodied by those who are "outside the groove of history" (443). The novel's counterarchival gaze is explicitly intimated in the subway platform episode when the narrator finally sees three zoot-suiters, those mysterious boys who, like Tod Clifton and later Invisible Man himself, are "living outside the realm of history" and who, crucially, are completely absorbed in the reading of comic books (441–42). *Invisible Man* thus exhibits a "whole different order of archival imaginary"[14] that challenges history by asking the central archival questions, voiced by the narrator in this episode: "Was this all that would be recorded? Was this the only true history of the times?" (443).

On the whole, this chapter is a means to reflect on the interrelation between the midcentury novel form's counterarchival functions of preservation and curation and how the contents of literary archives may offer a window into a correlative set of prescient collecting and novelistic practices. Literary archives can authorize new readings of canonized texts and reassessments of major authors, through a careful consideration of what the author chose to preserve and collect (drafts, research notes, specific subject files, photographs, print matter, and other ephemera), of outgoing and incoming correspondence touching on otherwise unattainable contextual and intimate information, and of genetic criticism—that is, microanalyses of multiple drafts of key texts and novelistic scenes.

HARLEM'S LITTLE BATMEN

When Ellison began writing *Invisible Man*, he reported reading Lord Raglan's work *The Hero* (1936), which traces the common characteristics of mythic heroes. As Ellison put it in an interview first published in 1961, Raglan's text "got [him] to thinking about the ambiguity of Negro leadership during that period."[15] Inspired by Kenneth Burke as well as by Joyce and Eliot's modernist techniques, Ellison studied folklore and myth as a way to inform and inflect his own time.[16] He saw in heroism and myth the ingredients of individual leadership; an introduction he wrote to *Invisible Man* in 1981 evinces his wish to imaginatively create an ideal sovereign figure who would transcend any and all restrictions, be they racial, societal, or merely human, through an unrelenting "personal vision of possibility." "At its most serious," Ellison writes, "fiction . . . is a thrust toward a human ideal."[17] For a novelist attuned to the reappearance of myth and heroism in novels and in contemporary fashion, comic books, then littering every corner of America,[18] evidently offered a new fantastic vision of possibility made manifest in the form of the superhero. Comic-book writers were practicing a similar plundering of myth in elevating individuals to superhuman status. As a hero who has no superpowers but rather actualizes the human's superhuman possibilities, the Batman, created by Bob Kane and Bill Finger in 1939, was a particularly seductive emblem. This explains why Ellison would refer to this character directly in his sociological observations published as "Harlem's America" in 1966.[19]

Throughout *Invisible Man*, Ellison seeks to enact a balance between tradition and change using the appeal to mass culture as a bridge, an approach to tradition echoing that of Ellison's close friend Albert Murray in *The Hero and the Blues* (1973). Tradition, Murray suggests, is "that which continues; it is also the medium by which and through which continuation occurs."[20] His statement should be understood not only in the context of African American cultural practices but also in the context of Ellison and Murray's interest in the national penchant for supernatural legends and fables, particularly as they are discussed in Constance Rourke's book *American Humor* (1931).[21] Murray's reading of Rourke's study suggests how this American production of tall tales might have evolved into comic books. Comics are an example of how "the traditional adapts itself to change, or renews itself through change" and thus represent an offshoot of the American "resilience"—Rourke's term—that "regenerates itself in the vernacular,"[22] a feature much discussed in the selected correspondence between Ellison and

Murray published as *Trading Twelves* and praised by Ellison in his foreword to the reprint of John Atlee Kouwenhoven's collection *The Beer Can by the Highway: Essays on What's "American" About America* (1961, reprint 1988).[23] Leslie Fiedler, one of the many New York intellectuals writing on comic books in the 1940s and 1950s, was quick to realize that the superheroes populating comics "are seen as inheritors, for all their superficial differences, of the *inner* impulses of traditional folk art."[24] Framed in this way, resilience becomes a defining characteristic of both African American literature and archivism, with the latter buttressed by a paradoxical combination of radical breaks within a persistence of tradition.

As for the fantasies pervading his youth in Oklahoma, Ellison notes that he and his friends strove to re-create the archetypes and legendary figures of American myth—those "which violated all ideas of social hierarchy and order"—and to recast them as *"Negro American."*[25] Ellison's yearning to appropriate for African Americans the archetypes traditionally reserved for whites served as an underlying motivation for taking the invariably white superhero and imagining a black counterpart for that figure. In his eulogy for his friend Romare Bearden, he directly points to comics as the source of archetypal figures to be reimagined as African American. He recollects the "hero of my childhood," a young neighbor in Oklahoma City, who

> filled his notebooks with cartoon characters who acted out visual narratives that I found far more interesting than those provided by the newspaper comic sections. More interesting because they were about us, about Negro boys like ourselves. He filled his notebooks with drawings which told the stories of Negro cowboys and rodeo stars like Bill Pickett, of detectives and gangsters, athletes, clowns and heroes. Indeed, he created such a variety of characters and adventures that our entire neighborhood took on a dimension of wonder.[26]

Rather uncannily, Ellison may as well be describing the first issue of Orrin C. Evan's *All-Negro Comics* (1947). Independently published in

Philadelphia by Evans, a journalist by trade, the issue featured a motley crew of "detectives and gangsters, athletes, clowns and heroes" and was entirely written and drawn by African Americans: "Every brush stroke and pen line in the drawings on these pages are by Negro artists," states Evans on the back cover of this first issue, adding, "All-Negro Comics will not only give Negro artists an opportunity gainfully to use their talents, but it will glorify Negro historical achievements."[27]

Ellison could see that the comics drawn by his childhood hero—and the art of his friend Bearden—"speak eloquently of a promise which goes far beyond the designs and figures displayed within their frames."[28] This sentiment echoes one he expressed at the Senate hearing *The Crisis in Our Cities* in 1966 and published as "Harlem's America." In his testimony, Ellison cast the city, Harlem specifically (the next neighborhood to take on a "dimension of wonder" for Ellison), as the site not only where the frustrations and restrictions faced by "Negro children" and African Americans as a whole can be overcome but also where a precious preservation of folklore takes place: "Harlem is a place where our folklore is preserved, and transformed. It is the place where the body of Negro myth and legend thrives. It is a place where our styles . . . find continuity and metamorphosis." As a repository in flux, the city should ideally be a "place for allowing the individual to achieve his highest promise." Ellison's sensibility for what he calls "promise" created a kind of ethereal matrix for his thoughts on mythic figures as they were found and reinvented in comics and in Harlem as well as, as I discuss in this chapter, for his relation to the great number of "juvenile delinquents" populating Harlem and America. At the hearing, speaking of the changes occurring in Harlem at the time, Ellison told members of the Senate that with the children of those African Americans who had migrated North to Harlem, "you had a different situation, because [these children] could see what is possible within the big city. They could see the wonderful possibilities offered by the city to define one's own individuality, to amplify one's talent, to find a place for one's self." At the same time, Ellison noted, many of these children had poor schooling, and sometimes their parents had no schooling at all. "This," he stated, "makes for a great deal of frustration."[29]

The period Ellison alluded to, from the 1930s to the 1950s, coincides with the rapid growth of the comic-book industry among millions of American children regardless of color. Having situated African American youth culture as caught between possibility and frustration, Ellison described the motivation for their dreams in terms of both nationalism and comics:

> Now, on the other hand, these are American children, and Americans are taught to be restless, to be mobile, to be daring. Our myths teach this, our cartoons teach us this, our athletic sports teach us this. The whole society is geared to making the individual restless, to making him test himself against the possibilities around him. . . . So you see little Negro Batmen flying around Harlem just as you see little white Batmen flying around Sutton Place. It is in the blood. But while the white child who is taken with these fantasies has many opportunities for working them into real life situations, too often the Negro child is unable to do so. This leads the Negro child who identifies with the heroes and outlaws of fantasy to feel frustrated and to feel that society has designated him the outlaw, for he is treated as one. Thus his sense of being outside the law is not simply a matter of fantasy, it is a reality based on the incontrovertible fact of race.[30]

In other words, the restless, mobile, and daring black youths fully engaged in the pursuit of the "infinite possibilities" that the city seemed to offer identified naturally with the outlaws of American fantasy because, like Batman, they were branded as such. But what Ellison was careful to underscore here is that "the incontrovertible fact of race" positioned the African American always already outside the law, where the fantasy of heroic action opened the possibility for the kind of vigilantism practiced by Batman. Indeed, the defiance and determination involved in bypassing the limitations imposed on Invisible Man's freedom, combined with the intention to develop himself "for the performance of many and diverse roles,"[31] reveal Ellison's protagonist to be quite the little Batman himself. Ellison's own phraseology in "Change the Joke and Slip the Yoke" associates his protagonist with the youth he described in his testimony, explaining that

Invisible Man "gets his restless mobility not so much from the blues or from sociology but because he appears in a literary form which has time and social change as its special province. Besides," Ellison adds, "restlessness of the spirit is an American condition."[32]

Ellison's work with Gordon Parks on the "Harlem Is Nowhere" project had given him a firsthand look at just how seriously local black boys were taking comics, as the photographer's archive can today bear witness. The untitled picture meant to accompany caption D in the original "Harlem Is Nowhere" photo-essay, discussed in chapter 3, shows five boys playing in garbage on the street, their positioning on the frame forming something like an ascending arc from left to right.[33] The first boy, on the left, is reading a comic book. An alternate frame from this scene, seen in a detail from a contact sheet in the Parks archive, focuses on this same boy reading the comic, while another depicts three of the boys huddled together around the comic (figures 5.2 and 5.3).

In the second frame, the boys appear to be in deep conversation about the horror comic that has now been passed from the boy in the leather jacket to the one wearing a cap in the middle. The importance these boys give to the comic belies the sentiment in the society of the time that comics were throwaways, akin to the burning garbage that surround the boys. Indeed, the images suggest that comics provide an escape from within the "foul landscape" of their lives and that horror comics in particular present "a sharper reflection of [their] world."[34] As I suggest, the trio of boys captured in these photographs are transported into Ellison's novel as the three comic-book-reading zoot-suiters in the subway, figures symbolizing a powerful new form of black leadership. These photographs are also further evidence that comics, far from being negligible garbage, harbored the transformative powers of a new, particularly American imaginary that thrived on the periphery, on the burning sidewalks of history's main thoroughfares.

FIGURES 5.2 AND 5.3 (*facing page*). Untitled, details from contact sheet, boys reading comics, Harlem, New York, 1948. Photographs by Gordon Parks.

Source: Courtesy of and copyright © The Gordon Parks Foundation.

THE BIRTHMARK

During his journalistic coverage of the Harlem riot of 1943, Ellison had already begun to think through the relations among crime, social change, youth, and blackness in America. As his archive shows, the young writer had witnessed and photographed the riot and then described it in an unpublished piece composed shortly after the event. In "Let Us Consider the Harlem 'Crime Wave,'" Ellison expressed his righteous anger at mainstream media's depiction of a "crime wave" in Harlem and argued that the crimes perpetrated in Harlem are fundamentally a "manifestation of our collective will to life." Of the many gangs that had sprouted in Harlem, including those that sold stolen goods (whom he called the "hotstuff men"), Ellison qualified their crimes as "good for the community." Echoing an underlying notion explored in Wright's novel *Native Son*, he declared: "the moment we seek to exert our own humanity we must commit a crime."[35]

Even before his work on the Harlem riot or the Lafargue Clinic, Ellison had already combined in literary form the themes of crime, comics, and racial discrimination at play in both *Invisible Man* and Wertham's social psychiatry. Testing out Kenneth Burke's "symbolic action" through the modernist method of dropping "a detail in its proper place in an action" so that "it gathers up associations and meanings,"[36] Ellison deployed comic strips in one of his earliest short stories, "The Birthmark," published in *New Masses* in 1940. In the story, the broken body of a black man lies in the grass by the side of the road. A white patrolman and his partner inform the dead man's brother and sister—Matt and Clara, who have been brought to the site to identify the body—that the man died in a car accident. But the body is so mangled and torn that the siblings, horrified, quickly understand that "HE WAS LYNCHED!" As Matt attempts to identify his brother's body by locating a birthmark on him, he sees that his brother has been "castrated." The birthmark has disappeared precisely because of the castration, a fact Matt could apprehend only through an unwanted handling of comics: when he first arrives at the scene, his brother's torn body—his groin area specifically—is covered with the news-paper's "colored comic sheets."[37]

In this early story, therefore, Ellison alludes to two cultural signifiers of American violence: first, the frontier figure of the corrupt, gun-swinging, hat-wearing lawman and, second, comics. The deployment of comics in "The Birthmark" is associated with the law's power literally to "cover up" the violence done to African Americans. In failing to depict African American heroes, newspaper comics adventures and the popular Western genre that elevates gunslinging sheriffs to mythic figures symbolically castrate the black man, circumscribing his sense of opportunity and access to power. This castration is the "reality based on the incontrovertible fact of race," Ellison lamented in 1966, a reality he inscribed into *Invisible Man* in the only scene where the narrator goes to the movies. At this early stage in his New York journey, a depressed and fearful Invisible Man goes to see a Western, described as "a picture of frontier life with heroic Indian fighting and struggles against flood, storm and forest fire, with the out-numbered settlers winning each engagement; an epic of wagon trains rolling ever westward" (170). The film is successful in providing the escapism the young man seeks, but it fails to reinvigorate him through identification. As he puts it, "I forgot myself (although there was no one like me taking part in the adventures)" (170). The politics of representation, dramatized in this need for African Americans to "take part in the adventures," is one of the chief underlying themes of Ellison's career as a public intellectual.

Frantz Fanon diagnoses the exact same problem with American comics in *Black Skin, White Masks*, published the same year as *Invisible Man*, when he stresses how the ubiquity of white heroes in comics leads black children to identify with magazines that "are put together by white men for little white men" and that often feature villains as "Negroes or Indians." "This is the heart of the problem," Fanon adds, because "the little Negro, quite as easily as the little white boy, becomes an explorer, an adventurer, a missionary 'who faces the danger of being eaten by the wicked Negroes.'" Since "all those 'comic books' serve actually as a release for collective aggression," Fanon demands "nothing more nor less than the establishment of children's magazines especially for Negroes."[38] Such comics would give material life to the fantasies of the colonized; as Fanon describes these fantasies in *The Wretched of the Earth*, they are straight out of superhero and adventure comics: "the dreams of the native are always of muscular prowess; his dreams are of action and of aggression. I dream I am jumping, swimming, running, climbing; I dream that I burst out laughing, that I span a river in one stride, or that I am followed by a flood of motorcars which never catch up with me."[39] Fanon's project echoes what Orrin C. Evans did in 1947 with *All-Negro Comics* and what Ellison's Oklahoma childhood hero did in his little notebooks. Just as Matt in "The Birthmark" wishes he had a gun of his own to face the law, Ellison appropriates for himself and his craft the same instruments of power. Thus, the "birthmark" not only serves as an overdetermined symbol of "the incontrovertible fact" of being born black in America but also connotes, more generally, the concept of origins ("it is in the blood"). Replaced with comics on the victim's absent phallus, the birthmark becomes the *arkhē* of Ellison's use of comics as literary allusion, pointing as it does to the commencement of the comics' power in his Oklahoma childhood.[40]

WRITE OR MURDER

In Ellison's novel, Invisible Man's fraught relationship to society and the law comes to the fore in the disturbing confessions of the prologue/epilogue, where, seen through the prism of comic-book ethics, *Invisible Man* exhibits an increasing sense of vigilantism. The narrator explains that "now, after first being 'for' society and then 'against' it, I assign myself no rank or any limit" and that "my world has become one of infinite possibilities" (576). Even though "there's still a conflict within" him, he is "coming out nevertheless" because "even an invisible man has a socially responsible role to play" (581). Vigilantes such as the Batman act under their own authority, tolerating "no rank or any limit," and come out of their lairs to make a difference in the world, motivated by their own individual sense of social responsibility and justice. It is precisely for these reasons that such vigilantism can be inspiring to a black boy, positioned "outside the law" as he is. Accordingly, Invisible Man sees his outlaw status—he steals electricity through "an act of sabotage" (7), he lives "off the grid" in his hole, he smokes marijuana, and he beats people up—as operating in the service of his aim to "protect the higher interests of society" (14). As the Batman himself puts it, "If you can't beat them 'inside' the law . . . you must beat them 'outside' it."[41] Resorting to violence seems to constitute part of Invisible Man's "socially responsible role" when, filled with rage, he attempts a kind of underlying justification for the vigilante stance he is adopting. In the prologue, he asks the reader to remember the man he head-butted and kicked:

> Take the man whom I almost killed: Who was responsible for that near murder—I? I don't think so, and I refuse it. I won't buy it. You can't give it to me. *He* bumped *me*, *he* insulted *me*. Shouldn't he, for his own personal safety, have recognized my hysteria, my "danger potential"? . . . And if he had yelled for a policeman, wouldn't I have been taken for the offending one? Yes, yes, yes! Let me agree with you, I was the irresponsible one; for I should have used my knife to protect the higher interests of society.
>
> (14, emphasis in original)

Responsibility here seems to also mean "answerability" in that the protagonist is not answerable for the violent actions he perpetrates upon those who fail to see him, even though the law, here in the form of the policeman, would incontrovertibly cast *him* as the criminal. In these circumstances, Invisible Man is exempt from blame in unleashing his "danger potential" because his actions are rather a consequence of what is wrong with American society. This kind of "irresponsibility," he claims, "is part of my invisibility" (14). But the extracted passage is even more alarming, for Invisible Man implies that he acted irresponsibly in *failing* to use his knife to "protect the higher interests of society," as he "should have," an implication that turns violent action—in this case murder—into a moral imperative. If we are to believe his call for a renewed sense of social "responsibility," which the prologue shows must come in the form of violent action, the resulting message is that Invisible Man finds the complicity between crime and social utility, the core contradiction of vigilantism, as his newfound worldview.

The boomeranging complicity between crime and social utility in *Invisible Man* is something Ellison had been pondering for years, as evidenced by his correspondence and editorial work from the early 1940s. Having just read Wright's book *12 Million Black Voices*, a deeply emotional Ellison shared with Wright in November 1941 how he had "learned to keep the bitterness submerged . . . so that those passions which could so easily be criminal might be socially useful." In Ellison's thinking, these passions are characteristic of those who, like his novel's protagonist, "shot up from the same region," those "for whom the trauma of passing from the country to the city of destruction brought no anesthesia of unconsciousness, but left our nerves peeled and quivering. We are not the numbed, but the seething. God! It makes you want to write and write and write, or murder."[42] With this astonishing phrase, Ellison seems to be offering only two alternatives, to write or to murder, yet either option "might be socially useful." This is precisely the dilemma at the heart of Invisible Man's stance toward society: he "should have used [his] knife to protect the higher interests of society," yet he ends up instead committing a "near murder" and writing down his story (14). Ellison's sense of writing as an alternative to murder can help explain why Invisible Man has been increasingly aligned with a kind of highbrow vigilantism, not as a "superhero" but as a writer. The two alternative reactions are not opposed; the last line of the novel—"Who knows but that, on the lower frequencies, I speak for you?" (581)—still contains a kernel of vigilantism in the sense that Invisible Man considers himself in a state of exception and takes on the task of acting on the reader's behalf without seeking society's permission. Like a comic book, the novel stresses the uncomfortable notion that under certain circumstances the individual will have to forgo the law and use violence as a means of ridding society of its evil. For the African American community of the 1950s, this sentiment was even more a reflection of reality than something out of comics.

In the early days of comics, the violent acts of superheroes always had productive consequences for society; redemptive violence is precisely the foundation of the outlaw hero's relation to society. Such heroes embody what Ellison yearned for in his letter to Wright: the harnessing of potentially criminal passions for social improvement. Positioning his hero in terms of these precarious ethics, Ellison invokes the world of "infinite possibilities" (576), where the fantasy that criminals can be heroes assures the reading public that antisocial and aggressive acts are not only healthy but necessary for upholding justice. What is inevitably simplified and idealized in superhero comics is made much more complex in a novel. Because exacting violence upon those we consider undesirable is ultimately undemocratic and often hardly redemptive (as in "The Birthmark"), Ellison is careful to stress that "there's still a conflict" within his protagonist; while Invisible Man "condemns" and "denounces," he also "affirms" and "defends" and, most important, commits only a *near* murder in the name of social justice. The comic-book tendency of divesting violent acts of their antisocial nature is too dangerous a slippage for Ellison to condone. It is also what Fredric Wertham's work at the Lafargue Clinic condemned. Nevertheless, Ellison does demonstrate in his novel the appeal of outlaw figures who, like the Batman, seize the right to operate "free of procedural and institutional restraint."[43] Invisible Man's "danger potential" includes his capacity for violence *and* his achievements as a writer, both of which have the potential to be socially redemptive. Indeed, Ellison went on record to say that "books represent socially useful acts."[44]

Operating outside institutional tethers was particularly appealing to an African American community that was disenfranchised to the point of invisibility. Booker T. Washington's Tuskegee Institute had fallen from grace as a symbol of black leadership, and the young Invisible Man overcomes his disillusionment once he understands that the answer to leadership lies in *individual* power. Indeed, the outlaw-hero ideal is about as far from Booker T's "cast down your bucket" ethics as one can get. Superheroes, as fantastic projections of a heightened mythical, although urbanist, imagination, are therefore apt symbols of what Ellison exploited as a writer and desired as a social activist.[45]

A COMIC-BOOK DAY IN A COMIC-BOOK WORLD

As a medium that combines words and images unbound by the exigencies of reality and the laws of physics, comics possess particular qualities that resonate with Ellison's aesthetic ideals. William W. Savage Jr. writes: "Comic books could carry heroes beyond the limits of possibility imposed by radio (sounds without pictures and thus without depth or significant personification) and film (sounds with pictures, but constrained by technology). . . . Comic-book artists and writers could produce that which could be conceived, which is more than the creators of motion pictures or radio programs could claim."[46] Ellison drew on comic books because, much like the Harlem of his description, they embody a space where his ideal "infinite possibilities" could be recorded on paper and because, as Bradford W. Wright explains, twentieth-century America required "a superhero who could resolve the tensions of individuals in an increasingly urban, consumer-driven, and anonymous mass society."[47] American frontier heroes such as Wyatt Earp and Davy Crockett no longer seemed capable of representing models of contemporary leadership, especially for African Americans.

Before the Comic Code Authority was implemented in 1954 (two years after the publication of *Invisible Man*), superheroes often acted directly against figures of established authority in the service of "true" justice. Comic books, despite their fantastic aspects, consistently addressed the sociopolitical reality of America and the world. They "epitomized so much of what was attractive and possible in the advanced consumer culture of the West. Their sheer thrill and accessibility made them subversive in the Communist society."[48] Almost a full year before the United States officially entered the struggle against the Axis nations, comic books went to war in 1941 with the cover of *Captain America Comics* number 1 when Jack Kirby's flag-wearing American hero punched Adolf Hitler squarely on the jaw. In their early stories, from 1938 up to the American involvement in World War II, comic-book superheroes took care of United States, watched out for their nation as philosopher kings endowed with the powers to make a difference.

Virtually every one of the early story lines sees the superhero fixing an array of problems, stopping all types of transgressions, from lynch mobs and domestic violence to political corruption. The first description of Superman, after all, was "champion of the oppressed." For any oppressed individual or community, such a figure was the embodiment of the promise of a better future through exceptional leadership.

Bradford Wright explains that Superman habitually "championed social reform and government assistance to the poor."[49] In an issue of the Superman comics from the late 1940s, when a boy is arrested for assault and battery, the boy's mother tells Superman that poor living conditions are the real reason for her boy's crimes. As Wright recounts the story, Superman "tells the neighbourhood boys, 'It's not entirely your fault that you're delinquent—it's these slums—your poor living conditions—if there was some way I could remedy it!' And remedy it he does, by demolishing the slums himself in defiance of the legal authorities, even fighting off the police and National Guard when they try to stop him. . . . In place of the demolished tenements, the government constructs splendid, shining public housing."[50] The scene recalls a late moment in *Invisible Man* when Dupre leads some men, including the protagonist, into the Harlem slum tenement where he lives and burns it down. Dupre addresses the Harlemite crowd: "My kid died from the t-bees in that deathtrap, but I bet a man ain't no more go'n be born in there" (547). In this context, Dupre takes on the role of Superman by suddenly entering the "scheme" to "remedy" the situation. Once the tenement has been set ablaze, however, it is Invisible Man who captures the hero's spotlight: "I burst into the air and the exploding sounds of the night. . . . I stood on the stoop with the red doorway behind me . . . lost in the clamour of shouts, screams, burglar alarms and sirens" (549). As the emerging hero, framed as he is by the blazing red doorway, the protagonist feels "the whole surface of [his] skin alert"; he has become "a dark mass in motion on a dark night, a black river ripping through the black land." His "personality blasted," he feels "as though a huge force was on the point of bursting" (550). Here Ellison is ascribing both power and a certain mystery to his hero, granting him entrance into "universal myth"[51] by virtue of the specific comic-book reality he has established from the beginning.

Indeed, *Invisible Man* opens by distancing itself from the Hollywood movie genre—"I am not . . . one of your Hollywood-movie ectoplasms," the narrator states in the prologue (3)—and closes with an illustration of what the protagonist dubs a "comic-book world" (458). Even from the outset, the very title of the novel, *Invisible Man*, is reminiscent of classic superhero eponyms such as "Superman" and "Batman" that had already been in vogue for more than a decade. In light of the fact that the protagonist remains unnamed, the hero's secret identity is preserved, for the reader knows him only as "Invisible Man." Readers become the equivalent of the denizens of Gotham, inhabiting the comic-book world, knowing only the heroic persona with its mythical aura of mystery and danger, an effect that Ellison clearly intends—recall Invisible Man's prologue declaration that others "never recognize me even when in closest contact with me" and "hardly believe that I exist" (13). At times, the protagonist seems invested in cultivating the mythical status of heroism, a facet of his personality that manifests perhaps most strongly in the Rinehart episode, when attire is the means through which a special social status is achieved. Like a superhero, Ellison's narrator displays a wish to be larger than life and to have an identifiable mark of superiority and power over the crowd. Facing the audience at his first lecture for the Brotherhood, Invisible fantasizes: "If only I were a foot taller and a hundred pounds heavier, I could simply stand before them with a sign across my chest, stating I KNOW ALL ABOUT THEM, and they'd be as awed as though I were the original boogey man . . . they'd simply thrill at the sight of me" (409, capitalization in the original). Imposing physical girth, insignia on the chest, the ability to induce thrills by mere presence—all are defining aspects of superheroes, whose costumes and size act as symbols of power in a burgeoning American mythology. Further, Invisible's desire to be "recognized at a glance—not by features, but by clothes, by uniform, by gait" (485) is a hint that the protagonist's superheroic (American) ambitions are on full display.

The indelible marks left by comics on Ellison's groping for popular allusions are also apparent in two earlier scenes that signify the narrator's entrance into a greater, mythical comic-book world. The Afrofuturistic overtones of the scene immediately following the explosion of the Liberty

Paints engine room imbue the novel with a narrative feeling akin to that of most origin stories of early superhero comics. Coming roughly at the halfway point of the novel, this scene also marks a clear change in the hero's personality and trajectory—a sort of rebirth of the hero: "My mind was a blank, as though I had just begun to live" (233). When the narrator first regains consciousness after the explosion, he finds himself completely ensconced inside a "machine" of some kind, surrounded by doctors/scientists. They seem to have implanted him with an unknown device, which is apparent when one of the doctors explodes, "Aha! You see! My little gadget will solve everything!" (235). In a kind of science-fictional scenario reminiscent of the period's horror comics and pulp tales, the narrator overhears the scientists explain what this gadget does: " 'The machine will produce the results of a prefrontal lobotomy without the negative effects of the knife,' the voice said. 'You see, instead of severing the prefrontal lobe, a single lobe, that is, we apply pressure in the proper degrees to the major centers of nerve control—our concept is Gestalt—and the result is as complete a change of personality as you'll find in your famous fairy-tale cases of criminals transformed into amiable fellows after all that bloody business of a brain operation'" (236). This lobotomy is akin to the castration in "The Birthmark," representing an embodied lesion of commencement. Of particular interest here is the allusion to fairy tales and the possibility of reforming criminals—the idea that there is but one degree of difference between the criminal and the "amiable fellow."

While Invisible Man is entrapped in a man-size glass case, the experiment grows bewilderingly stranger by the minute. After he is electroshocked, he begins to feel that he now exists "in some other dimension" (238), and he is suddenly force-fed a warm fluid. As the mysterious substance courses through his veins, his entire body begins to glow: "A huge iridescent bubble seemed to enfold me" (238), until the bubble—and apparently the glass case where he is trapped—explodes. He relates the fantastic event: "I felt myself bounce, sail off like a ball thrown over the roof into mist, striking a hidden wall beyond a pile of broken machinery and sailing back" (238). These narrative events are particularly reminiscent of comic-book superhero origin stories. Perhaps RZA of the Wu-Tang Clan puts it best when he observes that "in comics, when a scientific project goes wrong, it produces monsters. Or superheroes."⁵² Indeed, many superheroes' origins are linked with science gone wrong—for instance, the Flash (first appeared 1940) gains his powers following a laboratory explosion, and Steve Rogers (first appeared 1941) is injected with a "serum" that transforms his weak body into that of a supersoldier, Captain America (during the metamorphosis, supervised by a crew of scientists, a white glow surrounds Steve's body, pre-figuring the "iridescent bubble" that surrounds Invisible Man once he is injected with the "warm fluid"). In his essay "Black Power: Minstrelsy and Electricity in Ralph Ellison's *Invisible Man*," Johnny Wilcox even posits that the hero is transformed "into a black cyborg as a result of his several exposures to electricity."⁵³

After this first transformation, the protagonist is left alone, "fretting over [his] identity," wondering, "Who am I? . . . I felt like a clown. Nor was I up to being both a criminal and detective—though why criminal I didn't know" (242). Immediately upon waking, Invisible Man thinks of the affinities between the criminal and the detective, roles best embodied in the comic-book world by the vigilante known as the Batman. The scene easily lends itself to such a reading; indeed, as Invisible Man exits the machine, one of the doctors returns to examine him and notes that "he's surprisingly strong" (244). His newfound power thus instinctively tells him that he will be treated as a criminal. Once Invisible Man is freed and manages to make his way back to Mary Rambo's apartment, he stresses how Mary's talk serves as a constant reminder of "leadership and responsibility" (258). She repeatedly tells him that "something was expected of me, some act of leadership, some newsworthy achievement; and I was torn between resenting her for it and loving her for the nebulous hope she kept alive" (258). Through the character of Mary, the call of the hero beckons Invisible Man. His body transformed, his mind must come next, and, accordingly, "the obsession with [his] identity which [he] had developed at the factory hospital returned with a vengeance," leading him to ask two fundamental questions: "Who was I, how had I come to be?" (259). Notably, such questions would have been quite familiar to any Batman reader in that they are the first-person equivalent of Batman's oft-reprinted origin story, titled "The Legend of the

Batman—Who He Is and How He Came to Be!" First published in *Detective Comics* number 33 in 1939, this comic was also reprinted in *Batman* number 1 in 1940 and has been consistently reprinted throughout the years.

Regardless of whether Ellison was directly inspired by comics in the crafting of these scenes, the themes developed in the scenes as well as the language used to depict them are enough to create powerful correspondences between the novel and the folklore of comics. As readers of the novel know well, the answer Invisible Man conjures to his questions of identity arrives as a result of his wolfing down a yam. The yam salesman calls him "one of these old-fashioned yam eaters," leading him to proudly reply, "They're my birthmark . . . I yam what I am!" (266). Not only does the word *birthmark* directly hark back to Ellison's short story from 1940, containing the origin of Ellison's literary use of comics, but the phrase "I yam what I am" is yet another allusion to a superstrong cartoon character: Popeye. *I Yam What I Yam* is the title of the first official theatrical cartoon short in the *Popeye the Sailor* series, released in 1933 (the first had been part of a *Betty Boop* cartoon). Thus, the "secret origin" moment of Invisible Man, his "rebirth," is imbued with a twofold comics-related allusion, a novelistic move that Ellison subsequently redeploys at key moments in his hero's life, especially after he is recruited by the Brotherhood.

The events following the yam scene are in fact how the young hero is first brought to the Brotherhood's attention. The narrator sees an old African American couple being put out onto the street with all their earthly goods, and he is inspired to make his first impromptu public speech. His words, spoken to both the growing gathering crowd of Harlemites and the police officers supervising the eviction, center on the issue of the fraught relationship between African Americans and the law. The scene quickly reaches a boiling point, and fighting breaks out. In the immediate aftermath of the ruckus, the narrator encounters a strange white man who is, unbeknownst to the protagonist, a member of the Brotherhood. After this brief encounter, cop cars begin to arrive on the scene as backup to the first officers, and the cops start going into the building where Invisible Man is hiding. Filled with the adrenaline of his "action . . . action," the narrator is told that he will need to escape over the roof to evade arrest. A white girl gives him a golden piece of vigilante advice, "The longer you remain unknown to the police, the longer you'll be effective" (284). But at this point in the narrative, Invisible Man doesn't yet understand that the "incontrovertible fact of race" has made him an outlaw by default, and so the form of his vigilantism remains undefined at this stage in his evolution: "Effective? I thought. What did she mean?" (284).

The narrative frames the rooftop flight in visual cues that conjure both comics and the movies. With the cops just outside, Invisible Man hurries for the stairs, and the heroic adventure continues: "I took the flight in a bound and cautiously opened the door, and suddenly the sun flared bright on the roof and it was windy cold. Before me the low, snow-caked walls dividing the buildings stretched hurdle-like the long length of the block to the corner, and before me empty clotheslines trembled in the wind" (285). He makes his way "to the next roof and then to the next, going with swift caution" (285), but he suddenly realizes that a man is hurrying after him, "slipping, sliding, going over the low dividing walls of the roofs with puffing, bustling effort" (285). An air of mystery is added to the chase in that the man does not yell "Halt!" nor does he shoot at the narrator, as the latter keeps expecting. Once our hero finally makes his way down and out of the building, he steps "into the street with a nonchalance copied from characters I had seen in the movies" (286). Soon, the man does catch up to him, and he is revealed to be Brother Jack, leader of the Brotherhood.

In their ensuing dialogue, Jack awakens Invisible Man to the proximity of criminal and socially useful action, telling him that "sometimes the difference between individual and organized indignation is the difference between criminal and political action" (293). But the narrator is not quite yet ready for the heroic role the events have already made him experience, as he thinks back upon the day's adventure and dejectedly concludes, "I must have looked silly hurtling across the roofs, and like a black-face comedian shrinking from a ghost when the white pigeons shot up around me" (294). At this early stage, it seems Invisible Man still considers the role of the roof-hopping vigilante hero to belong exclusively to whites. It will take his showdown with Ras the Destroyer to convince him that he, too, can be Batman.

It is in the novel's closing sections that the narrator—along with all the other Harlemites he has met—comes closest to behaving like a comic-book character. We must recall that, as Ellison's essay "Harlem Is Nowhere" testifies, "the most surreal fantasies are acted out upon the streets of Harlem." Here "life becomes a masquerade; exotic costumes are worn every day."[54] At the height of the Harlem riot sequence, Ras the Destroyer, the hero's archenemy, appears before the hero in full supervillain-like regalia— "dressed in the costume of an Abyssinian chieftain; a fur cap upon his head, his arm bearing a shield, a cape made of the skin of some wild animal around his shoulders"—and tries to spear Invisible Man in the middle of a Harlem street (556). In response to his enemy's spectacular costume, Invisible Man fashions a costume of his own. First, he searches for his dark Rinehart glasses, only to find they have been crushed. Desperate, he slips Tarp's leg chain over his knuckles (as he had done in earlier situations of distress) and "closed the flap, locking it" (481). As soon as he locks in the link, a "new mood" settles over him; he has a "certain new sense of self" and knows "suddenly what [he] had to do" (557). Moreover, *Invisible Man*'s riot scene is crammed with exciting brawls and chases padded with the prominence of dialogue articulated in urgent exclamations, such as "Look!" "Betrayer!" and "Grab him!" (557–58). The comic-book world the protagonist prophesized in his eulogy for Tod Clifton has come to life; Ras the Destroyer and his henchmen attack and "want the streets to flow with blood; your blood, black blood and white blood" (483). It becomes clear that the next likely victim of a "comic-book killing" (457) might just be Invisible Man himself. This clash was foreshadowed early on: Ras is the first figure the protagonist encounters upon arriving in Harlem, giving Invisible "a sensation of shock and fear," and the anger of Ras's men makes him feel "as though a riot would break any minute" (159–60). When the riot does finally erupt, and the hero is forced into physical combat, he wrenches free Ras's spear, "gripping it midshaft, point forward" (558), and takes down his nemesis. The precise physical descriptions allow the reader to clearly visualize the scene as it might be depicted in a comic book or through a series of snapshots.[55]

Although there is no denying the dynamic sense of agency conveyed in this scene, the scene also suggests the danger of such aggressive action. It is charged with an ambivalence given voice by the protagonist, who, taking in the scene's "unreality," attempts an ironically antiheroic self-definition that stands in stark contrast to the self-magnifying tendency of the violent madness unfolding around him: "I no hero, but short and dark with only a certain eloquence and a bottomless capacity for being a fool to mark me from the rest . . . I was now, just now, a leader" (558–59). Although he unequivocally feels himself to be "no hero" and draws attention to his physical inadequacy for the role (recalling his earlier wish to be "a foot taller and a hundred pounds heavier" [409]), the historical moment nevertheless positions him as a leader, and he is baptized as such through violent prowess. As he lets that spear fly, he states, "It was as though for a moment I had surrendered my life and begun to live again" (559–60), marking yet another turning point in his metamorphosis. When the henchmen raise their guns toward him, he hits one with Tarp's leg chain and another with his briefcase; his costume and choice of weapons are determined, and he emerges victorious. Significantly, moments after Invisible spears Ras, "the madman in a foreign costume" (558), Ellison slips in an allusion to comic-book culture: overhearing some men speak of how Ras had hurled a spear at a cop, one of the men says that Ras's horse "shot up the street leaping like Heigho, the goddam Silver!" (564). Most major superheroes of the day—say, the Lone Ranger (who rode Silver) and Superman—had both their own comic books and their own radio serials, both of which enjoyed a tremendous following. In fact, Superman's famous motto, "Truth, justice, and the American way," along with the iconic questions, "Is it a bird? Is it a plane? No, it's Superman!" originated on the radio serial.[56] The casual allusion to the Lone Ranger here not only serves to plant the scene in a comic-book-like fantasy but also illustrates how natural it was for Americans—and Harlemites—to use the reality of fantastic heroes as a method for apprehending the surrealist aspects of the urban world. Significantly, Ellison's protagonist harbors some reservations about how the spectators trivialize the scene by comparing it to something out of the *Lone Ranger* and thinks: "Ras was not funny, or not only funny, but dangerous as well, wrong but justified, crazy and yet coldly sane. . . . Why did they make it seem funny, *only* funny?" (564, emphasis and ellipses in the original). Here the presence of the term *comic* in *comic book* underlies Invisible's statement. In this way, Ellison covertly advises the reader that the fantasies of American popular culture should not be apprehended as simply trivial.

The novel makes a similar gesture three times earlier in alluding to both high- and lowbrow comic strips and cartoons, and in each instance the allusions continue to serve as a sharper reflection of the protagonist's own sense of reality. The first is the *Popeye the Sailor* allusion, and the second comes during the narrator's intimate rendezvous with the married and lonely Sybil. After a few too many strong drinks, Invisible's appalled reaction to Sybil's proposal to join her "in a very revolting ritual" is to wonder: "Had life suddenly become a crazy Thurber cartoon?" (517). This reaction marks Invisible as a reader of the highbrow magazine the *New Yorker*, specifically the work of humorist James Thurber, whose contributions to the magazine as editor, writer, and cartoonist began in 1930. Thomas Inge, in his study *Comics as Culture*, states that in order to truly "understand and appreciate" Thurber's cartoons, the reader "must be well-read, in touch with culture of the past and present, sensitive to the eccentricities of human nature, and familiar with the latest trends in society, politics, and the mass media"[57] By following what Cold War culture would probably have dubbed a sexually perverted suggestion with an allusion to an upper-class publication such as the *New Yorker*, Ellison again engages the debate over mass culture by suggesting that the moral depravity that some diagnosed in comics could also be found in more socially sanctioned publications.

The third allusion to a specific comic strip occurs when Invisible Man's relationship to the Brotherhood begins to unravel, leading Jack to question Invisible's loyalty. During the argument, Invisible's frustration with Jack's Manichean worldview leads him to ask aloud, "Is everyone reading Dick Tracy these days?" Jack immediately replies, "This is no matter of Dick Tracy. . . . The movement has many enemies" (404), acknowledging the comic strip as a widespread cultural marker for a certain kind of American fantasy. *Dick Tracy*, enormously popular throughout the 1930s and 1940s—and centered on another detective figure—was created by Chester Gould and featured stock fantastic noir characters with names such as "Flattop," "the Brow," and "Shoulders." Eminent social theorist C. L. R. James was particularly fond of *Dick Tracy* and weighed in on the strips by claiming that they were "a result of the depression, rage, anger and bitterness [that] were surging through the people of the United States."[58] Invisible Man's question to Jack insists on a realism that is more nuanced than that of comics, even while it evokes the comic-book world of Dick Tracy as an analogy appropriate for the situation. The (correct) accusation that everyone is "reading Dick Tracy these days" becomes even more judicious once the protagonist realizes that the riot was instigated by the Brotherhood under orders from Jack "the Cyclops."

Through these specific allusions and key scenes of scientific transformation, law-defying attacks, and rooftop adventures, Ellison develops a comic-book reality as the novel progresses, a reality that partakes of both danger and dynamism and culminates in a Dick Tracyesque Harlem riot. Indeed, just before Invisible's loyalty to the Brotherhood is called into question, the news-picture-magazine man who interviewed Invisible tells him that "we need all the heroes we can get" (396). This world has become, as Invisible Man realizes, one in which an "obsession with enemies" (405) is alive and well. It is always the heroes who have privileged insight into the villains who populate their world, yet these heroes are nevertheless obliged to prove the danger that such villains pose before society can accept the heroes' violent acts to contain that danger. A hero's failure to provide such proof brands him as a vigilante. In crafting the origin-story confession of the hero's "pre-invisible days" (18), Ellison prepares the reader to see how such a heroic insight can eventually allow even a near-homicidal "I" to "speak for you" and bear the promise of redemptive action in the world. We are, after all, told that "great deeds are yet to be performed," that "legends are still to be created" (133). The underground location of Invisible Man's headquarters again associates him most with the vigilante figure of the Batman, who operates from the depths of the Batcave. In short, the correspondences with comic-book features allow the novel to draw on the appeal of youth culture by engaging with its antisocial undercurrents and with the felt need for a champion of the oppressed to finally emerge for African Americans.

SOLVING THE ZOOT-SUIT RIDDLE

Addressing Ellison's work on the novel's final sections, Arnold Rampersad notes: "To the very end, he searched for allusions and inferences that would make his novel resound with greatness."[59] Alongside this modernist impulse to pepper novels with allusions to popular culture, the novel form expresses anxiety over becoming a "victim of the topical," to use Kenneth Warren's phrase.[60] For Ellison, "archetypes are timeless, novels are time-haunted," and, as a consequence, "if the symbols appearing in a novel link up with those of universal myth they do so by virtue of their emergence from the specific texture of a specific form of social reality."[61] Ellison believed that the American novelist could transcend the novel's "time-haunted" topicality only by achieving "some imaginative integration of the total American experience."[62] Put another way, one has to preserve—in an archival sense—a holistic America through novelistic practice. During the years in which Ellison composed *Invisible Man*, between 1945 and 1952, just before televisions appeared in almost every home in America, the unprecedented popularity of comics on a national scale provided Ellison with a solution to the "question of how to fashion strategies of communication that will bridge the many divisions of background and taste which any representative American audience embodies."[63] In ways that may not have been obvious to readers at the time, much of what underlies Ellison's critique of American society in *Invisible Man* was mirrored by the efforts of Entertainment Comics (EC). The Cold War saw EC rise into an extremely popular publisher that produced horror and crime tales rather than superhero comics—such as the horror comic the three boys are reading in figure 5.3—weaving together innovative story lines that overtly criticized the naiveté with which most superhero comics tackled serious social issues.

EC did not depict American society as a melting pot "that dissolved racial, religious, ethnic, and political differences into a national consensus," and its comics were popular precisely "*because* of [their] willfully antagonistic cultural stance."[64] The challenge for the novelist, therefore, was to find a way to capture the EC reader's sense of America as "a society at war with itself" without alienating a more conservative audience.[65] As Ellison explains in "The Little Man at Chehaw Station," an essay in which he explores the relationship between the American artist and his audience, there are particular sites—or "contact zones"[66]—in the American landscape where "the many divisions of background and taste" can unexpectedly collide to expose this potential societal strife and difference. "As a point of arrival and departure for people representing a wide diversity of tastes and styles of living," the Chehaw Station of Ellison's Tuskegee days is one such symbolic site, and in his novel the site for the "motley mixtures of people" is brought to the underground: the New York City subway system.[67] It is important to note that the underground is the hero's as well as the Lafargue Clinic's future home.

The subway platform episode of *Invisible Man* specifically addresses the antagonistic youth culture growing within the bowels of the city, an outreach that Ellison attempts through an allusion to comic books.[68] The narrator waits on the subway platform, focusing his thoughts on types of people who never appear in history books because they are "too obscure for learned classification":

> All things, it is said, are duly recorded—all things of importance, that is. But not quite, for actually it is only the known, the seen, the heard and only those events that the recorder regards as important that are put down, those lies his keepers keep their powers by. . . . Where were the historians today? And how would they put it down?
>
> . . . What did they ever think of us transitory ones? . . . birds of passage who were too obscure for learned classification, too silent for the most sensitive recorders of sound; of natures too ambiguous for the most ambiguous words, and too distant from the centers of historical decision

to sign or even applaud the signers of historical documents? We who write no novels, histories or other books [(and who must discover invisibility before trying a memoir?)] What about us? I thought, seeing Clifton again in my mind.[69]

(439)

Engrossed in thought, the narrator sits on a bench close to the subway staircase watching people coming down onto the platform: "Yes, I thought, what about those of us who shoot up from the South into the busy city?" (439). The familiar phrase "shoot up from the South" used here shows that the community Invisible Man has in mind is precisely the one Ellison alluded to in his letter to Richard Wright in November 1941 and used in "Harlem's America." Invisible Man's gaze surveys the scene and settles on three tall and slender black boys, "harsh as a cry of terror in their quietness," zoot-suiters who mystify him with their novelty: "It was as though I'd never seen their like before" (440). He follows them as they sway forward, "their black faces secret," "men outside of historical time," wise enough, like Tod Clifton, to reject the "mysteries" of the Brotherhood (440). Still staring at the zoot-suiters, Invisible Man wonders at their power and asks himself the types of questions one would ask in the face of overwhelming conquerors or gods: "Do they come to bury the others or to be entombed, to give life or to receive it?" (440–41). He eventually comes to a crucial series of observations that position these young men as a strange breed of fleeting, invisible archivists:

Do the others see them, think about them, even those standing close enough to speak? And if they spoke back . . . ? What would they say? For the boys speak a jived-up transitional language full of country glamour, think transitional thoughts, though perhaps they dream the same old ancient dreams. They were men out of time . . . who would soon be gone and forgotten. . . . But who knew (and now I began to tremble so violently I had to lean against a refuse can)—who knew but that they were the saviors, the true leaders, the bearers of something

| 271 |

precious? The stewards of something uncomfortable, burdensome, which they hated because, living outside the realm of history, there was no one to applaud their value.

(441)

Like the lives of Foucault's "infamous men," the boys are "men out of time, who would soon be gone and forgotten;" theirs are "lives of a few lines or a few pages. . . . Brief lives, encountered by chance."[70] But in their role as "bearers" and "stewards" of that which stands outside history—that trembling thought—the zoot-suiters are also akin to Derrida's archons, those overseers and guardians of documents who also have "the power to interpret the archives."[71] The narrator follows the boys, only to witness one of them take out three comic books from his inner pocket, "passing two around and keeping one for himself." Immediately, the bearers begin to "read in complete absorption" (442).

As transitional mobile archons of otherwise invisible pop-cultural artifacts, the boys symbolically protect that which, like Harlem, is "nowhere," that which slips out of the archive: "What if history was not a reasonable citizen, but a madman full of paranoid guile and these boys his agents, his big surprise! His own revenge? For they were outside . . . taking it on the lambo with my fallen brother, Tod Clifton (Tod, Tod) running and dodging the forces of history instead of making a dominating stand" (441). In partaking of the protagonist's invisibility and his leadership potential, and by further being relegated to the "outside," the zoot-suiters are also identified with those "little Negro Batmen" running around Harlem. The conjuring of Tod Clifton is natural; this character is described earlier as "a hipster, a zoot-suiter, a sharpie" (366) who spoke with "zoot-suiter characteristics in his speech" (367). This connection is crystallized when one of three boys lifts up his comic book, and the bloody and violent scene depicted on its cover reminds Invisible Man of the murder of Clifton: "The shining rails, the fire hydrant, the fallen policeman, the diving-birds and in the midground, Clifton, crumbling" (442). The details on the cover match the deadly encounter between Clifton and the cops the narrator had witnessed: "I saw the rails in the asphalt and a fire plug at the curb and the

flying birds" (435). Indeed, their clash had been a ballet of exaggerated movements, like a fight in comics: after spinning "on his toes like a dancer,"
Clifton had swung "forward and to the left in a motion that sent the box
strap free as his right foot traveled forward and his left arm followed through
in a floating uppercut that sent the cop's cap sailing into the street and his
feet flying, to drop him hard" (436). Even the nearby child describes the
fight in comic-book clichés: "Your friend sure knows how to use his dukes.
Biff, bang! One, two, and the cop's on his ass!" (438). The "vivid scene" (442)
of the comic-book cover is thus the source of the narrator's allusions in his
funeral eulogy for Clifton.

The source of the three zoot-suiters, however, returns us to the photographic origins of *Invisible Man*'s later sections, as discussed earlier. The
contact sheets of Gordon Parks's photos featuring three black boys reading
comics outside appear to be the archival origin of Ellison's three zoot-
suiters—boys captured a few years before their metamorphosis into the
mesmerizing figures of the fictional subway encounter. A manifestation of
yet another lifecycle for the aborted "Harlem Is Nowhere" project, these
photographs certainly give Ellison a model of complete absorption into
comics and demonstrate the genuine seriousness with which the black boys
on the subway are taking the comic.

In having its invisible hero internalize this brush with history's outside,
Ellison's novel distances itself from a purely positivist relation to the archive
and instead demonstrates "the degree to which the archive is unable to convey to us more than a vaguely enunciated intimation of the considerably
vaster body of unwritten acts of witness and behavior."[72] The fateful encounter forever alters the narrator's way of seeing: he is now "painfully aware of
other men dressed like the boys, and of girls in dark exotic-colored stock-
ings, their costumes surreal variations of downtown styles" (443). The education in perception leads the narrator to voice the novel's archival logic in
terms of a necessary task: "They'd been there all along, but somehow I'd
missed them. . . . They were outside the groove of history, and it was my
job to get them in, all of them" (443). Now bearing the pain of his counterarchival gaze, his literary role as writer-ranter is to ensure that they "all"
get "in." Carried aboveground onto the sidewalk with the swaying of the

crowd, the narrator suddenly hears "the growing sound of a record shop loudspeaker blaring a languid blues" and stops dead, wondering: "Was this all that would be recorded? Was this the only true history of the times?" (443). These archival questions seem to seal the novelist's destiny: he now bears the knowledge that what gets written, recorded, engraved, "grooved," and played back is only a fragment of history.

In "Going to the Territory," Ellison confirms the dual nature of American history: "we possess two basic versions of American history: one which is written and as neatly stylized as ancient myth, and the other unwritten and as chaotic and full of contradictions, changes of pace, and surprises as life itself."[73] Such a "[f]urtive, implacable and tricky" novelistic moment as the subway scene, to quote Ellison's introduction to *Invisible Man*, "inspirits both the observer and the scene observed, artifacts, manners and atmosphere and it speaks even when no one wills to listen."[74] Part of the novel's archival power is to endow with "lasting value" forgotten lives and dismissed cultural artifacts, to effect a literary metamorphosis of them into "something precious" that is nevertheless "burdensome, uncomfortable" (recall the narrative's lament that outside history there is "no one to applaud their value" [441]). In fact, "Going to the Territory" directly associates this underground novelistic moment with "the underground of our unwritten history" and argues that "in spite of what is left out of our recorded history, our unwritten history looms as its *obscure* alter ego" and remains "always active in the shaping of events."[75] Tellingly, the zoot-suiters belong to those transitory subjects considered "too *obscure* for learned classification" (439). Obscurity—playfully edging close to blackness—here further implies the systematic exclusion of a recorded African American history.

Inserted into this underground encounter, comics complement the "zoot-suit riddle" Ellison posed as early as 1943. In his editorial comment in *Negro Quarterly*, he expressed a need for black leaders to "come to terms with their own group," just as Invisible Man struggles to do in this scene. "Indispensible [*sic*] to the centralization and direction of power," Ellison claimed in 1943, "is that of learning the meaning of the myths and symbols which abound among the Negro masses."[76] In the comment, he went on to pose the zoot-suit riddle that has inspired and intrigued many critics:[77]

"Much in Negro life remains a mystery; perhaps the zoot suit conceals profound political meaning; perhaps the symmetrical frenzy of the Lindy Hop conceals clues to great potential power—if only Negro leaders would solve this riddle. . . . The problem is psychological; it will be solved only by a Negro leadership that is aware of the psychological attitudes and incipient forms of action which the black masses reveal in their emotion-charged myths, symbols, and wartime folklore."[78] Ellison adapts the novel's form to accommodate the return of the zoot-suit riddle. He first reintroduces the mystery of the zoot-suit through the questions the narrator asks as he beholds the three youths and then implies that comics offer the solution to this riddle. The comic books that the zoot-suiters carry, shoved in Invisible Man's face as they are, reveal these young black men as ephemeral carriers of the new "myths, symbols, and wartime folklore" that make up the invisible archive of an emergent American counterculture. Ellison's contact with the Lafargue Clinic and his efforts to document the Harlem community photographically with Gordon Parks gave him an understanding of the psychological intricacies of Harlem's young delinquents and their fondness for comic books. He in turn gave his protagonist awareness into "the psychological attitudes and incipient forms of action" revealed by the intense symbolic charge created by the convergence of the zoot suit and the comic book.

During the funeral eulogy for Tod Clifton, the orator confirms that he has been bequeathed part of the archons' interpretive power when he describes Clifton's murder to the gathering crowd: "The blood ran like blood in a comic-book killing, on a comic-book street in a comic-book town on a comic-book day in a comic-book world" (457–58). These two moments—the subway encounter and the funeral speech—in a way inseparable, are striking for congealing a whole matrix of concerns underlying Ellison's project: leadership, history, youth and pop culture, preservation of folklore, migration to the city, violence, Harlem, fantasy, myth, power. The heroic images associated with the boys—running and dodging nimbly outside history, invisible harbingers of some upcoming historical revenge—are problematized by the description of them as at once beings he identifies with and beings he doesn't quite understand. The notion that the boys can be both "true leaders" bearing "something precious" and yet also avid readers of material that portrays lurid violence is at the heart of the debate over comics that overtook America during the Cold War, a period that directly associated comic-book reading and zoot-suits with juvenile delinquency.[79]

THE ARCHIVAL FATE AND PROMISE OF JUVENILE DELINQUENTS

The comic-book industry did not take lying down all the criticism directed at it, and one of the early lines of defense for comic books was reiterated in Ellison's position regarding youth culture. This defense came from William Moulton Marston, a psychologist and feminist theorist who happened also to be the creator and writer of *Wonder Woman* comics (and who is also credited as being one of the inventors of the polygraph). As Bart Beaty recounts, Marston believed that superhero comics "were good for children because they cultivated a wish for power."[80] Marston argued for a brand of typical American toughness and violence based on the underlying assumption that humans are inherently violent conquerors: "Do you want [your child] to cultivate weakling's aims, sissified attitudes? . . . The wish to be super-strong is a healthy wish, a vital, compelling, power-producing desire. The more the *Superman–Wonder Woman* picture stories build up this inner compulsion by stimulating the child's natural longing to battle and overcome obstacles, particularly evil ones, the better chance your child has for self-advancement in the world."[81]

Although this perspective was mostly criticized for not only accepting but also fostering violence (and ultimately fascism), the underlying notion of self-reliance and courage in overcoming obstacles would have appealed to Ellison. When speaking of American children, whether in lectures or essays, he almost always emphasizes the need to go beyond inherited notions of what is "possible to achieve and to become in this country."[82] In "What These Children Are Like," a lecture Ellison gave in 1963, he explains that the education he received at Tuskegee "cultivate[d] weakling's aims," as

Marston would say, by offering "an education *away* from the uses of the imagination, away from the attitudes of aggression and courage." Ellison's solution for dropouts and other delinquent youth, objectionably called "culturally deprived" children, fosters a contrary spirit: "We need aggressiveness. We need daring. We need the little guy who, in order to prove himself, goes out to conquer the world. Psychologically Napoleon was not different from the slum kid who tries to take over the block; he just had big armies through which to amplify his aggression."[83] In *Black Skin, White Masks*, Fanon also stresses the need for black children to release their aggression through "the idea of a *collective catharsis*," and he speaks of comic books as "a release for collective aggression," a release marred by their sole reliance on white heroes.[84] Similarly, Ellison emphasizes how "it does me no good to be told that I'm down on the bottom of the pile and that I have nothing with which to get out. I know better. It does me no good to be told that I have no heroes."[85] Daring and aggression—marks of heroism in Ellison's thinking—are necessary to "endure in a hostile world," as he puts it in his essay "Harlem Is Nowhere,"[86] to which I now turn because it is there that he fleshes out the blueprint of the "comic-book world" one finds in *Invisible Man*.

In discussing the Lafargue Clinic and the work of anticomics crusader Fredric Wertham, "Harlem Is Nowhere" points to comic books and their influence upon American youth. The importance of "Harlem Is Nowhere"— and of its many drafts—to the composition of *Invisible Man* is deeper than most accounts suggest. Genetic analysis of the essay's manuscripts reinforces biographer Arnold Rampersad's claim that in "Harlem Is Nowhere" one finds the source "for both the substance and the style of *Invisible Man*."[87] Before Ellison's gaze, Rampersad points out, Harlem had become a "masquerade," a madhouse of terror and violence to which Ellison thought the Lafargue Clinic could provide an "antidote." There are many reasons why Ellison was able to perceive the clinic in this favorable light; as I discuss in chapter 3, when Lafargue opened in 1946, it was the only interracial clinic in New York, and, in fact, Wertham, the clinic's founder, was directly involved in key desegregation battles. The clinic was, in short, "a leading New York center for the promotion of civil rights."[88] This explains why in

"Harlem Is Nowhere" Ellison calls Lafargue "an underground extension of democracy" that represents "perhaps the most successful attempt in the nation to provide psychotherapy for the underprivileged."[89] Conducted at Lafargue at the behest of the NAACP, Wertham's studies of the psychological effects of segregation among black and white children as well as his subsequent courtroom testimony were instrumental in the *Brown v. Board of Education* Supreme Court decision in 1954.[90]

Yet in his psychiatric treatment of Harlem youth, Wertham became convinced that comic books acted as a "school for sadism" that perpetuated violence and brutality among children. He concluded that "comic-book reading was a distinct influencing factor in the case of every single juvenile delinquent or disturbed child" he had studied in Harlem.[91] Beaty notes that when the clinic opened, *Time* magazine reported that "Harlem accounted for more than half of New York City's delinquency cases."[92] In the "Fredric Wertham" folder of the Ralph Ellison Papers at the Library of Congress (which contain multiple pieces by Wertham beginning in the mid-1940s and spanning his lifetime), an article by the doctor titled "The Comics . . . Very Funny!" argues that the "common denominator" of many of the youth crimes in America was comic books, an argument he would famously elaborate in his book *Seduction of the Innocent*. In the article, Wertham speaks only briefly of the violence between young citizens and the police: "A twenty-year-old in New York City has just killed a policeman. Is that so astonishing when he can see anywhere a typical comic book cover showing a man and a woman shooting it out with the police . . . ?"[93] This confrontational scene is exactly like the one depicted on the comic-book cover that Ellison puts in the hands of his fictional zoot-suiters and that is carried out when Tod Clifton is murdered by a city cop.

In sifting through the draft fragments for "Harlem Is Nowhere" in Ellison's archive, one finds that the section of the published essay describing "the most surreal fantasies" that were "acted out on the streets of Harlem" underwent multiple revisions. The list of fantasies could easily have been taken straight from horror comics, and indeed the presence of Judith Crist's article "Horror in the Nursery" (1948)—the first publication to reveal in detail Wertham's argument against comics—in the Ellison Papers Subject

Files lends credence to the influence of comics on Ellison's thought. Ellison's final, published list of the "surreal fantasies" runs as follows:

A man ducks in and out of traffic shouting and throwing imaginary grenades that actually exploded during World War I; a boy participates in the rape-robbery of his mother; a man beating his wife in a park uses boxing "science" and observes Marquis of Queensberry rules . . .; two men hold a third while a lesbian slashes him to death with a razor blade; boy gangsters wielding homemade pistols (which in the South of their origin are but toy symbols of adolescent yearning for manhood) shoot down their young rivals. Life becomes a masquerade; exotic costumes are worn every day.[94]

In a late draft, slightly different than the final version, Ellison follows the list with this explanation: "This is a world in which the major part of the imagination goes not into the creation of works of art, but into overcoming the limitations placed upon it by social discrimination."[95] Taken together, these observations diagnose the frustration faced by the little Batmen of "Harlem's America" in terms of typical horror-comic scenarios, the kind the three boys in the Parks photograph are discussing.

Yet in the essay's earliest drafts, this entire section was not labeled "fantasies" at all but rather "crime." Box 100 of the Ellison Papers quite literally archives the text's transformations, leaving persistent traces of gradual erasures. In what appears to be the essay's first draft, Ellison states baldly that in Harlem, "adolescents commit crimes learned from comic books."[96] Several subsequent drafts offer the following variation: crimes are learned "from movies and comic books." Microanalysis shows that only later in the history of the manuscript do crimes go from being "learned" to being "inspired by" movies and comics, until suddenly the emphasis on crime is dropped in favor of a focus on "surreal fantasies." These later drafts no longer directly allude to comics, nor do they focus only on "adolescents" but move to encompass all Harlemites. In fact, in the published essay Ellison omits any mention of possible media sources for these fantasies, in effect heightening the sense of unreality his essay tries to diagnose and present. By refraining from identifying direct sources for either crimes or fantasies, Ellison not only paints a more complex picture of what was currently gripping Harlem and America but also distinguishes his essay from the argument of the Lafargue Clinic's founder. Where the early drafts saw Ellison buying into Wertham's theory, his subsequent elision of comics—it is the first medium to appear and the first to disappear in the essay drafts—suggests that he felt differently over time. The fondness with which he recalls his comic-drawing Oklahoma friend in eulogizing Romare Bearden exists in striking contrast to the murderous undertones of the comic-book world in the eulogy for Tod Clifton. Similarly, the reading of comics by the transitional warmth of a bonfire of street garbage in alternate takes for caption D of the "Harlem Is Nowhere" photo-report and the conversations provoked by these comics among black youth make it counterintuitive for Ellison to pinpoint comics solely as a source of criminality. To use one of Ellison's own rejected—yet compelling—images in his "Nowhere" drafts, the allusions to comics in the essay and the novel have "sunk" into the archive "but, like a sunken log that shapes the currents between a river's banks, remain[] to affect the tide of the speaker's moods."[97]

In his archival hoarding, Ellison also kept a file on the Lafargue Clinic in which a yellow sheet addressed "Dear Dick" (Richard Wright), dated April 4, 1946, offers a little advertisement and praise for the clinic and seems to be one of Ellison's earliest attempts at what would eventually become "Harlem Is Nowhere." At the bottom of the sheet, as a kind of note to self, Ellison wrote: "Wright as example of fate and promise of juvenile delinquents, i.e. BLACK BOY."[98] This wonderfully resonant line—"fate and promise"—is an indication that Ellison never abandoned the association of juvenile delinquency with the "fate and promise" that became the core of his stance toward comic books—symbols of the boomeranging contradiction, especially for African Americans, of crimes perpetrated for the communal good. As I stated earlier, Ellison could see how criminality could be an exertion of humanity, a comingling of both the antisocial absurdism and optimistic dynamism characteristic of midcentury comics.

In the same "Lafargue Clinic" folder, Ellison kept an article from *Headlines and Pictures: A Monthly Negro News Magazine* entitled "Harlem

Pioneers with Mental Clinic," one of many pieces on the clinic he collected. In that particular magazine, however, the two-page article that immediately follows the one on the clinic in the July 1946 issue is a testament to how closely linked the clinic, comic books, and juvenile delinquency really were. The anonymous article "Super Democrat of the Radio" is about Clayton (Bud) Collyer, better known as "Superman of the radio," and how the radio adventures of Superman would now have "the new tolerance theme lasting through mid-July," after which "the show will tackle juvenile delinquency in August and September, and school absenteeism as school starts again in October."[99] The accompanying photographs are revelatory; one shows "Superman" reading his own comic, while the other shows him happily shaking the hand of a young smiling Harlemite named Richard Gibson, the twelve-year-old "chairman of the Youth Builders conference," glowing with "fate and promise."

Accordingly, Ellison also collected materials on juvenile delinquency, and his archive contains articles on that theme dating from the mid-1940s through the late 1950s. Among the articles, a big spread from *Life* magazine dated April 8, 1946, and titled "Juvenile Delinquency: War's Insecurity Lifts Youthful Crime 100%" includes several photographs taken of both black and white gangs in Harlem and concludes by offering a portrait of a "reformed" juvenile delinquent. The youth's progress is represented by a picture of a muscular former gang leader lifting weights with one arm, an image whose iconography recalls a famous and oft-reprinted issue of *Detective Comics* from 1939 that shows how Bruce Wayne, also lifting weights with a single arm, trained to become the Batman.[100] Most of the "Juvenile Delinquency" folder in the Ellison Papers consists of articles depicting the trials of delinquent youth who have suffered from sudden migration to the urban North from the rural South. Focusing on certain gang leaders, Ellison's choice of articles to preserve further underscores the promise Invisible Man sees in the zoot-suiters, in Tod Clifton, and in the type of "culturally deprived" delinquents discussed in "What These Children Are Like." Of particular note in Ellison's papers is the presence, in a folder labeled "Harlem, New York, NY," of Gordon Parks' first *Life* magazine byline, "Harlem Gang Leader," from 1948, as discussed in chapter 3. A chronicle of seventeen-year-old "delinquent" Red Jackson, leader of the Midtowners gang, the piece represents a documented historical example of a black delinquent who is nevertheless presented as a leader.[101]

It should be noted, however, that by the late 1970s Ellison seems to have become somewhat disillusioned by the idea of the "fate and promise of juvenile delinquents" and the leadership potential of criminals in general: "During the Sixties," Ellison told his interviewers, "this myth of the redeemed criminal had a tremendous influence on our young people, when criminals guilty of every crime from con games, to rape, to murder exploited it by declaring themselves political activists and Black leaders." Perhaps having grown more conservative with the passage of time or simply having seen too much crime perpetrated without a sense of justice, Ellison lamented that as a result of this tendency to make "heroes out of thugs" in the 1960s, "many sincere, dedicated leaders of an older generation were swept aside. I'm speaking now of courageous individuals who made sacrifices in order to master the disciplines of leadership and who created a continuity between themselves and earlier leaders of our struggle. The kids treated such people as if they were Uncle Toms, and I found it outrageous." What Ellison bemoaned here are precisely the kinds of criticisms that were directed at him personally in the wake of the Black Arts Movement, and what he regretted most in this failure of young thugs to live up to their "fate and promise" was that it "gave many kids the notion that there was no point in developing their minds . . . all that was required was a history of criminality."[102]

But back when Ellison was a young novelist bursting with promise, back when he was "mastering the disciplines of leadership," he seemed to be suggesting that the restless, mobile, and daring little Batmen whom society regarded as delinquents may have in fact been "protecting the higher interests of society," not despite but *because* of their outlaw status. This watchful protection occurring outside the law was akin to the vigilance provided by those zoot-suiters outside history, and it was the novelist's job to make sure they "get in." Precisely because they were "not the numbed, but the seething," their "fate and promise" might have enabled them to become the kind of leaders African Americans needed most. The

"I no hero" who also becomes "just now, a leader" after spearing Ras the Destroyer thus embodies this seeming contradiction.[103] Insofar as Ellison adopted this contradictory logic when he wrote of black heroism, he can be seen less as a prisoner of his era's contradictions and more as a strategist employing the comic's necessarily fraught ethics. All allusions to comic books or cartoons in the novel have something in common: in each instance, they offer the protagonist the most accurate analogy for his own holistic sense of reality, a sense intimately grounded in what Ellison calls the "unreality that haunts Harlem."[104] This is the register on which we can understand Ellison's striking statement, quoted at the beginning of this chapter, that "the individual man . . . is more apt to get a sense of wonder, a sense of self-awareness and a sharper reflection of his world from a comic book than from most novels."

Through such comic-book allusions, Ellison is able to infuse his novel with this self-awareness and "sharper reflection" of the world, granting the novel a radical counterarchival ability to "speak even when no one wills to listen."[105] The zoot-suiters episode reminds us, in the form of a revelation, that unlikely archons are roaming unseen in our ranks—like so many little men of the world's Chehaw Stations—custodians of an otherwise invisible archive. They are the "unseen eye" not just watching but rather watching over us in "a world so fluid and shifting that often within the mind the real and the unreal merge, and the marvelous beckons from behind the same sordid reality that denies its existence."[106] In other words, Ellison's gaze sees the promise behind the delinquency, the justice behind the crime, the vigilance behind the surveillance, just as Invisible Man sees the "principle on which the country was built" beckoning from behind "the men who did the violence" (574). The novel offers a glimpse of a world where criminal passions can be harnessed to socially useful ends. As an answer to the narrator's questions, "Was this all that would be recorded? Was this the only true history of the times?" (443), Ellison gives us the novel as counterarchive, as history's "obscure alter ego," its "own revenge." History's "big surprise!" might just be that comics have lasting value, that those ephemeral artifacts we so easily dismiss or fail even to see belong in the archive.

CODA

DISAPPOINTED BRIDGES

A Note on the Discovery of *Amiable with Big Teeth*

I am saying that a journey is called that because you cannot know what you will discover on the journey, what you will do with what you find, or what you find will do to you.

—JAMES BALDWIN TO JAY ACTON, JUNE 30, 1979

"What happens to a dream deferred?" asks Langston Hughes in his poem "Harlem" (1951) and proceeds to speculate on a few possibilities. One he omits, however, is that sometimes, without anyone being told, and while we're busy making other plans, such dreams get buried in the archive. That place where everything is always already over and the place where it all begins. Considering *Amiable with Big Teeth*'s brush with eternal obscurity, the old Latin saying *"Habent sua fata libelli"*—"Books have their own destiny"—seems particularly salient in the case of Claude McKay's last novel. Prior to its unexpected discovery in the summer of 2009, no one—well, no one alive, that is—knew it even existed. When I came upon the manuscript in Columbia University's Rare Book and Manuscript Library, I was entering my third year as a doctoral student in the Department of English and Comparative Literature at Columbia and for about a month had been processing the papers of the notorious Jewish American writer, publisher, and recidivist Samuel Roth.

It was with disbelief that I looked upon the bound typescript whose title page read, "Amiable with Big Teeth: A Novel of the Love Affair Between the Communists and the Poor Black Sheep of Harlem by Claude McKay, Author of Home to Harlem." As a student of twentieth-century American literature who just a year earlier had written a seminar paper on *Home to Harlem*, encountering this typescript was both tremendously exciting and highly suspect. Was the novel truly written by the renowned Jamaican-born poet, novelist, and scholar Claude McKay? And if so, what could it possibly be doing in the papers of Samuel Roth, that all-around schemer who is perhaps best known for being the appellant in a notorious Supreme Court obscenity case in 1957—following his conviction for mailing obscene materials—and for his status as the target of James Joyce's famous "International Protest" in 1927, a petition "signed by 167 writers, artists, and intellectuals," for publishing unauthorized excerpts from Joyce's *Ulysses* in the United States.[1]

It was Roth's status as the villainous "*bête noire* of modernism"[2] that had brought me to process his papers in the first place when I was hired to intern at the Rare Book and Manuscript Library for a program in primary sources funded by the Mellon Foundation. I was an international student on an F-1 Visa, so my only means of summer remuneration was to secure employment through the university, and this opportunity seemed ideal. After a few weeks of training in archival science under the deft supervision of processing archivist Alix Ross, the time came for each intern—we were an interdisciplinary bunch, hailing from diverse departments such as music, religion, philosophy, history, literature, anthropology, and more—to be assigned a collection to process from Columbia's "backlog." The conceit behind this internship, the brainchild of Michael Ryan, then the library's director, was for students to be matched with collections related to their field of study or interest. Such a rationale made the initiative doubly useful: graduate students were exposed to rich new avenues of knowledge within their field while gaining "alt-ac" skills, and the host institution had a specialized workforce chipping away at its backlog.

Though Roth's name was not on the list I was given to choose from, I remembered seeing an announcement that his papers had been acquired by

FIGURE 6.1. Samuel Roth at his desk, ca. 1961. Could the *Amiable* typescript be lurking somewhere on Roth's desk? Photograph by John Gruen.

Source: Adelaide Kugel, "WrothWrackt Joyce: Samuel Roth and the 'Not Quite Unauthorized' Edition of Ulysses," *Joyce Studies Annual* 1992:243.

Columbia. After a short administrative delay, I received the good news that Roth was mine to process. The material in the Roth collection was semi-arranged, having first been transferred for transportation to Columbia from the basement of 151 Central Park West, New York, the building in which Roth's daughter, Adelaide Kugel, had lived until her passing in 2006. A total of fifty-three "transitional" document boxes and five record cartons were moved to Butler Library. Despite these transfers, the material was kept in the order in which Adelaide Kugel (whose own materials are also part of the collection) had left it prior to donation. Adelaide had already imposed a new order on parts of the collection during her years trying to write her father's biography (a book she intended to call *Plain Brown Wrapper*), but the majority of the material had no discernable order. After an initial survey phase, I began the slow, meticulous process of cataloging the collection. It was only when I undertook the actual filing of material in the Writings series that I first took hold of the typescript for *Amiable*, which was ensconced in a deteriorating black-colored binder with floppy covers. From a visual standpoint, the manuscript looked like the majority of the other writings present in the collection; many of Roth's unrealized projects, such as "A Calendar of Sorrow for Cynics" and "A Day-Book of Solace for Scientists," were kept in such DIY black binders. As I added the information about the manuscript to the container list and transferred its unbound three-hundred-plus pages into new folders, the potential gravity of this moment both nagged at me and needed to be shrugged off so that I could finish the day's work. I remember turning to a colleague at the adjacent desk to announce, "There's a Claude McKay novel in here," to which he replied, "Which one?" "'Amiable with Big Teeth,'" I answered. "Don't think I've read that one," he said. "Me neither," I added before moving on to the next item in the box.

When I returned home, I began rummaging through library databases, the Internet at large, and my own McKay books for references to a novel titled *Amiable with Big Teeth*. The searches were unsuccessful; there was no mention of this title or any such manuscript either in McKay's published work or in the secondary scholarship on his career by critics and biographers such as Wayne Cooper, Winston James, Tyrone Tillery, and William Maxwell. Increasingly excited, I temporarily abandoned my processing of the Writings series the next day to look through the correspondence boxes that for the most part had already been kept in alphabetical order by the creators. There, astonished and delighted, I found two letters from Claude McKay to Roth as well as a contract between McKay and Roth for a book to be titled "Descent Into Harlem."

The initial rush of discovery was tempered by my knowledge that Roth had hired ghost writers to compose fake "sequels" to modern classics, such as *Lady Chatterley's Husbands* (1931), and works falsely attributed to famous authors, such as *My Sister and I* (1951), a sensational hoax in which a repentant Friedrich Nietzsche ("the boy who grew up in a house full of manless women," as Roth described him[3]) confesses to years of incestuous love with his sister, Elizabeth, and ultimately disavows his allegiance to the

Übermensch in order to follow, of all things, the teachings of Jesus. To spur sales, Roth would send his clients all sorts of gimmicks as incentives, such as "Skin Edge Micro-Blades," the sharpest razors imaginable! Or a manual that could teach you how to "Drink and Stay Sober!" Or, for the especially forlorn on his subscribers' list, three-foot-high blow-up replicas of women—"Living Dolls"—that came dressed or undressed and with three choices of hair color.

In short, the specter of Roth, his salesmanship and forgeries, loomed over the discovery, yet the byline "by Claude McKay, Author of Home to Harlem," on the typescript's cover page, the letters McKay sent Roth, and that book contract warranted further investigation. After a week or so of additional research that resulted in nothing more substantive than a short list of individuals both men may have had in common (such as Max Eastman, Joseph Freeman, Frank Harris, Louise Bryant, John Reed, Harry Roskolenko, and Maxwell Bodenheim), I shared the discovery and preliminary findings with my then graduate adviser and McKay expert Brent Hayes Edwards. I recall expecting him to rectify the misunderstanding by revealing his extensive knowledge of *Amiable*, but Brent had never heard of this novel. We decided the best way to proceed was to make a copy of the novel, read it over the weekend, and then reconvene to share our thoughts.

The novel's presence in Roth's papers was at once indisputable and inexplicable. It felt like a challenge of reverse engineering, a Cold War scenario in which one nation gets hold of the other's previously unsuspected invention and has somehow to understand how it was put together. Instead of making things clearer, the other McKay materials in the Roth Papers only added to our confusion. There was a book contract, yes, but for something called "Descent Into Harlem," not "Amiable with Big Teeth." And the contract was actually for a ghostwriting job: it stipulated that although "Descent" would be written by Claude McKay, its author would publicly be known as Dante Cacici; McKay was also to provide an introduction, though this time under his own name.[4] The letters make it clear that "Descent Into Harlem" was meant to be a first-person account of an Italian immigrant living in Harlem, a conceit clearly different from what is found in *Amiable with Big Teeth*. There was another puzzling element: with the

"Amiable" typescript , Roth had bound something titled "Proem," written in a very different voice and composed in a visibly different typeface from the rest of the typescript. The three-page "Proem" is written in the first person of a young Italian American coming back from years spent traveling and then going to Harlem to search for his family. It was presumably written by Cacici as an example of what he had in mind for "Descent Into Harlem." Yes, Dante Cacici was a real person; he wrote the afterword to Roth's novel *Bumarap: The Story of a Male Virgin* (1947), a book someone named Norman Lockridge described as "a novel of incredible richness; the most amusing I have read since *Don Quixote*."[5] "Norman Lockridge" was, of course, an alias for Roth himself. Roth published a few successful books under that pseudonym—*World's Wit and Wisdom, Waggish Tales of the Czechs, The Sexual Conduct of Men & Women*—and would use it to correspond with authors such as T. S. Eliot, who would not have replied to Samuel Roth. The two of them, Roth and Cacici, most likely met in jail in the 1930s; Cacici had done time for counterfeiting ten-dollar-bills, and Roth had been imprisoned for the sale and possession of obscene books. The only letter from Cacici in the Roth collection is from 1960—twenty years after the "Descent Into Harlem" contract—sent just days after Roth was released from his last jail sentence, a five-year stint in Lewisburg. Cacici, now a bookseller in the Bronx, touchingly wrote, "Welcome back to the world of the uncaught."[6]

But as far as Brent and I have been able to determine, even though the contract was signed by McKay, Roth, and Cacici in September 1941, the "Descent Into Harlem" project was never realized. In fact, one of Roth's checks to McKay bounced, which greatly distressed the nearly penniless writer. In one of his letters to Roth, McKay writes:

> Any incident like a returned cheque upsets me in a way that perhaps I can never explain to you. It has never happened to me before, although I have had terribly difficult times. But you must know that Harlem is just a little village. A thing like that is whispered around and I have enemies.
>
> More important is the fact that I do my writing on a very delicate balance. And an incident like this will upset me for many days. I heard

about it Saturday night, Sunday I remained worried and all of today I had to give to it.[7]

Although we were somewhat perplexed by the ancillary documents in the Roth Papers, one of our initial assumptions was that "Descent Into Harlem" and "Amiable with Big Teeth" were the same project—that McKay had perhaps started writing "Descent Into Harlem" for Roth and that it had somehow morphed into a very different book during the creative process. Whatever the mysteries of the composition of the "Amiable with Big Teeth" manuscript, we were excited by it. We were struck by the many circumstantial clues that McKay had indeed written it: tell-tale quirks such as his predilection for the compound word *Aframerican*, his singular fondness for Sufi Abdul Hamid, as well as a preponderance of themes familiar to readers of McKay's later work (labor agitation in Harlem, black internationalism, anticommunism). The clues *were* admittedly circumstantial, but it was also hard to imagine who else—even among black writers in Harlem in the period—could have written this novel. We decided to contact the McKay Estate to inform it of the discovery and outlining our preliminary sense of the novel's provenance. We requested permission to bring the novel to publication. After consulting with an outside legal adviser, however, the estate was not yet ready to confirm the authenticity of the manuscript; given the fact that no one had ever heard of this novel, the estate wanted irrefutable evidence. Although this roadblock was initially frustrating, it spurred us into many months of research in archives around the country, eventually giving us not only overwhelming evidence of the typescript's authenticity (as we later outlined in the introduction to our edition of the novel) but also a much fuller understanding of the history of the novel and of McKay's late career. We eventually came to realize that the novel had *already* been written by the time McKay entered into a contract with Roth and quite probably before the two men even met. Quite contrary to our earliest assumptions, Roth had nothing whatsoever to do with the novel's composition.

In other words, this discovery was an education in the need to remain vigilant and suspicious when encountering those ever-seductive material traces of the past. Some of the clues in the Roth Papers were false trails we had to follow before doubling back to the artifact to begin anew. It quickly became apparent that "the archive" could lie just as easily as "fiction" and could in fact lie better than fiction because of its "sacral character," to use Antoinette Burton's phrase.[8] This realization reminded me that, more often than we might initially suspect, both genuine and inauthentic documents are literally *bound* together . . . like the garden in Vladimir Nabokov's novel *Ada* (1969), with its real and fake flowers mixed together, or like Lij Alamaya's "imperial" letter in *Amiable with Big Teeth*. And the best means of distinguishing between the genuine article and impostors was to trace documents back to the beginning: *provenance* was key. The research journey Brent and I undertook allowed us to determine the exact provenance of the novel—when McKay conceived of the project, when and where he composed it, which publisher paid him to write it, and so on. But the authentication work that the novel required paved the way for a whole array of new discoveries. The more I learned about the novel's provenance, the more it began to speak back to the archive and to a buried history lying within it—a history McKay had helped to build and out of which he had composed his novel.

Amiable with Big Teeth is McKay's "shadow book," as Kevin Young would call it, an example of the third type in Young's taxonomy, the "lost": it was "written" but was "now gone."[9] Yet in the strange case of *Amiable*, because we did not know that it had been written in the first place, its loss could ironically only be felt after it was found. It was, to use the infamous phrase, one of those "unknown unknowns." With *Amiable*'s subsequent emergence from the shadow realm—moving from unwritten to lost to found—many questions that had remained latent about McKay's writing career and about the final decade of his life could suddenly be asked, and some even answered. At the same time, the authentication process was an education in the American publishing scene of the early 1940s, in the inner workings of the Federal Writers' Project in the 1930s, and in African Americans' response to Italy's invasion of Ethiopia in 1935—the topic around which the novel's plot revolves. It lifted the lid on a cluster of beguiling historical figures that had often remained peripheral to most studies of the period. In other words, authentication acted like a domino effect—a slew of other texts that had lain dormant were suddenly dug up, revived, and reread in light of the new artifact, making "them glow alive by new manipulation," as McKay writes in his preface to *Harlem Shadows*.[10]

As a scholarly process involving textual study, historicization, and the scouring of multiple repositories to find scraps of documentary evidence proving that the text in question belongs to a specific author, authentication doubles as a "genesis effect"—to use a concept from *Star Trek II: The Wrath of Khan* (Nicholas Meyer, 1982)—and is thus a significant example of the unpredictable "lifecycles" of documents, not to mention a key aspect of history of the book. Even the "dead ends" can mend invisible gaps and foster comparative analyses—across texts, across fields, across communities, or at the material level: between documentary types (between, say, correspondence and photographs or newspaper clippings and poems). On another register, authentication forces the literary scholar to re-create what in *The Archive and the Repertoire* Diana Taylor calls a "*scenario*" as opposed to a "narrative." Each authenticating fragment, including details offered by *Amiable*'s own performative acts (notably its climactic staging of the ritual of the Society of the Leopard Men), enrich the scenario until it can finally "allow commentators to historicize specific practices" that go beyond the demands of authentication.[11] In short, the resultant scenario allows us to glimpse where and how collections, fields, and even periodization have been split and artificially scattered as well as how the novel's sociopolitical thematics are inscribed in McKay's own archive and private repertoire.

I am often asked, "How do you authenticate a novel, anyway?" The answer is that there are many paths one can follow, and digital humanities are constantly increasing the number of potential avenues for material and textual analysis. For instance, though Brent and I did not resort to this measure, it would have been possible to feed all of McKay's extant writings into an algorithm that would have tested the likelihood that *Amiable* was composed by his hand. In our extensive authentication memo sent to the McKay Estate in 2012 and to the three independent experts who were asked to evaluate our findings—Henry Louis Gates Jr., Wayne Cooper, and William Maxwell—we included an appendix of "handwriting analysis" where we had charted every word that McKay had personally hand-edited on three of his available typescripts: "Romance in Marseilles" (written around 1930, still unpublished), "Harlem Glory" (written in 1936–1937), and "Amiable" (written in 1941). Whenever the same word was holographically added by McKay on each of the different documents, we visually brought the three instances adjacent to one another to compare the particularities of the calligraphy. We then isolated the most recurring words—*black, might, color, New York* (which together form a kind of uncanny poem)—to underscore the striking similarity of handwriting style across the three typescripts. Paleographic comparison taps into some of literary studies' roots in philology, and its novelty—for those of us who work with twentieth-century materials—brings with it an ancient pleasure of the text.

But the bulk of the authentication process involved more traditional research tasks: traveling to repositories that house McKay or McKay-related materials, making reproduction requests for documents that would be too cost prohibitive to see in person, and reading published scholarship and biographies. The overarching principle is to immerse oneself as deeply as possible into the "scenario" of the text in question, a process that is often best rewarded via the reading of correspondence. In pre-email literary studies, letters were often one's best chance of uncovering the kind of contextual information that would otherwise leave no trace—passing anecdotes, remarks about a conversation or a party, not to mention details such as addresses, dates, and names of people. The tricky aspect of literary papers is that in most cases an author's collection will include the letters that he or she has received but not necessarily those he or she sent out (unless that author made carbon copies or found an alternative means of duplication). Therefore, if one ends up finding a particularly promising set of letters from one specific correspondent, it becomes tantalizing—if not necessary—to find the recipient's papers in the hopes of reading the letters sent by the author in question. Largely thanks to chance but also to the increasing rise of institutional interest in literary papers, the letter recipient's archive may indeed be available somewhere. In our case, the Max Eastman Mss. in the Lilly Library at Indiana University houses letters by McKay from 1941 in which he directly discussed his progress on *Amiable*. Most of the time, how-ever, history is not so kind.

We also rummaged through the publisher E. P. Dutton's records at Syr-acuse University hoping to find the *Amiable* book contract. Alas, as we discovered, standard practice among publishers is to destroy records related to rejected manuscripts. What we did find, however, proved valuable for our authenticating purposes: budget sheets from 1940 and 1941 listed pay-ments made out to McKay even after he had received full payment for *Har-lem: Negro Metropolis*, a book published by Dutton in 1940. Comparing the payment amounts and their scheduled frequencies with information obtained in the correspondence between Eastman and McKay as well as between McKay and Dutton, we were able to make exact matches, provid-ing more evidence that Dutton was paying McKay an advance for writing a new book. Although the Dutton records were useful in this rather direct manner, the richness of the files regarding *Harlem: Negro Metropolis* would later prove valuable to my ongoing research on McKay beyond the confines of authentication. Everything was always potentially doubled in this fashion; what failed to yield evidence for authentication provided other kinds of insights into McKay's world.

As these unexpected double epiphanies accumulated across several years—and would occur in the context of research in other novelists' archives—I became increasingly aware of the quasi-ubiquitous presence of serendipity in archival research. From a methodological perspective, I kept stumbling upon documents that I had not set out to find yet that would later prove not only relevant but essential. To absorb the potential future relevance of such documents required mental malleability, what Arlette Farge calls "soak[ing] up the archive" or "remain[ing] sufficiently open to the forms the archive contains that you are able to notice things that were not a priori of interest . . . but could, later on—you never know—turn out to be invaluable."[12] Although there seems to be "no ideal way to do this," as Farge claims,[13] these recurring experiences brought to mind the situation-ist Guy Debord's theory of the *dérive* and its goal of reconfiguring one's psychogeographic relation to urban space.

In "Théorie de la dérive," Debord defines the *dérive* as a "technique of hurried passage" in which an individual must renounce for the duration of this hurried passage all that is most familiar, including all "relations, work and leisure activities," everything and anything that usually fills one's days and habitual reasons for activity. One must instead let go and embrace the solicitations of the new, foreign terrain and the encounters that lie therein. At first glance, it may seem as if Debord is inviting pure randomness to the *dérive*, but he goes on to specify how the apparent aleatory nature of the experiment is not as decisive as one might think; once one is engaged on a new path, one nevertheless cannot escape one's own "psychogeographical contours," and one thus perceives "fixed points and vortexes that strongly discourage entry into or exit from certain zones."[14]

Although Debord is clearly speaking of a method for renewing one's relationship to the city in an increasingly industrial, modern, and deadening world of routine, his theory of the *dérive* is equally applicable to the archive. For what is the reality of archival research but a necessarily hurried passage that forces one to abandon previously acquired notions and intimations of a given subject? And what are finding aids if not precisely those psychogeographical contours whose fixed points and vortexes lead scholars to and fro among surprising encounters? Architects design cities, archivists arrange collections. *Dérive* allows one to alter the landscape by reconceptualizing its psychogeography, and, similarly, the archive ideally offers the scholar alternatives to the main thoroughfares used and abused by past scholarship. All disciplines—say, literary criticism—come with their own more or less ossified psychogeography, and a process such as the *dérive* can lead scholars to new destinations, to cut the Gordian knot. This is not a matter of seeking the new for its own sake, but a way of reckoning with and pushing back against the gentrification of one's disciplinary habitat.

Debord specifies that a *dérive* should last on average around the length of a work day. In this sense, it corresponds to the usual hours most special-collections libraries remain open daily. If the *dérives* are of "sufficient intensity," then they can last three or four days or more, punctuated, of course, by sleep (a pattern most archival researchers will have experienced during their archival plundering). All this navigating requires that a bit of homework be done beforehand. Debord insists on the study of maps, old and new, of the terrain about to be scoured, just as the researcher needs to study the finding aid prepared by the archivist and perhaps even contact the archivist directly if the psychogeographic arrangement of the collection (intellectual control) demands deeper insight into its secret machinations.

Since the completion of the McKay authentication project, I have implemented the use of *dérives* in most of my archival visits. In other words, once I have looked through the relevant folders I prioritized beforehand, I wander into some of the other folders in the same box and often request other boxes—sometimes based on a whim or sometimes by pretending to be another researcher working on a completely different project. The reasoning behind some of my choices is a kind of hunch—a hope and a desire that there just might be "something" relevant hiding in there. In the end, the method amounts to a form of calculated improvisation where the archive looms before you like an urban jungle, a naked city to be navigated through the concept of the *dérive*. As a result, every single chapter in this book includes the use of documents obtained through this method as well as its fair share of "organic" serendipities that blessedly accompany most archival encounters.

All this returns us to the idea of the lifecycles of documents. *Amiable* is a novel whose unexpected discovery necessitated a long process of authentication, which entailed years of rummaging through multiple documents, but what I want to underscore here is that none of the documents we dug up, encountered, and used had been created with the need for authentication in mind. In other words, authentication is a process that bestows documents with a new lifecycle or value. A researcher's project inevitably reorganizes the hierarchy of a document's value and thus always speaks to the politics of the archive. As a literary scholar, I am particularly invested in how the emergence of a novel can be the agent for a necessary reorganization of values, a recalibration of the materiality we preserve and use to reconstruct our histories.

There are two processes here: the way a novel can have an agency, a life of its own independent of the author's plans or intentions—posthumous publications and other targets of recuperation are examples—where the mere existence or recovery of a novel changes our relation to the materiality of the past, regardless of the author's original sense of what is valuable, though obviously in an oblique relation to it. But the recalibration can sometimes be built into the novel; in other words, novelists such as McKay perform an alternative, parallel function of "appraisal"—the process of determining whether documentary materials have sufficient value to warrant acquisition or preservation—that serves to destabilize the configurations of archival institutionalization (one collection's "miscellaneous" can be a scholar's holy grail). Other practices—such as collecting or scrapbooking—can serve an analogous function, but the novelist as archivist is in dialectical tension with the ruling ideology of his or her own era and with his or her unique sense of posterity, which allows fiction to become "active in the shaping of events," to quote Ralph Ellison.[15]

In the wake of the authentication process, it was evident that the archive McKay had gathered in his work for the FWP and in writing his nonfiction book *Harlem: Negro Metropolis* was repurposed for *Amiable*, his immediate follow-up. Repurposing—a common practice for fiction writers (and academics!)—is a privately undertaken shift in a document's lifecycle. But what makes *Amiable* a particularly fascinating case study in understanding the novelist's craft as a genetic series of lifecycles is the way McKay dramatizes repurposing—the application of an "old" document toward a new use—as a practice in the novel's plot. The novel repeatedly stages scenes where evidentiary challenges surrounding authentication are foregrounded, as I demonstrate in chapter 2. Although repurposing suggests the potential unreliability of archival records, it also opens the door for creative refashioning of documents in ways that much of postwar experimental and digital poetics have pursued.[16] With all of this taken into consideration, therefore, the authenticating research Brent and I were doing resonated with the concerns and challenges present in the novel and with those McKay was facing at the time of its composition, a resonance that forges a rich statement on both the aesthetics and the politics of literary papers.

We still don't and may never know exactly why and how Roth became the custodian of McKay's typescript. As Carolyn Steedman reminds us, archives are "made from selected and consciously chosen documentation from the past and also from the mad fragmentations that no one intended to preserve and that just ended up there."[17] The earliest evidence we have of a confirmed encounter between Roth and McKay is a signed copy of Roth's book of poetry *Europe: A Book for America* (1919) inscribed "For Claude McKay with the unqualified admiration of Samuel Roth," dated September 11, 1941.[18] Based on the evidence Brent and I unearthed between discovery and publication of *Amiable*, we conjectured that McKay gave the manuscript to Roth to read in the late summer or early fall of 1941 (immediately after the Dutton deal floundered and shortly before McKay's illness was severely aggravated) or perhaps as late as 1943 (prior to his move to Chicago). But an addition to the Max Eastman collection at the Lilly in 2017 helped add clarity to why Roth, in possession of the typescript for so many years, apparently never tried to publish it. Indiana professor Christoph Irmscher, who had been working on a new biography of Max Eastman, stumbled upon a document that had eluded us all these years: the original rejection letter that John Macrae, then president of E. P. Dutton, the publisher that had contracted McKay to write the novel, sent to McKay.[19] Through the course of his research, Irmscher had access to Eastman's former residence in Martha's Vineyard and found the letter in an old filing cabinet, along with two more McKay had composed in the wake of the rejection— one to Macrae and one to his friend Max Eastman.

The letters are full of revelations, notably that the novel was submitted to Dutton under the much-better title *God's Black Sheep*, the same title that McKay's literary agent, Carl Cowl, had used in a letter to Jean Wagner alluding to McKay's "lost" novel.[20] Brent found Cowl's letter to Wagner, by the way, purely by accident. John Macrae's rejection letter included a financial threat to McKay that clarified, rather devastatingly, why the manuscript was left stranded. Macrae informed McKay that he would have to pay back the entirety of the advance he had received if he wanted to get the novel published elsewhere: "We have paid you an advance of $475. It is

agreed in the contract that you will return this $475 if you sell the manu-
script to another publisher or receive any monies from any source whatsoever in connection with the publication of the manuscript."[21] For the destitute McKay, this clause would, for all intents and purposes, have killed any
hope he may have had of finding a reputable home for the novel. It may
also help explain why the manuscript eventually found its way to Samuel
Roth—whom Eastman had known (or at least known of) since the 1920s.

What this latest turn in the McKay manuscript saga further underscores
is the importance and impact of "additions" to collections—a common phenomenon among archives and literary papers in particular. Additions can
arrive at any time and are a reminder that archives are the opposite of static,
lifeless things but rather ceaselessly in motion, gestating in hibernation. The
phenomenon of additions and the timing of their arrival can potentially
alter the course of an entire project. Had the rejection letter from Macrae
already been part of the Eastman papers when we consulted them in 2009,
the authentication would have been an easier and quicker process. If we cast
aside our late involvement entirely, it seems more than likely that earlier
researchers, such as Wayne Cooper and Winston James, who consulted the
Eastman papers in the 1970s, would have come across the letter and thus
realized that by August 1941 McKay had actually completed a novel manuscript called "God's Black Sheep," writing it under contract for E. P. Dutton. Though this letter alone would not have led them to the manuscript's
physical location among the Samuel Roth Papers, it would have alerted
scholars that McKay indeed had a "shadow book"—beyond the unfinished
"Harlem Glory" and his late poetry—and thus prepared the literary community for the novel's possible appearance, just as it would have likely
launched quite a few archival quests.

To this day, Roth is largely portrayed with derision. For example, Michael
Chabon's Pulitzer Prize–winning novel *The Amazing Adventures of Kavalier & Clay* includes a harsh description of "an almost comically shifty-
looking and heavily perspiring walleyed loser named Samuel Roth."[22] Yet
Roth was hardly a mere "loser" or smut peddler. The scholar Milton Hindus, whose book on Louis-Ferdinand Céline, *The Crippled Giant*, was published by Roth in 1950, explained Roth this way: "Whoever dared to defy

convention and the authorities, for any reason whatever, found a sympathetic ear in Roth."[23] As Jay Gertzman underscores in his definitive biography *Samuel Roth: Infamous Modernist*, Roth was widely known in the New York publishing scene as someone who regularly represented maverick authors whose works had trouble finding an audience. A daring publisher, Roth printed early books on queer life (*A Scarlet Pansy*, 1932), alleged corruption among prominent politicians (*The Strange Career of Mr Hoover Under Two Flags*, 1931), erotic adventures of contemporaries (*The Private Life of Frank Harris*, 1931), and other taboo subjects. This boldness may have attracted a radical writer such as McKay, especially in the context of the contractual bind in which he found himself. Money matters aside, the potentially incendiary subject matter of *Amiable*, which constitutes a direct attack on the Communist Party—and as such is part of McKay's hardnosed turn against the party late in life also in evidence in his now published Cycle poems—and provides a scathing account of what he calls "the Black Sheep of Harlem," could have attracted Roth. McKay may have sought out Roth after his novel was rejected—perhaps on the advice of Eastman or simply on his own—because of Roth's reputation as both a risk taker in terms of subject matter and his occasional unscrupulous disregard for the fine print.

In all likelihood, McKay probably gave Roth the "God's Black Sheep" manuscript a few days after inking the "Descent Into Harlem" contract in September 1941 (a month after the Dutton rejection), perhaps to see if something could be done. Alas, the "Descent" project was quickly abandoned, and Roth apparently misplaced the only copy of McKay's final novel. Because it was too expensive or risky to release the novel in 1941, he may have decided to wait for a later opportunity or forgot about it altogether. Indeed, other publishers, not to mention McKay himself, had forgotten about his manuscripts before. When Yale librarian Bernhard Knollenberg contacted Harper & Brothers in 1941 to request the typescript for *Banana Bottom* at McKay's behest, the editor had not only forgotten that he had it but ended up finding another manuscript by McKay titled "Lafala" (an alternate title to his as yet unpublished work "Romance in Marseilles"). The editor wrote:

I am glad to send you by express today this typescript [for *Banana Bottom*] together with a shorter typescript of 88 pages which was attached to it. . . . I have been out of touch with McKay for a number of years and Harpers do not seem to know his present whereabouts, so I should be very glad to have you take charge of both typescripts, notifying Mr. McKay of their safe arrival in your hands. These unclaimed scripts had been stored in my files for some time, and I should have been unaware of their presence had word not come to me from you of Mr. McKay's wishes.[24]

When word of this rediscovery reached McKay, he excitedly wrote to Van Vechten: "I especially want to have back Banana Bottom and the unfinished manuscript of Lafala, which I had forgotten about and don't want to be in any collection."[25]

The announcement of McKay's death in 1948 may have similarly reminded Roth that he owned the "Amiable" typescript because, as Brent and I explain in the published edition's "Note on the Text," he composed a misleading "Publisher's Note" where he claims that McKay wrote the novel "just before his death" in 1948 (whereas in fact he wrote it in the spring of 1941). Nothing ever came of this half-hearted effort, and soon Roth was back to facing more legal troubles for his mail-order business. The binder in which Roth had inserted the "Amiable" typescript listed Roth's address in New York's Upper West Side, an apartment that the police raided and ransacked in 1954 (see figure 1.2). The police had also raided his downtown office, and the chaos left in their wake forced Roth to rearrange all his files. It may even be during this forced reorganization that he realized he still had this McKay manuscript and composed his "note." Yet Roth's reacquaintance with the typescript after 1948 seemed only to lead to a new binder that would go on to gather dust and stain its contents for another half-century.

Though Roth was not involved with the genesis of McKay's novel, part of the poetry of archival research entails following the romance of the trace down all those dead-end trails, temporary assumptions, and lingering mysteries that unfold with each acid-free folder. The archive's promise, as

FIGURE 6.2 Claude McKay's "Amiable with Big Teeth" typescript, 1941.
Photograph by Brent Hayes Edwards and Jean-Christophe Cloutier.

Source: Box 29, folders 7–8, Samuel Roth Papers, Rare Book and Manuscript Library, Columbia.

Brent Edwards writes in *The Practice of Diaspora*, "necessarily involves a process of linking or connecting gaps,"[26] yet in reality it always falls a little short. Edwards pushes this thought further in his later essay "The Taste of the Archive," where he stresses how "there is never only one archive. And one way to read an archive critically is to read it in concert with another archive, supplementing the blind spots and biases of one repository with the additional and differently classified documents in another. Still, the gaps remain."[27]

In *Ulysses*, the young artist and teacher Stephen Dedalus asks one of his students, "What is a pier?" The perplexed boy replies, "A pier, sir . . . A thing out in the water. A kind of bridge." Dedalus agrees, "Yes, a disappointed bridge."[28] So it goes for the archive. The more backlog I see and the more research I undertake in the archive, the more I come to regard it as a movable yet disappointed bridge, allowing us to glimpse but not quite reach the other shore. As such, there is a kinship between the archive and twentieth-century literature's unwillingness to solve every plot mystery, its tendency to keep open the possibilities of meaning. If we adhere to a naive hope that the archive can provide an answer to everything, it will always feel incomplete. Why Samuel Roth? How and when *exactly* did Roth get ahold of this novel? Why did McKay forget to retrieve it? Why would McKay or Eastman never again mention a book they both seemed to admire? But to think of the archive this way would be to treat history as a kind of catechism awaiting completion, an impulse James Joyce mocks in the "Ithaca" chapter of *Ulysses*. It would be to assume that every conversation, every interaction, every transaction has miraculously been recorded and preserved. Although this disappointed bridge can never quite carry us across the aporias of history, some things sometimes do serendipitously, indeed eerily, drift back to our side. Samuel Roth was not just "blundering all over the two worlds," as Joyce claimed about the publisher;[29] he was also bridging them—and he did so, as he said, "for the increase of the gaiety of nations!" as the subtitle to Roth's journal *Two Worlds Monthly* states.[30] Roth may have stood in the shadow of modernism, but his papers provide undeniable proof that some of the traditional categorizations and specializations we have erected within the humanities have artificially kept apart worlds that in the end are as intertwined as Swann's and Guermante's ways. Roth's check to McKay may have humiliatingly bounced, yet his preservation of the man's novel might act as symbolic payback. Although neither one lived to see the published novel— sadly enough—Roth did end up, in that strange archival way, seeing to its publication after all.

APPENDIX

ARTIFACT BIOGRAPHIES OR VAGABOND ITINERARIES OF KEY DOCUMENTS DISCUSSED IN THIS BOOK

AMIABLE WITH BIG TEETH / GOD'S BLACK SHEEP

Created in 1941; found in 2009.

- February–March 1941: Living in North Wayne, Maine, Claude McKay begins writing "Amiable with Big Teeth," a novel manuscript he is then calling "God's Black Sheep" under contract with E. P. Dutton.
- March 1941: McKay sends the first fifty pages of the novel to Max Eastman, who is then living in Florida. It remains unclear whether these pages are duplicates or if they are the only copy.
- April 1941: McKay receives encouraging feedback from Eastman on the first fifty pages of the novel, and he works tirelessly to complete the story.
- April–July 1941: McKay, in considerable physical discomfort, returns to New York, completes his novel, and submits it to Dutton. Due to lack of time, he works only on the original and does not make a duplicate.
- August 1941: The novel is officially rejected by Dutton, and the only extant copy of the manuscript is returned to McKay.
- September–October 1941: McKay falls ill. He also enters into a contract with the independent publisher Samuel Roth to ghostwrite a

novel manuscript called "Descent Into Harlem." In all likelihood, it is during this period that McKay gives Roth the "God's Black Sheep" typescript. The typescript remains in Roth's possession but is never published.

- 1941–1954: The typescript is either in Roth's Upper West Side apartment or in his office on Lafayette Street.

- 1943–1948: McKay moves to Chicago; he does not retrieve the "Amiable/God's Black Sheep" typescript. McKay dies in 1948.

- April 1954: Roth's office on Lafayette and his apartment on West Eighty-First Street are ransacked by police officers looking for obscene books. Many items are confiscated, and everything is left in disarray. Several documents are lost, and a complete inventory proves impossible. The "Amiable" typescript somehow survives this raid, but its exact whereabouts within Roth's files remains unknown.

- 1955–1960: Roth serves a five-year sentence in Lewisburg Penitentiary; in the meantime, his affairs are handled by his wife, Pauline, but his files do not change location.

- 1960: Returning home from prison, Roth undertakes a more systematic survey of his files. During this process, he puts many of the manuscripts in his possession into black binders—including the "Amiable" typescript. Roth binds the novel with a short "Proem" likely written by his friend Dante Cacici (the "Proem" may have already been kept in the same folder as the McKay typescript prior to binding) and writes a short "Publisher's Note," which he also inserts into the same binder. At this time or perhaps earlier, Roth also lightly edits a few of the first pages of the typescript as well as some of the final pages but does not make any holograph edits to any of the leaves in between. It is also possible that Roth composed his publisher's note in the immediate wake of McKay's death in 1948, but not earlier.

- 1974: Samuel Roth dies in July. His daughter, Adelaide Kugel, inherits her father's affairs and files.

- 1974–2006: Adelaide Kugel works intermittently on a biography of her father to be entitled "Plain Brown Wrapper," which is never published. During this process, she rearranges some of her father's records, including classifying some of the correspondence in alphabetical order and creating a series of index cards related to themes and people. One of the index cards indicates that she has located from within her father's files the two letters by McKay to Roth from October 1941 as well as the "Descent Into Harlem" book contract. This "McKay" index card, however, does not record any indication of her having found the "Amiable" typescript. She goes on to do some preliminary research into the Roth–McKay relation but finds no promising leads. The bound typescript remains somewhere hidden among the files. Adelaide passes away in 2006.

- 2008: Samuel Roth's grandchildren want to find a home for their grandfather's collection and contact Columbia University's Rare Book and Manuscript Library (Roth is a Columbia alum). More than fifty boxes and five record cartons are packed and shipped to Columbia's Butler Library, where a literary appraiser, Bart Aeurbach, goes through the contents to evaluate its value and advise the Rare Book Library staff regarding its acquisition. Given the size of the collection, Aeurbach only has time to give the "Amiable" typescript "a superficial look." The Samuel Roth Papers are donated to Columbia University's Rare Book and Manuscript Library.

- July 2009: An archival intern begins processing the Roth collection and finds the bound "Amiable" typescript. The typescript is subsequently unbound and put in two acid-free folders, which are then put into box 29 of the Samuel Roth Papers in Columbia University's Rare Book and Manuscript Library, sixth floor, Butler Library. It remains there to this day.

- 2017: The manuscript for a novel originally intended to be titled "God's Black Sheep" is published as *Amiable with Big Teeth: A Novel of the Love Affair Between the Communists and the Poor Black Sheep of Harlem*, a title I suspect was coined by Samuel Roth as one of his last and best pranks played on the literary establishment.

THE "HARLEM IS NOWHERE" PHOTOGRAPHS

Created 1948; "found" in 2014.

- November 1947–March 1948: Gordon Parks and Ralph Ellison roam Harlem taking photographs for their "Harlem Is Nowhere" photo-report, under contract with *'48: The Magazine of the Year.* Ellison appears to develop most of the materials. Multiple contact sheets and some prints are made following their numerous photo shoots. At this stage, the photographs sit in darkrooms and in Ellison's and Parks's apartments in Manhattan and Westchester, respectively, where Ellison also writes some of the essay text.
- March 1948: Both the text and the photographs are now ready. Ellison and Parks meet twice with Richard Lauterbach, editor at *'48*, to go over the layout of the photo-essay.
- April 1948: Ellison receives the final layout of the photo-report and begins composing captions for the selected images. Twelve or thirteen photographs in total appear to have been chosen—the editors ascribe a letter of the alphabet, from A to M, to each photograph to be used, but no reference to a letter L can be found among Ellison's caption drafts (it may have been dropped from the initial layout plan).
- May 1948: *Magazine of the Year* suspends publication and files for bankruptcy. It keeps the final materials for "Harlem Is Nowhere" in its files for potential use in its bankruptcy case.
- June–August 1948: Although the final prints of the photographs for "Harlem Is Nowhere" are now held by the *Magazine of the Year* editors, a few duplicate prints, along with contact sheets and negatives for the project are dispersed among Parks's files at his Westchester house. A few of the alternate prints and negatives are also in Ellison's apartment, including some of Ellison's own attempts at or versions of the images he wanted Parks to capture for the essay.
- August 1948: Parks puts some of the duplicate photographs from the "Harlem Is Nowhere" project into his photographer's portfolio, along

with some of his fashion photography and Farm Security
Administration work, and shows it to Wilson Hicks, *Life* magazine's
photography editor. *Life* hires Parks as a staff photographer.

- September 1948: Ellison writes to the *Magazine of the Year* editors and
  demands that "the set of photographs prepared for its illustration be
  returned" to him. The magazine's lawyers refuse to return the
  materials, and they remain tied up in litigation. That same month,
  Hesketh Wertham—Dr. Fredric Wertham's wife—informs Ellison
  that she has submitted two photographs by Gordon Parks to the
  Encyclopedia Britannica's contest for the year's best photographs of
  documentary journalism—the winners would be published in the
  yearbook titled *The Great Pictures*. One of the two photographs
  submitted, of an African American patient waiting to be seen by a
  doctor at the Lafargue Clinic, matches what is described in caption M
  of the "Harlem Is Nowhere" photo-report. The photos are not selected
  for the *Great Pictures* yearbook and are subsequently returned to the
  Lafargue Clinic by the publishers of *Encyclopedia Britannica*. They
  remain in Wertham's personal papers until the latter are acquired and
  processed by the Library of Congress in 2010.
- November 1948: *Harlem Rooftops*, a photograph by Parks taken for the
  "Harlem Is Nowhere" project and corresponding to caption C, is used as
  the opening two-page spread of Parks's first byline at *Life*, "Harlem
  Gang Leader." In the process and due to the close proximity in time,
  space, and theme of both the "Nowhere" and the "Gang Leader" projects,
  the negatives, contact sheets, and prints in Parks's possession become
  intermingled and are seamlessly filed together in the *Life* magazine
  offices (though a few may have remained at Parks's residence in White
  Plains). Deracinated from their provenance in the "Harlem Is Nowhere"
  projects, some of these photographs slowly begin to enter circulation as
  part of Parks's oeuvre, including *Harlem Rooftops*, *Off on My Own*
  (corresponding to caption B), and *Street Scene* (corresponding to caption J).
- August 1951: Bankruptcy Case 85638 in the matter of the petition of
  Associated Magazine Contributors, Inc., owners of *Magazine of the
  Year*, for relief under Chapter 11, section 128, in the United States

District Court, Southern District of New York, is closed. Deemed "unimportant" by the court, the "Harlem Is Nowhere" photographs, used as evidence in the case, are destroyed.

- 1952: Ralph Ellison's novel *Invisible Man* is published. Ellison and Parks collaborate on an experimental, promotional photo-text titled "A Man Becomes Invisible" to celebrate the novel in *Life* magazine. They revisit some of the same themes they had explored four years earlier, including the focus on "Harlem Mysticism," a theme associated with the photograph for caption K of "Harlem Is Nowhere" but updated for the *Life* feature.

- 1964: Under contract with Random House to publish his first collection of nonfiction work, *Shadow and Act*, Ralph Ellison informs the press that photographs taken by Gordon Parks had originally accompanied "Harlem Is Nowhere," an essay to be included in the book. Indicating that he no longer has access to them, Ellison tells Random House he believes the images are now owned by *Life* magazine. Internal memos between editors Jim Silberman and Tony Wimpfheimer at Random House show interest in having the essay appear with Parks's photographs, if they can be found.[1] It appears this search is unsuccessful because "Harlem Is Nowhere" is published in *Shadow and Act* without photographs.

- August 1964: Ralph Ellison again publishes "Harlem Is Nowhere," though this time in truncated form in *Harper's Magazine*. This version appears with four photographs by Roy DeCarava, including two (*Graduation* and *Man Sitting on Stoop with Baby*) that had first appeared in DeCarava's and Langston Hughes's book *The Sweet Flypaper of Life* in 1955. However, the print of *Man on Sitting Stoop with Baby* used in the *Harper's* version of the essay is slightly different from the one that appeared in *Sweet Flypaper*, suggesting that Ellison was able to look through DeCarava's negatives to select this alternate take.

- 1971: Gordon Parks leaves his employ as a *Life* magazine staff photographer and takes many of his files with him to his estate in White Plains, New York.

- 1971–1994: Over the years, a few prints and contact sheets from the "Harlem Is Nowhere" project appear to be in circulation on the art market and are purchased by private hands. Confirmed purchases include a large print of *Off on My Own*, later acquired by the Art Institute of Chicago for its exhibition *Invisible Man: Gordon Parks and Ralph Ellison in Harlem* in 2016, as well as a contact sheet.
- 1994: Ralph Ellison passes away at the age of eighty-one. His papers are eventually acquired by the Library of Congress.
- 2006: Gordon Parks passes away at the age of ninety-three.
- 2007: The Library of Congress Prints and Photographs Division processes a batch of Ralph Ellison's photographic holdings obtained in 1998. In this initial batch, none of the prints, contact sheets, or negatives appear to match the "Harlem Is Nowhere" captions. There is, however, one contact sheet print that includes both Parks and Ellison and that was taken during the 1947–1948 winter photo-shoot for "Harlem Is Nowhere." The shot of Ellison is an outtake of the Ellison portrait Parks included in his book *Camera Portraits: Techniques and Principles of Documentary Portraiture* (1948).
- 2008: The Gordon Parks Foundation is born, and it begins processing what will become the Gordon Parks Archive.
- 2010: The Library of Congress receives an additional batch of Ellison's photographic holdings. In this latest addition, a few prints from the "Harlem Is Nowhere" project are present, including a small-size print of *Harlem Rooftops*, the photograph of the "cynical adolescent" used for caption I, and large-format alternatives of Harlem garbage prints associated with caption D. Perhaps as an indication of how close Ellison and Parks's initial collaboration was, on the back of one of these oversize prints Fanny Ellison wrote "Photo by R.E.," even though the image was in fact taken by Parks. Contact sheets also show alternate shots of *Off on My Own* and *Harlem Mysticism*.
- Also in 2010: The Fredric Wertham Papers at the Library of Congress become accessible to researchers. The photograph of a patient waiting to see a doctor described by caption M for "Harlem Is Nowhere" is put

in box 215, folder 6, and is found by Gabriel Mendes during his research on the Lafargue Clinic. Mendes eventually includes the photograph in his book *Under the Strain of Color: Harlem's Lafargue Clinic and the Promise of an Antiracist Psychiatry* (2015).

- 2014: At a meeting in The Gordon Parks Archive, research materials and information pooled from those present (archivist, curator, historian, literary scholar) are combined and, through this collaboration, enable the group to discern and identify the prints, contact sheets, and negatives originally belonging to the "Harlem Is Nowhere" project. The meeting results in conclusive evidence that many of the "Harlem Is Nowhere" images had been intermingled and kept with the "Harlem Gang Leader" file boxes. At the time of this meeting, the "Harlem Gang Leader" boxes are labeled "Harlem Gang Wars," reflecting what must have likely been their internal filing title at *Life* magazine headquarters prior to acquisition by The Gordon Parks Foundation. Parks likely made the shift from "Wars" to "Leader" in the title in an effort to celebrate and redeem Red Jackson rather than pathologize juvenile violence in Harlem.

- 2015: For consistency across its publications, The Gordon Parks Foundation abandons the original label "Harlem Gang Wars" and retitles the files "Harlem Gang Leader."

- May–August 2016: All known extant prints from the "Harlem Is Nowhere" project are exhibited for the public at the Art Institute of Chicago and published in the accompanying catalog, *Invisible Man: Gordon Parks and Ralph Ellison in Harlem* (2016).

- *Note*: Thus far, no print, contact sheet, or negative by Gordon Parks matching what is described in caption A—a black psychiatrist with a white patient—has been located in either The Gordon Parks Archive or the Ellison Papers or the Wertham Papers or in private hands. If you have this print or contact sheet, please get in touch.

NOTES

ABBREVIATIONS

APC   Ann Petry Collection, Howard Gotlieb Archival Research Center,
            Boston University
CMC   Claude McKay Collection, Collection of American Literature,
            Beinecke Rare Book and Manuscript Library, Yale University, New
            Haven
CMPA   Claude McKay Papers (Additions), Schomburg Center for Research
            in Black Culture, New York Public Library
CVVP   Carl Van Vechten Papers Relating to African American Arts and
            Letters, James Weldon Johnson Collection in the Collection of
            American Literature, Beinecke Rare Book and Manuscript Library,
            Yale University, New Haven
CVV NYPL   Carl Van Vechten Papers, Manuscripts and Archives Division, New
            York Public Library
FWP   Fredric Wertham Papers, Manuscript Division, Library of Congress,
            Washington, DC
IGP   Ida Guggenheimer Papers, Schomburg Center for Research in Black
            Culture, New York Public Library
LCR   Lafargue Clinic Records, Schomburg Center for Research in Black
            Culture, New York Public Library
NYPL   New York Public Library
REP   Ralph Ellison Papers, Manuscript Division, Library of Congress,
            Washington, DC
RWP   Richard Wright Papers, Collection of American Literature, Beinecke
            Rare Book and Manuscript Library, Yale University, New Haven

SRP   Samuel Roth Papers, Rare Book and Manuscript Library, Columbia University, New York

UPBS   University Place Book Shop Records, Rare Book and Manuscript Library, Columbia University, New York

WPN   Writers' Program, New York City, Negroes of New York Collection, 1936–1941, New Manuscripts, Archives, and Rare Books Division, Schomburg Center for Research in Black Culture, New York Public Library

INTRODUCTION: "NOT LIKE AN ARROW, BUT A BOOMERANG," OR THE LIFECYCLES OF TWENTIETH-CENTURY AFRICAN AMERICAN LITERARY PAPERS

1. Richard Wright, *Later Works: Black Boy (American Hunger); The Outsider,* ed. Arnold Rampersad (New York: Library of America, 1991), 365. This volume established the definitive version of *Black Boy* that has since been used for subsequent editions.

2. Richard Wright, *American Hunger* (New York: Harper and Row, 1977), 146.

3. *American Hunger* was supposed to be the title of Wright's complete autobiography but instead became the title of the posthumously released part 2 of what we now know as *Black Boy.* Among other titles Wright proposed to Harper were "Shadow-land," "On the Margin," "The Valley of Darkness," "Dark Awakening," and "In a Strange Land." He rejected the use of the word *autobiography* in the subtitle in favor of "A *Record* of Childhood and Youth," thus giving the text an archival feel. Details regarding *Black Boy*'s complex publication history are chronicled in Toru Kiuchi, ed., *Richard Wright: A Documented Chronology, 1908–1960* (Jefferson, NC: McFarland, 2014).

4. See Langston Hughes, *Montage of a Dream Deferred* (New York: Holt, 1951).

5. Kevin Young, *The Grey Album: On the Blackness of Blackness* (Minneapolis: Greywolf Press, 2013), 11.

6. Young, *The Grey Album,* 12.

7. Young, *The Grey Album,* 12. See also Roland Barthes, "Death of the Author," in *The Book History Reader,* ed. David Finkelstein and Alistair McCleery (London: Routledge, 1977), 277–80, which considers the literary as a form of eduction rather than production in a Kantian sense—that is, to bring out from a state of latent or potential existence, as addressed in *The Critique of Judgement.*

8. Young, *The Grey Album,* 14.

9. See Kiuchi, *Richard Wright,* loc. 6271 of 12871, Kindle.

10. Arnold Rampersad, quoted in Eleanor Blau, "The Works of Richard Wright, as Written," *New York Times,* August 28, 1991.

11. Blau, "The Works of Richard Wright, as Written"

12. Lisa Stead, introduction to *The Boundaries of the Literary Archive: Reclamation and Representation*, ed. Carrie Smith and Lisa Stead (Surrey, UK: Ashgate, 2013), 4.

13. *American Archivist*, quoted in H. G. Jones, "Introduction to the 2003 Reissue," in Theodore R. Schellenberg, *Modern Archives: Principles and Techniques* (1956; reissue, Chicago: Society of American Archivists, 2003), xi.

14. "National Archives History," https://www.archives.gov/about/history.

15. Jones, "Introduction," xi.

16. For a useful historicized summary of Jenkinson's interwar principles of archival custodianship and Schellenberg's intent to "supplant" him, see Paul Saint-Amour, *Tense Future: Modernism, Total War, Encyclopedic Form* (New York: Oxford University Press, 2015), 157–69, "old fossil" on 164 n. 31.

17. Schellenberg, *Modern Archives*, 37–38.

18. Schellenberg, *Modern Archives*, 37.

19. Elizabeth Shepherd and Geoffrey Yeo, *Managing Records: A Handbook of Principles and Practice* (London: Facet, 2003), 5.

20. Shepherd and Yeo, *Managing Records*, 4.

21. See Shepherd and Yeo, *Managing Records*, 23–24. For more on the hardware of digital storage, see Matthew G. Kirschenbaum, *Mechanisms: New Media and the Forensic Imagination* (Cambridge, MA: MIT Press, 2008).

22. Giorgio Agamben, *Remnants of Auschwitz: The Witness and the Archive*, trans. Daniel Heller-Roazen (New York: Zone Books, 1999); Saidiya Hartman, *Lose Your Mother: A Journey Along the Atlantic Slave Route* (New York: Farrar, Straus and Giroux, 2006); Ann Laura Stoler, *Along the Archival Grain: Epistemic Anxieties and Colonial Common Sense* (Princeton, NJ: Princeton University Press, 2010).

23. NourbeSe Philip, *Zong!* (Middletown, CN: Wesleyan University Press, 2008).

24. Achille Mbembe, "The Power of the Archive and Its Limits," trans. Judith Inggs, in *Refiguring the Archive*, ed. Carolyn Hamilton, Verne Harris, Jane Taylor, Michele Pickover, Graeme Reid, and Razia Saleh (Dordrecht, Netherlands: Kluwer, 2002), 21.

25. For a particularly adroit example, see Dagmawi Woubshet's recent book *A Calendar of Loss: Race, Sexuality, and Mourning in the Early Era of AIDS* (Baltimore, MD: Johns Hopkins University Press, 2015).

26. Salamishah Tillet, *Sites of Slavery: Citizenship and Racial Democracy in the Post–Civil Rights Imagination* (Durham, NC: Duke University Press, 2012); Christina Sharpe, *In the Wake: On Blackness and Being* (Durham, NC: Duke University Press, 2016).

27. Amiri Baraka, *Black Music: Essays by Leroi Jones (Amiri Baraka)* (New York: Akashi-Classics, 1968). See also Margo Natalie Crawford, "'What Was *Is*': The Time and Space of Entanglement Erased by Post-blackness," in *The Trouble with Post-blackness*, ed. Houston A. Baker Jr. and K. Merinda Simmons (New York: Columbia University Press, 2015), 21–43.

28. Wallace Thurman, *Infants of the Spring* (1932; reprint, Boston: Northeastern University Press, 1992), 283.

29. Mbembe, "The Power of the Archive and Its Limits," 21, 25.

30. For more on the records-continuum concept, see James M. O'Toole and Richard J. Cox, *Understanding Archives & Manuscripts* (Chicago: Society of American Archivists, 2006), 93.

31. U.S. National Archives and Records Administration, "What's a Record?" http://www.archives.gov/about/info/whats-a-record.html.

32. Philip C. Bantin, "Strategies for Managing Electronic Records: A New Archival Paradigm? An Affirmation of Our Archival Traditions?" *Archival Issues* 23, no. 1 (1998): 19. For Bantin's own source on the lifecycle concept, see Ira A. Penn, Gail Pennix, and Jim Coulson, *Records Management Handbook*, 2nd ed. (Hampshire, UK: Gower, 1994), 12–17.

33. Ralph Ellison, "The Shadow and the Act" (1949), in *The Collected Essays of Ralph Ellison*, rev. and updated, ed. John F. Callahan (New York: Modern, 2003), 305, 303.

34. See Carlo Ginzburg and Carlo Poni, "La micro-histoire," *Le Débat*, no. 17 (December 1981): 133–36, and Carlo Ginzburg, "Microhistory: Two or Three Things That I Know About It," *Critical Inquiry* 20 (1993): 10–35.

35. My use of the term *scenario* is informed by Diana Taylor's definition as outlined in her book *The Archive and the Repertoire: Performing Cultural Memory in the Americas* (Durham, NC: Duke University Press, 2003).

36. For more on the "fevers" of archival scholarship, see Carolyn Steedman, *Dust: The Archive and Cultural History* (New Brunswick, NJ: Rutgers University Press, 2002).

37. Jerome McGann, *A New Republic of Letters: Memory and Scholarship in the Age of Digital Reproduction* (Cambridge, MA: Harvard University Press, 2014), 19.

38. McGann, *A New Republic of Letters*, 19.

39. Stead, introduction to *The Boundaries of the Literary Archive*, 1–2.

40. Jacques Derrida, *Archive Fever: A Freudian Impression*, trans. Eric Prenowitz (Chicago: University of Chicago Press, 1995), 18.

41. Toni Morrison, *Beloved* (New York: New American Library, 1987), 210.

42. Brent Hayes Edwards, *The Practice of Diaspora: Literature, Translation, and the Rise of Black Internationalism* (Cambridge, MA: Harvard University Press, 2003), 13.

43. Edwards, *The Practice of Diaspora*, 13–14.

44. Steedman, *Dust*, 7.

45. The phrase "wreckage upon wreckage" is from Walter Benjamin, "Theses on the Philosophy of History," in *Illuminations*, trans. Harry Zohn (New York: Schocken Books, 1969), 249.

46. Margo N. Crawford, *Blackness Post-blackness: The Black Arts Movement and Twenty-First-Century Aesthetics* (Champaign: University of Illinois Press, 2017), 2–3, emphasis in the original. See also Nathaniel Mackey, "An Interview with Kamau

Brathwaite," in *The Art of Kamau Brathwaite*, ed. Stewart Brown (Bridgend, Wales: Seren, 1995), 13–32.

47. Stoler, *Along the Archival Grain*, 4, emphasis in original.

48. Stephen Enniss, "In the Author's Hand: Artifacts of Origin and Twentieth-Century Reading Practices," *RBM: A Journal of Rare Books, Manuscripts, and Cultural Heritage* 2 (Fall 2001): 115.

49. See David Greetham, "Uncoupled : Or, How I Lost My Author(s)," *Textual Cultures: Texts, Contexts, Interpretation* 3, no. 1 (Spring 2008): 44–55.

50. Mbembe, "The Power of the Archive and Its Limits," 19.

51. Mbembe, "The Power of the Archive and Its Limits," 25, 19.

52. Enniss, "In the Author's Hand," 109.

53. Enniss, "In the Author's Hand," 109.

54. Enniss, "In the Author's Hand," 110.

55. Mark McGurl, *The Program Era: Postwar Fiction and the Rise of Creative Writing* (Cambridge, MA: Harvard University Press, 2009).

56. Lawrence P. Jackson, *The Indignant Generation: A Narrative History of African American Writers and Critics, 1934–1960* (Princeton, NJ: Princeton University Press, 2011).

57. Lisa Gitelman, *Paper Knowledge: Toward a Media History of Documents* (Durham, NC: Duke University Press, 2014); Hal Foster, "An Archival Impulse," *October* 110 (Fall 2004): 3.

58. Claude McKay, *Harlem: Negro Metropolis* (1940; reprint, New York: Harvest, 1968), and *Amiable with Big Teeth: A Novel of the Love Affair Between the Communists and the Poor Black Sheep of Harlem*, ed. Jean-Christophe Cloutier and Brent Hayes Edwards (New York: Penguin Classics, 2017).

59. Jackson, *The Indignant Generation*, 143–44.

60. Terry Cook, "What Is Past Is Prologue: A History of Archival Ideas Since 1898, and the Future Paradigm Shift," *Archivaria* 43 (Spring 1997): 24.

61. Henry James, "The American Scene" (1907), in *Collected Travel Writings: Great Britain and America* (New York: Library of America, 1993), 684.

62. Steedman, *Dust*, 77.

63. Stoler, *Along the Archival Grain*, 3.

64. Steedman, *Dust*, 68.

65. Michel-Rolph Trouillot, *Silencing the Past: Power and the Production of History* (Boston: Beacon Press, 1995).

66. Ralph Ellison to Richard Wright, November 3, 1941, RWP. See also Richard Wright and Edwin Rosskam, *12 Million Black Voices* (New York: Viking, 1941).

67. Arlette Farge, *The Allure of Archives*, trans. Thomas Scott-Railton (New Haven, CT: Yale University Press, 2013), 76, 77. The French original, *Le goût de l'archive*, was published in 1989. For another source of scholarship that grapples with the question of

how to ethically narrate from the archive, see also Saidiya V. Hartman, "Venus in Two Acts," *Small Axe* 12, no. 2 (2008): 1–14.

68. Steedman, *Dust*, 69.

69. Suzanne Keen, *Romances of the Archive in Contemporary British Fiction* (Toronto: University of Toronto Press, 2001), 4.

70. David Bradley, *The Chaneysville Incident* (New York: Harper and Row, 1981), 140.

71. Bradley, *The Chaneysville Incident*, 264, 268.

72. Hartman, "Venus in Two Acts," 11.

73. Bradley, *The Chaneysville Incident*, 271–72 (ellipses in original), 273, 140.

74. Don DeLillo, *Libra* (1988; reprint, New York: Penguin Books, 2006), vii, xi.

75. Marco Codebò, *Narrating from the Archive: Novels, Records, and Bureaucrats in the Modern Age* (Madison, NJ: Fairleigh Dickinson University Press, 2010), 13, 14.

76. Ralph Ellison, *Invisible Man* (1952; reprint, New York: Vintage-Random, 1995), 439. For a typical example of this approach, see Allan H. Pasco, "Literature as Historical Archive," *New Literary History* 35, no. 3 (Summer 2004): 373–94.

77. Linda Hutcheon, *A Poetics of Postmodernism: History, Theory, Fiction* (London: Routledge, 1988), 76, quoted in Keen, *Romances of the Archive*, 13.

78. See Hayden White, "Historical Pluralism," *Critical Inquiry* 12, no. 3 (Spring 1986): 480–93.

79. On this notion of "archival poetics," see Paul J. Voss and Marta L. Werner, "Toward a Poetics of the Archive: Introduction," *Studies in the Literary Imagination* 32, no. 1 (Spring 1999): i–viii.

80. Aarthi Vadde, "National Myth, Transnational Memory: Ondaatje's Archival Method," *Novel: A Forum on Fiction* 45, no. 2 (Summer 2012): 257. Even though Vadde does not refer to these literary trends, we could say that she is reading *The Collected Works of Billy the Kid* by Michael Ondaatje according to the archival poetics of the *Archivroman* and reading *Anil's Ghost* as a counterarchive that "magnif[ies] the instabilities of history, myth, and memory" (258).

81. See the following works by Catherine Hobbs: "The Character of Personal Archives: Reflections on the Value of Records of Individuals," *Archivaria* 52 (Fall 2001): 126–35; "New Approaches to Canadian Literary Archives," *Journal of Canadian Studies* 40, no. 2 (2006): 109–19; "Reenvisioning the Personal: Reframing Traces of Individual Life," in *Currents of Archival Thinking*, ed. Terry Eastwood and Heather Mac-Neil (Santa Barbara, CA: Libraries Unlimited, 2010), 213–41; and "Personal Ethics: Being an Archivist of Writers," in *Basements and Attics, Closets and Cyberspace*, ed. Linda M. Morra (Waterloo, Canada: Wilfrid Laurier University Press, 2012), 181–92. See also Jennifer Douglas, "What We Talk About When We Talk About Original Order in Writers' Archives," *Archivaria* 76 (Fall 2013): 7–25.

82. Hobbs, "Personal Ethics," 181.

83. David C. Sutton, "Diasporic Literary Archives: Questions of Location, Ownership, and Interpretation," keynote address, Silences of Archives conference, Helsinki, November 6, 2014, 8.

84. See Cook, "What Is Past Is Prologue," and Terry Cook, "The Concept of Archival Fonds in the Post-custodial Era," *Archivaria* 35 (Spring 1993): 24–37.

85. Tyler O. Walters, "Contemporary Archival Appraisal Methods and Preservation Decision-Making," *American Archivist* 59 (Summer 1996): 332.

86. Cook, "The Concept of Archival Fonds in the Post-custodial Era," 25.

87. Jacques Derrida, "No Apocalypse, Not Now (Full Speed Ahead, Seven Missiles, Seven Missives)," in "Nuclear Criticism," special issue of *Diacritics* 14, no. 2 (Summer 1984): 20–31. See also Saint-Amour, *Tense Future*, 25–33.

88. Cook, "The Concept of Archival Fonds in the Post-custodial Era," 24–25.

89. Hobbs, "Personal Ethics," 181–82.

90. Walters, "Contemporary Archival Appraisal Methods," 332.

91. Cook, "The Concept of Archival Fonds in the Post-custodial Era," 27.

92. See Cook, "What Is Past Is Prologue."

93. Phillip N. Cronenwett, "Appraisal of Literary Manuscripts," in *Archival Choices: Managing the Historical Record in an Age of Abundance*, ed. Nancy E. Peace (Lexington, MA: Lexington Books, 1984), 109.

94. Mark A. Greene and Dennis Meissner, "More Product, Less Process: Revamping Traditional Archival Processing," *American Archivist* 68 (Fall–Winter 2005): 208–63.

1. BLACK SPECIAL COLLECTIONS AND THE MIDCENTURY RISE OF THE INSTITUTIONAL COLLECTOR

1. Jessie Carney Smith, "An Overview, Including the Special Collections at Fisk University," in *Black Bibliophiles and Collectors: Preservers of Black History*, ed. Elinor Des Verney Sinnette, W. Paul Coates, and Thomas C. Battle (Washington, DC: Howard University Press, 1990), 60.

2. Stephen Enniss, "In the Author's Hand: Artifacts of Origin and Twentieth-Century Reading Practices," *RBM: A Journal of Rare Books, Manuscripts, and Cultural Heritage* 2 (Fall 2001): 112.

3. James F. English, *The Economy of Prestige: Prizes, Awards, and the Circulation of Cultural Value* (Cambridge, MA: Harvard University Press, 2008).

4. Melissa Barton, *Gather out of Star-Dust: A Harlem Renaissance Album* (New Haven, CN: Yale University Press, 2017), 6.

5. Jeremy Braddock, *Collecting as Modernist Practice* (Baltimore, MD: Johns Hopkins University Press, 2012).

6. Emily Bernard, *Carl Van Vechten and the Harlem Renaissance* (New Haven, CN: Yale University Press, 2012); Michele Birnbaum, *Race, Work, and Desire in American Literature, 1860–1930* (Cambridge: Cambridge University Press, 2003).

7. For an informative summary of Van Vechten's wide-ranging cultural work, see Kirsten MacLeod, "The 'Librarian's Dream-Prince': Carl Van Vechten and America's Modernist Cultural Archives Industry," *Libraries & the Cultural Record* 46, no. 4 (2011): 360–87.

8. For instance, Van Vechten spent years assisting Gertrude Stein, at her request, putting her papers in order. For more on Van Vechten as collector and archivist, see Emily Bernard, ed., *Remember Me to Harlem: The Letters of Langston Hughes and Carl Van Vechten, 1925–1964* (New York: Knopf, 2001); Birnbaum, *Race, Work, and Desire in American Literature*; Braddock, *Collecting as Modernist Practice*; and MacLeod, "The 'Librarian's Dream-Prince.'"

9. Arnold Rampersad, *The Life of Langston Hughes*, vol. 2: *1941–1967* (New York: Oxford University Press, 2002), 30. See also Bernard, *Remember Me to Harlem*.

10. Library of Congress, "Archibald MacLeish (1892–1982)," https://www.loc.gov/item /n80015459/archibald-macleish-1892-1982-2/.

11. Library of Congress, "Archibald MacLeish (1892–1982)."

12. Carl Van Vechten, "The J. W. Johnson Collection at Yale," *The Crisis*, July 1942, 222.

13. See "Booknotes," C-SPAN, April 20, 2001.

14. Bernard, *Carl Van Vechten*, 228, 254.

15. Bernard Knollenberg to Lillian G. Lewis, March 15, 1941, box 12, folder 1, CVV NYPL.

16. Knollenberg to Lewis, March 26, 1941, box 12, folder 1, CVV NYPL; see also Bernard, *Carl Van Vechten*, 255.

17. Quoted in Bernard, *Carl Van Vechten*, 257.

18. Morris Dickstein, "Carl Van Vechten and the Harlem Renaissance," *Times Literary Supplement*, May 4, 2012, http://www.morrisdickstein.com/articles/carl-van-vechten -and-the-harlem-renaissance/.

19. Porter's own papers are now at Yale, purchased at auction in 2012. For more on Dorothy Porter Wesley, see Thomas C. Battle, "Moorland-Spingarn Research Center, Howard University," *Library Quarterly: Information, Community, Policy* 58, no. 2 (April 1988): 143–51; Janet Sims-Wood, *Dorothy Porter Wesley at Howard University: Building a Legacy of Black History* (Stroud, UK: History Press, 2014); Kara Bledsoe, "What Dorothy Porter's Life Meant for Black Studies," *JSTOR Daily Newsletter*, August 22, 2018, https://daily.jstor.org/what-dorothy-porters-life-meant-for-black -studies/; Zita Cristina Nunes, "Cataloguing Black Knowledge: How Dorothy Porter Assembled and Organized a Premier Africana Research Collection," *Perspectives on History*, November 20, 2018, https://www.historians.org/publications-and -directories/perspectives-on-history/december-2018/cataloging-black-knowledge

-how-dorothy-porter-assembled-and-organized-a-premier-africana-research
-collection.

20. Quoted in Minnie Clayton, "Special Collections at the Atlanta University Center,"
in *Black Bibliophiles and Collectors*, ed. Sinnette, Coates, and Battle, 95.

21. Smith, "An Overview," 59.

22. Arturo A. Schomburg, "The Negro Digs Up His Past," *Survey Graphic*, March 1925,
670.

23. Smith, "An Overview," 59, 60.

24. Smith, "An Overview," 59.

25. Claude McKay to Carl Van Vechten, July 31, 1941, CVV NYPL; see also Bernard,
Carl Van Vechten, 270.

26. McKay to Van Vechten, October 26, 1941, box 12, folder 2, CVV NYPL; see also
Bernard, *Carl Van Vechten*, 271. McKay's mention of Slaughter piqued Van Vech-
ten's interest and led him to ask the collector for his duplicates, just as he had asked
Arthur Spingarn for his duplicates for the JWJ Collection. See Van Vechten to
Knollenberg, October 31, 1941, box 12, folder 2, CVV NYPL.

27. For more information on "Descent Into Harlem," the history of the "Amiable" typescript, and the McKay–Roth relationship, see the coda of this book as well as Jean-
Christophe Cloutier and Brent Hayes Edwards, "Introduction" and "A Note on the
Text," in Claude McKay, *Amiable with Big Teeth: A Novel of the Love Affair Between
the Communists and the Poor Black Sheep of Harlem*, ed. Jean-Christophe Cloutier
and Brent Hayes (New York: Penguin Classics, 2017), xiii–xlvi and li–liii.

28. McKay to Van Vechten, October 26, 1941.

29. McKay to Van Vechten, October 26, 1941.

30. Bernard, *Carl Van Vechten*, 271.

31. Finding aid for the Claude McKay Collection, Beinecke Rare Book and Manuscript
Library, Yale University, http://drs.library.yale.edu/HLTransformer/HLTransServ
let?stylename=yul.ead2002.xhtml.xsl&pid=beinecke:mckay&query=claude%20
mckay&clear-stylesheet-cache=yes&hlon=yes&filter=&hitPageStart=1. Aside
from the materials donated by Hope Virtue McKay, some materials were also donated
by Liliane Blary, Sister Mary Conroy, Wayne Cooper, and William Schenck. Yale's
McKay finding aid seems unsure about its own provenance history; it specifies that
McKay's original outgoing letters "*appear* to have come into the collection with the
original purchase in 1964" (my emphasis).

32. McKay to Van Vechten, September 11, 1941, box 12, folder 2, CVV NYPL.

33. Appraisal report of the McKay Collection, Walter Goldwater to Donald Gallup,
May 12, 1963, box 5, folder 7, CVV NYPL.

34. In a letter to Carl Van Vechten, Hope McKay Virtue wrote, "I shall be happy to
offer some worthwhile material when I receive my father's literary remains" (June 23,
1948, box 46, folder 866, CVVP).

35. Braddock, *Collecting as Modernist Practice*, 224. For a focalized consideration of Hughes's archival practices, see Birnbaum, *Race, Work, and Desire in American Literature*. For more on the assistants Yale provided Hughes, see Hughes's correspondence with Donald Gallup, boxes 2–5, CVV NYPL.

36. Birnbaum, *Race, Work, and Desire in American Literature*, 125.

37. Langston Hughes to Van Vechten, October 30, 1941; see also Bernard, *Carl Van Vechten*, 284.

38. Birnbaum, *Race, Work, and Desire in American Literature*, 125.

39. William J. Maxwell, *F.B. Eyes: How J. Edgar Hoover's Ghostreaders Framed African American Literature* (Princeton, NJ: Princeton University Press, 2015).

40. Bernard, *Carl Van Vechten*, 283–84.

41. Quoted in Braddock, *Collecting as Modernist Practice*, 224.

42. For more on the fire and DuVal's role in saving some of Hurston's manuscripts, see T. C. Palm, "Manuscripts of Fort Pierce's Zora Neale Hurston Almost Burned as Trash," *Palm Beach Post*, January 27, 2010, https://www.palmbeachpost.com/entertainment/manuscripts-fort-pierce-zora-neale-hurston-almost-burned-trash/1gyfCbBqATeHUodTufSFHI/. The Hurston collection was donated to the University of Florida in 1961 by her friend and neighbor Marjorie Silver. See the finding aid for the Zora Neale Hurston Collection, Smathers Libraries, University of Florida, at http://www.library.ufl.edu/spec/manuscript/hurston/hurston.htm.

43. Van Vechten to Langston Hughes, October 11, 1959, quoted in Birnbaum, *Race, Work, and Desire in American Literature*, 126; full letter in *Remember Me to Harlem*, ed. Bernard, 304.

44. Melissa Barton to Jean-Christophe Cloutier, email, February 19, 2017.

45. Arnold Rampersad, *Ralph Ellison: A Biography* (New York: Knopf, 2007), 182–83.

46. Hughes to Van Vechten, August 24, 1944, in *Remember Me to Harlem*, ed. Bernard, 230.

47. Van Vechten to Hughes, August 29, 1944, in *Remember Me to Harlem*, ed. Bernard, 231.

48. James Babb, copy of receipt sent to Van Vechten, May 2, 1944, box 13, folder 1, CVV NYPL.

49. Ellison quoted in Rampersad, *The Life of Langston Hughes*, 2:277.

50. Van Vechten to Hughes, September 4, 1952, in *Remember Me to Harlem*, ed. Bernard, 272, capitalization and emphasis in the original. *Invisible Man* was published in April 1952.

51. David Sutton, "The Destinies of Literary Manuscripts: Past, Present, and Future," *Archives & Manuscripts* 42, no. 3 (2014): 296.

52. Ellison, quoted in Rampersad, *Ralph Ellison*, 551.

53. For Grace Nail Johnson's reservations about Yale, see Van Vechten to James Babb, May 2, 1945, box 12, folder 2, CVV NYPL, and Bernard, *Carl Van Vechten*, 275.

54. Rampersad, *Ralph Ellison*, 555, 528.

55. Bart Auerbach, interview by Jean-Christophe Cloutier, New York City, July 23, 2018.

56. Rampersad, *Ralph Ellison*, 625, 528–29.

57. Charles Hobson, *Great Libraries* (London: Weidenfeld and Nicolson, 1970), 303.

58. Hobson, *Great Libraries*, 309.

59. "The Great Paper Chase," *Time*, April 6, 1962.

60. Hobson, *Great Libraries*, 307.

61. See Hobson, *Great Libraries*, 309.

62. "The Great Paper Chase."

63. My thanks to Bart Auerbach for providing the details on Lew David Feldman, the man who became Ransom's agent at auctions until the Humanities Research Funds ran out in the early 1970s.

64. Hobson, *Great Libraries*, 307.

65. Hobson, *Great Libraries*, 307.

66. Robert K. Elder, "Prestige Files: Hunter Thompson's Gonzo Archives Are Looking for a Home. Libraries, Line Up," *Chicago Tribune*, March 10, 2005.

67. "The Great Paper Chase."

68. Hobson, *Great Libraries*, 309.

69. Cyril Connolly, "The Egghead Shrinkers," *Sunday Times* (London), April 15, 1962.

70. Connolly, "The Egghead Shrinkers." Often thought to be wholly fictitious, Victor Galbraith was a Prussian émigré who enlisted in the U.S. Army in the 1840s and was unfairly executed. The circumstances of his death are recorded in Samuel Chamberlain, *My Confession* (1861; reprint, New York: Harper and Brothers, 1956), 224–25. Chamberlain's book inspired Cormac McCarthy's novel *Blood Meridian*.

71. Quoted in Elder, "Prestige Files."

72. Elder, "Prestige Files."

73. See Ron Mexico, "Johnny Depp Purchases Hunter S. Thompson Archive," *Totally Gonzo*, July 28, 2008, https://totallygonzo.org/2008/07/28/johnny-depp-purchases -hunter-s-thompson-archive/.

74. The papers of some white women have also fetched hefty sums; most recently, a few items from the Sylvia Plath and Ted Hughes estates were sold at auction at Bonhams in London. See John Dugdale, "Is Sylvia Plath's Driver's License Worth More Than a Letter from Dickens?" *Guardian*, March 22, 2018.

75. See Hope McKay Virtue to Van Vechten, ca. 1948–1949, box 46, folder 866, CVVP.

76. McKay Virtue to Van Vechten, ca. 1948–1949.

77. Large collections of black authors' materials, in contrast to smaller personal records, were purchased earlier—including Arturo Schomburg's collection sold to the NYPL in 1926 and Arthur Spingarn's private collection sold to Howard University in 1946. The convoluted appraisal history of the Spingarn Library is a fascinating example of how ill equipped most white repositories were in ascribing a monetary value to

black materials in this period. Dorothy Porter, in charge of the Spingarn acquisition, was instrumental in finding a solution for the collection's appraisal and for years
was often called upon to perform appraisals. See Dorothy Porter Oral History, Oral
History Collection, Moorland-Spingarn Research Center, Howard University, and
Nunes, "Cataloguing Black Knowledge."

78. Goldwater to Gallup, May 12, 1963.
79. Gallup to Van Vechten, June 27, 1963, box 5, folder 7, and appraisal report, Goldwater to Gallup, May 12, 1963. See also boxes 1–4, UPBS.
80. Appraisal report, Goldwater to Gallup, May 12, 1963.
81. Gallup to Van Vechten, June 18, 1963, box 5, folder 7, CVV NYPL, and Goldwater
to Gallup, May 12, 1963.
82. Gallup to Van Vechten, June 27, 1963.
83. Appraisal report for the Lester A. Walton Collection, Goldwater to the Schomburg Collection of the NYPL, March 28, 1979, UPBS. Goldwater was also a chess
enthusiast and an expert in incunabula (see his contribution to *Rare Book Tapes* [New
York: Antiquarian Booksellers Center, 1978] and radical leftist publications (see
Walter Goldwater, *Radical Periodicals in America, 1890–1950* [New Haven, CN: Yale
University Library, 1964]).
84. Biographical note on Walter Goldwater, undated, box 3, UPBS.
85. Goldwater to Fred McRae, November 27, 1978, box 3, UPBS.
86. Flagg Kris, acquisitions librarian at Howard University, to Goldwater, December 11,
1973, box 1, folder 10, UPBS.
87. Robert Darnton, "What Is the History of Books?" *Daedalus* 111, no. 3 (Summer 1982):
65–83, passim.
88. Photocopied page from *Africa Guide*, ca. 1968, box 1, folder 2, UPBS.
89. Goldwater to John Smith, University of California, Irvine, December 10, 1974, box 2,
folder 6, UPBS.
90. Robert Hill, "On Collectors, Their Contributions to the Documentation of the
Black Past," in *Black Bibliophiles*, ed. Sinnette, Coates, and Battle, 54, 52, 54.
91. Hill, "On Collectors," 51.
92. The finding aid for the Countee Cullen Collection notes that the collection was
reprocessed in 2009 "to include a 1986 addendum." As a result, "the collection was
reorganized into series and material postdating Cullen's life and collected by Ida
Cullen Cooper was transferred to the Ida Cullen Cooper papers" (http://amistadre
searchcenter.tulane.edu/archon/?p=collections/controlcard&id=41).
93. In March 2018, Holly Snyder, curator of American Historical Collections and the
History of Science at Brown University, was kind enough to send me the university's
"preliminary finding aid" for the Redding Papers. This unfinished document makes
clear that the processing is dependent on intermittent funding from the administration and donors.

94. Hill, "On Collectors," 55.

95. The JWJ Collection is also sometimes called the James Weldon Johnson Memorial Collection. This naming discrepancy actually reflects how Yale names the collection. See "About the James Weldon Johnson Memorial Collection," n.d., https:// jwj.yale.edu/about-james-weldon-johnson-memorial-collection.

96. See "Processing Notes" in the finding aid for the James Weldon Johnson and Grace Nail Johnson Papers, Beinecke Rare Book and Manuscript Library, Yale University, at http://drs.library.yale.edu/HLTransformer/HLTransServlet?stylename=yul .ead2002.xhtml.xsl&pid=beinecke:jwj&clear-stylesheet-cache=yes#ai.

97. The original finding aid for the Richard Wright Papers consists of photocopies of cards listing manuscripts and correspondence. The sequence of numbers used in this catalog was the one used by Michel Fabre in his bibliography and biography of Richard Wright, *The Unfinished Quest of Richard Wright* (New York: William Morrow, 1973).

98. See Alan McLeod/Claude McKay Research Collections, MS Sc MG750, Schomburg Center for Research in Black Culture, NYPL.

99. Thanks to a privileged relationship with Wright's widow, Ellen—both Constance Webb and Ellen were white women who had married radical black intellectuals— Constance Webb was given access to materials that no one else would have been able to see at the time ("I had access to all of Wright's letters and unpublished manuscripts, which are considerable," she wrote). Constance visited Wright's final workspace in Paris, which "had been kept in its original state by the new owners and the maps he'd pasted on the walls were still clinging with just a slight yellowing of their colors" (no title, no date, Constance Webb Papers, box 6, folder 9, Rare Book and Manuscript Library, Columbia University, New York). Consultation of and access to papers while they are still in private hands is another example of how literary papers can make their way into public knowledge prior to institutionalization.

100. Horace Cayton to Constance Pearlstein Webb, May 23, 1969, box 4, folder 15, Constance Webb Papers.

101. David Bradley, *The Chaneysville Incident* (New York: Harper and Row, 1981), 129–30.

102. Mapping the Stacks website, http://mts.lib.uchicago.edu/.

103. See the finding aid for the Frederick Douglass Papers, Library of Congress, at http://findingaids.loc.gov/db/search/xq/searchMfer02.xq?_id=loc.mss.eadmss .ms000009&_faSection=usingThisCollection&_faSubsection=usingThisCollecti on&_dmdid=d15023e14.

104. Information regarding the existence and location of a possible Siefert collection was obtained through the efforts made by Robert Hill, Brent Hayes Edwards, Diana Lachatanere, Susan Pevar, and Laura Helton.

105. See Catherine Hobbs, "The Character of Personal Archives: Reflections on the Value of Records of Individuals," *Archivaria* 52 (Fall 2001): 126–35.

106. Sam Lim-Kimberg and Sebastian Mazza, "Black Radicalism and the Politics of Writing: Lessons from the Archive: An Interview with Brent Hayes Edwards," *Columbia Journal of Literary Criticism*, Spring 2018, http://c-j-l-c.org/portfolio/black -radicalism-50-and-the-politics-of-writing-lessons-from-the-archive-an-interview -with-brent-hayes-edwards/.

107. Lim-Kimberg and Mazza, "Black Radicalism and the Politics of Writing."

108. Jennifer Douglas, "What We Talk About When We Talk About Original Order in Writers' Archives," *Archivaria* 76 (Fall 2013): 10, 25, 13, 12 14, 15, 22.

109. See Terry Cook, "The Concept of the Archival Fonds in the Post-custodial Era," *Archivaria* 35 (Spring 1993): 24–37.

110. McKay to Catherine Latimer, February 19, 1941, box 1, folder 2, General Correspondence, N–Z, Schomburg Center for Research in Black Culture, NYPL.

111. McKay to Van Vechten, September 11, 1941, box 12, folder 2, CVV NYPL.

112. McKay to Carl Cowl, July 28, 1947, box 2, folder 44, CMC.

113. A rather elaborate example is Norman Mailer, who hired a growing cadre of typists and secretaries as early as 1955 to help organize his swelling archive. See the administrative information on the finding aid for the Normal Mailer Papers, Harry Ransom Research Center, University of Texas at Austin, http://norman.hrc.utexas .edu/fasearch/findingAid.cfm?eadid=00480/.

114. Finding aid for the Lorraine Hansberry Papers, Sc MG 680, Schomburg Center for Research in Black Culture, NYPL.

115. Finding aid for the Langston Hughes Papers, Beinecke Rare Book and Manuscript Library, Yale University, https://archives.yale.edu/repositories/11/resources /969.

116. See "Processing Notes" in the finding aid for the Langston Hughes Papers, https:// archives.yale.edu/repositories/11/resources/969.

117. "Processing Notes," Langston Hughes Papers. Another collection, the Chester Himes Papers at the Amistad Research Center, which were acquired as a gift from his wife, E. M. Lesley Himes, underwent a similar extraction of records.

118. Phillip N. Cronenwett, "Appraisal of Literary Manuscripts," in *Archival Choices: Managing the Historical Record in an Age of Abundance*, ed. Nancy E. Peace (Lexington, MA: Lexington Books, 1984), 105, 107.

119. David C. Sutton, "Diasporic Literary Archives: Questions of Location, Ownership, and Interpretation," keynote address, Silences of Archives conference, Helsinki, November 6, 2014, and Sutton, "The Destinies of Literary Manuscripts."

120. Cronenwett, "Appraisal of Literary Manuscripts," 106.

121. Cronenwett, "Appraisal of Literary Manuscripts," 105. Michael Forstrom at the Beinecke Library has also compiled a list of fourteen various ways in which literary

collections have been "split" (cited in Sutton, "The Destinies of Literary Manuscripts," 296).

122. Cronenwett, "Appraisal of Literary Manuscripts," 105.

123. Quoted in Elder, "Prestige Files."

124. In some cases, allowing for the sale of a unique item at auction allows a repository to afford the price of the rest of the collection, as was the case for the Jack Kerouac Papers—by selling the *On the Road* scroll to a private collector for $2.43 million, the NYPL could purchase the rest of the collection and assure that it would be kept in the same location.

125. Stephen Enniss, quoted in Jennifer Schuessler, "Inside the Battle for Arthur Miller's Archive," *New York Times*, January 9, 2018.

126. Michael Ondaatje Collection, Library and Archives Canada, https://www .collectionscanada.gc.ca/literaryarchives/027011-200.097-e.html . See also the press release issued by the Harry Ransom Center regarding its acquisition of the Ondaatje materials, http://www.hrc.utexas.edu/press/releases/2017/ondaatje.html.

127. Quoted in Chris Branch, "Do Toni Morrison's Papers Belong at Princeton or Howard?" *Huffington Post*, October 23, 2014, https://www.huffingtonpost.ca/entry/toni -morrison-papers-princeton-howard_n_6035026.

128. See J. Morgan, "bell hooks Archive Finds a Home at Berea College," *Berea College Magazine*, June 2017, https://www.berea.edu/magazine/article/bell-hooks-archive -finds-home-berea-college/.

129. As the *New York Times* put it in its obituary of the Boston University archivist, Howard Gotlieb "cajoled, charmed, wheedled and . . . groveled to snare the papers of notables like the Rev. Dr. Martin Luther King Jr. and Bette Davis, not to mention Fred Astaire's dancing shoes" (Douglas Martin, "Howard Gotlieb, an Archivist with Persistence, Dies at 79," *New York Times*, December 5, 2005). For more on Charles Abbott's establishment of the Poetry Collection at Buffalo, see Braddock, *Collecting as Modernist Practice*, 209–28.

130. Cronenwett, "Appraisal of Literary Manuscripts," 106.

131. Cronenwett, "Appraisal of Literary Manuscripts," 106.

132. Ammiel Alcalay, *a little history* (Los Angeles: UpSet Press, 2013), 8–9. For a stark portrait of how the same author's papers can be split into many different locations and repositories, see the information compiled by Peter K. Steinberg on Sylvia Plath, which lists more than forty-four collections, at http://www.sylviaplath.info/collec tions.html.

133. Alcalay, *a little history*, 8–9.

134. Cronenwett, "Appraisal of Literary Manuscripts," 112.

135. See Rachel Sagner Buurma and Laura Heffernan, "The Classroom in the Canon: T. S. Eliot's Modern English Literature Extension Course for Working People and *The Sacred Wood*," *PMLA* 133, no. 2 (March 2018): 264–81.

136. Cronenwett, "Appraisal of Literary Manuscripts," 109.

137. Sutton, "Diasporic Literary Archives."

138. Mark A. Greene and Dennis Meissner, "More Product, Less Process: Revamping Traditional Archival Processing," *American Archivist* 68 (Fall–Winter 2005): 208–63.

139. Alcalay, *a little history*, 9.

140. Alcalay, *a little history*, 9.

141. All information and quotes related to the story of the Toomer Collection are, unless otherwise noted, from District Judge Higgins, "Memorandum," in *Yale University v. Fisk University*, No. 82-3158, U.S. District Court, M.D., Tennessee, Nashville Division, October 1, 1985, https://www.leagle.com/decision/198567666 ofsupp161672.

142. The Amistad Research Center has been at the Tulane University campus in New Orleans since 1987. For more on the Amistad's peripatetic journey, see https://www .amistadresearchcenter.org/about.

143. See the finding aid for the Jean Toomer Papers, Beinecke Rare Book and Manuscript Library, Yale University, http://drs.library.yale.edu/HLTransformer /HLTransServlet?stylename=yul.ead2002.xhtml.xsl&pid=beinecke:toomer& clear-stylesheet-cache=yes.

144. For more on the reasons listed for the transfer of the Toomer Papers from Fisk to Yale, see *Yale University v. Fiske University*.

145. Quoted in D. T. Max, "Final Destination: Why Do the Archives of so Many Great Writers End Up in Texas?" *New Yorker*, June 11, 2007.

146. In a similar story, the Harold Cruse Papers were first given to Virginia Commonwealth in 1994; the agreement was then voided the following year, and the materials returned to the estate. In 1996, the Cruse Papers were donated to the Tamiment Library at New York University, where they were processed seven years later, in 2003.

147. See "Explanatory Note Concerning Manuscript Collections Cataloged in the Card Catalog," appended to all of the Harry Ransom Center collections acquired before 1990. An example from its Baldwin collection can be found at http://norman.hrc .utexas.edu/fasearch/findingAid.cfm?eadid=00551.

148. "Processing Notes" section of the finding aid for the Bruce Nugent Papers, Beinecke Rare Book and Manuscript Library, Yale University, http://drs.library .yale.edu/HLTransformer/HLTransServlet?stylename=yul.ead2002.xhtml.xsl &pid=beinecke:nugent&query=bruce%2onugent&clear-stylesheet-cache=yes& hlon=yes&filter=&hitPageStart=1#ai, and, with a slight variation, for the Lisbeth Tellefsen Papers, http://drs.library.yale.edu/HLTransformer/HLTrans Servlet?stylename=yul.ead2002.xhtml.xsl&pid=beinecke:tellefsen&clear-style sheet-cache=yes.

2. CLAUDE MCKAY'S ARCHIVAL REBIRTH: PROVENANCE AND POLITICS IN *AMIABLE WITH BIG TEETH*

In the letter quoted in the chapter epigraph, Max Eastman was writing about McKay's progress on his manuscript "God's Black Sheep," a novel unknown to the public until 2009 (see "A Note on the Text," in Claude McKay, *Amiable with Big Teeth: A Novel of the Love Affair Between the Communists and the Poor Black Sheep of Harlem*, ed. Jean-Christophe Cloutier and Brent Hayes Edwards [New York: Penguin Classics, 2017], li–liii).

1. Quoted in Frank Budgen, *James Joyce and the Making of Ulysses* (London: Oxford University Press, 1972), 69.

2. Claude McKay, *A Long Way from Home* (1937; reprint, New Brunswick, NJ: Rutgers University Press, 2007), 190, hereafter *ALWFH*. Claude McKay to Max Eastman, April 25, 1932, in *The Passion of Claude McKay: Selected Poetry and Prose, 1912–1948*, ed. Wayne F. Cooper (New York: Schocken Books, 1973), 151, hereafter *PCM*.

3. Wayne F. Cooper, *Claude McKay: Rebel Sojourner in the Harlem Renaissance, a Biography* (Baton Rouge: Louisiana State University Press, 1987), 255. See also Brent Hayes Edwards, *The Practice of Diaspora: Literature, Translation, and the Rise of Black Internationalism* (Cambridge, MA: Harvard University Press, 2003), 189.

4. For the implications of the connection between McKay's "plotlessness" and the practice of diaspora, see Edwards, *Practice of Diaspora*.

5. Marilyn Booth uses these terms to explain the agenda behind Zaynab Fawwaz's nineteenth-century historical fiction in her essay "Fiction's Imaginative Archive and the Newspaper's Local Scandals: The Case of Nineteenth-Century Egypt," in *Archive Stories: Facts, Fictions, and the Writing of History*, ed. Antoinette Burton (Durham, NC: Duke University Press, 2005), 275, 277.

6. Ann Laura Stoler, *Along the Archival Grain: Epistemic Anxieties and Colonial Common Sense* (Princeton, NJ: Princeton University Press, 2010), 1.

7. *Negroes of New York (an Informal Social History)*, chapter 9, "I, too, Sing America," Reel 4, WPN.

8. William J. Maxwell, *F.B. Eyes: How J. Edgar Hoover's Ghostreaders Framed African American Literature* (Princeton, NJ: Princeton University Press, 2015), 207.

9. Maxwell, *F.B. Eyes*, 207.

10. See "Ways and Means Committee for a New Negro Magazine," CMC.

11. Alain Locke, "Spiritual Truant," *New Challenge* 2 (Fall 1937): 84.

12. William J. Maxwell, *New Negro, Old Left: African-American Writing and Communism Between the Wars* (New York: Columbia University Press, 1999), 3.

13. McKay, *ALWFH*, 267.

14. Cooper, *Claude McKay*, 306.

15. Cooper, *Claude McKay*, 306.
16. Ronald R. Thomas, *Detective Fiction and the Rise of Forensic Science* (Cambridge: Cambridge University Press, 1999), 4.
17. Edwards, *Practice of Diaspora*, 3.
18. Lawrence P. Jackson, *The Indignant Generation: A Narrative History of African American Writers and Critics, 1934–1960* (Princeton, NJ: Princeton University Press, 2011), 18. Jackson's informative treatise traces African American writing following the "formal end of the Renaissance" as a continuous evolution, not as a radical break. The works of Sterling Brown, Gerald Early, and Brent Edwards, among others, have also stressed this approach.
19. From "For a Negro Magazine," CMPA, in McKay, *PCM*, 202, full capitals in the original. This text was circulated in the summer of 1934.
20. Claude McKay to Edwin R. Embree, April 30, 1935, Julius Rosenwald Fund Archives (microfilm), Amistad Research Center, Tulane University, New Orleans, quoted in Cooper, *Claude McKay*, 307.
21. Claude McKay, "Plan of Work," September 9, 1937, box 4, folder 115, CMC.
22. McKay to Lewis Gannet, September 18, 1937, Lewis Gannett Papers, MS Am 1888–Am 1888.4, Houghton Library, Harvard University, Cambridge, MA.
23. Scholars have suggested that *Harlem Glory*, an incomplete novel published posthumously in 1990, was written while McKay was doing the research for *Harlem: Negro Metropolis* because it contains thinly veiled portraits of Father Divine and Sufi Abdul Hamid, both of whom feature prominently in *Harlem: Negro Metropolis*. However, letters in McKay's papers to his agent at the time, Laurence Roberts, attest that *Harlem Glory* was written in or around 1936–1937.
24. McKay to Embree, April 30, 1935.
25. Cooper, *Claude McKay*, 317.
26. McKay, *ALWFH*, 85 (see also 111). Kenneth W. Warren also touches on this point in *What Was African American Literature* (Cambridge, MA: Harvard University Press, 2012).
27. Gold was first published in *The New Masses*, penning an article referring to Gertrude Stein as "a literary idiot" and another calling Marcel Proust the "master-masturbator of the bourgeois literature." For the Stein comment, see Mike Gold, "Gertrude Stein: A Literary Idiot," in *Change the World!* (New York: International Publishers, 1936), 29; for the Proust comment, see Mike Gold, "Proletarian Realism," in *Mike Gold: A Literary Anthology*, ed. Michael Folsom (New York: International Publishers, 1972), 206.
28. McKay, *ALWFH*, 111, emphasis in original.
29. McKay to Max Eastman, March 29, 1941, Max Eastman Mss. 1892–1968, Lilly Library Manuscript Collections, Indiana University, Bloomington.
30. McKay to John Macrae, August 8, 1941, Max Eastman Mss. II, Addition 1, Lilly Library Manuscript Collections. Thanks to Christoph Irmscher for drawing my

attention to this letter and to the other correspondence in this addition to the East-man collection made in 2017.

31. Claude McKay, Notebook, box 11, folder 338, CMC. For the "Miscellaneous" folder, see box 17, CMC. For McKay's "Subject Files" series, see the CMC finding aid, http://drs.library.yale.edu/HLTransformer/HLTransServlet?stylename=yul.ead2002.xhtml.xsl&pid=beinecke:mckay&query=claude%20mckay&clear-stylesheet-cache=yes&hlon=yes&filter=&hitPageStart=1.

32. McKay, *ALWFH*, 270.

33. "McKay Says Schuyler Is Writing Nonsense," *New York Amsterdam News*, November 20, 1937, in McKay, *PCM*, 256.

34. Claude McKay, "Where the News Ends," *New Leader*, June 10, 1939, in McKay, *PCM*, 231.

35. Arturo A. Schomburg, "The Negro Digs Up His Past," *Survey Graphic*, March 1925.

36. McKay, "Where the News Ends," in *PCM*, 231–32.

37. Late in life, relocated in Chicago, McKay abandoned notions of writing about con-temporary events. In response, intellectuals in New York said he was "a coward to turn [his] back on politics." Hearing these accusations, McKay told Eastman: "Really it is silly for I have never been a political writer; I never claimed to be one" (McKay to Eastman, August 28, 1946, in McKay, *PCM*, 310–12). Despite McKay's ongoing belief in his apolitical output, his articles from the late 1930s as well as both *Harlem: Negro Metropolis* and *Amiable* are the works of a highly politicized if not political writer.

38. McKay, "Where the News Ends," in *PCM*, 232.

39. Claude McKay, *Harlem: Negro Metropolis* (1940; reprint, New York: Harvest, 1968), 216, hereafter *HNM*.

40. McKay, *ALWFH*, 184.

41. McKay to A. Schomburg, August 20, 1935, quoted in Cooper, *Claude McKay*, 313. In *HNM*, McKay included a photograph of the Schomburg Collection reading room by Martin Smith and Marvin Smith.

42. McKay to Orrick Johns, September 11, 1936, quoted in Cooper, *Claude McKay*, 314.

43. McKay, *HNM*, 240.

44. Claude McKay, "Labor Steps Out In Harlem," *The Nation* 145 (October 16, 1937): 399–402, in McKay, *PCM*, 243–49.

45. "Claude McKay Versus Powell," *New York Amsterdam News*, November 6, 1937, in McKay, *PCM*, 250.

46. "McKay Says Schuyler Is Writing Nonsense," in McKay, *PCM*, 253, 255, 257. Schuyler and McKay had apparently reconciled by 1940 because McKay names Schuyler one of the "excellent types" of black Harlem intellectuals (McKay, *HNM*, 218).

47. McKay, *HNM*, 199. See also page 203, where he explains visiting the Sufi's offices "to get some facts."

48. See, for example, McKay's letter to Catherine Latimer about librarians and the history of the Schomburg Collection, June 24, 1940, box 1, folder 3, "Reference Correspondence, 1928–1948, A–W," Schomburg Center Records, Schomburg Center for Research in Black Culture, NYPL. Another good example is his letter to Judge James S. Watson about Harlem political elections, May 2, 1940, box 12, folder 9, "Claude McKay, 1938, 1940, 1942, n.d." James S. Watson Papers, Schomburg Center for Research in Black Culture.

49. Zora Neale Hurston, "Review of *Harlem: Negro Metropolis*," *Common Ground*, 1 (Winter 1941): 95–96; Grace Nail Johnson to McKay, October 22, 1940, box 4, folder 121, CMC.

50. A. Phillip Randolph to McKay, April 4, 1941, box 6, folder 173, CMC.

51. John Dewey to McKay, November 29, 1940, box 2, folder 61, CMC.

52. See McKay to Archibald MacLeish, December 18, 1941, box 5, folder 144, CMC. By 1945, McKay was also compiling reports for Reverend Bernard J. Sheil that consisted of transcribed articles on different topics such as politics, the "minority problem," labor, religion, and "the Negro." Two of these reports are in box 9, CMC.

53. McKay to Simon Williamson, May 29, 1941, box 1, folder 2, CMPA.

54. McKay, *HNM*, vii.

55. See the WPN collection.

56. The Negro Writers' Guild was to include an "Aframerican Book of the Month Club," along with a "catalogue" of recommended books by black authors. See McKay to James Weldon Johnson, January 9, 1937, box 13, folder 309, James Weldon Johnson and Grace Nail Johnson Papers, Collection of American Literature, Beinecke Rare Book and Manuscript Library, Yale University.

57. Claude McKay, "Circular Letter for the Creation of a Negro Writers' Guild," October 23, 1937, box 4, folder 108, CMC, in McKay, *PCM*, 233–34, my italics.

58. Countee Cullen to McKay, July 24, 1938, box 2, folder 53, CMC. For a compelling look into *The African* journal, see Hillina Seife, "A New Generation of Ethiopianists: The Universal Ethiopian Students Association and *The African: Journal of African Affairs*, 1937–1948," *African and Black Diaspora: An International Journal* 3, no. 2 (2010): 197–209.

59. McKay to Embree, November 16, 1940, Julius Rosenwald Fund Archives (microfilm).

60. Cooper, *Claude McKay*, 325.

61. McKay to James Weldon Johnson, April 1935, quoted in Cooper, *Claude McKay*, 325.

62. McKay, *ALWFH*, 213.

63. Cooper, *Claude McKay*, 319.

64. McKay, *ALWFH*, 269–70.

65. As Lawrence Jackson explains, "Wright hoped to see McKay's body of work over-turned. He desired a complete repudiation of the Harlem Renaissance" and privately asked Locke to review McKay's autobiography (*The Indignant Generation*, 75).

66. Locke, "Spiritual Truant," 84. See also Cooper, *Claude McKay*, 319–20.

67. James Weldon Johnson to McKay, March 26, 1937, box 13, folder 309, James Weldon Johnson and Grace Nail Johnson Papers.

68. McKay to James Weldon Johnson, April 1935, quoted in Cooper, *Claude McKay*, 326; see also McKay, *HNM*, 221.

69. Cooper, *Claude McKay*, 323; McKay to Helen Boardman, July 18, 1937, box 1, folder 12, CMC. In a wonderful parallel fictionalized scene from *Amiable*, Pablo Peixota ridicules the idea, proposed by Prudhomme Bishop, that there should be at least one white person in every colored organization and suggests the reverse instead: "Your campaign might be of greater national significance and symbolic effect, if you made it a campaign to put a colored person in every white institution. You might take the Government first" (59–60).

70. Cooper, *Claude McKay*, 323.

71. McKay to Helen Boardman, July 18, 1937, box 1, folder 12, CMC. See also McKay, *HNM*, 246–49.

72. Boardman to McKay, September 4, 1937, box 1, folder 12, CMC, quoted in Cooper, *Claude McKay*, 327.

73. McKay, *ALWFH*, 267–68.

74. McKay, *ALWFH*, 267.

75. McKay, *Amiable*, 269.

76. Edwards, *Practice of Diaspora*, 7.

77. McKay, *ALWFH*, 263.

78. This section's title is from Eastman to McKay, April 20, 1941, box 3, folder 69, CMC.

79. McKay, *Amiable*, 28, subsequently cited parenthetically by page number in text; ellipses indicate omission of text unless otherwise noted.

80. When *Amiable* appeared in print in 2017, many of the reviews of the novel stressed this particular point. See, for instance, Jennifer Wilson, "A Forgotten Novel Reveals a Forgotten Harlem," *Atlantic*, March 9, 2017; Sarah Begley, "A Found Novel of Harlem Works as a Time Capsule," *Time*, February 2, 2017; Steve Nathans-Kelly, "Claude McKay's *Amiable with Big Teeth*: How a Hidden Manuscript's Discovery Brings 1930s Harlem to Life," *PASTE Magazine*, February 10, 2017; Ross Barkan, "Claude McKay's Long-Lost Novel Brings the Harlem Renaissance to Life," *Village Voice*, March 22, 2017.

81. See David Shaftel, "The Black Eagle of Harlem: The Truth Behind the Tall Tales of Hubert Fauntleroy Julian," *Air and Space Magazine*, January 1, 2009.

82. McKay also mentions the Lindy Hop in *HNM*, 21–22.

83. Julian is featured among the many "portraits" gathered by the writers of the Federal Writers' Project in the WPN collection.

84. Aarthi Vadde, "National Myth, Transnational Memory: Ondaatje's Archival Method," *Novel: A Forum on Fiction* 45, no. 2 (Summer 2012): 273.

85. William Solomon, *Slapstick Modernism: Chaplin to Kerouac to Iggy Pop* (Champaign: University of Illinois Press, 2016).

86. Claude McKay, "For Group Survival," *Jewish Frontier* 4 (October 1937): 19–26, in McKay, *PCM* 234–39.

87. See McKay, *HNM*, 226.

88. In *HNM*, McKay conjures a Harlem of 1920 "blink[ing] at the sizzling splendor" of Marcus Garvey's "wonderful parade," describing Garvey as wearing "a magnificent uniform of purple, green, black, and a plume hat. He stood in the car and saluted the cheering crowds that jammed the sidewalks" (155).

89. McKay to Langston Hughes, April 30, 1927, Langston Hughes Papers, James Weldon Johnson Collection, Collection of American Literature, Beinecke Rare Book and Manuscript Library.

90. McKay freely used the abbreviation C.P.T., "Colored People's Time"— for example, in a note to Carl Van Vechten sent around the time he was completing the "Amiable" typescript: "I shall be at your place on Friday at 4, but you must make allowance for C.P.T. in case" (July 24, 1941, box LO–MJ, folder "McKay, Claude," CMC).

91. McKay, *HNM*, 176.

92. McKay, "For Group Survival."

93. McKay, *HNM*, 217.

94. The Interlink emphasizes the international networks at play within the novel and positions Harlem as a hub. See McKay, *Amiable*, 169.

95. See Claude McKay, "Negro Author Sees Disaster If the Communist Party Gains Control of Negro Workers," *New Leader*, September 10, 1938, in McKay, *PCM*, 228–29.

96. Claude McKay, "Everybody's Doing It: Anti-Semitic Propaganda Fails to Attract Negroes," *New Leader*, May 20, 1939. For more on the links between Tasan and "Communist hyenas," see Jean-Christophe Cloutier and Brent Hayes Edwards, introduction to McKay, *Amiable*, xxvii.

97. Sadie Hall and Larry Jordan, "Chappy Gardner," reel 1, WPN.

98. See box 15, folder 454, CMC.

99. See reels 1 and 2, WPN. The humorous headlines from July 1935 deteriorate steadily from positive portrayals to "Princess Is Disavowed: Ethiopian Foreign Minister Says Woman Here Is Imposter" and "Finds Princess Is a Maid—with a Press Agent." Even though "Princess Tamanya," whose real name was Mrs. Iselyn Harvey, was ousted as a fraud, she nevertheless went on tour, giving concerts across the country

between 1935 and 1940, just as Alamaya in *Amiable* "becomes the manager of Princess Benebe" (286).

100. McKay, *HNM*, 221.

101. For more details on some of the historical antecedents of Lij Alamaya and other characters, see Cloutier and Edwards, introduction to McKay, *Amiable*, xvii–xxiii.

102. William R. Scott, "Malaku E. Bayen: Ethiopian Emissary to Black America, 1936–1941," *Ethiopia Observer* 15, no. 2 (1972): 5.

103. McKay, *HNM*, 176; photograph, 113.

104. See the card that the Communist Party produced to attack Willis Huggins and his efforts in the Aid to Ethiopia campaign, describing his work as "fascist activities," reproduced in McKay, *HNM*, 189. As McKay writes there, "Hundreds of these cards were mailed to the Board of Education" (189).

105. Williamson to McKay, March 16, 1941, box 1, folder 2, CMPA.

106. "Charles Seifert, Collector and Teacher of Black History," n.d., https://aaregistry .org/story/charles-seifert-collector-and-teacher-of-black-history/.

107. Robert Hill, "On Collectors, Their Contributions to the Documentation of the Black Past," in *Black Bibliophiles and Collectors: Preservers of Black History*, ed. Elinor Des Verney Sinnette, W. Paul Coates, and Thomas C. Battle (Washington, DC: Howard University Press, 1990), 47.

108. Hill, "On Collectors," 47.

109. Elmer Wendell Dean, dedication in *An Elephant Lives in Harlem* (New York: Ethiopic Press, n.d.), 1. In "Labor Steps Out in Harlem," McKay also used the expression "an elephant in Harlem," but in reference to Sufi Abdul Hamid.

110. McKay to Eastman, August 24, 1934, in McKay, *PCM*, 199. See also Cooper, *Claude McKay*, 297.

111. Sufi Abdul Hamid—born Eugene Brown—was a labor organizer. He was profiled through the Federal Writers' Project, and McKay wrote of him often and fondly in his articles in the 1930s and 1940s, as well as dedicating the final chapter of *HNM* to him, 181–262.

112. McKay, *HNM*, 102. Casper Holstein, whom McKay thanks in the acknowledgments to *HNM*, was also involved in a fascinating kidnapping case carefully recounted in *HNM* (102–5). Holstein is also the likely inspiration behind the character Oscar Holcombe in George Schuyler's story "The Ethiopian Murder Mystery," *Ethiopian Stories*, ed. Robert A. Hill (Boston: Northeastern University Press, 1994), 51–122.

113. McKay, *HNM*, 102.

114. See McKay, *HNM*, 104.

115. McKay, *HNM*, 114–15.

116. Cooper, *Claude McKay*, 131.

117. "Claude McKay Versus Powell."

118. "Claude McKay Versus Powell."

119. Cooper, *Claude McKay*, 306.

120. As part of his work for the Federal Writers' Project, McKay did extensive research for a report titled "Negro Artists in New York," in which he personally profiled the following artists: William Ernest Braxton, Melvin Gray Johnson, Albert Alexander Smith, Charles H. Alston, Henry W. Bannarn, Richmond Barthé, Sara Murrell, Romare Bearden, E. Simms Campbell, Aaron Douglas, Beauford Delaney, Richard Bruce Nugent, Robert Savon Pious, Earle Wilton Richardson, and Augusta Savage. See reel 1, WPN. McKay also lived in the same building at 33 W. 125th Street in Harlem as Romare Bearden and Jacob Lawrence in the late 1930s.

121. For an in-depth study of the relation between the rise of international fascism and twentieth-century African American literature, see Vaughn Rasberry, *Race and the Totalitarian Century: Geopolitics in the Black Literary Imagination* (Cambridge, MA: Harvard University Press, 2016). Rasberry notably takes a multifaceted approach to understanding the "love affair" between African Americans and communism.

122. Tyrone Tillery, *Claude McKay: A Black Poet's Struggle for Identity* (Amherst: University of Massachusetts Press, 1992), 87.

123. Claude McKay, "Group Life and Literature," ca. 1939, box 8, folder 287, CMC. McKay's examples of such writers are Du Bois and Walter White, and he added (by hand on his typed essay) that "a recent startling phenomenon is Richard Wright's picture of Uncle Tom's Children."

124. All quotes in this paragraph are from McKay, "Group Life and Literature."

125. McKay, "Group Life and Literature."

126. See Jeremy Braddock, "Media Studies 1932: Nancy Cunard in the Archive of Claude McKay," *Modernism/modernity* 3, cycle 2 (May 30, 2018), https://doi.org/10 .26597/mod.0050.

127. McKay, "Group Life and Literature."

128. McKay to Macrae, August 8, 1941.

129. McKay to Eastman, August 6, 1941.

130. Quoted in McKay, *ALWFH*, 196.

131. "Claude McKay Replies to Poston on Solution of Negro Problems," *New Leader*, December 7, 1940, in McKay, *PCM*, 261–64.

132. Booth, "Fiction's Imaginative Archive," 275.

133. Booth, "Fiction's Imaginative Archive," 275.

134. McKay to Edwin Embree, November 10, 1940, Julius Rosenwald Fund Archives (microfilm).

135. Saidiya V. Hartman, "Venus in Two Acts," *Small Axe* 12, no. 2 (2008): 14.

136. Claude McKay, notebook, box 11, folder 338, CMC.

137. Laura Winkiel, *Modernism, Race, and Manifestos* (Cambridge: Cambridge University Press, 2008), 166.

138. Ralph Ellison, *Invisible Man* (1952; reprint, New York: Vintage-Random, 1995), 13.
139. Ellison, introduction (1981) to *Invisible Man*, xx.
140. Moretti's argument is summarized in Joseph Jonghyun Jeon, "Memories of Memories: Historicity, Nostalgia, and Archive in Bong Joon-ho's *Memories of Murder*," *Cinema Journal* 51, no. 1 (Fall 2011): 76, emphasis in original. See also Franco Moretti, *Signs Taken for Wonders: On the Sociology of Literary Forms* (New York: Verso, 1983), 145–46, and Carlo Ginzburg, "Clues: Roots of an Evidential Paradigm," in *Clues, Myths, and the Historical Method*, trans. John Tedeschi and Anne C. Tedeschi (Baltimore, MD: Johns Hopkins University Press, 1989), 96–125.
141. Arlette Farge, *The Allure of Archives*, trans. Thomas Scott-Railton (New Haven, CT: Yale University Press, 2013), 30.
142. Ellison, introduction to *Invisible Man*, xxii.
143. Hartman, "Venus in Two Acts," 12.
144. Braddock, "Media Studies 1932."
145. McKay to Eastman, August 6, 1941, and McKay to Macrae, August 8, 1941.
146. Williamson to McKay, June 1, 1941, box 1, folder 1, CMPA.

3. "AT ONCE BOTH DOCUMENT AND SYMBOL": RICHARD WRIGHT, RALPH ELLISON, AND THE LAFARGUE CLINIC PHOTOGRAPHIC ARCHIVE

1. Back cover, *'48: The Magazine of the Year*, June 1948, box 3, LCR.
2. See the exhibition catalog *Invisible Man: Gordon Parks and Ralph Ellison in Harlem* (Göttengen, Germany: Steidl; Chicago: Art Institute of Chicago; New York: Gordon Parks Foundation, 2016), hereafter *IM* catalog.
3. Ralph Ellison, "Harlem Is Nowhere" ([1948] 1964), in *The Collected Essays of Ralph Ellison*, rev. and updated, ed. John F. Callahan (New York: Modern, 2003), 320.
4. See Sara Blair, *Harlem Crossroads: Black Writers and the Photograph in the Twentieth Century* (Princeton, NJ: Princeton University Press, 2007); J. Bradford Campbell, "The Schizophrenic Solution: Dialectics of Neurosis and Anti-psychiatric Animus in Ralph Ellison's *Invisible Man*," *Novel: A Forum on Fiction* 43, no. 3 (Fall 2010): 443–65; Jean-Christophe Cloutier, "The Comic-Book World of Ralph Ellison's *Invisible Man*," *Novel: A Forum on Fiction* 43, no. 2 (Summer 2010): 294–319; Shelly Eversley, "The Lunatic's Fancy and the Work of Art," *American Literary History* 13, no. 3 (Autumn 2001): 445–68; Jay Garcia, *Psychiatry Comes to Harlem: Rethinking the Race Question in Twentieth-Century America* (Baltimore, MD: Johns Hopkins University Press, 2012); James E. Reibman, "Ellison's Expanding Circle: Legal and Psychological Ramifications of Invisibility: Ralph Ellison, Fredric Wertham, M.D., and the Lafargue Clinic: Civil Rights and Psychiatric

Services in Harlem," *Oklahoma City University Law Review* 26 (2001): 1041–55; Catherine A. Stewart, "'Crazy for This Democracy': Postwar Psychoanalysis, African American Blues Narratives, and the Lafargue Clinic," *American Quarterly* 65, no. 2 (June 2013): 371–95. Based on his dissertation work, in *Under the Strain of Color: Harlem's Lafargue Clinic and the Promise of an Antiracist Psychiatry* (Ithaca, NY: Cornell University Press, 2015), Gabriel N. Mendes offers a thorough history of the clinic.

5. Richard Wright, "Psychiatry Comes to Harlem," *Free World*, September 1946. For unknown reasons, the first word in the printed title appeared with a typo as "Phychiatry." Having just relocated to Paris, Wright first tried to have the article published in *The Nation*, but the editors of that journal changed their minds when *The New Republic* ran a piece on Wertham and the clinic. He then asked Wertham to see if Dorothy Norman would run his essay in her journal *Twice a Year*. In the end, it appeared in the magazine *Free World*. See Richard Wright to Fredric Wertham, July 9, 1946, box 67, folder 8, FWP.

6. Richard Wright and Edwin Rosskam, *12 Million Black Voices* (New York: Viking, 1941); Gordon Parks, *Voices in the Mirror: An Autobiography* (New York: Doubleday, 1990), 110.

7. Roland Barthes, *Camera Lucida: Reflections on Photography*, trans. Richard Howard (1981; reprint, New York: Hill and Wang, 2010), 89.

8. Sara Blair, "Nation Time: Richard Wright, Black Power, and Photographic Modernism," in *The Oxford Handbook of Global Modernisms*, ed. Mark Wollaeger and Matt Eatough (Oxford: Oxford University Press, 2015), 131.

9. Ralph Ellison to Albert Murray, March 16, 1956, in *Trading Twelves: The Selected Letters of Ralph Ellison and Albert Murray*, ed. Albert Murray and John F. Callahan (New York: Vintage Books, 2000), 118.

10. Ellison, "Harlem Is Nowhere," in *Collected Essays*, 322.

11. Paul Saint-Amour, *Tense Future: Modernism, Total War, Encyclopedic Form* (New York: Oxford University Press, 2015), 32.

12. Richard Wright, introduction to St. Clair Drake and Horace Cayton, *Black Metropolis: A Study of Negro Life in a Northern City*, 2 vols. (1945; reprint, New York: Harcourt, 1970), xvii–xxxiv.

13. Ellison to Richard Wright, February 1, 1948, box 97, folder 1314, RWP.

14. Hilde L. Mossé, "Child Psychiatry and Social Action: An Integral Part of the History of American Child Psychiatry" (1981), p. 3, box 2, folder 1, LCR.

15. Father Bishop is one of the figures featured in the photographs included in both Wright, "Psychiatry Comes to Harlem," and Gordon Parks, "Harlem Gang Leader," *Life*, November 1, 1948.

16. Mossé, "Child Psychiatry and Social Action," 4–5.

17. Lafargue Clinic pamphlet, box I:203, REP. The pamphlet featured a photograph of the man for whom the clinic is named, Paul Lafargue, a Cuban-born black French physician who married Karl Marx's daughter.
18. Mossé, "Child Psychiatry and Social Action," 6.
19. See Constance Curtis, "Dr. Tweed's Appointment Sets National Precedent," *New York Post*, n.d., 1946, clipping in box OV 1, FWP.
20. Quoted in Ralph G. Martin, "Doctor's Dream in Harlem," *New Republic*, June 3, 1946.
21. Quoted in Martin, "Doctor's Dream in Harlem." For a comprehensive study of the clinic, its aims, history, and legacy, see Mendes, *Under the Strain of Color*.
22. Reibman, "Ellison's Expanding Circle," 1048. Charles Sumner of Boston had in fact used such an approach in 1849, though unsuccessfully, during what became known as the "Roberts case." See Charles Sumner, *Equality Before the Law: Unconstitutionality of Separate Colored Schools in Massachusetts* (Washington, DC: Rives & Bailey, 1870).
23. Reibman, "Ellison's Expanding Circle," 1047–48.
24. Quoted in Reibman, "Ellison's Expanding Circle," 1049.
25. Reibman, "Ellison's Expanding Circle," 1049. Although Dr. Wertham is today most remembered as the man who tried to ban comic books in the 1950s, he was also quite forward thinking and courageous. As early as 1948, he publicly advocated desegregation and "the repeal of all laws against homosexual acts by consenting adults" (Mossé, "Child Psychiatry and Social Action," 16).
26. Mossé, "Child Psychiatry and Social Action," 12.
27. Hilde L. Mossé to Dr. Paul H. Hoch of New York State of Mental Hygiene, undated, box 1, folder 1, LCR.
28. The broadcast date was Sunday, October 27, 1957.
29. Wright to Ida Guggenheimer, July 13, 1945, box 1, IGP. Guggenheimer was also Ellison's patron.
30. Wright to Guggenheimer, August 24, 1944, box 1, IGP.
31. Wright to Guggenheimer, July 13, 1945. In the letter, Wright goes on to add: "I've written Ralph twice, but have no answer from him; he must [be] busy." Actually, letters reveal that Ellison had not received Wright's letters, and Ida eventually had to send him her own letter to read (see box 97, folder 1314, RWP).
32. Wright, introduction to Drake and Cayton, *Black Metropolis*, xxx, xxviii.
33. Wright, introduction to Drake and Cayton, *Black Metropolis*, xvii.
34. Wright, introduction to Drake and Cayton, *Black Metropolis*, xvii, xviii.
35. Wright, introduction to Drake and Cayton, *Black Metropolis*, xviii.
36. Richard Wright, *Black Boy (American Hunger): A Record of Childhood and Youth* (1945; reprint, New York: HarperPerennial, 2006), 376.

37. Wright, introduction to Drake and Cayton, *Black Metropolis*, xix.
38. Richard Wright, "How Bigger Was Born," lecture, March 12, 1940, included in *Native Son* (1940; reprint, New York: Perennial Library, 1987), vii.
39. Wright, introduction to Drake and Cayton, *Black Metropolis*, xx.
40. See Richard Wright, "The Position of the Negro Artist and Intellectual in American Society," unpublished lecture, box 5, folder 19, Constance Webb Papers, RBML.
41. Wright, introduction to Drake and Cayton, *Black Metropolis*, xx.
42. Wright, "The Position of the Negro Artist and Intellectual in American Society."
43. Wright, introduction to Drake and Cayton, *Black Metropolis*, xix.
44. Ralph Ellison brought up the same point in his critique of Langston Hughes's autobiography, *The Big Sea*. See Ralph Ellison "Stormy Weather," *The New Masses*, September 24, 1940.
45. Wright, introduction to Drake and Cayton, *Black Metropolis*, xix.
46. Wright, introduction to Drake and Cayton, *Black Metropolis*, xx.
47. Wright, introduction to Drake and Cayton, *Black Metropolis*, xxiv.
48. Wright, introduction to Drake and Cayton, *Black Metropolis*, xxvi–xxvii.
49. Wright, introduction to Drake and Cayton, *Black Metropolis*, xxvii.
50. Wright, *Native Son*, 69–70; subsequent references are given parenthetically by page number in the text; ellipses indicate omission of text unless otherwise noted.
51. Richard Wright, "The Man Who Lived Underground," in *Eight Men: Short Stories* (New York: HarperPerennial, 1996), 74.
52. Wright, "How Bigger Was Born," xx.
53. The subtitle of *Black Boy* is *A Record of Childhood and Youth*.
54. William Faulkner to Wright, undated (ca. 1945), Constance Webb Papers.
55. Wertham to Wright, March 16, 1945, RWP.
56. Wright, introduction to Drake and Cayton, *Black Metropolis*, xxviii.
57. Notably, the Lafargue Clinic became the first psychiatric facility to be officially designated by the Veteran's Administration "for the psychiatric treatment of white and colored veterans alike" (John Hohenberg, "Harlem Clinic Now Official VA Agency: An Unprecedented Action; White Veterans Also Treated," *New York Post*, February 24, 1947).
58. See *Wiltwyck School for Boys*, promotional leaflet, Subject Files, box 139, RWP.
59. Robert Cooper to Wright, August 3, 1944, box 139, RWP.
60. Toru Kiuchi, ed., *Richard Wright: A Documented Chronology, 1908–1960* (Jefferson, NC: McFarland, 2014), loc. 4,420 of 12,871, Kindle. Even earlier, in November 1944 Wright had met with Helen Levitt, who had exhibited at the Museum of Modern Art in 1943, to discuss his plans to create a "photographic documentary" of Harlem children (Kiuchi, *Richard Wright*, loc. 4,425 of 12,871).
61. Richard Saunders (1922–1987) later relocated to Pittsburgh, where, under Roy Stryker, he was one of the primary photographers for a project documenting the

Steel City's urban renewal. He had a successful career as a photojournalist in the United States, Latin America, and Africa, contributing work to major publications and the United States Information Agency. For more information on Saunders, see Deborah Willis-Thomas, *An Illustrated Bio-bibliography of Black Photographers, 1940–1988* (New York: Garland, 1989), 121–22.

62. Wright, "Psychiatry Comes to Harlem."
63. Wright, "Psychiatry Comes to Harlem."
64. Garcia, *Psychiatry Comes to Harlem*, 1.
65. Wright, "Psychiatry Comes to Harlem."
66. Wright, "Psychiatry Comes to Harlem."
67. Ellison, "Harlem Is Nowhere," in *Collected Essays*, 322.
68. Ellison, "Harlem Is Nowhere," in *Collected Essays*, 320.
69. Wright, "Psychiatry Comes to Harlem."
70. Wright, "Psychiatry Comes to Harlem."
71. Wright, "Psychiatry Comes to Harlem."
72. Wright, "Psychiatry Comes to Harlem."
73. Contact sheets of photographs taken by Richard Saunders for "Psychiatry Comes to Harlem," box 215, folder 5, FWP.
74. Upon closer inspection, the folder the nurse is holding bears the name of the photographer, "Richard Saunders," another hint that these images are staged.
75. Wright, "Psychiatry Comes to Harlem."
76. Wright to Guggenheimer, June 6, 1946, box 1, IGP. Wright departed New York for Paris on May 1, 1945.
77. For a fascinating discussion of Wright's evolving engagement with photographic practice, see Blair, *Harlem Crossroads* and "Nation Time."
78. Incidentally, *Rite of Passage* is littered with allusions to Superman, a character who was then a fledgling new figure of heroism that was beginning to capture the imagination of urban youths across the nation and whom Dr. Wertham was closely investigating (see chapter 5).
79. Ellison, "Harlem Is Nowhere," in *Collected Essays*, 321.
80. Shelly Eversley, "The Lunatic's Fancy and the Work of Art," *American Literary History* 13, no. 3 (Autumn 2001): 455, 458.
81. Lawrence P. Jackson, *Ralph Ellison: Emergence of Genius* (New York: Wiley, 2002), 333.
82. Robert G. O'Meally, "Checking Our Balances: Ellison on Armstrong's Humor," *Boundary 2* 30, no. 2 (Summer 2003): 131.
83. Jackson, *Ralph Ellison*, 331.
84. Ralph Ellison, "Harlem 24 Hours After—Peace and Quiet Reign," *New York Post*, August 3, 1943.
85. This contact sheet appears on page 89 in the *IM* catalog. The first frame on the sheet, that of a teenage boy holding a toy rifle, corresponds with a line in "Harlem Is

Nowhere": "Boy gangsters wielding homemade pistols (which in the South of their origin are but toy symbols of adolescent yearning for manhood) shoot down their young rivals" (in *Collected Essays*, 322).

86. Ralph Ellison, *Invisible Man* (1952; reprint, New York: Vintage-Random, 1995), 8, subsequent references given parenthetically by page number in the text; ellipses indicate omission of text unless otherwise noted.

87. Blair, *Harlem Crossroads*.

88. See the "Photography" reference file in box I:207 and Ellison's correspondence with his wife, Fanny, in box I:15, REP. For published examples of Ellison's photography, see Ellison and Murray, *Trading Twelves*, and the *IM* catalog.

89. Lawrence Lee to Ellison, July 30, 1947, box I:162, REP.

90. Wertham to Ellison, August 2, 1947, box I:77, REP.

91. Ellison to Wertham, August 17, 1947, box I:77, REP.

92. See Lee to Ellison, October 15, 1947, box I:162, REP.

93. "Problem Kids: New Harlem Clinic Rescues Ghetto Youth," *Ebony*, July 1947. I am grateful to John Edwin Mason for sharing this information. See also John Edwin Mason, "Revisiting Gordon Parks' Classic Photo Essay, 'Harlem Gang Leader,'" *Time*, September 21, 2014, http://time.com/3461593/revisiting-gordon-parks-classic -photo-essay-harlem-gang-leader/. Years later Ellison and Clark would engaged in public debates on the psychological and social life of African Americans; see Ralph Ellison, "A Very Stern Discipline" (1967), in *Collected Essays*, 730–58.

94. Richard E. Lauterbach to Ellison, January 29, 1948, box I:162, REP.

95. Ralph Ellison, working notes, "Lafargue Clinic" folder, box I:203, REP. Although these sheets are undated, Ellison's opening statement, "in the two years since [the clinic's] establishment," indicate that they were composed in 1948.

96. "One-shot" or "color-separation cameras" produced three separate single-color negatives to create the three primary-color elements of the photographed subject. By the 1930s, the three negatives were made simultaneously. These cameras were fitted with "internal arrangements of half-silvered mirrors to divide the light from the lens into three parts, and direct each part to a plate"; it was these parts that combined to form full-color images. See "Three-Color Camera," n.d., http://camera-wiki.org /wiki/Three-color_camera.

97. Ellison, working notes, "Lafargue Clinic" folder.

98. Gordon Parks, *A Choice of Weapons* (New York: Harper and Row, 1965).

99. Sara Blair, "Ellison, Photography, and the Origins of Invisibility," in *The Cambridge Companion to Ralph Ellison*, ed. Ross Posnock (Cambridge: Cambridge University Press, 2005), 57.

100. Ellison, "Harlem Is Nowhere," in *Collected Essays*, 326.

101. Ellison, "Harlem Is Nowhere," in *Collected Essays*, 326.

102. Ellison, "Harlem Is Nowhere," in *Collected Essays*, 327.

103. Ellison to Wright, June 24, 1946, box 97, folder 1314, RWP.
104. Ellison to Murray, March 16, 1956, in *Trading Twelves*, 118. In that same letter, Ellison added: "My camera went bad on me recently and I'm falling behind on my photo notes, I've just written the states to see what I can do about getting a 35mm job, so if you're dissatisfied with the Leica why not give me a chance to buy it[?] . . . [I]t'll take a pictorial record to help us make the most of my year here" (118).
105. Ellison to Edward Weinfeld, September 29, 1948, box I:100, REP.
106. Ellison to Weinfeld, September 29, 1948.
107. Gordon Parks, *Camera Portraits: Techniques and Principles of Documentary Portraiture* (New York: Watts, 1948); Arnold Rampersad, *Ralph Ellison: A Biography* (New York: Knopf, 2007).
108. Ralph Ellison, drafts of "Harlem Is Nowhere," box I:100, REP.
109. Ralph Ellison's appointment calendar for 1948, box I:212, REP.
110. Jere Daniel to Ellison, April 19, 1948, box I:100, REP.
111. Ellison to Weinfeld, September 29, 1948, box I:100, REP.
112. Ellison to Wright, February 1, 1948, box 97, folder 1314, RWP.
113. Ellison to Wright, February 1, 1948.
114. Ellison to Constance Webb, July 7, 1967, box 5, folder 7, Constance Webb Papers.
115. For more on Wright's work with the Wiltwyck School, see Mendes, *Under the Strain of Color*, 46–52. See also Garcia, *Psychology Comes to Harlem*.
116. Ralph Ellison, preparatory notes for "Harlem Is Nowhere," box I:100, REP.
117. Blair, *Harlem Crossroads*, 124.
118. Ralph Ellison, "Pictorial Problem," shooting script for "Harlem Is Nowhere," box I:100, REP. One draft of "Pictorial Problem" is reproduced in *IM* catalog, 44–45.
119. Ellison, "Pictorial Problem."
120. For instance, Dorothy Norman, "A World to Live In: Help for the Troubled in Harlem," *New York Post*, March 18, 1946; Ralph G. Martin, "Doctor's Dream in Harlem," *New Republic*, June 3, 1946; "Harlem Pioneers with Mental Clinic," *Headlines and Pictures: A Monthly Negro News Magazine*, July 1946; Sidney M. Katz, "Jim Crow Is Barred from Wertham's Clinic," *Magazine Digest*, September 1946; "Lafargue Clinic Gives Harlem Free Expert Psychiatric Aid," *New York State Journal of Medicine* 46, no. 20 (October 15, 1946): page numbers not known; James L. Tuck, "Here's Hope for Harlem!" *New York Herald Tribune*, January 26, 1947. Both Ralph Ellison and Richard Wright kept copies of these pieces, which are currently housed in their respective papers.
121. Ralph Ellison, holograph notes for "Harlem Is Nowhere," box I:100, REP. The reference to "comic books, horror stories" is a reminder of Dr. Wertham's focus on the problem of comic-book reading by Harlem youth (see chapter 5).
122. Ellison, holograph notes for "Harlem Is Nowhere."
123. Ellison, "Pictorial Problem."

124. Ellison, "Pictorial Problem." The section in square brackets and the crossed-out passage are taken from an alternate, earlier draft of "Pictorial Problem," I:100, REP.
125. Blair, "Ellison, Photography, and the Origins of Invisibility," 58.
126. Ellison to Wright, January 21, 1953, box 97, folder 1314, RWP.
127. Blair, "Ellison, Photography, and the Origins of Invisibility," 59.
128. See Jean-Christophe Cloutier, "Harlem Is Now Here," in *IM* catalog, 30. The discovery was made possible by the analysis of the Parks records done by the Art Institute of Chicago curator Michal Raz-Ru and The Gordon Parks Foundation archivists Amanda Smith and James L. Jordan as well as by my own research into Ellison's papers. For additional examples of the mixing of images from "Harlem Is Nowhere" and "Harlem Gang Leader," see Russell Lord, *Gordon Parks: The Making of an Argument*, exhibition catalog (Göttengen, Germany: Steidl, 2013), plates 51, 53, 95.
129. All captions were reconstituted from two drafts located in box I:100, REP. Ellison's directives were heeded in reconstructing a "final" version for each caption, and these final versions are available with the photos in the *IM* catalog, 57–62. Because some of the information in both drafts is repetitive or presents alternate versions of the same caption, the clearest or most complete version was selected in the reconstituting process.
130. Ellison, "Pictorial Problem."
131. Gordon Parks, *Harlem Rooftops*, caption by Ralph Ellison for "Harlem Is Nowhere," in *IM* catalog, 59. A small print of *Harlem Rooftops* was also found in Ellison's papers, PR 13 CN 2010:045, container 5, folder 9, REP.
132. For one example of such attempts, see *IM* catalog, 34. The frontispiece for Claude McKay's study *Harlem: Negro Metropolis* (1940; reprint, New York: Harvest, 1968) is a *Bird's-Eye View of Harlem* by photographer "Lewis," which closely recalls Parks's photo *Harlem Rooftops*; both capture Harlem rooftops in winter. The "Lewis" in question is likely African American photojournalist and newsreel director Edward W. Lewis.
133. Ellison, "Pictorial Problem."
134. Gordon Parks, *Off on My Own*, caption by Ralph Ellison for "Harlem Is Nowhere," in *IM* catalog, 59, 61.
135. Contact sheet, in *IM* catalog, 35. This same contact sheet also includes a frame of a pile of comic books.
136. Ellison, "Pictorial Problem."
137. Caption D by Ralph Ellison for "Harlem Is Nowhere," in *IM* catalog, 68.
138. Gordon Parks, untitled print for "Harlem Is Nowhere," reproduced in *IM* catalog, 69. For more on this photograph and variant images taken of these same boys, one of whom is reading a comic book, see chapter 5.
139. Blair, *Harlem Crossroads*, 120.

140. Ellison, "Pictorial Problem."

141. Ellison, "Pictorial Problem." In Ellison's copy of Robert Bendiner's article "Psychiatry for the Needy," *Tomorrow*, May 1946, which describes Dr. Wertham's efforts at the clinic, Ellison jotted a notation in the margins—"Later maze / End of piece"—next to a penciled line indicating the sections to which the note refers (box I:197, REP).

142. Caption M by Ralph Ellison for "Harlem Is Nowhere," in *IM* catalog, 84. The caption as quoted is written on a typescript glued to the copy of the photo associated with caption M found in box 215, folder 6, FWP, and is different from the extant drafts for caption M in Ellison's files. Gordon Parks's photograph accompanying caption M is reproduced in *IM* catalog, 85. I thank Gabriel Mendes for locating this photograph, which also appears in his book *Under the Strain of Color*, 116.

143. John Callahan, "Ralph Ellison and Gordon Parks in the Labyrinth of Harlem," in *IM* catalog, 12.

144. In his manuscripts, Ellison also identifies the name of the patient by hand: "Patient Beine interviewed at Lafargue Psychiatric Clinic." Only a few patient files are preserved in the Lafargue Clinic Records, and none of the extant records appears to be related to a patient named "Beine." Note that none of the images found at The Gordon Parks Foundation—or elsewhere—corresponds to what is being described by caption A—that is, an African American doctor with a white patient. The image described is now the only "missing" one from the "Harlem Is Nowhere" photo-essay from 1948.

145. Captions E, F, and G by Ralph Ellison for "Harlem Is Nowhere," in *IM* catalog, 70.

146. Caption drafts for images to be used in "Harlem Is Nowhere," in *IM* catalog, 59.

147. The photographs discussed in this paragraph appear in *IM* catalog, 70–75.

148. Caption drafts for images to be used in "Harlem Is Nowhere," box I:100, REP.

149. *Street Scene* appears in *IM* catalog, 81, and in multiple Gordon Parks catalogs.

150. Caption H by Ralph Ellison for "Harlem Is Nowhere," in *IM* catalog, 76. The contact sheet upon which the frame associated with caption H appears is reproduced in *IM* catalog, 77.

151. W. E. B. Du Bois, *The Souls of Black Folk* (1903; reprint, New York: Penguin, 1989), 5.

152. Erika Doss, "Visualizing Black America: Gordon Parks at *Life*, 1948–1971," in *Looking at* Life *Magazine*, ed. Erika Doss (Washington, DC: Smithsonian Institution Press, 2001), 231.

153. Maren Stange, "Gordon Parks: A World of Possibility" (interview), in *Bare Witness: Photographs by Gordon Parks* (Stanford, CA: SKIRA in association with Iris and B. Gerald Cantor Center for Visual Arts at Stanford University, 2006), 17.

154. Ellison to Stanley Edgar Hyman, August 13, 1948, box I:51, REP.

155. Ralph Ellison and Gordon Parks, "A Man Becomes Invisible," *Life*, August 25, 1952. For an in-depth look at this collaboration in 1952, see Michal Raz-Russo, "Visible Men," in *IM* catalog, 13–28.

156. Raz-Russo, "Visible Men," 25.

157. Raz-Russo, "Visible Men," 26.

158. Ellison to Wright, January 21, 1953.

159. Campbell, "The Schizophrenic Solution," 458.

160. Ellison, "Harlem Is Nowhere," in *Collected Essays*, 327.

161. Ralph Ellison, "Out of the Hospital and Under the Bar" (n.d.), in *Soon, One Morning: New Writing by American Negroes, 1940–1962*, ed. Herbert Hill (New York: Knopf, 1968), 242–290; Campbell, "The Schizophrenic Solution," 457.

162. Campbell, "The Schizophrenic Solution," 456.

163. Ellison, "Out of the Hospital and Under the Bar," 247–48.

164. Ellison, "Out of the Hospital and Under the Bar," 248.

165. Ellison, "Out of the Hospital and Under the Bar," 254, 269, 271.

166. Ellison, "Out of the Hospital and Under the Bar," 287, 258–59.

167. Ellison, "Out of the Hospital and Under the Bar," 278, 266, 267.

168. Ellison, "Harlem Is Nowhere," in *Collected Essays*, 321.

169. Ellison, "Out of the Hospital and Under the Bar," 268.

170. Ellison, "Out of the Hospital and Under the Bar," 275.

171. See note 148.

172. Despite the four-year gap between Parks's photograph *Mysticism, Harlem Mysticism, New York* and Ellison's contact sheet, a copy of the same *Afro Dream Book* appears in prints in both Parks's and Ellison's archives. See *IM* catalog, 36–37.

173. Ellison, "Pictorial Problem."

174. Lauterbach to Ellison, May 17, 1948, box I:100, REP.

175. See the documents issued by the U.S. District Court, Southern District of New York; correspondence from the law offices of Nemeroff, Jelline, Danzig & Paley; and the memo from the law offices of Krause, Hirsch, Levin & Heilpern pertaining to the bankruptcy case of Associated Magazine Contributors, Inc., July–October 1948, box I:100, REP. *Magazine of the Year* was owned by Associated Magazine Contributors, Inc.

176. Ellison to Weinfeld, September 29, 1948. By September 9, 1948, the debtor was officially adjudged a bankrupt. On July 22, 1948, Ellison had filed a claim to receive the payment he was owed, $306.40, for "an article, at the agreed price of ten cents a word, consisting of 2770 words, titled: HARLEM IS NOWHERE; plus picture captions numbering 295 words." See legal claim in the matter of Associated Magazine Contributors, Inc., box I:100, folder 3, REP, and docket for Bankruptcy Case 85638, National Archives and Records Administration for the Northeast Region, U.S. District Court, Southern District of New York.

177. Office of the Editor, *Harper's Magazine*, to Ellison, January 4, 1949, box I:50, REP.
178. In a letter to Robert O'Meally dated March 7, 1984 (box II:32, REP), Ellison referred to his personal papers as his "cluttered files." See also Richard Avedon and Ralph Ellison, *Nothing Personal* (New York: Atheneum, 1964).
179. Willie Morris to Lisel Eisenheimer, May 4, 1964, box I:50, REP.
180. Langston Hughes and Roy DeCarava, *The Sweet Flypaper of Life* (New York: Hill and Wang, 1955). The photographs by DeCarava used in Ralph Ellison, "Harlem Is Nowhere," *Harper's Magazine*, August 1964, are *Man Sitting on Stoop with Baby* (1952); *Graduation* (1949); *Half Man* (1953); and an untitled image on page 57 that I was not able to locate in any other of DeCarava's published works.
181. Ellison, "Harlem Is Nowhere," *Harper's*; Hughes and DeCarava, *The Sweet Flypaper of Life*, 67.
182. For a fascinating study of a similar case—the use of the same image in drastically different publications—see Justin Parks, "On Making Graven Images: The Racial Meanings of Death in a Walker Evans Photograph and Its Double," *Plot*, no. 18, June 9, 2017, http://www.plot.online/plot/points/on-making-graven-images-the-racial-meanings-of-death-in-a-walker-evans-photograph-and-its-double/. Parks uncovers how both James Agee's book *Let Us Now Praise Famous Men* (1941; reprint, New York: Penguin, 2006) and Wright and Rosskam's book *12 Million Black Voices* use the same Walker Evans photograph of a "sparsely adorned grave," just as *Man Sitting on Stoop with Baby* appears in both *Sweet Flypaper of Life* and *Harper's* version of "Harlem Is Nowhere."
183. In fact, August 1964 saw the publication of DeCarava's photographs in two major magazines; not only in *Harper's* for Ellison's essay but in *Newsweek* on August 3, where he also had his first cover for a piece that also, like "Harlem Is Nowhere," touched on the unrest in Harlem. See John Edwin Mason, "Roy DeCarava, the Kamoinge Workshop, and *Newsweek* Magazine, 1964," July 18, 2013, http://johnedwinmason.typepad.com/john_edwin_mason_photogra/2013/07/decarava-kamoinge-newsweek.html.
184. Editors' headnote to Ellison, "Harlem Is Nowhere," *Harper's*, 53.
185. Daniel Matlin, *On the Corner: African American Intellectuals and the Urban Crisis* (Cambridge, MA: Harvard University Press, 2013), 58. See also Kenneth B. Clark, *Dark Ghetto: Dilemmas of Social Power* (New York: Harper and Row, 1965).
186. Sharifa Rhodes-Pitts, *"Harlem Is Nowhere": A Journey to the Mecca of Black America* (London: Granta, 2011), 116.
187. Ellison, "Harlem Is Nowhere," in *Collected Essays*, 326.
188. Farah Jasmine Griffin, *Harlem Nocturne: Women Artists and Progressive Politics During World War II* (New York: Basic Civitas, 2013), 125, 128, 122.
189. Teju Cole, *Known and Strange Things: Essays* (New York: Random House, 2016), 144.

4. AN INTERLUDE CONCERNING THE VANISHING MANUSCRIPTS OF ANN PETRY

1. "Information for Researchers," Howard Gotlieb Research Center, Boston University, website, http://hgar-srv3.bu.edu/researchers.
2. Nellie Y. McKay, "Ann Petry's *The Street* and *The Narrows*: A Study of the Influence of Class, Race, and Gender in Afro-American Women's Lives," in *Women and War: The Changing Status of American Women from the 1930s to the 1950s*, ed. Maria Diedrich and Dorothea Fischer-Hornung (New York: Berg, 1990), 127. "At least six birth dates" from Elisabeth Petry, *At Home Inside: A Daughter's Tribute to Ann Petry* (Jackson: University of Mississippi Press, 2009), 3.
3. E. Petry, *At Home Inside*, 3.
4. Farah Jasmine Griffin, "Ann Petry: Brief Life of a Celebrity-Averse Novelist: 1908–1997," *Harvard Magazine*, January–February 2014, https://harvardmagazine.com/2014/01/ann-petry.
5. Quoted in E. Petry, *At Home Inside*, 1.
6. E. Petry, *At Home Inside*, 3. For more details on Petry's many birth dates, see pages 20–21.
7. E. Petry, *At Home Inside*, 13, 14.
8. E. Petry, *At Home Inside*, 1.
9. Stephen Best, *None Like Us: Blackness, Belonging, Aesthetic Life* (Durham, NC: Duke University Press, 2018), 12 and passim.
10. Ann Petry, quoted in E. Petry, *At Home Inside*, 14.
11. E. Petry, *At Home Inside*, 14.
12. E. Petry, *At Home Inside*, 1.
13. Quotations from the journal are in E. Petry, *At Home Inside*, 14, 1, 14.
14. Arlette Farge, *The Allure of Archives*, trans. Thomas Scott-Railton (New Haven, CT: Yale University Press, 2013), 14, 74.
15. E. Petry, *At Home Inside*, 15.
16. E. Petry, *At Home Inside*, 15.
17. Quoted in E. Petry, *At Home Inside*, 16.
18. Elisabeth Petry, ed., *Can Anything Beat White? A Black Family's Letters* (Jackson: University Press of Mississippi, 2005).
19. E. Petry, *At Home Inside*, 15.
20. E. Petry, *At Home Inside*, 15.
21. Lawrence P. Jackson, *The Indignant Generation: A Narrative History of African American Writers and Critics, 1934–1960* (Princeton, NJ: Princeton University Press, 2011), 143–44.
22. Farah Jasmine Griffin, *Harlem Nocturne: Women Artists and Progressive Politics During World War II* (New York: Basic Civitas, 2013), 94–95.

23. Jackson, *The Indignant Generation*, 143.

24. Quoted in Griffin, "Ann Petry."

25. Phillip N. Cronenwett, "Appraisal of Literary Manuscripts," in *Archival Choices: Managing the Historical Record in an Age of Abundance*, ed. Nancy E. Peace (Lexington, MA: Lexington Books, 1984), 106.

26. As reported in the *New York Times*, Arthur Miller donated "13 boxes of material, including multiple manuscripts and working notebooks for the plays that made his name—including 'Death of a Salesman,' 'All My Sons' and 'The Crucible'—in exchange for a tax deduction" (Jennifer Schuessler, "Inside the Battle for Arthur Miller's Archive," *New York Times*, January 9, 2018).

27. Michael Rips, "Painters Deserve Their Deduction," *New York Times*, April 21, 2017, https://www.nytimes.com/2017/04/21/opinion/painters-deserve-their-deduction.html.

28. E. Petry, *At Home Inside*, 13.

29. Rips, "Painters Deserve Their Deduction."

30. Rips, "Painters Deserve Their Deduction."

31. Schuessler, "Inside the Battle for Arthur Miller's Archive." The matter was not settled until 2018, when the Harry Ransom Center officially purchased the Miller Archive after a late-in-the-game competitive bid from Yale University.

32. For more on Nixon's tax return for 1969 as the underlying cause of the tax-code change, see Rips, "Painters Deserve Their Deduction," and Eric Pace, "Edward Morgan, 61, Nixon Aide Convicted in Tax Fraud Case," *New York Times*, August 20, 1999, https://www.nytimes.com/1999/08/20/us/edward-morgan-61-nixon-aide-convicted-in-tax-fraud-case.html.

33. Cronenwett, "Appraisal of Literary Manuscripts," 106.

34. See "Papers of Ann Petry, 1938–2000 (Inclusive), 1973–2000 (Bulk)," Schlesinger Library, Harvard University, Cambridge, MA, https://hollis.harvard.edu/primo-explore/fulldisplay?docid=01HVD_ALMA21220609370000394&context=L&vid=HVD2&lang=en_US&search_scope=default_scope&adaptor=Local%20Search%20Engine&tab=books&query=any,contains,ann%20petry%20collection&sortby=rank.

35. See "Ann Petry Portrait Collection," Schomburg Center for Research in Black Culture, NYPL, https://browse.nypl.org/iii/encore/record/C__Rb11487294__Sann%20petry%20portrait__Orightresult__U__X6?lang=eng.

36. Jackson, *Indignant Generation*; Keith Clark, *The Radical Fiction of Ann Petry* (Baton Rouge: Louisiana State University Press, 2013); Griffin, *Harlem Nocturne*. The four collections listed in Griffin are the one at BU; the portrait collection at the Schomburg Center (see the previous note); as well as the James E. Jackson and Esther Cooper Jackson Papers in the Elmer Holmes Bobst Library and the Robert F. Wagner Labor Archives in the Tamiment Library, both at New York University.

37. Clark, *The Radical Fiction of Ann Petry*, 1.

38. Rather than imposing any classificatory system on the perpetually accumulating material making its way into The Factory, Warhol—starting in 1974—decided instead to allow the stuff to build every month, at the end of which he swept everything into a box, closed it up, and labeled it by date. These "Time Capsules," as they are called, now represent unique, raw, uncurated exposures to the chaos of American culture that was manifest in material form and that bombarded the postwar working celebrity-artist. The Andy Warhol Museum in Pittsburgh keeps the contents of one of these capsules on display for visitors, rotating the contents of a different capsule as the cataloging of the 610 boxes continues. See Desi Gonzalez, "Unboxed: A New App at the Warhol," the Warhol, February 3, 2016, https://www.warhol.org/unboxed-a-new-app-at-the-warhol/.

39. Ann Petry, *The Street* (New York: Houghton Mifflin, 1946), 1–2; ellipses indicate omission of text unless noted otherwise.

40. Petry, *The Street*, 11, 12, 29, 31, 50, 56, 91, 94.

41. Petry, *The Street*, 128.

42. Carl Van Vechten to Ann Petry, May 4, 1946, APC.

43. E. Petry, *At Home Inside*, 165.

44. Griffin, *Harlem Nocturne*, 86.

45. Van Vechten to Petry, June 22, 1946, APC, capitalization and emphasis in the original.

46. Van Vechten to Petry, undated, APC, capitalization in the original.

47. Van Vechten to Petry, April 30, 1947, APC, capitalization in the original.

48. Van Vechten to Petry, September 25, 1947, APC, capitalization in the original.

49. Van Vechten to Petry, September 30, 1947, APC, capitalization and emphasis in the original.

50. James T. Babb to Petry, January 21, 1949, APC.

51. Babb to Petry, January 21, 1949, APC, second letter with same date.

52. Babb to Petry, January 24, 1949, APC.

53. Babb to Petry, December 1950, APC.

54. Van Vechten to Petry, August 16, 1952, APC, capitalization in the original.

55. Elizabeth Riley to Petry, October 26, 1964, APC.

56. Donald Gallup to Riley, November 1964, APC.

57. Petry to aspiring writer, March 30, 1966, APC, emphasis in the original. In this letter, Petry also names Flannery O'Connor as a writerly model to emulate. And in an interview for *Ebony* in 1946 after the release of her first novel, Petry named Richard Wright, Theodore Dreiser, and James Joyce as the authors she most admired ("First Novel," *Ebony*, April 1, 1946).

58. Babb to Van Vechten, January 21, 1949, box 13, folder 6, CVV NYPL.

59. Petry to Van Vechten, May 7, 1946, box 39, folder 699, CVVP.

60. Petry to Van Vechten, May 7, 1946.

61. Petry to Van Vechten, April 29, 1947, box 39, folder 699, CVVP.
62. Frances Reckling to Van Vechten, April 29, 1947, box 39, folder 723, CVVP.
63. "Carl Van Vechten Catalog," box 62, folder 1068, CVVP, emphasis in original.
64. Petry to Van Vechten, February 10, 1949, box 39, folder 699, CVVP.
65. Petry to Van Vechten, January 9, 1950, box 39, folder 699, CVVP.
66. Petry to Van Vechten, August 13, 1952, box 39, folder 699, CVVP.
67. Van Vechten to Gallup, August 20, 1952, box 4, folder 2, CVV NYPL.
68. Petry to Van Vechten, August 14, 1953, box 39, folder 699, CVVP.
69. See "The Inventory of the Ann Petry Collection #1391," listings of the first shipment, June 1968, Howard Gotlieb Archival Research Center.
70. Melissa Barton to Jean-Christophe Cloutier, email, July 27, 2018.
71. Barton to Cloutier, email, August 6, 2018.
72. Tayari Jones, "In Praise of Ann Petry," *New York Times*, November 10, 2018, https://www.nytimes.com/2018/11/10/books/review/in-praise-of-ann-petry.html.
73. Elisabeth Petry to Jean-Christophe Cloutier, email, July 26, 2018.

5. "TOO OBSCURE FOR LEARNED CLASSIFICATION": COMIC BOOKS, COUNTERCULTURE, AND ARCHIVAL INVISIBILITY IN *INVISIBLE MAN*

1. Scott McCloud, *Understanding Comics: The Invisible Art* (New York: Perennial-Harper, 1993).
2. Michel Foucault, "Michel Foucault explique son dernier livre," in *Dits et écrits*, vol. 1: *1954–1975* (Paris : Éditions Gallimard, 2001), 800. All translations from the French are mine.
3. Ralph Ellison, *Invisible Man* (1952; reprint, New York: Vintage-Random, 1995), 443, subsequently cited parenthetically by page number in the text; ellipses indicate omission of text unless otherwise noted.
4. Ralph Ellison, "The Essential Ellison," in *Conversations with Ralph Ellison*, ed. Maryemma Graham and Amritjit Singh (Jackson: University Press of Mississippi, 1995), 362.
5. Ralph Ellison, "What's Wrong with the American Novel?" *American Scholar* 24 (Autumn 1955): 472.
6. Ralph Ellison, "Society, Morality, and the Novel" (1957), in *The Collected Essays of Ralph Ellison*, rev. and updated, ed. John F. Callahan (New York: Modern, 2003), 717.
7. See the brochure that advertised an exhibition at the Charles-Fourth Gallery, *School for Sadism* (box I:203, REP), which states, "The collection, based on the studies of Dr. Frederic [*sic*] Wertham . . . is a thought-provoking exposé of the violence,

sadism, and general underlying damage perpetrated by the popular 'comic' books on American children today." Note the choice of comics displayed, emphasizing violence in their titles: "CRIME," "GUNS," "MURDER," "LAWBREAKERS," "TARGET," and "THE HUMAN TORCH." In the context of a nation with a history of lynching and racial profiling, these titles take on tragic connotations. The Fredric Wertham Papers also hold a photograph of Dr. Wertham standing next to this rack of comics, browsing through its contents.

8. David Hajdu, *The Ten-Cent Plague: The Great Comic-Book Scare and How It Changed America* (New York: Farrar, 2008).

9. The phrase "fate and promise" is from Ralph Ellison to Richard Wright, April 4, 1946, box I:203, REP. A copy of this letter can also be found in the RWP.

10. For Ellison's particular use of the term *groping*, see Ellison, "The Essential Ellison," 345–46.

11. Antoinette Burton, "Introduction: Archive Fever, Archive Stories," in *Archive Stories: Facts, Fictions, and the Writing of History*, ed. Antoinette Burton (Durham, NC: Duke University Press, 2005), 16–17.

12. Carolyn Hamilton, Verne Harris, and Graeme Reid, introduction to *Refiguring the Archive*, ed. Carolyn Hamilton, Verne Harris, Jane Taylor, Michele Pickover, Graeme Reid, and Razia Saleh (Cape Town, South Africa: David Philip, 2002), 9.

13. Foucault, "Michel Foucault explique son dernier livre," 800.

14. Burton, "Introduction," 17.

15. Ralph Ellison, "That Same Pain, That Same Pleasure: An Interview" (1961), in *Collected Essays*, 76.

16. See Ralph Ellison, "Change and Joke and Slip the Yoke" (1958), in *Collected Essays*, 111–12.

17. Ellison, introduction to *Invisible Man* (1981), xxii, xx.

18. David Hajdu reports that in the mid-1940s "the comic book was the most popular form of entertainment in America. Comics were selling between eighty million and a hundred million copies every week, with a typical issue passed along or traded to six to ten readers, thereby reaching more people than movies, television, radio, or magazines for adults" (*The Ten-Cent Plague*, 5).

19. Ralph Ellison, "Harlem's America," *New Leader*, September 26, 1966.

20. Albert Murray, *The Hero and the Blues* (Columbia: University of Missouri Press, 1973), 72.

21. Constance Rourke, *American Humor: A Study of the National Character* (1931; reprint, New York: New York Review of Books, 2004).

22. Murray, *The Hero and the Blues*, 72.

23. Ralph Ellison, foreword (November 1987) to John Atlee Kouwenhoven, *The Beer Can by the Highway: Essays on What's "American" About America* (1961; reprint, Baltimore, MD: Johns Hopkins University Press, 1988), . For Murray and Ellison, Constance

Rourke casts "resilience as a prime trait" (Murray, *The Hero and the Blues*, 18) of the American national character and uses the term *resilience* multiple times in her book *American Humor*. Albert Murray appropriates the term in his own work (see, for example, *The Omni-Americans: Black Experience and American Culture* [New York: Da Capo, 1970], 16–17). In *Trading Twelves*, the collected letters between Ellison and Murray also use this term as well as *nimbleness* in an analogous way (Ralph Ellison and Albert Murray, *Trading Twelves: The Selected Letters of Ralph Ellison and Albert Murray*, ed. Albert Murray and John F. Callahan [New York: Modern, 2000]).

24. Leslie Fiedler, "The Middle Against Both Ends," in *Arguing Comics: Literary Masters on a Popular Medium*, ed. Jeet Heer and Kent Worcester (Jackson: University Press of Mississippi, 2004), 126.

25. Ralph Ellison, introduction to *Shadow and Act* (1964), in *Collected Essays*, 53–54, italics in original.

26. Ralph Ellison, "Bearden" (1988), in *Collected Essays*, 836.

27. Orrin C. Evans, *All-Negro Comics*, no. 1 (Philadelphia: All-Negro Comics, June 1947), back cover.

28. Ellison, "Bearden," 839.

29. Ellison, "Harlem's America."

30. Ellison, "Harlem's America."

31. Ellison, introduction to *Shadow and Act*, 54.

32. Ellison, "Change and Joke and Slip the Yoke," 111.

33. This photograph appears in *Invisible Man: Gordon Parks and Ralph Ellison in Harlem*, exhibition catalog (Göttengen, Germany: Steidl; Chicago: Art Institute of Chicago; New York: Gordon Parks Foundation, 2016), 69.

34. "Foul landscape" is from Ralph Ellison, caption D for "Harlem Is Nowhere," in *Invisible Man* catalog, 68; "a sharper reflection of his world" is from "What's Wrong with the American Novel?" 472.

35. Ralph Ellison, "Let Us Consider the Harlem 'Crime Wave'" (1943), box I:101, REP.

36. Ellison, "The Essential Ellison," 373, paraphrasing Burke.

37. Ralph Ellison, "The Birthmark," *New Masses*, July 2, 1940, 16–17.

38. Frantz Fanon, *Black Skins, White Masks*, trans. Charles Lam Markmann (1952; reprint, New York: Grove Press, 1967), 146, 148.

39. Frantz Fanon, *The Wretched of the Earth*, trans. Constance Farrington (New York: Grove Press, 1963), 51.

40. For more on *arkhē*, origins, and commencement, see Jacques Derrida, *Archive Fever: A Freudian Impression*, trans. Eric Prenowitz (Chicago: University of Chicago Press, 1995), 1–2, 91.

41. Quoted in Michael L. Fleisher, *The Encyclopedia of Comic Book Heroes*, vol. 1: *Batman* (New York: Collier, 1976), 110.

42. Ralph Ellison to Richard Wright, November 3, 1941, RWP.

43. Bradford W. Wright, *Comic Book Nation: The Transformation of Youth Culture in America* (Baltimore, MD: Johns Hopkins University Press, 2001), 17.
44. Ralph Ellison, "On Initiation Rites and Power: A Lecture at West Point" (1969), in *Collected Essays*, 541.
45. One contact sheet from Ellison's photographic archive includes a frame with a representative sample of the types of comics Ellison was looking at in the late 1940s. The contact sheet's bottom-right frame shows a few issues of comics spread out on a surface. The following titles can be discerned—two are superhero comics and two are Westerns: "Captain Marvel Fights the Battle of Electricity," *Captain Marvel Adventures*, no. 94 (March 1, 1949); *Blue Bolt* 9, no. 7 (released 1948; February 1949); *Gabby Hayes Western*, no. 4 (released 1948; March 1949); and *Tim McCoy Comics*, no. 17 (December 1948). The other issues in the frame are too small to identify their titles with certainty. See Prints and Photographs Division, PR 13 Call Number 2010:045, container 7, folder 5, REP.
46. William W. Savage Jr., *Comic Books and America, 1945–1954* (Norman: University of Oklahoma Press, 1990), 7.
47. B. Wright, *Comic Book Nation*, 10.
48. B. Wright, *Comic Book Nation*, x.
49. B. Wright, *Comic Book Nation*, 12.
50. B. Wright, *Comic Book Nation*, 12–13.
51. Ellison, "Change and Joke and Slip the Yoke," 111.
52. The RZA, *The WU-TANG Manual* (New York: Penguin Books, 2005), 86.
53. Johnny Wilcox, "Black Power: Minstrelsy and Electricity in Ralph Ellison's *Invisible Man*," *Callaloo* 30, no. 4 (Fall 2007): 987.
54. Ralph Ellison, "Harlem Is Nowhere" ([1948] 1964), in *Collected Essays*, 322.
55. My reading of the comics allusions in the Harlem riot scene must necessarily disagree with Sara Blair's stipulation that Ellison "strategically suppresses the visual referents or resources of *Invisible Man* in its climactic episodes" and that in the novel "visual culture remains conspicuously, even puzzlingly, absent" (*Harlem Crossroads: Black Writers and the Photograph in the Twentieth Century* [Princeton, NJ: Princeton University Press, 2007], 151). For more on visual culture in *Invisible Man*, see Lena M. Hill, "The Visual Art of *Invisible Man*: Ellison's Portrait of Blackness," *American Literature* 81, no. 4 (December 2009): 775–803, and Kimberly Lamm, "Visuality and Black Masculinity in Ralph Ellison's *Invisible Man* and Romare Bearden's Photomontages," *Callaloo* 26, no. 3 (Summer 2003): 813–35.
56. The Lone Ranger radio series began in 1933, and the comic strip in 1938. The comics were so popular that by 1952 even Silver, the Lone Ranger's horse referred to in this scene, had his own title. A whole slew of superheroes, including Superman, the Shadow, and Green Hornet, had radio serials in the 1930s and 1940s. In the 1940s, Superman's "radio adventures," consisting of "four 15 minute radio serials," were

broadcast over the Mutual Network "between 5 and 6 pm every weekday afternoon" (Jack Curtin, "What a Long Strange Journey It's Been: Memories of Superman," in *Wizard: Superman Tribute Edition*, ed. Gareb S. Shamus and Patrick Daniel O'Neill [New York: Wizard Press, 1993], 10).

57. M. Thomas Inge, *Comics as Culture* (Jackson: University Press of Mississippi, 1990), 114.

58. C. L. R. James, "Letter to Daniel Bell," in *Arguing Comics*, ed. Heer and Worcester, 144.

59. Arnold Rampersad, *Ralph Ellison: A Biography* (New York: Knopf, 2007), 246.

60. Kenneth W. Warren, *So Black and Blue: Ralph Ellison and the Occasion of Criticism* (Chicago: University of Chicago Press, 2003), 4.

61. Ellison, "Change and Joke and Slip the Yoke," 111.

62. Ellison, "On Initiation Rites and Power," 529.

63. Ralph Ellison, "The Little Man at Chehaw Station" (1978), in *Collected Essays*, 498.

64. B. Wright, *Comic Book Nation*, 142, 149.

65. B. Wright, *Comic Book Nation*, 142.

66. See Burton's discussion of "the archive as contact zone" in her introduction to *Archive Stories*, 9–13.

67. Ellison, "The Little Man at Chehaw Station," 503–4.

68. In an important essay, Robert O'Meally reads this same scene in terms of *Invisible Man*'s relation to history ("On Burke and the Vernacular: Ralph Ellison's Boomerang of History," in *History and Memory in African-American Culture*, ed. Geneviève Fabre and Robert O'Meally [New York: Oxford University Press, 1994], 255–71).

69. The crossed-out passage is from an earlier draft of this episode (*Invisible Man* drafts, box I:143, REP) and hints at the hurdles that must be transcended before such an invisible history can be recorded.

70. Michel Foucault, "La vie des hommes infâmes," in *Dits et écrits*, vol. 2: *1976–1988* (Paris: Éditions Gallimard, 2001), 237.

71. Derrida, *Archive Fever*, 2.

72. Andrew John Miller, "Fables of Progression: Modernism, Modernity, Narrative," in *Modernism and Theory: A Critical Debate*, ed. Stephen Ross (London: Routledge, 2009), 179.

73. Ralph Ellison, "Going to the Territory" (1979), in *Collected Essays*, 600.

74. Ellison, introduction to *Invisible Man*, xvi.

75. Ellison, "Going to the Territory," 600, 598.

76. Ralph Ellison, "Editorial Comment," *Negro Quarterly* 1, no. 4 (1943): 299, 301. Ellison coedited this issue with Angelo Herndon.

77. See, for instance, the chapter "The Riddle of the Zoot: Malcolm Little and Black Cultural Politics During World War II," in Robin D. G. Kelley, *Race Rebels: Culture, Politics, and the Black Working Class* (New York: Free Press, 1994), 161–82, and Larry

Neal, "Ellison's Zoot Suit," in *Ralph Ellison's* Invisible Man: *A Casebook*, ed. John F. Callahan (Oxford: Oxford University Press, 2004), 81–108.

78. Ellison, "Editorial Comment," 301–2.

79. Although juvenile delinquency was regarded as a national problem, it was associated especially with Harlem. An article present in the Lafargue Clinic folders in both Wright's and Ellison's papers states, "Harlem's 400,000 population produces 53 per cent of the juvenile delinquency in Manhattan, which has a total population of 2,000,000" ("Lafargue Clinic Gives Harlem Free Expert Psychiatric Aid," *New York State Journal of Medicine* 46, no. 20 [October 15, 1946]: 2299). Ellison also scribbled this statistic on the margins of various drafts of "Harlem Is Nowhere" (box I:100, REP).

80. Bart Beaty, *Fredric Wertham and the Critique of Mass Culture* (Jackson: University Press of Mississippi, 2005), 114.

81. Quoted in Beaty, *Fredric Wertham*, 114–15.

82. Ralph Ellison, "What These Children Are Like" (1963), in *Collected Essays*, 546.

83. Ellison, "What These Children Are Like," 546–47, 549–50.

84. Fanon, *Black Skin, White Masks*, 145–46.

85. Ellison, "What These Children Are Like," 547. Ellison reiterates elsewhere that not only children but also all African Americans "understandably are hungry for heroes and redeemers" ("The Essential Ellison," 366).

86. Ellison, "Harlem Is Nowhere," in *Collected Essays*, 327.

87. Rampersad, *Ralph Ellison*, 220.

88. Beaty, *Fredric Wertham*, 89.

89. Ellison, "Harlem Is Nowhere," in *Collected Essays*, 320.

90. Multiple copies of Wertham's tract "The Psychological Effects of School Segregation," *American Journal of Psychology* 6 (1952): 94–103, can be found in Ellison's papers. For a full account of the legal ramifications of Wertham's work commissioned by the NAACP, see Beaty, *Fredric Wertham*, 94–97, and James E. Reibman, "Ellison's Expanding Circle: Legal and Psychological Ramifications of Invisibility: Ralph Ellison, Fredric Wertham, M.D., and the Lafargue Clinic: Civil Rights and Psychiatric Services in Harlem," *Oklahoma City University Law Review* 26 (2001): 1041–55.

91. Judith Crist, "Horror in the Nursery," *Collier's*, March 27, 1948.

92. Quoted in Beaty, *Fredric Wertham*, 90.

93. Fredric Wertham, "The Comics . . . Very Funny!" *Saturday Review of Literature*, May 22, 1948. See also Fredric Wertham, *Seduction of the Innocent: The Influence of Comics on Today's Youth* (New York: Rinehart, 1954).

94. Ellison, "Harlem Is Nowhere," in *Collected Essays*, 322.

95. Ralph Ellison, drafts of "Harlem Is Nowhere," box I:100, REP.

96. Ellison, drafts of "Harlem Is Nowhere," box I:100, REP.

97. Ellison, drafts of "Harlem Is Nowhere," box I:100, REP.

98. Ellison to Wright, April 4, 1946.

99. "Super Democrat of the Radio," *Headlines and Pictures: A Monthly Negro News Magazine*, July 1946. A complete copy of this magazine can also be found in Richard Wright's papers (box 139, folder 2028, RWP). A few key passages in *Black Boy* describe a Richard Wright whose juvenile delinquency has more than a mere passing affinity to the kind of youth being treated at the Lafargue Clinic. Wright reveals his fascination with pulp magazines such as *Flynn's Detective Weekly* and *Argosy All-Story Magazine* as well as with adventure stories such as Zane Grey's *Riders of the Purple Sage* (1912). Wright ultimately realized that these enthralling stories were racist publications and that, in fact, their racism was deployed in "lurid cartoon" form (Richard Wright, *Black Boy [American Hunger]: A Record of Childhood and Youth* [1945; reprint, New York: Perennial-Harper, 2006], 129–30). And let's not forget Bigger Thomas's wish to "buy a ten-cent magazine" at the beginning of *Native Son* (1940; reprint, New York: Perennial Library, 1987), 13.

100. For reproductions of these images, see Jean-Christophe Cloutier, "The Comic Book World of Ralph Ellison's *Invisible Man*," *Novel: A Forum on Fiction* 43, no. 2 (Summer 2010): 314–15.

101. In the same "Harlem" folder, Ellison also kept a copy of a comic book: "YOUTH IN THE GHETTO and the Blueprint for Change" *Harlem Youth Report*, no. 5 (Custom Comics, 1964), the voice of Harlem Youth Unlimited. The comic was distributed only around Harlem and was commissioned by the social activism organization HARYOU, spearheaded by Kenneth Clark. See Daniel Matlin, *On the Corner: African American Intellectuals and the Urban Crisis* (Cambridge, MA: Harvard University Press, 2013).

102. Ellison, "The Essential Ellison," 366.

103. For a compelling elucidation of the hero-leader figure created in the closing scenes of *Invisible Man*, see chapter 3 of John S. Wright, *Shadowing Ralph Ellison* (Jackson: University Press of Mississippi, 2006).

104. Ellison, "Harlem Is Nowhere," in *Collected Essays*, 327.

105. Ellison, introduction to *Invisible Man*, xvi.

106. Ellison, "Harlem Is Nowhere," in *Collected Essays*, 322.

CODA. DISAPPOINTED BRIDGES: A NOTE ON THE DISCOVERY OF *AMIABLE WITH BIG TEETH*

1. Jay Gertzman, "Not Quite Honest: Samuel Roth's 'Unauthorized' *Ulysses* and the 1927 International Protest," *Joyce Studies Annual* 2009:35

2. Paul K. Saint-Amour, "Soliloquy of Samuel Roth: A Paranormal Defense," *James Joyce Quarterly* 37, no. 3 (Spring 2000): 468.

3. Samuel Roth, advertisements for *My Sister and I*, box 40, folder 7, SRP.

4. "Descent Into Harlem" book contract, September 19, 1941, box 36, folder 26, SRP.

5. Norman Lockridge [Samuel Roth], advertisements for *Bumarap*, box 48, folder 5, SRP.

6. Dante Cacici to Samuel Roth, 1960, SRP. See also Jay Gertzman's authoritative biography *Samuel Roth; Infamous Modernist* (Gainesville: University Press of Florida, 2013).

7. Claude McKay to Roth, October 6, 1941, box 36, folder 26, SRP.

8. Antoinette Burton, "Introduction: Archive Fever, Archive Stories," in *Archive Stories: Facts, Fictions, and the Writing of History*, ed. Antoinette Burton (Durham, NC: Duke University Press, 2005), 5.

9. Kevin Young, *The Grey Album: On the Blackness of Blackness* (Minneapolis: Greywolf Press, 2013), 13.

10. Claude McKay, *Harlem Shadows: The Poems of Claude McKay* (New York: Harcourt, Brace, 1922), xxi.

11. Diana Taylor, *The Archive and the Repertoire: Performing Cultural Memory in the Americas* (Durham, NC: Duke University Press, 2003), 33.

12. Arlette Farge, *The Allure of Archives*, trans. Thomas Scott-Railton (New Haven, CT: Yale University Press, 2013),69–70.

13. Farge, *The Allure of Archives*, 70.

14. Guy Debord, "Théorie de la dérive," *La Revue des Ressources*, 2002, https://www.larevuedesressources.org/IMG/_article_PDF/article_38.pdf ; English translation available at Bureau of Public Secrets, http://www.bopsecrets.org/SI/2.derive.htm.

15. Ralph Ellison, "Going to the Territory" (1980), in *The Collected Essays of Ralph Ellison*, rev. and updated, ed. John F. Callahan (New York: Modern, 2003), 598.

16. These correspondences become doubly fascinating when we take into consideration the historical origins of literary archives in the eighteenth century. As Roger Chartier has shown in his work tracing the reasons behind why literary archives came into being in Europe, material in "the author's hand"—autograph manuscripts—became the means though which forgeries could be exposed and authenticity guaranteed (*The Author's Hand and the Printer's Mind: Transformations of the Written Word in Early Modern Europe* [Cambridge: Polity Press, 2013]).

17. Carolyn Steedman, *Dust: The Archive and Cultural History* (New Brunswick, NJ: Rutgers University Press, 2002), 68.

18. The signed book is part of the Claude McKay Collection at the Beinecke. See Samuel Roth, *Europe: A Book for America* (New York: Boni and Liveright, 1919).

19. Christoph Irmscher, "Rejecting Claude McKay: An Author's Lost, and Last, Novel." Library of America blog, August 21, 2017, https://loa.org/news-and-views/1318 -rejecting-claude-mckay-an-authors-lost-and-last-novel.
20. Carl Cowl to Jean Wagner, February 7, 1970, discussed in Jean-Christophe Cloutier and Brent Hayes Edwards, introduction to Claude McKay, *Amiable with Big Teeth: A Novel of the Love Affair Between the Communists and the Poor Black Sheep of Harlem*, ed. Jean-Christophe Cloutier and Brent Hayes Edwards (New York: Penguin Classics, 2017), xi.
21. John Macrae to Claude McKay, August 7, 1941, Max Eastman Mss. II, Addition 1, Lilly Library, Indiana University, Bloomington.
22. Michael Chabon, *The Amazing Adventures of Kavalier & Clay* (New York: Picador, 2000), 614.
23. Milton Hindus, "Samuel Roth," unpublished essay, Milton Hindus Papers, Robert D. Farber University Archives, Brandeis University, Waltham, MA, 36; Milton Hindus, *The Crippled Giant: A Literary Relationship with Louis-Ferdinand Céline* (New York: Boar's Head Books, 1950).
24. John B. Turner to Bernhard Knollenberg, October 3, 1941, CVV NYPL.
25. McKay to Carl Van Vechten, October 26, 1941, CVV NYPL.
26. Brent Hayes Edwards, *The Practice of Diaspora: Literature, Translation, and the Rise of Black Internationalism* (Cambridge, MA: Harvard University Press, 2003), 14.
27. Brent Hayes Edwards, "The Taste of the Archive," *Callaloo* 35, no. 4 (2012): 961.
28. James Joyce, *Ulysses*, Gabler ed. (New York: Vintage, 1986), U2.30–39, ellipses in the original.
29. James Joyce, *Finnegans Wake* (1939; reprint, New York: Penguin Books, 1999), 422. Joyce is here taking a dig at Samuel Roth ("Rot him!") by subtly referring to the title of Roth's journals from the 1920s, *Two Worlds* and *Two Worlds Monthly: For the Increase of the Gaiety of Nations*, in which excerpts from both *Work in Progress* and *Ulysses* appeared.
30. *Two Worlds Monthly: For the Increase of the Gaiety of Nations*1–3, (1926–27).

APPENDIX: ARTIFACT BIOGRAPHIES OR VAGABOND ITINERARIES OF KEY DOCUMENTS DISCUSSED IN THIS BOOK

1. See box 656, "Ellison, Ralph, The Shadow and The Act Production" folder, Random House Records, Rare Book and Manuscript Library, Columbia University, New York.

PERMISSIONS

INDEX

Abbott, Charles, 57, 86

Acker, Kathy, 90

Acton, Jay, 285

Ada (Nabokov), 292

aesthetics, 17, 22, 77, 103, 111, 135, 139, 154, 155, 165, 178, 185, 193, 258, 298; archival concepts and, 21, 99, 106, 108, 142; documentary, 156; ethics and, 100; politics and, 9, 18, 24, 104, 138, 146, 148, 212

Aframericans (McKay's term), 126, 136; ghettoized status of, 124; Judaism and, 125; Popular Front and, 135

African, The: A Journal of African Affairs, 99, 109

African American authors, 10, 12, 14, 68, 172; sociopolitical challenges of, 44; tax law and, 216; twentieth-century American novel and, 148; wary of Van Vechten, 52

African American community, of 1950s, 256

African American studies, 7, 9, 18, 35; afterlives and, 10; establishing, 46; at Howard University, 86. *See also* black studies

African Studies Association, 64

Afrofuturism, 17, 260

Afromodernism, 21

afterlives, 2, 6, 10, 18

Agamben, Giorgio, 7

agency, 128, 184, 193, 266; of novels, 297; provenance and, 79; "Psychiatry Comes to Harlem" and, 167

Aid to Ethiopia organizations (*Amiable with Big Teeth*), 98, 121

Alcalay, Ammiel, 87–88, 89, 90

All-Negro Comics (Evans), 247–48, 254

Allure of Archives, The (Farge), 26

Almanac for New Yorkers 1938 (FWP), 129

Along the Archival Grain (Stoler), 25

American Animals (2018), 237

American Archivist (journal), 5

American Dream, 176

American Gothic, Washington, DC (photograph), 44

American Humor (Rourke), 246

American Hunger (Wright), 1, 3, 314n3

Amiable with Big Teeth (McKay), 13, 17, 22, 66, 96–97, 115; archival practices and, 108, 143; "Descent Into Harlem" and, 291; discovery of, 99, 285, 297; Ethiopia and, 114; historical record and, 129; lower-class black life and, 138; manuscript for, 80, 285–304;

INDEX

Debord, Guy, 94, 295–97
décalage, 15–16
DeCarava, Roy, 189, 202, *203, 204*
delay, as related to archives, 2, 4, 14, 15, 17,
18, 21, 23, 37, 41, 68, 72, 76, 128, 202–3,
220, 234. *See also* hibernation
DeLillo, Don, 30–31
democratization, 24
Depp, Johnny, 61
dérive, 295–97
Derrida, Jacques, 14, 32, 34, 272
"Descent Into Harlem," 288, 289, 290, 301;
Amiable with Big Teeth and, 291
desegregation, 277
Detective Comics, 262–63
determinism, 158
Dewey, John, 107
diaspora, 15, 94, 123, 140; black diasporic
archive, 9
Dickstein, Morris, 44
Dick Tracy (fictional character), 267–68
Dictee (Cha), 32
digital humanities, 158, 293
discourse control, 25
discovery, 128, 288, 289, 291, 302; of
Amiable with Big Teeth, 13, 96, 285, 297;
archival discovery, 96, 297
"Doctor's Dream in Harlem" (Martin), 152
documents, 30, 51, 77, 128, 167, 202, 230, 275;
accessible only by appointment, 218;
afterlives of, 2, 6, 10, 18; as alive, 8;
ancillary, 291; archival documents, 129;
authenticity of, 118; bureaucratic,
12; counterarchival imaginative
documentation, 32; creation of, 17;
differently classified, 303; documentary,
28, 65, 100, 146, 167, 172; documentary
aesthetics, 156; documentary evidence,
149; documentary means of persuasion,
166; documentation with objectivity of
science, 157; expressionist form,
documentary practice and, 183; genuine

and inauthentic bound together, 292;
guardians of, 272; itineraries of, 97;
neglected, 24; novels grounded in key
documents, 22; photography's power
to document, 147, 171, 177, 185; plots
revolving around, 126; preservation of,
41; produced by administrators, 25; as
product and process, 34; realism of,
160; reproduction requests for, 294;
shift from documentary to archival,
148; sociohistory of, 14; transitional,
287; unpredictable itinerary of, 18.
See also lifecycles
Dodson, Howard, 54
Doisneau, Robert, 174
Dorn, Ed, 90
Doss, Erika, 193
Double V campaign, 44
Douglas, Jennifer, 77, 78
Douglass, Frederick, 55
Doyle, Arthur Conan, 60
Drake, St. Clair, 154, 159, 164
Du Bois, W. E. B., 65, 109, 191
Dubus, Andre, 60
Dumas, Henry, 19
DuVal, Patrick, 51

Earp, Wyatt, 258
Eastman, Max, 95, 103, 299; McKay and,
132, 138, 143, 295; Roth and, 300
Eberhart, Richard, 89
Ebony (magazine), 175, 221
EC. *See* Entertainment Comics
Edwards, Brent Hayes, 15, 77, 96, 101, 113,
289, 303
Eight Men (Wright), 3
Eliot, T. S., 246, 290
Ellison, Fanny McConnell, 56, 180
Ellison, Ralph, 2, 12, 22, 31, 145, 147, 150,
153, 172, 173, *206*; aesthetic ideals of,
258; "And Hickman Arrives," 202;
archival sensibility of, 21, 205–6, 208;

"Harlem Is Nowhere" (Ellison), 145, 146, 147, 165, 172, 173, 200, 265; belatedness of, 204; comic books and, 251; concluding sentence of, 190; Ellison captions for, 192, 198, 280; Ellison repurposing, 195; Ellison shooting script for, 182, 183–84, 197, 198; excavation and reconstitution of, 193; *Harper's Magazine* and, 202; importance of, 277; *Invisible Man* and, 195; lifecycle of, 273; Parks and Ellison working on, *179*; *Photography on Parade* (exposition) and, 178; prehistory of, 203; in print, 174; published version of, 177; research for, 180; *Street Scene* and, 191; working on "Harlem Is Nowhere," *179*
Harlem: Negro Metropolis (HNM) (McKay), 22, 48, 97, 104, 106, 115, 135; communism and, 129–30; conspiracy of silence against, 109–10; factual exactitude of, 108; Holstein and, 133; Huggins and, 131–32; McKay notes on, 141; Powell and Schuyler in, 107; repurposing and, 298; research for, 330n23; reviews of, 112; richness of files regarding, 295
Harlem Nocturne (Griffin), 207, 217
"Harlem Pioneers with Mental Clinic" (*Headlines and Pictures: A Monthly Negro News Magazine*), 280–81
Harlem Renaissance, 41, 63, 99, 159; end of, 101; evolution of, 99; height of, 96, 128; Van Vechten and, 41–42. *See also* New Negro movement
Harlem riots, 173, 174, 204, 242; comic books and, 354n55; Ellison journalistic coverage of, 252; *Invisible Man* and, 265
Harlem Rooftops (Parks), 186, *186*, 195
"Harlem's America" (Ellison), 242, 246, 248, 279
Harlem Shadows (McKay), 293

"Harlem 24 Hours After—Peace and Quiet Reign" (Ellison), 173
Harlem United Aid to Ethiopia, 130
Harper and Row, 91
Harper & Brothers, 4, 48, 301
Harper's Magazine, 149–50, 201, 205; "Harlem Is Nowhere" and, 202
Harriet Tubman (A. Petry), 230
Harrington, Virginia, 217
Harrison, Hubert H., 46
Harry Ransom Center, 20, 40, 60, 85–86, 92, 93
Hartman, Saidiya, 8, 9, 29, 141
Harvard University, 72, 86; Schlesinger Library, 212
Harvey, Iselyn, *131*
HBCUs. *See* historically black colleges and universities
Headlines and Pictures: A Monthly Negro News Magazine, 280–81
Heartman, Charles F., 46
Heffernan, Laura, 89
Hellman, Lillian, 60
Hero, The (Raglan), 245
heroism, 242
hibernation, 2, 142, 148, 300
Hill, Robert, 65, 66, 72, 82, 132
Himes, Chester, 52, 71
Hindus, Milton, 300
Hip Hop Archive and Research Institute at Harvard University, 36
Hip Hop History Archive, 36
historically black colleges and universities (HBCUs), 39, 45; black special collections outside of, 68
Hitler, Adolf, 135, 258
HNM. See Harlem: Negro Metropolis
Hobbs, Catherine, 33, 34, 77, 85
Hobson, Charles, 56
Holstein, Casper, 133–34, 141
Home to Harlem (McKay), 134, 136, 286
hooks, bell, 86

INDEX

"Horror in the Nursery" (Crist), 278
House I Enter, The: A Portrait of the
American Doctor (NBC program), 153
House of El Dieff, Inc., 57
Howard Gotlieb Archival Research
Center, 209, 216, 217, 218, 220, 231, 237
Howard University, 74, 86; Moorland
Collection, 64
"How Bigger Was Born" (Wright), 157
Huggins, Willis N., 131–32, 141
Hughes, Langston, 1, 42, 54, 75, 83, 101, 202,
285; letters to Cunard, 90; McKay and,
122; Papers, 73, 82; Van Vechten and, 49
Huntington, Henry Edwards, 56, 57
Hurston, Zora Neale, 51, 101, 107
Hutcheon, Linda, 30, 31
Huxley, Aldous, 60

"In Darkness and Confusion" (A. Petry),
207
independent black nations, 114
Indiana Jones and the Last Crusade
(1989), 28
Indignant Generation, The (L. Jackson),
213, 217
Infants of the Spring (Thurman), 10
Inge, Thomas, 267
institutional acquisition landscape, 63
institutional libraries, 5
integration, 172
international communism, 100
International Protest petition (Joyce), 286
interwar years, 42, 66
"In the Author's Hand: Artifacts of
Origin and Twentieth-Century
Reading Practices" (Enniss), 20
In the Wake: On Blackness and Being
(Sharpe), 9
invisibility, 51, 124, 160, 166, 207, 241, 244,
257; Ellison and, 175, 193, 245, 255, 272
Invisible Man (Ellison), 2, 22, 53, 149, 253;
Batman and, 249; central concepts

from, 208; comic-book ethics and, 254;
comic books and, 241–42, 260, 272;
concluding chapters of, 174, 184; crime
and social utility in, 256; critique of
American society in, 269; early years
of composition of, 178; epilogue of,
254; guiding principle behind, 193;
"Harlem Is Nowhere" and, 195;
Harlem riots and, 265; Hollywood
movie genre and, 260; introduction to,
246, 274; Luke Cage (fictional
character) and, 244; magical-realist
elements of, 194; mythic heroes and,
260; Parks and, 199; photography and,
201; prologue of, 254, 255, 256;
promotion of, 185; protagonist of, 164;
revisions of, 196; socially responsible
leadership and, 243; symbolic action
of, 165; themes of, 242; universal
myth and, 259; vigilantism and,
264; violence and, 255; Wall Street
and, 192
Invisible Man: Gordon Parks and Ralph
Ellison in Harlem (exhibition),
145, 185
Irmscher, Christoph, 299
"Island of Hallucination" (Wright), 3, 73
Italo-Abyssinian crisis. See Second
Italo-Ethiopian War
Ivy League, 45, 86
I Yam What I Yam (theatrical cartoon
short), 263

Jackman, Harold, 43, 44, 54
Jackson, Lawrence P., 21, 101, 213, 217
Jackson, Red, 187, 282, 312
James, C. L. R., 71, 74, 268
James, Henry, 24, 139
James, Winston, 288, 300
James Baldwin Papers, 86
James Weldon Johnson (JWJ) Collection,
41–47, 218, 225; black scholars and, 45;

| 372 |

West, Dorothy, 72
West, Herbert (fictional character), 19
Western genre, 253
"What These Children Are Like"
    (Ellison), 276
White, Hayden, 32
White, Poppy Cannon, 55
White, Walter, 50, 54, 99
whiteness, 191
Wilcox, Johnny, 262
Wilde, Oscar, 58
Wilhelm Meister's Journeyman Years
    (Goethe), 32
Williamson, Simon, 108, 132, 143
Wilson, Logan, 57
Wiltwyck School for Boys, 163, 172;
    Wright and, 182–83
Winkiel, Laura, 141
Wonder Woman (comic book), 276
Woodson, Susan Cayton, 56
Woodward, Bob, 60
Works Progress Administration, 20, 177
WorldCat.org, 217
World War II, 97, 123, 159, 213; Axis
    nations in, 258; Double V campaign
    of, 44; United States entering
    into, 47
Woubshet, Dagmawi, 315n25
Wretched of the Earth, The (Fanon), 254
Wright, Bradford W., 258, 259
Wright, Ellen Poplar, 56
Wright, Julia, 56
Wright, Richard, 1–4, 12, 17, 21, 22, 66,
    153, 155, 167, *168, 169,* 190; *American
    Hunger,* 1, 3, 314n3; archival sensibility
    of, 21; on archives, 160; Baldwin and,
    149; Beinecke Rare Book and
    Manuscript Library at Yale University
    and, 40–41; *Black Boy,* 1, 3, 154, 157, 160,
    162, 314n3; *Black Power,* 171; Book-of-
    the-Month-club and, 4; *The Color
    Curtain,* 171; *Eight Men,* 3; Ellison

and, 146, 165, 257; fame of, 154; *A
Father's Law,* 3; Faulkner and, 162;
FWP and, 157; Guggenheimer and,
158; "How Bigger Was Born," 157;
"Island of Hallucination," 3, 73;
Lafargue Mental Hygiene Clinic and,
150, 162, 163; large-scale research
practices of, 157; *Lawd Today!,* 3; *The
Long Dream,* 3; *Native Son,* 4, 22, 66,
160, 161, 162, 166; "Out of the
Hospital" and, 197; *The Outsider,* 4,
171; Papers, 73; Parks and, 163;
photography and, 147; "The Position
of the Negro Artist and Intellectual
in American Society," 158–59; possible
titles for autobiography, 314n3; praise
for *Black Metropolis* (Cayton), 163;
"Psychiatry Comes to Harlem," 146,
147, 154, 163, 165, 166, 167, *168, 169,* 170,
189, 190; psychoanalytic theory and,
171–72; *Rite of Passage,* 3, 171, 172;
Sartre and, 159; *Savage Holiday,* 171;
shadow books and, 3; sociological
pieces by, 149; *12 Million Black Voices,*
26, 146, 160, 256; unused images by,
170; vagabond experiences of, 156;
Wertham and, 146, 150, 162, 189;
Wiltwyck School for Boys and,
182–83
Wronoski, John, 61
Wu-Tang Clan, 261–62

Yale University, 93, 227; Carl Van
Vechten Papers Relating to African
American Arts and Letters at Yale,
234; *Country Place* and, 71; Fisk
University and, 92; Langston Hughes
and, 49, 53, 62, 82, 83, 225; original order
and, 83; A. Petry and, 69, 71, 225, 229,
231, 237; purchase of Claude McKay
Collection, 61; reprocessing at, 83;
Richard Wright Papers and, 73;